# THE ETHICS OF SEX

# THE

# ETHICS OF SEX

*By Helmut Thielicke*

*Translated by John W. Doberstein*

*Harper & Row, Publishers*

*New York, Evanston, and London*

Published by arrangement with Fortress Press, publishers of *Theological Ethics* by Helmut Thielicke.

FIRST EDITION

M-N

LIBRARY OF CONGRESS CATALOG CARD NUMBER: 64-10366

# Preface: *To My American Readers*

Among Americans German professors are—not altogether un-justly—reputed to require dreadfully long and dreadfully theoretical introductions before they finally get to the point. This can be some-what irritating to persons of a more practical temper. Some years ago when I was a visiting professor in the United States I illustrated for my students this rather unattractive habit of my profession, and sometimes of mine, with this little anecdote. When a German pro-fessor delivers a lecture on the kangaroo the first paragaraph (and we are lucky if he ever gets to the second one) is likely to begin: "Prolegomena to some introductory considerations of the question whether and to what extent the kangaroo belongs to the category of mammals." A more pragmatic-minded American, I said, would be more inclined to begin at once with the question: "Can the kangaroo carry passengers?"

Well, no man can entirely shed his nature; nor should he even wish to do so! And certainly in this book the German professor is by no means completely concealed. For here the sexuality of man is dealt with in the broad context of Christian anthropology, in the light of the doctrine of creation and redemption, of fellow humanity and the orders. And in order to familiarize the reader with this approach, the introductory section begins at once with a rather theoretical treatment of basic principles.

The historical aspects of the subject also recur frequently, since one cannot understand the extraordinary changes which have taken place in man's views of sexual ethics unless one sees them in the context of the changed view of man and his understanding of reality. Insights which have long since become familiar to us through the hermeneutical study of the biblical texts we must now learn to apply in the realm of ethics.

I therefore cannot promise the reader that I shall relieve him entirely of some very fundamental consideration of basic principles. On the other hand, I may perhaps also say that if he is willing to go through this part of the book, he will also be confronted with the whole range of very concrete problems of sex. I believe I can say that I have not wished to evade dealing with any aspect of the subject, however ticklish it may be. One need only to examine the subjects dealt with in part IV, "Borderline Situations," to assure oneself that even the most touchy problems, which are often passed over in silence in Christian ethics, are here discussed *in extenso*.

The reason why, despite the above qualifications, this discussion of the ethics of sex is on the whole treated in a very concrete way is explained by the fact that the theological foundations for it have been laid elsewhere. In other words, this book constitutes a chapter in a comprehensive system of "theological ethics," which is now complete in four volumes. The first part of the larger work, to be published in the near future in an English version by the Fortress Press of Philadelphia, is being translated and edited by Professors William H. Lazareth and Geoffrey W. Bromiley. I may suggest that theological readers of *The Ethics of Sex* consult this English edition if they wish to know the framework of thinking in which this anthropology of the sexes is incorporated.

The circumstance which prompted the removal of the ethics of sex from the whole and its separate publication was that I delivered the substance of it in a series of lectures at the Divinity School of the University of Chicago in the fall of 1963. In this connection the presentation was so framed as to constitute a complete whole and also in terms that would be intelligible to medical men, jurists, and all educated persons who are concerned with the problems of sex.

Again I wish to extend my cordial thanks to my friend and translator, John W. Doberstein, for placing his sovereign skill as a translator at the disposal of this work. If my books have hitherto met with a lively response in the United States, I am well aware that I owe this above all to him and that English readers will find in me an author who has been elevated beyond himself by the translator.

HELMUT THIELICKE

## Translator's Note

There is no need for the translator to expatiate upon the value and significance of this work on the ethics of sex. I think it is safe to say that at the present time there is available no other single study which covers this whole area, including its thorny and "boundary line" problems, from the point of view of biblical theology, particularly a biblically Christian anthropology. Its great value lies in its confrontation of the subject with the whole complex of relevant factors, biblical, historical, social and cultural, medical, psychological, and legal. It addresses itself as a responsible social ethics to ministers, sociologists, physicians, psychiatrists, and jurists, a well as to the general reader. The reader may wish to pursue the presupposition upon which this study is based in the first volume of the author's *Theological Ethics,* which will be published by the Fortress Press, Philadelphia. The publisher and the translator desire to express here their appreciation for the gracious consent of the Fortress Press to the publication of this portion as a separate volume of the entire work.

The format of the text follows, with some exceptions, that of the German editions of the *Theological Ethics.* In this arrangement the main line of the discussion is presented in standard type, while material that supports, develops, or illustrates the central argument appears in reduced type. The reader should be warned, however, that matter in reduced type is not less important and may often be of greater interest and practicality than the normal text. The translator has substituted English titles of books in the biblical references where these works are available in English translation and also supplied the indexes. He has also had the benefit of constant collaboration with the author.

J. W. D.

# List of Abbreviations

AG—*Entwurf für eine neue Trauungsagende, 5. Ev. Landeskirchentag Württemberg.*

BGB—*Bundesgesetzbuch* (German Federal Republic).

CL—*Luthers Werke in Auswahl,* ed. by Otto Clemen.

Denzinger—*The Sources of Catholic Dogma,* trans. by Roy J. Defarrari from the Thirteenth Edition of Henry Denzinger's *Enchiridion* (St. Louis: Herder, 1957).

EA—*D. Martin Luthers sämmtliche Werke* (Erlangen edition).

EvTh—*Evangelische Theologie.*

FR—Dombois-Schumann, *Familienrechtsreform,* 1958.

NTD—*Das Neue Testament Deutsch.*

RE—*Realencyclopädie für protestantische Theologie und Kirche.*

RGG—*Die Religion in Geschichte und Gegenwart.*

STRACK-BILLERBECK—H. L. Strack, and Paul Billerbeck, *Kommentar zum Neuen Testament aus Talmud und Midrasch.*

ThBl—*Theologische Blätter.*

ThE—Helmut Thielicke, *Theologische Ethik,* Bd. I, 1 Aufl., 1955, 2 Aufl., 1958. Bd. II, 1, 2 Aufl., 1959; Bd. II, 2, 1 Aufl., 1958.

TWNT—*Theologisches Wörterbuch zum Neuen Testament,* ed. by G. Kittel.

WA—*D. Martin Luthers Werke. Kritische Gesamtausgabe.* (Weimar).

W.BR—*D. Martin Luthers Werke. Briefwechsel.* (Weimar).

ZKR—*Zeitschrift für evangelische Kirchenrecht.*

ZEE—*Zeitschrift für evangelische Ethik.*

ZsyTh—*Zeitschrift für systematische Theologie.*

ZThK—*Zeitschrift für Theologie und Kirche.*

# Contents

# I    INTRODUCTION

# The Duality of Man:
# Biblical Anthropology of the Sexes

Reference to the sexual differentiation in man is one of the axioms repeatedly stressed in biblical anthropology. Apart from this differentiation, it would be impossible to conceive of the *humanum*, of "humanness," in any expressible terms—at any rate in all respects that affect human existence in this world. Whereas all racial differences are "variations of one and the same structure"[1] and thus are miscible and therefore inconstant, the sexes have an indelible character.[2] Our Lord says in Matthew 19:4, 6: "Have you not read that he who made them from the beginning made them male and female . . .? What therefore God has joined together, let not man put asunder." This *logion* indicates a line that connects the order of creation with the order of redemption.

The differentiation of the sexes is so constitutive of humanity that, first, it appears as a primeval order (Gen. 1:27; 2:18 ff.) and endures as a constant despite its depravation in the Fall (Gen. 3:16),

---

[1] As Karl Barth quite rightly says in *Church Dogmatics,* III, 2, p. 286.

[2] The fact of homosexuality, which, anthropologically speaking, rests upon a latent—that is, to a large extent somatically indetectable—mixture of the two sexes in one individual (cf. O. Weininger, *Geschlecht und Charakter* [1922], *Sex and Character* [English trans. of earlier edition, 1906]), does not disprove this thesis. First, because this acquired immanental bisexuality bears witness to the polarity of the sexes, instead of ignoring it, and also because it can actually be adduced as a help in understanding the phenomenon. Second, because the homosexual must always understand himself in terms of his disparity with the "normal" polarity of the sexes and to this extent also remains bound to it. (Cf. the chapter on homosexuality.)

3

and, second, that to it is attributed symbolic value for the fundamental structure of all human existence, that is to say, for the existence of man in his relationship to his fellow man, for the fact that he is defined by his being as a Thou in relationship to a Thou. Barth rightly says that man does not have the "choice to be fellow-human or something else. . . . Man *exists* in this differentiation, in this duality." And "this is the *only* structural differentiation in which he exists."[3]

The creation of the woman from Adam's rib (Gen. 2:21 ff.) parabolically suggests this constitutive character of the fact that man and woman belong together. At the same time the very ground and goal of this act of creation points to the fact that man's being has been determined by God as a "being in fellow-humanity" [*Mitmenchlichkeit*], the representative expression of which is that man and woman belong together.

With respect to his other works of creation God speaks his word of approval and says that they are *good*. Only with respect to the creation of man does he utter the negative judgment "not good": "It is not good that the man should be alone" (Gen. 2:18). The solitary Adam is not yet "man"; he is still not the fulfillment of the creation of man. Accordingly, the woman is created as his "helper." And what is meant by this is a partnership, such as is intended, for example, in the idea of a fellow worker (*synergos*) referred to in II Corinthians 1:24. The idea here is that of a vis-à-vis which has the character of a Thou, of that which corresponds to the man, as, indeed, the Hebrew text requires to be translated, "I will make him a helper as his opposite."[4]

This means that the relationship of fellow humanity, represented by the man-woman relationship, is emphasized and given privileged status over against all I-It relationships. For among man's animal fellow creatures there was not a partner that was "fit for him" (Gen. 2:20), whereas Adam, confronted with the Thou of the female being created for him, breaks out in the cry, "This at last is bone of my bones and flesh of my flesh" (Gen. 2:23). Therefore he gives her his own name ("Woman") and in this way, too, singles her out in the naming of the animals.

[3] *Church Dogmatics*, III, 2, p. 286.
[4] H. Greeven, "Die Weisungen der Bibel über das rechte Verhältnis von Mann und Frau," in *Kirche und Volk*, XII, p. 4, or "a helper fit for him" (Gerhard von Rad, *Genesis, A Commentary*, trans. by John H. Marks [Philadelphia: Westminster Press, 1961]), p. 80, or a "mirror of himself, in which he recognizes himself" (F. Delitzsch, *Neuer Kommentar über die Genesis* [1887], on Gen. 2:18).

The duality of the sexes expresses with great precision and strong symbolism this dependence of the one upon the other. For in this passage the
emphasis is not only upon their dependence upon each other in the realm
of working together (*synergeia*), but rather upon a mutual dependence
that extends even to the biological, somatic realm. Alongside of the specifically theological significance which this reference to the sexes in the
creation story possesses, we must not overlook this symbolical value
which it has for the concept of fellow humanity as a whole. The sex
reference is, so to speak, not a subsection within the rubric "fellow
humanity," but is rather the representation and prototype of fellow
humanity. Man cannot understand himself in his creaturely relationship
to God without at the same time expressing his relationship to the Thou of
the neighbor. This double relationship constitutes his humanity. To this
extent we have here an adumbration of Jesus' correlation between love
of God and love of one's neighbor (Luke 10:27). Therefore when Emil
Brunner says that "God has created two kinds of human beings, male and
female,"[5] we must say that this is really an unfortunate way of putting it.
What is meant here is not the coexistence of two sorts of human beings,
but rather a polarity which is constitutive of man as such. Therefore man
and woman do not find each other, as it were, *subsequently;* they rather
come to each other from each other.

It is true, of course, that the theological relevance of this sex differentiation has not always remained undisputed. That is to say, when
theology is "eschatologistic" instead of eschatological, and, to use
Bonhoeffer's terms, it overlooks the "penultimate" in its preoccupation with the "Ultimate" and thus becomes visionary and utopian
[*schwärmerish*], the result is a leveling down of everything that is
concrete and distinctive. So this kind of theology, appealing to the
promise that in the Kingdom of God there shall be no marrying or
giving in marriage (Matt. 22:30), perpetrates a relativizing of the
sex difference, which in some ascetic schools of thought has frequently resulted in the actual defamation of sex.[6] This is to sidestep
and evade in visionary fashion our "being-in-the-world," which, after
all, is the very context which shows us that our love, hate, faith, and

---

[5] *The Divine Imperative,* trans. by Olive Wyon (Philadelphia: Westminster
Press, 1947), p. 374. Cf. the criticism by M. C. van Asch van Wijk, *op. cit.,*
p. 19.
[6] Cf. Fr. Hauck, *Markus-Evangelium* (1931), p. 146; Strack-Billerbeck IV,
p. 891.

the assaults upon our faith occur only as we encounter the concrete media of this world. In other words, my faith comes into being only as I face certain definite, concrete events and circumstances and believe in the face of them and in spite of them. Therefore faith can never be detached from the media of the world within which and in spite of which it prevails, just as the assaults upon my faith come to me by way of these media. In the same way, my loving is influenced and determined by the concrete framework within which I love, whether it be erotic love or love of parents and children, love of friends or love of enemies, whether it be a matter of spontaneous loving emotions— influenced possibly by tenderheartedness or temperament—or of real struggle to love a person whom I know I "should" love. Whenever human existence is thus illegitimately "eschatologized" the result is that we overleap these media within which the spiritual acts occur and come into being. And by the same process the result is also the tendency to ignore the sex difference, which then produces an abstract concept of "man" which has been stripped of all reality. In this kind of thinking Adam is made the representative of man as such, rather than Adam *and* Eve together.

On the other hand, the theological ontology of human existence must not go so far as to imagine that it can express the idea of *imago Dei only* by means of this sex differentiation.[7] It is true that this differentiation is very important as a medium of our relationship to God and our fellow man and thus is one of the media in which, through which, and despite which that relationship is realized. The *imago Dei*, however, both in its implications for our creaturehood and its Christological implications,[8] expresses our unmediated relationship to God.

This explains why it is that when we are dealing with this immediacy to God and thus with the eschatological aspect, the sex differentiation loses its force and validity. This becomes apparent, first, in the reference already mentioned to the effect that there is neither marrying nor giving in marriage in the Kingdom of God (Mark 12:25). It is apparent again in Paul's complete disassociation of life from all

[7] Thus van Asch van Wijk, *op. cit.*, p. 13.
[8] Cf. *ThE* I, §690 ff. and §829 ff.

sexuality "in the dim twilight of changing aeons" (I Cor. 7:1 ff.).[9]
It is apparent again in the question of our status in the sight of God:
under the Law "all" of us are *sinners*, without any distinction (*diastole*) whatsoever, and hence without sexual distinction (Rom. 3:23),
and under the Gospel we receive justification "freely" (i.e., without
having to meet any conditions and without any possibility that any
differences whatsoever could bring us closer to or take us farther away
from grace). In *this* dimension, therefore, we are "equally pardoned"
without differentiation.[10] When it is a question of this form of immediacy to God and therefore of the eschatological dimension of humanity, it is a level beneath all differentiations that is addressed.

It is true that a relationship of higher or lower status in the "penultimate" realm is altogether consistent with this solidarity in the "ultimate" dimension.[11] And yet this ultimate solidarity before God will
also make itself apparent in these "penultimate" areas. The equality
of status which arises in the encounter of I and Thou in the presence
of God will also break through the hierarchy of superiority and subordination and inform it with personal, mutual responsibility.

In this connection it is worth noting that even from a purely quantitative point of view the references to this partnership under God in
the biblical anthropology greatly outnumber the references to possible differences of superiority or subordination in the earthly, penultimate realm.

In the first account of creation there is no indication whatsoever of
any distinction of rank between man and woman (Gen. 1:26-28).
The threefold reference to God's "creating" in verse 27 leaves no
room for any distinction of value. Both, man and woman, are equally
immediate to the Creator and his act. Furthermore, both together receive (v. 28) the blessing as well as the command to subdue the
earth (1:28 f.).

We have already discussed the second account of the creation of

[9] The words quoted are those of G. Gloege. Cf. the description of the
eschatological background of I Cor. 7:29 ff. in H. W. Wendland (*NTD* VII,
p. 37).

[10] Ch. von Kirschbaum, *op. cit.*

[11] An extreme expression of this possibility occurs in Paul's letter to Philemon
in which he recognizes the hierarchy of master and slave, though at the same
time he speaks of the brotherhood of both in Christ. Cf. *ThE* II, 1, §2060 ff.

man (Gen. 2:7 ff.) and described the element of partnership between man and woman in it. The story of the Fall does indeed say
that the man has superior rank: "He shall rule over you" (3:16).
But that this is not a commandment but rather a prognostic curse is
evident from the parallel *logia*: "in pain you shall bring forth children"; "thorns and thistles it shall bring forth to you"; "in the sweat
of your face you shall eat bread" (3:16-19). In this context the fact
that one shall "rule" over the other is not an imperative order of creation, but rather the element of disorder that disturbs the original
peace of creation: for the domination of the man spoken of *here* is
the result of the desire (the libido) of the woman. This indicates that
sexuality has lost its original form. Whereas originally its purpose, in
conformity with the common origin of both man and woman, was to
maintain this original unity and make them "one flesh" (Gen. 1:24),
now it is promised that the sexes will be "against" each other and the
question is who shall triumph and who shall be subjugated. Now
libido-thralldom on the one hand and despotism on the other constitute a terrible correspondency. This antagonism between the sexes
immediately becomes apparent in the fact that now one partner proceeds to denounce the other (3:12). But all this is, of course, not in
accord with the order of creation, but rather a disruption of the order
of creation.

According to the Synoptics, Jesus dealt with woman as a human being,
as a sister. When he did this he was addressing her, so to speak, as she
was originally meant to be in God's creation; he was looking beyond the
disturbed relationship spoken of in the story of the Fall. We can properly
evaluate Jesus' dealings with women and his words to them and about
them only if we view them against the background of the time in which
he lived. The despised status of woman in rabbinical Judaism as well as in
the contemporary Greek world is actually a kind of paradigm of this
*disturbanc*e of the created order of the sexes, and Jesus' attitude is really
a protest against it. Although late Judaism exhibits isolated statements in
praise of the virtuous woman[12] and is also capable of saying that women
have equal if not higher rights before God than men,[13] the *general*
attitude toward women presents a totally different picture: One should not

[12] *Theologisches Wörterbuch zum Neuen Testament* I, 782, 21 ff.; hereinafter referred to as TWNT.
[13] *Ibid.*, p. 781, 30.

converse with a woman, not even with one's own wife; women are greedy eaters, curious listeners, indolent, jealous, and frivolous; "many women, much witchcraft"; "ten cabs of garrulousness descended upon the world, nine came down upon the women, one upon the rest of the world." "Blessed is he whose children are male and woe to him whose children are female"—in the light of the attitude toward woman expressed in these quotations this outcry of ben Kiddushin is understandable.[14] When women headed funeral processions the etiological explanation of this custom is to be found in the role she played in the Fall: they stand closer to the doom of death than the man. Likewise, the anthropological thesis of Philo to the effect that man represents the intellect (*nous*), whereas the woman represents sensuality (*disuesis*), goes back to the story of the Fall and the judgment of God.[15]

Only if we see them against this background will the seemingly quite unpolemical and almost incidental references in the Gospels to Jesus' attitude toward women take on the significance of an extraordinary protest against the status quo. The very fact that he spoke with women at all meant that he was notoriously disregarding the written and unwritten laws of the community in which he lived. Thus he healed the daughter of the Canaanite woman (Matt. 15:21 ff; Mark 7:24), the mother-in-law of Peter (Matt. 8:14 f.), Mary Magdalene (Luke 8:2 ff.); out of compassion for his mother he raised the young man of Nain (Luke 7:11 ff.) and restored to life the daughter of Jairus (Matt. 9:18 f.). If we keep in mind that women were excluded from cultic life (the Torah should rather be burned than transmitted to women, says the Jerusalem Talmud; and the women were required to sit behind screens in the synagogues [*TWNT* I, 782]), we shall see how shocking is the account that it was the women who remained at the cross of Jesus (Matt. 27:55 f.; Mark 15:40 f.; Luke 23:49; John 19:25) and finally were also among the witnesses of the resurrection (Matt. 28:1 ff.; Mark 16:1 ff.; Luke 24:10; John 20:1 ff.). Even though Jesus definitely rejected divorce (Matt. 19:4 ff.) and insisted that at most it must be regarded as a "regulation of necessity" (because of men's *sklerokardia,* 19:8), he dealt mercifully and forgivingly with the adulteress (John 7:53-8:11). He bestowed his regard even upon the harlots who were particularly despised (Luke 7:36 ff.). Here the equality of woman before God and the created solidarity of man and woman is dealt with in real earnest over against the contemporary cultic and social degradation of woman.

[14] *Ibid.,* 781, 41.
[15] *Ibid.,* 782, 17. On the contemporary background cf. A. Oepke, *TWNT* I, 781 ff.; J. Leipoldt, *Die Frau i. d. antik. Welt u. i. Urchristent.* (1954); K. H. Rengstorf, *Mann u. Frau i. Urchristent.,* in *AG für Forschg. d. Landes Nordrh.-Westf., Geistesw.* 12 (1954), pp. 7 ff.

Undoubtedly another nuance of this determination of the relationship of the sexes is to be found in Paul. The repeated statement that the man is the head of the woman is enough to indicate this (I Cor. 11:3; Eph. 5:23). Nevertheless, closer examination shows that even here the solidarity of the sexes *coram Deo* is upheld.

In this connection the most difficult factor is the exegesis of I Corinthians 11, because here Paul's argument is interfused with two extraneous elements.

First, with the Gnostic doctrine of emanation by means of which the later creation of the woman (11:8 f.) is interpreted as meaning that the man was at a higher stage of emanation than the woman and consequently was a more immediate reflection of God (*eikon* and *doxa*), whereas the woman was at most an indirect reflection of this glory, since she was the *doxa* of the man (11:7).

Here, of course, the use of the doctrine of emanation for the interpretation of the story of creation reaches its limit in that the very thing that Paul does not do is to draw the implication that is inherent in it, namely, that the woman lacks completely the character of *imago Dei*.[16] Moreover, his statement with regard to the man-woman relationship is made more difficult by the fact that here it is not a thetical and independent statement, but is meant merely to support the argument that the man should keep his head uncovered in the service of worship and the woman should keep hers covered (11:4 f.). A certain uncertainty and discontinuity in the argument (it is nothing more than this—this is not a "kerygmatic" statement!) arises from the fact that, alongside of the argument from the creation story and the doctrine of emanations, he also employs the obscure—again probably a Gnostic, mythological—reference to the doctrine of angels (11:10).

Besides these Gnostic elements, the passage contains a second extraneous element in which Paul argues that "nature" commands that men and women should wear their hair differently, indicating their difference in status (11:14). What Paul meant here by "nature" (*physis*) is undoubtedly social custom (and therefore a *thesis!*). But precisely this identification, which is *post festum* and therefore questionable because of the time interval, points to the real aim of Paul's argument here, namely, that the social difference in the role of man and woman and all the customs connected with it (which were understood not only by Paul but by all his contemporaries as being "natural") should not be revolutionized by appeal to the fact that men and women are in solidarity *coram Deo*. For he, too, proceeds to emphasize this solidarity (11:11 f.). The emphatic stress he puts upon it here is meant to prevent us from drawing

---

[16] Cf. Greeven, *op. cit.*, p. 8.

from the dissimilar social ("natural") position of the sexes the erroneous conclusion that such differences could have any validity in the sight of God. In exactly the same way, of course, we can also infer from the text what he is fighting against on the opposite front, namely, the threatening and equally erroneous conclusion that by appealing to this solidarity before God one can now postulate the social identification or leveling of the sexes. In saying this, Paul is employing the same kind of polemic that Luther used against the rebellious peasants, namely, forbidding them to demand their social freedom by appealing to the solidarity of master and servant under the gospel.

In summary we may say that here Paul is making a conservative judgment sociologically but a revolutionary judgment theologically, for certainly the equal status of the sexes before God was in contradiction to the social customs of the times. The double intention which he here pursues is directed against the fanatical, "eschatologistic" leveling of the sexes as well as the orthodox Jewish differentiation of the sexes. It is only in this *intention* and not in the argumentation that the kerygmatic content of the passage lies. We are therefore dealing with the same kind of Pauline criticism and interpretation as we encounter when we are obliged to separate the aim of his theological statements from the form of his rabbinical exegesis (e.g., Gal. 4:21 ff.).

Moreover, the thesis stated in Ephesians 5:23, that the man is the head of the woman, cannot be understood as an *isolated* thesis, without taking into account the theological context. But if this is kept in mind, then again the same equality of status and equality of obligation before God appear, and here with the added emphasis that both have their effect upon the concrete, "worldly" cohabitation of the sexes.

The statement that the man is the head of the woman—which has reference only to the *married* woman and therefore contains no sociological statement concerning the status of the woman—is inserted in a more general framework, namely, in the commandment to "be subject *to one another,*" and to be so "in the fear of Christ" (*upotassomenoi allelois,* Eph. 5:21). Hence this cannot mean any one-sided domination on the part of the man; on the contrary, their common dependence upon the Lord, who is above them and is to be feared, places man and wife in a relationship of mutual service to each other, which is characteristic of our whole relationship to our fellow men (Gal. 5:13; I Pet. 4:10, etc.); for Christ is himself the prototype of the servant (*diakonon,* Luke 22:27).

This understanding of Christ as the one who serves must be kept in view when in the following text (Eph. 5:22 ff.) use is made of the analogy that as Christ is the head of his church so the husband is the head of the wife (5:23). From what has just been said it is already clear that what is meant here is something more and something different from a simple relationship of superiority, a kind of "leadership principle" [*Führerprinzip*] in marriage. The analogy can be understood only if we also see the way in which Christ is the head. But once this is seen, then both the limitations and the validity of the analogy become clear. The limitations lie above all in the fact that Christ has saving significance for the body (*soma*), of which he is the head (5:23b). This distinguishes his headship from that of the man, who does not possess this saving significance. On the contrary, he stands together with the wife *under* this salvation. And this is precisely what gives its peculiar stamp to his relationship to his wife. Apart from Ephesians 5, this is stated with unusual expressiveness in the first epistle of Peter where the author says that the husband should bestow honor on his wife as "the weaker sex" (*asthenestero skeuei*) because they are "joint heirs of the grace of life" (*sygkleronomois charitos zoes*, 3:7). This allusion to the wife as the weaker sex naturally cannot be interpreted in the sense of modern chivalry. It should rather be understood as a concessive clause: "though the wife is the weaker sex" honor should be bestowed on her. Even though she cannot demand this respect by reason of an equal partnership in the natural sense, she nevertheless can do so by reason of an "alien dignity" (*dignitas aliena*): she is equal before God. Here we have an instance of how Christian anthropology "infiltrates" the contemporary attitude toward, and evaluation of, woman.[17]

This in itself gives us a lead as to how the headship of the man in Ephesians 5 is to be understood. For this understanding it is important to note that verses 25 ff. are addressed to the husband. Their intent is not to be an objective doctrine of the sexes, but rather an appeal to the husband not to regard and act upon his position as the head in the sociological sense as being one of simple superiority, but rather in the soteriological sense of the imitation of Christ. In view of the prevailing contempt for women which we mentioned above, it is no wonder that this should be emphasized here, as in I Peter, and clearly directed against the man-wife hierarchy in the Jewish and pagan environment. Josephus, for example, thought of the headship of the husband purely in terms of "bridling" the wife and "ruling over" her.[18]

But now that the headship of the husband is to be understood in analogy with Christ we perceive a new and unprecedented tone: husbands should love their wives as Christ loved us all—men and women (5:25). And here "love" is to be understood not in the sense of *eros* but of *agape*. This is the new note which appears nowhere else in late antiquity. What *agape* means here is made amply clear in statements that follow (5:25 ff.) in reference to the service of Christ to his church. The respect the

---

[17] *ThE* II, I, §2057 ff.
[18] Greeven, *op. cit.*, p. 10.

woman should show toward the husband therefore has its correspondence in the sustaining love the husband bears toward her. It is a living, personal relationship which reminds us of the "golden rule" (Matt. 7:12).

We may leave out of account here the passage in I Timothy 2:11 which departs from the rest of the New Testament tradition. The etiological explanation of the subordination of the woman as resulting from her taking the initiative in the Fall is in contradiction to the statements which Paul makes on this question (Rom. 5:14). Furthermore, the employment of rabbinical teachings which are alien to the Bible is evident in this passage.[19]

We may sum up by saying that the male-female duality of man remains as a constant within the history of salvation [*Heilsgeschichte*]. It was ordained in creation and continues to endure through the crisis of the Fall, except that here it becomes a *disturbed* relationship (though it still remains a relationship!). Even in the distorted state caused by the libido and the urge to power, the indestructible correspondence of the sexes remains; the distortion occurs, so to speak, "within" this correspondence. In the order of redemption men are called back to the original design of creation in that the relationship of the sexes is oriented upon the Christological analogy: man and wife are again related to each other as persons who stand equally under the grace of God. The man's position as the "head" implies no patent of authority (since the correspondence of domination and servitude is the very mark of the disturbance caused by the Fall). It rather means only a primacy within a fellow-human relationship determined by love and willingness to serve. This provides a scope for freedom which allows us to distinguish the theological norm from its contemporary actualization and to leave this actualization to historical—including modern—modification. Every time is in *its own* way directly subject to that theological norm.

[19] *Ibid.*, p. 11.

# II  EROS
## AND
## AGAPE

*Theological Phenomenology*

*of the Human*

*Sex Relationship*

# Introduction

Having set forth the biblical framework for the duality of the sexes
—it will be given more detailed contours in the chapter on marriage
—we shall now try to see the phenomena of human sexuality *within*
this framework. In marriage, sexuality, at least sexuality in the narrower sense, is only *one* of its constitutive elements. And, inversely, in
sexuality marriage is only *one* of the areas in which it actualizes itself; long before marriage the young person is drawn into the field of
sex, and the person who remains unmarried is still a sexual being.
Therefore even in theological ethics the problem of sex is one that is
not to be treated only within the framework of marriage. On the contrary, it is a problem that is a part of the basic province of general theological anthropology.

In dealing with it here, our analysis will be concerned with two
main points.

First, our concern is not to present something like a timeless typol-
ogy of human sexuality and arrive, as it were, at the "Platonic idea"
of man as a sexual being. Rather, we must examine the specific forms
that sexuality has taken in our *present* situation, its phenomena, its
hazards, its crises, and its problems. That is to say that, knowing that
there is something like a stable and, in my opinion, "timeless" original, primeval relationship of the sexes, we take into account the historical variability of this relationship and try to discover our, i.e., the
*present* generation's, place in the process of these changes in the primeval, original relationship.

This will also be important for the later question of the way in which the biblical statements concerning marriage, the relationship of the sexes (whether superordination or subordination), and parents and children are to be considered binding and put into practice in our situation today. This hermeneutical problem can be solved only if we get it clear in our minds first that we today are structured essentially differently, historically, sociologically, and finally also in our general feeling about life, from the men of the Bible. We would therefore be doing great violence to the pertinent directions of the Bible, for example those of the Apostle Paul, if we were simply to transfer them "legalistically" and without translation to our situation. We would also be doing violence to ourselves. And we know how frequently this has actually happened within Christendom. Therefore, in order that we may arrive at the place where we can legitimately transpose the biblical statements into our situation, we must first know what this situation is. Hence the phenomenology of sex and its interpretation in the light of the present situation is a proper preparation for the real theological task.

Second, a further emphasis in our analysis consists in the fact that even this phenomenology *itself* is already subject to a "theological" principle. It is one of the axioms of biblical anthropology that man in all dimensions of his existence can be understood only in his relationship to God. And his sexuality cannot be excluded from this. This means that the biological side of sex cannot be isolated and viewed as being autonomous. Rather it is only a mode of the being and functioning of the one, whole, indivisible man, who as this one, whole, indivisible man is from God, to God, and under God. If this is not to be a mere doctrinaire, generalized statement, then we must be able to establish and show how this indivisible totality of the man becomes manifest, how the biological and the personal sides of his being interpenetrate each other, point to each other, and cannot be understood at all apart from their correlation with each other.

But in the attempt to show and establish this, we shall have to deal at length with biological and psychological phenomena and thus with empirical data. Therefore it is of great importance to note right from the beginning the key signature which is prefixed to the stave containing the sum of phenomena: it is the key signature of that foundational God-man relationship which encloses all dimensions of human existence and therefore constitutes its indivisibility. Therefore the sexuality of man cannot be explained simply in terms of the biological aspect of his nature (*bios*).[1] On the contrary, even in its most subtle ramifications it is *human* sexuality through and through. The biological aspect is thoroughly integrated in the *humanum;* and the *humanum* lives and moves and has its being in the *divinum*. This is the basic thesis which we now propose to develop.

The title of this section, "Eros and Agape," with its combination of divine and human love, is also intended to convey this basic concept.

[1] The Greek term *bios* is used here and throughout in the sense of physical, biological life. (Trans.)

# A. The Problem: The Interconnection of Bios and Person in the Realm of Eros

## 1. THE CRISIS OF ANTHROPOLOGY

He who no longer knows what man is, also cannot know what it is on which his peculiarity as a sexual being is based. He who disregards this *anthropological* motif of sexuality degrades it to a mere biological question. (The decline of sexual morality and countless marriage breakdowns are connected with this.) Not that sexuality has no essential relation to the biological. Only a doctrinaire moralist could ignore or refuse to admit this. But the mystery of man consists in the interconnection of personhood and bios, not merely in the sense that bios affects and puts its stamp upon his personality—to say this is by now almost a commonplace—but also in the sense that bios is given its character by the personhood of the human being; this, however, is something that has not yet been appreciated to the same degree. But if it is true that the bios of man is not simply identical with the bios of the animal, then the sexuality of man, despite the parallelism in physiological processes, is also not simply identical with the sexuality of the animal. Therefore it is important that we should examine the relationship of person and bios in order by this means to discover the peculiar, unique nature of human sexuality.

Once we take into account the totality of man, which means his thinking, feeling, and willing, and also the products of these activities as they occur in his sexual existence, we find again and again that they resolve themselves into two main dimensions. Characterizing them somewhat abstractly to begin with, we may say that in one dimension it is a matter of man in his *being* and in the other of man in his *function*.

By man in his *being* we mean man as he is related to God, man insofar as he is the bearer of a responsibility and an infinite value and insofar as he thus has the dignity of being an "end in himself" (Kant), that is, never to be used as a means to an end.[2] By man in his *function*, on the other hand, we mean man as he actively steps out of himself, accomplishes and effects something, becomes, so to speak, "productive"—whether this has to do with things or with persons.

When we are dealing with man, no matter in what area, we are constantly meeting with these two dimensions. And this co-ordination of two dimensions is especially acute in the social area.

Karl Marx, for example, accused capitalist society of valuing the workingman merely in terms of his function, that is, his capacity as a labor force. It was therefore treating him as a means of production (and thus as a means to an end) and failing to respect him as a human being. In capitalist society the being of man was disregarded in favor of his function. But to regard man merely as the bearer of a function, a "functionary," is to dehumanize and make a thing of him, and therefore to enslave him. On the other hand, one might take a look at Goethe's *Werther,* for example, and ask how human society is to function at all, if man is to attribute such excessive importance to his being, for example his being as one who loves and is loved, and in this way cultivate his entelechy as an end in itself. We ask ourselves whether this Werther had no functions to perform (did he not have to have a student job or work as a candidate for a degree?) and, if he had been obliged to perform such functions, would he not have had far less trouble with his hypertrophied being and his love-sick sufferings and sorrows?

It becomes apparent that the being and the function of man are co-ordinated in a way that still needs to be defined, and that when the

---

[2] Kant illustrated this degrading of man to a mere means to an end by reference to prostitution and slavery.

two are isolated from each other the immediate and inevitable result is the emergence of pathological conditions of a psychic or social kind. (Perhaps one could approach the whole social question as it affects us today from this point of view.)

One must immediately add, of course, that being and function can be related to each other in very different ways. In purely mechanical functions, for example, such as those performed on an assembly line or operating the controls of automatic processes, the person and the function become widely separated; these are "nonpersonal" forms of work. A poet, on the other hand, or a dedicated physician will be able to perform his function only as he becomes personally engaged and puts "his heart" into his functions.

Now, there can be no doubt that the extreme of immediacy in the interconnection of these two dimensions, that of being and that of function, the personal and—in this case—the biological-functional sphere, is to be found in the area of *sexuality*. The details of this interconnection we shall deal with more fully later. At this point we merely recognize that it exists. In order merely to indicate for our present purpose what this interconnection means, we may point out that it is present in the choice of the erotic partner, where the personal element is extremely different in different cases. We have only to think of the Platonic myth of a bisexual primordial man in the *Symposium* to see a symbol of how the being of two persons is correlated and therefore how both are involved in this their being. If sexuality were merely a matter of physiological function (and thus a glandular problem) or of the business of reproduction (and thus again of a function), it would be difficult to see why the partners should not be just as interchangeable as the bearers of any other biological or mechanical functions, such as draft animals, for example, or machines.

Then it would be hard to see why Don Juan and Casanova should not be regarded as the typical, ideal representatives of *eros*, which, as a matter of fact, they are in the eyes of many. We propose to show that just the opposite is the case, namely, that despite their erotic artistry these very figures missed the mystery of *eros* and in the end were deserted by it. The aging "Casanova," the lover "in retirement," who, so to speak, no longer performs his "function" and is put out to pasture in the field of "beingless" senility after having exhausted his amorous promptings, is really a macabre figure. Can we believe that he was ever really in league with *eros*, if he is left in solitude even before death comes to fetch him?

So, once more, if sexuality were merely a function, we would hardly be able to understand why the partners should not be exchangeable at will and why promiscuity should not be legalized and made a social institution. The fact that this is not so, or that in any case it is felt that it is something which should not be, the fact that on the contrary we prefer to uphold monogamy and thus respect the uniqueness of the choice of partner and thus the uniqueness of the other person's being, makes it clear that we see something more and something other in sexuality than a mere function, that here we recognize that the being of the person is involved and engaged.

In the light of what we have said above, the fact that this individual character of choice of partner has been, not institutionally but yet *de facto*, largely lost in the modern world, and replaced by a certain discrimination in the sense of promiscuity, points to far deeper defects than mere moral laxity or unbridled passions. What is evident here is rather that the interconnection of person and bios, of personal being and biological function, is no longer realized. But where bios is taken by itself and given the monopoly, the bearers of the function of bios become interchangeable at will and the ability to perform the (erotic) function becomes the sole criterion of the exchange.

This law of interchangeability of function-bearers can also be observed in other areas of life. One can actually state it as a formula that to the degree that this tendency to regard the person as a thing increases and the person is impugned at the point of his substantial being, men become stereotypes which are interchangeable at will. In *economic* materialism man becomes an impersonal bearer of a labor force, and when his ability to work is gone he is "finished" (liquidated). The ant in the production process of the termite state can be replaced at any time with another member to perform the function. In *biological* materialism man becomes completely analogous to an impersonal bearer of a propagative apparatus and thus becomes mere raw material for population politics and biological selection. Laws, which are in this sense ideologically determined, then have a habit of decreeing that in cases where only one of the married partners is capable of procreation, and hence capable of performing a function in accord with the population policy, divorce is to be favored. Marriage which is viewed as being merely instrumental no longer binds the partners together at the level of being, but rather makes continuance or exchange of partners dependent upon the function.[3] Only the "being" of a person is unique, irreplaceable, and unrepeatable.

Wherever sexual chaos, i.e., exchange of partners at will, prevails, we are confronted with a crisis, a breakdown of *personal* being, of personhood. Therefore, it would be misleading to look for the causes of certain manifestations of sexual deterioration in the destruction of morality. Where such destruction is present it is itself the effect of this deeper crisis. Moreover, it is altogether possible that this crisis in the being of a person may evidence itself only partially. That is to say, the result may be a very specific loss of the ability to see the interconnection of bios and person and thus may lead one to degrade one's partner to the status of a mere function-bearer in this one area of sex. Experience teaches that this occurs frequently. People who are otherwise "ethically intact" and capable of friendship and fellow humanity may perpetrate this degradation of another human being in this *one* area of sex. When they do this, they are allying themselves (at least partially) with an anthropology which they certainly would not accept theoretically and generally, and they would be horrified if they were confronted with this consistent interpretation of their actions.

It is the task of pastoral care in this area to communicate this interpretation. That is to say, pastoral care must point out what one makes of his erotic partner when he isolates bios and person from each other (namely, a selfishly misused function-bearer); and inversely, it must show that he separates person and bios from each other when he allows certain forms of sex to have power over him. But pastoral care will move on *this* level of thought and interpretation in the positive sense too; it will not attempt to combat the insistent libido with the moral appeal: "You dare not do this"; because this appeal does not touch the root of the problem at all and is therefore fruitless. The Law reaches only the "outside of the cup and of the plate" (Matt. 23:26 ff.) and not always even this; but it certainly never reaches the "inside." The libido can be attacked only by the kind of pastoral care which is aware of the anthropological problem and challenges the person to engage in a particular kind of meditation or exercise of his own thinking. The aim of this meditation is to arrive at the conviction that the desired body belongs to the "being" of a human being who himself belongs to another; a human being, that is, who has been

---

[3] H. Dölle, *Grundsätzliches zur Ehescheidungsrecht* (1946), pp. 8 f.

bought with a price (I Cor. 6:20; 7:23), and has a temporal and eternal destiny, a destiny in which one who claims this other person in his totality responsibly participates. Only through this meditation do we come to see that *whole* human being, who alone is capable of disclosing the full richness of sexuality. For among the conclusions of our study will be the realization that focusing one's intention upon the whole man, upon his indivisible unity, does not merely curb sex, but rather liberates it and brings it to its fullness. He who seeks only the partial—only the body, only the function, and again possibly only a part of this—remains unfulfilled even on the level of *eros,* because, having lost the wholeness of the other person, he also loses the other person's uniqueness. The general part of the functions, however, he shares with everybody. Hence there is something like a communism in the erotic. It evidences itself in the fact that that which evokes the peripheral manifestations of eroticism are present everywhere as public property in the form of sex appeal, revealing styles of clothing, and the illustrations and content of advertising in general.[4]

The same uncertainty and reduction which evidence themselves in the loss of the wholeness of the person are also discernible in much of the "technical" literature dealing with sex knowledge and marriage, at least insofar as it is offered to the broad public as an aid. When we say this we are not even referring to the great mass of publications which are intended to be merely stimulants to erotic fantasy under the guise of aids to marriage. We are thinking rather of some of the serious literature in this field. To cite one which is representative of many others, we mention the well-known marriage manuals written by Th. van de Velde,[5] without disparaging their importance for the physiological and technical side of sexual life.

Since sexual life requires an art of loving (*ars amandi*) and therefore has its techniques, it is justifiable and even necessary that prophylactic and therapeutic measures be taken against sexual crises from this angle too. This conclusion is fully consistent with our basic starting point, which was to emphasize and keep in view the whole person; for, since the psychophysical nexus is an indivisible whole, injuries in one sector inevitably have their effect upon the others. It would be pseudotheological one-sidedness to think only in terms of primary injuries in the area of the person—such as disregard of the person of the other partner and merely making use of his bios function—without at the same time taking into account the opposite source of difficulty, namely, that something may be

[4] Cf. Friedrich Sieburg, "Vom Unfug der Entblössung," in *Constance* (1951), 9.

[5] E.g., *Ideal Marriage, Its Physiology and Technique,* trans. by Stella Browne (New York: Random House, 1930).

wrong in the elementary bios relationship, the physiology and technique of the sexual relationship. This too can threaten and undermine the person-relationship. Hence there are many marriage crises which are not primarily the province of the pastoral counselor, but rather the gynecologist or the neurologist or the psychotherapist. The subject matter dealt with by van de Velde therefore has its importance also from the standpoint of a theological anthropology which puts the emphasis upon the whole man; and it is an indication of a lack of openness to the whole realm of created life and vitality to regard van de Velde from this quarter with the reserve of prudery.

The difficulty, however, is that the total intention of van de Velde's books creates the fatal impression that in the sexual area it is all more or less *only* a problem of techniques and that all that it requires to stabilize a marriage is to give the partners erotic training in order to develop their ability to function properly. Therefore, what lies behind it may again be that functional idea of man in which the personal concept of *community* in marriage has no place. In view of this inadequacy, we ought to recommend with praise theological and medical works in our generation which stress the wholeness of man and the interconnection of bios and person, especially in the realm of sex, but also within the framework of an expanded medical anthropology.[6]

## 2. The Terms Eros and Agape

When the totality of the person is engaged in the sex community it will not be sufficient to regard *eros* as being the only thing that establishes communication. It must be admitted—contrary to a slander not infrequently expressed—that *eros* positively does not direct itself only to the erotic function. Undoubtedly it also addresses itself to the other person's being, at any rate if we assume that the term is being used in its Platonic sense. The only question is whether I can see the whole person if I do not see him in his relationship to God and therefore as the bearer of an "alien dignity."[7] If I am blind to this dimension, then I can give the other person only a partial dignity insofar as I estimate his importance "for me"—even if this includes far more than his mere *functional* importance for me!—but not insofar as I see in him his importance "for God."

[6] Here the works of Otto A. Piper and Theodor Bovet are especially recommended. Cf. also R. Siebeck, V. v. Weizsäcker, P. Christian, and H. Gödan.
[7] See *ThE* I, index, "Dignitas aliena."

It is obvious what the result of this distinction must mean in the context of human communication. For even though there are stages in human relationships in which the other person's importance "for me" decreases, my regard for him will remain as long as in my consciousness I realize that he means something "for God," that he was "bought with a price." Correspondingly, communication between the partners will be preserved where this insight is present. And yet the reverse is also true: if this communication with the other person depends only upon the importance which he has "for me," then there is always a certain tendency that causes the other's being to recede behind his function, in order to benefit, complement, and stimulate me, and then, when these functions diminish or disappear, I also tend to write him off in reality. At this point the *agape* relationship acquires its relevance, for it allows the other person to appear, not merely in his being, his "being as he is," but rather in his "being before God." Whereas the English word "love" has many connotations, ranging all the way from calf love to married love and the feeling of sympathy to the love of Francis of Assisi and Friedrich von Bodelschwingh, the Greek language differentiates more precisely and helpfully.

Anders Nygren, in this two-volume book *Eros and Agape,* has assembled an immense body of material for the diagnosis of these two terms. When Nygren interprets *eros* as meaning the longing of the soul upward, for example toward the beautiful or the idea of the beautiful, and *agape* as self-giving, self-sacrificing love, love that is directed downward, this may well be a proper characterization of the *ideal types* of these two forms of love. However, the problem of their relationships to each other really begins with the question of how they fit together and are dialectically interconnected with each other. Thus, for example, *agape* never directs itself to an abstract concept of one's neighbor, but always to another person, whether I stand in an *eros* relationship to him, in the broadest sense of a mental, physical, or generally sympathetic kind of relationship, or whether I am indifferent to him, or even whether he evokes dislike or hatred in me. *Agape* can realize itself only in the framework of these interhuman media, and depending upon *which* medium is present, it acquires other tasks and also other tones. Its form changes according to whether it is practiced with respect to "enemies" (Matt. 5:44) or "friends" (Matt. 5:46; John 15:13), a "stranger" (Luke 10:34) or one's "wife" (Eph. 5:25). Hence *agape* cannot be defined at all without taking into account the concrete medium to which it happens to be attached. It therefore cannot be defined apart from the given, or not given, kind of *eros* through which the specific interhuman relation is determined. This indicates the limitations of the view that concerns itself with defining only the ideal type, a view with which Nygren is essentially satisfied and which in our own approach to the theology of sexuality we shall seek to break away from.

In order, then, to secure a preliminary orientation, we define the differing motives of *eros* and *agape* in the form of two theses. First, in *eros* the *worth* of the other person is the object; in *agape* the *authentic being* [*Eigentlichkeit*] of the other person is the object. Secondly, in this connection sexual community represents the point at which these two strivings intersect. We shall explain what we mean by these two theses in what follows. But this requires that we take a brief glance at what Plato understands by *eros*.

In the *Phaedrus* as well as the *Symposium* Plato introduces an *eros* myth. In the *Phaedrus* he distinguishes between a desirous, unreasonable *eros* and an *eros* guided by reason. The unreasonable *eros* arises when the blind and irrational desires are directed exclusively to beautiful *bodies*. This kind of *eros* then remains on the level of the act of momentary physical possession. The beauty of the other person is only a means to kindle passion and satisfy it. Thus the other person does not enter into consideration at all as a "human being," that is, as a bearer of values which transcend him (for example, as a symbol of the beautiful). Moreover, he is not even intended to be such. On the contrary, in our line of reasoning and quite in line with Platonic thought, one can say that he is thought of merely as an interchangeable means, which I need in order to stimulate the erotic feeling.

Now, it would be quite wrong to think of *reasonable eros*—the correlate of its irrational variant—as being a kind of domesticated, unecstatic, well-mannered *eros*. For it too is thoroughly ecstatic. But this ecstasy is a completely different state of "being beside oneself." That is to say, it is aroused by the fact that what is loved in the other person is the idea of beauty and that therefore the other person is regarded as a symbol, and relationship is established with that which transcends him. But then, since the reason is likewise directed to the Ideas—for example, the idea of the beautiful—the reason plays its part in the erotic movement thus defined. Consequently, it is by no means the case that the erotically excited "nerves" must assert themselves and prevail against the reason in order to give expression to their impulse. The erotic act is not, as it were, bowdlerized and moralized by the fact that reason participates in it, or better, is capable of participating in it; it is rather made fuller and weightier by the fact that reason is present in it. Perhaps it can be expressed this way: since man is essentially a bearer of reason, his real self is present in the erotic act, whereas in the lower form of *eros* his real self is excluded, because in the erotic act he is employing only part of himself, namely, the area of impulse and desire. He delegates, as it were, only certain organs, and thus only his partial self, to deal with his erotic needs. In this idea of the reasonable *eros* Plato is undoubtedly concerned to humanize the erotic act. His aim is to fill it with human content, for he is concerned that the *whole* man should be engaged in it.

Then this reasonable *eros* actually does have an upward-striving tendency. And, as the conversation of Socrates with Diotima in the *Symposium* shows, this ascent passes through three states.[8] At the lowest stage the love of one form (or body) leads one to "recognize that the beauty in every form is one and the same." At the second stage appears the beauty of the other person's mind (*to en tais psychais kallos*), which "improves" me when I come into contact with it, which produces, as it were, a personal and ethical communication. The third stage leads one up to the beauty of the sciences (*epistemon kallos*). Thus beauty becomes increasingly formless and bodiless, more immediate and more independent of the forms and bodies in which it incarnates itself. So it is understandable that toward the end of this last stage beauty "in itself" is suddenly (*exaiphnes*) perceived and the ecstatic vision (*theoria*) occurs. This idea of the beautiful is everlasting, imperishable, and unchangeable (*to aei on*). All other beauty—beauty that is bound to form, to a young *body,* and therefore subject to "growing and decaying, waxing and waning"—is beauty only because it participates in the idea of beauty itself.

Of the many relationships of *eros* implied in these stages we mention only two because they are important for our theme. First, *eros* relates itself to the worth of the other person—whether this worth or value that incarnates itself in the other person be beauty or virtue (*agathon*) or goodness (*arete*). Second, *eros* strives to complete itself by means of this worth. The myth of the spherical man introduced by Aristophanes,[9] but especially the section in which Socrates speaks of what he learned from the wise Diotima, make this point. If *eros* shows desire, this indicates that it lacks something. "We love only that which we do not have and what we lack"; for "who in all the world would desire that which he already has?"

This is why Socrates "demythologizes" Eros a bit. That is, he denies him divine character and makes him a daemon, an intermediate being.

---

[8] See *Symposium,* 210 ff.; English trans. in *The Dialogues of Plato,* by B. Jowett (Oxford University Press, 1891), I, 580 ff. (Trans.)

[9] *Symposium* 190; *ibid.,* p. 559. (Trans.)

The gods are perfect. And this is precisely the reason why they do not have this erotic defect; they do not have that need to complete themselves which Aristophanes defined in his myth of the original man as the really basic tendency of *eros*. So Eros is an intermediate power, an in-between power (*metaxu*). He lies in an intermediate zone between wisdom and ignorance, between beauty and ugliness. And because man himself dwells in this "mean," and the gods live in immortal completeness, *eros* is a specifically "human" passion and it is wrongly considered to be a divine passion. The gods cannot love because they have everything. (As Fr. Hebbel says, they "have no fate but they ordain fate.")

So, because *eros* is determined by the fact that it dwells in this intermediate state, it is always self-love. It is never pure surrender in the sense of giving oneself away, but it always has in it the element of monopolizing, of fulfilling oneself, and appropriating. (Cf. the verses on Eros in Goethe's *"Urworten, orphisch"* ["Words of Ancient Wisdom, Orphic"[10]].) When we say that *eros* has an egocentric tendency, we do so only with the understanding that we must assume that, depending upon the stage of purification it has gone through, *eros* is capable of reaching a very sublime form of *amor sui*. For the higher form of *eros* is, after all, love of the "better" self, the self that strives to complete itself through the highest values and finally to attain the vision of the Ideas. So when we say that this is a kind of spiritual *amor sui,* this does not imply any moral disparagement. On the contrary, this is only to state that it has in it an *inversio in me ipsum,* which as such is regarded either as being completely meta-ethical (as is, for example, the *amour de soi-même* in contrast with *amour propre* in Rousseau) or as a "turning in upon my self" which strives for the ethical triumph of the higher, authentic self over the lower self (in the same sense in which Augustine's idea of self-love is doubtless to be understood).[11]

Now, when we proceed to deal with the concept of *agape,* we enter into completely different territory.

The very fact that the New Testament never uses the term to mean love for ideas, norms, and values, and thus for "the" good and "the" beautiful, would inevitably strike us as being different in atmosphere if we came to it from the Greek way of thinking. But it becomes intelligible as soon as

[10] Prose trans. in *The Penguin Book of German Verse,* ed. by Leonard Foster (Baltimore: Penguin Books, 1959), pp. 230 f.:
"That is not withheld! He swoops from heaven, whither he had risen from ancient wastes, he flutters to us with airy wings and hovers all through the spring day round our heads and breasts, sometimes he seems to retreat, but returns from his retreating; then there comes joy in suffering, so sweet and tremulous. Many a heart tends to diffusion, but it is the noblest that gives itself to the One." (Trans.)

[11] Cf. *ThE* I, §1713.

we remember that in New Testament thought there are no norms and values in the sense of autonomous qualities alongside of, and apart from, their personification in God. For biblical thinking it is impossible (though the heretical attempt to do so occurs again and again in the history of theology) to conceive that there can be such a thing as a given and knowable system of values in which God is then incorporated as the apex of the value hierarchy, the "Idea of ideas."

Then, too, we are struck by the fact that, in contrast with the *eros* world, the term *agape* is used, not only for the love of men for one another, but primarily for the love of God for men (John 3:16). The very fact that the idea of a "love of God," that God is the Subject of loving, is conceivable at all shows that here we are on a completely different level of thinking. We have seen why it is that the gods of Plato cannot love in the real sense of the word.

In attempting now to say what *agape* is on the positive side, we can only note several central points. We shall define it with reference to the significance the *eros-agape* relationship has for the sexual relationship.

1. The love of God is above all the love which loves that which is like it. It loves in man the *imago Dei*.[12] And this tendency of the love of God evidences its real character precisely in the fact that it addresses itself to fallen man, who, so to speak, no longer has any worth (in the *eros* sense) and thus is no longer worth loving. God loves in him the buried image of himself. He loves him *nevertheless*. God does not love the dust in which the pearl lies, but he loves the pearl lying in the dust. The parable of the Prodigal Son shows how the Father's gaze penetrates beneath the grubby surface and sees the real person. This real, authentic man, this *imago Dei*, is not the image we show to others; it is the image the Father has of us.[13]

2. This real being of man is not an ontically producible attribute, such as the reason, for example.[14] For, as Goethe said, the reason can also serve to make man "even more beastly than any beast." Luther declared that if we were to see the *imago Dei* in ontic qualities, we should have to describe the devil as the most perfect image, since he possesses all these qualities in superlative form.[15] The real being of man therefore does not consist in a sum of attributes, but rather in a relationship. That is to say that this man was created in order to live in fellowship with his Father and not merely to develop himself as a mere entelechy. And he retains this dignity of fellowship with God even when he loses his ontic qualities, when he becomes, as Pascal said, a "king with a broken scepter and

[12] Cf. *ThE* I, §837 ff.
[13] Cf. *ThE* I, §817-820, 842.
[14] Cf. *ThE* I, §800 ff.
[15] Cf. *ThE* I, §808.

decayed purple," when one can no longer tell by looking at the returning son that he is the son of this Father.

3. Because God's *agape,* as it took on historical form in Christ, and the *agape* practiced by men in imitation of God directs itself to this authentic being in the other person, it has a liberating effect. (This effect of liberation can be seen in Jesus' loving association with sinners, the people who are not "worth" loving.) It performs the function of a photographic developer which brings out the latent image. *Agape* is not a response to a "loveworthiness" which is already there; it is rather the creative cause that produces this "loveworthiness." Nor is trust, which is nourished by this *agape,* a reaction to a trustworthiness already demonstrated; it rather initially elicits this trustworthiness. God does not love us because we are valuable and worthful; we are worthful because God loves us. This describes again the creative significance of *agape.*

4. In this connection we should repeat the statement made at the beginning, namely, that the real being of the person to which *agape* directs itself is not its immanent being, but rather its "alien dignity," the fact that it stands in relationship to God and thus is under his protection. Therefore the person, thus understood as being in "relationship," remains intact even when the immanent attributes and the ability to perform functions disappear. Thus understood, the value of a person lies in a totally different level from that of his utility value. Hence there can never be any question of a "life that is not worth being allowed to live" (and all the consequences of this notion). And hence a community like that of marriage cannot simply cease to exist when the importance of the other person for me (say his importance in fulfilling myself in the *eros* sense) diminishes or disappears and he fails functionally. *Agape* discerns in him other, abiding elements.

5. On this basis—and only on this basis—can we understand how it is possible to love our enemies.[16] In *agape* I no longer identify the other person with the opposition in which he stands to me; nor do I identify him with his functions, which he directs upon me. I see in him the child of God (and hence the relationship that constitutes the real being of his person), and therefore I see him in a dimension which transcends his functions. When—to take an instance of what is meant by the Sermon on the Mount—I am delivered over to the enemy of my faith and I suffer because of him, then God's sorrow for his erring child becomes my sorrow. And this is what creates the bond of *agape* with one's enemy. The sin of the elder brother who remained at home was that he could neither rejoice nor sorrow with his father, in short, that he had no *agape.*[17]

[16] Cf. *ThE* I, §455.
[17] Luke 15:25 ff.; cf. Thielicke, *The Waiting Father,* trans. by John W. Doberstein (New York: Harper & Row, 1959), pp. 30 ff.

6. This *agape* is not at man's disposal; nor is it like *eros,* inherent in his nature. It can be bestowed upon him only by God. Man can be empowered to possess *agape* only by allowing himself to receive it from God and so pass it on to his neighbor. He who does not receive it cannot pass it on, and he who does not pass it on loses what he has received.[18]

All of these important points together bring out at the same time the characteristic marks that distinguish *agape* from *eros.* Without restating them in detail, we shall now try to show how these two lines— that of *eros* and that of *agape*—intersect in the actual sex community. And here again we shall content ourselves for the present with indicative statements, since we shall have to go back repeatedly and elaborate this relationship on the basis of concrete data.

1. Since the sex community is a connection between two human beings—leaving out of account for the present whether it be a married, and thus a lifelong relationship, or a "free" and passing connection—and since it therefore always has a personal character, the *agape* relationship must always play a part in it. Because the other party is a person, because he has an eternal destiny which he can miss, and because I can be a party to his missing his destiny, I must respect the "alien dignity" within him. His real being can never be a mere means to an end for me, which, in this connection, means a mere instrument of sexual ecstasy, in the same way that prostitution, the extreme development of this attitude, entails the instrumentalizing of a human being. One could also very simply describe this *agape* relationship in the sex community by saying that for me the other person is a "neighbor."[19]

2. On the other hand, however, not just any "neighbor" can become my partner in the sex community. In order to become this, he must rather fulfill certain conditions which lift him out in a very specific way from the general classification of "neighbor." Among these conditions are that, apart from certain borderline cases, he belongs to the opposite sex, that his age be in a proper relation to mine, that he be my "type," in physique, character, and mind, to mention only a

---

[18] Matt. 18: 21 ff.; cf. Thielicke, *The Waiting Father,* pp. 93 ff.

[19] Many of our marriage liturgies express this in the words: "that one may bring the other with him to heaven."

few respects, and thus be in a highly specialized complementary relationship to me. Thus the other person must fulfill the requirement of being the bearer of some very definite values. To this extent the *eros* relationship comes into play here.

Briefly stated, the two aspects can be related to each other as follows: The person to whom I relate myself erotically must be my "neighbor" and hence the object of my *agape*. Otherwise, I dehumanize him. On the other hand, however, not everyone who is my neighbor and therefore stands in *agape* relationship to me can be the object of my *eros*. I cannot, for example, give myself erotically or even marry out of sympathy. Anyone who attempts this enters, not *into* marriage, but definitely into something *alongside* of marriage. *Sex community is a special case of human communication with conditions attached to it.*

We see, therefore, how *agape* and *eros* are both at work in the sex community and how they point to each other. We may expect, however, that the antithetical structure of the two motives will also come into play. And though we can assert with certainty that in *eros* and *agape* the two basic strivings of all human existence find expression, we can also expect that in sex community the mystery of human existence will manifest itself in its most direct and concentrated form.

# B. The Libido, Animal and Human

## 1. The Nature of the Sex Impulse

The sex impulse is the desire, accompanied by pleasure and the urge to consummate this pleasure in ecstasy, for psychophysical union with another human being.

In speaking of the desire for "union" we are already employing a concept of "community" which is central to sexual ethics, although for reasons which will immediately become apparent we still cannot use the term at this point. So we ask what "union" means here, our specific purpose being to learn how this concept is related to that of "community" or union of two persons.

According to our definition, the urge to union is characterized by the following factors:

First, the pleasure and the ecstasy. When we examine these two emotions with regard to their power to produce community, the first thing that strikes us is their fleeting [*punktuelle*] character. They are not continuous, they do not last. For pleasure and ecstasy are excitements that rise and fall in definite and steep curves. Nobody can be excited all the time and even pathological manic states are usually followed by depressions. Ecstasy rises up, as it were, from dead center and falls back into it. Fulfillment is followed by relapse into apathy and then again by reawakened desire:

> Thus in desire I hasten to enjoyment,
> And in enjoyment pine to feel desire.[1]

[1] Goethe, *Faust,* I, 14, trans. by Bayard Taylor (New York: Modern Library, 1950), p. 125. (Trans.)

All pleasure, all joy, according to Nietzsche, "wants eternity—wants deep, wants deep eternity,"[2] and yet because it is fleeting its plea to the "moment", "Ah, still delay—thou art so fair!"[3] remains fundamentally unheard.[4] There are far more oaths (of eternal love) sworn on park benches on summer nights than on the witness stands of the courts. Why is it that a full moon and the scent of roses should turn the formula of an oath into everyday speech? After all, everybody knows that such oaths are usually broken. It would appear that the only explanation that presents itself is that these are not so much oaths as earnest entreaties and adjurations. People entreat the "moment," whose ecstatic fullness stands in such frightening contrast to its brevity, to linger longer and become "deep, deep eternity."

In this whole connection some attention must be given to this practice of adjuration in the realm of *eros*. In our generation there is a widespread tendency to make fun of the reticence concerning erotic matters in polite society prescribed by Victorian times. This lack of any "direct" statements concerning sex is obvious even in the literature of the time. Where would you find in Goethe's *Wilhelm Meister* or in the works of Gottfried Keller or Adalbert Stifter even the remotest analogy to what is now accepted as a matter of course as being part of the stock material for a novel even by a novelist like Thomas Mann? We feel compelled to ask whether this was prudery, whereas we moderns acknowledge the existence of the impulse and therefore do not allow it to smolder in secrecy and be stunted, starved, and smothered beneath the universal silence. To be sure, it would not be wrong to say that this was prudery, insofar as it confused the psychic form of what manifests itself here with the thing itself which is manifested. What is manifesting itself here, or better, what is concealing itself in prudery, is again an act of adjuration. We know that these things must not be invoked, because mentioning them by name might loose powers which could not be restrained. Just because we are aware of the elemental dynamic of *eros*, we seek to banish it in silence. Even the most sublimated signs of suggestion are sufficient to insure its presence. Whereas postpsychoanalytical literature usually gives us extensive guided tours through the cellars and lumber rooms of human nature, Stifter's *Nachsommer*, for example, shows us only the architectural symmetry of lives

[2] *Thus Spoke Zarathustra;* see Walter Kaufmann, *The Portable Nietzsche* (New York: The Viking Press, 1954), p. 436. (Trans.)

[3] Goethe, *Faust*, II, V, 6; *op. cit.*, p. 241. (Trans.)

[4] This passage from *Faust* also refers to this "moment" which cannot be seized and retained, though here it is filled with a different content.

that are sound and healthy. It is left to the reader to what extent he is going to conclude that these buildings simply do not rise from the flat surface of the ground, but rather extend down into the earth and therefore have cellars. The darkness is there, but it is left unexpressed; it is relegated to its proper place, and we are protected from its power. Stifter, especially, was conscious of its presence, and it was the tragedy of his life that this subterranean power caught him in its grip and the forces of despair rose up from the cellars of his soul. Yet it was kept out of his works; this is proved by his own words. Only in his letters do we hear it, as it were, knocking on the wall.

Today we speak not only about the power but also about the details of *eros* even in the best society. We talk in a free and easy way about our complexes and are capable of revealing things about ourselves in the code language of objective terminology which were formerly uttered only in the confessional. This, however, does not reveal a more intact *eros,* but rather an *eros* that has been domesticated, exhausted, and robbed of its elemental character. We no longer need to be exorcised. Since it has changed from a wild, rushing torrent, confined to a narrow riverbed, into stagnant flood waters that inundate the whole country and since we are always wading in it and coming into touch with it everywhere (in nudifying concealments and concealing nudifications, in the omnipresent exploitation of sex appeal on stage and screen, in magazines and newspapers), it ceases to be something ecstatically seductive and enjoys the prescriptive right to have at its beck and call *at any time* those whom it formerly had to seduce.[5] Already there are highly civilized countries in which even young children are given sex education by means of films and talks in order that the ecstatic demands of nature may be normalized and reduced to "second nature" at an early enough age, and in order that what is by nature a mystery may be shown to be merely an objective triviality and thus make it harmless. And as a matter of fact, here adjurations and reticences are no longer needed in order to prevent the elemental force from coming too close. The stagnant waters surround us on all sides. The fleeting moment of *eros* has become an extended flat surface. Has this brought us closer to *eros*?

The fleeting character of the libido evidences itself, however, not only in the alternation of pleasure and apathy, euphoria and depression, but also in the law of attraction and repulsion which operates here. The more erotic behavior is merely a matter of releasing an instinctive impulse the more it is subject to this law. And it is a well-

[5] Cf. Sieburg, *op. cit.*

known phenomenon that sexual intercourse between partners who meet each other only in the animal pleasure of the moment—as, for example, in prostitution—usually changes immediately after the orgasm into aversion and disgust, that is, "repulsion." Actually, the criterion of that which is *more* than merely instinctive, namely, the personal character of the sexual intercourse, is that gratitude and fulfillment survive the moment of ecstasy and that these moments are only the expression, culmination, and concentration of a continuing relationship which outlasts all changes of mood and feeling.

In any case, the steep curve of the purely instinctive reactions shows us that in the sex urge something is expressing itself which is qualitatively different from sympathy or love or trust. Inherent in these attitudes there is a certain permanence and steadiness which is the very thing the urge does not possess. And the urge does not have it because the interhuman contact which it establishes is tied up with definite functions, or to express it still more concretely, with definite *hormonal* functions, which have a totally different effect upon the psyche, depending upon the time of the year, the person's age, the kind of stimulation present in a particular milieu, the stage which desire or satiation has reached in the rhythmical pattern of the urge.

In this matter of attitude toward community, if we wish to draw a parallel from a completely nonsexual area, we might perhaps be inclined to think first of *comradeship*. For comradeship means—distinguished from "friendship," in which the being of two persons constitutes a *communio*—the relationship of persons who are confronted with particular practical tasks, and therefore are performing the same functions which serve to fulfill these tasks. Thus school comrades are bound together by the education which they share, the common struggles and difficulties they have with certain teachers and examination situations. These comradeships are frequently characterized by the fact—and herein lies the point of comparison with the inconstancy of the urge—that they remain confined to definite functions and thus their duration is also limited to the performance of these functions. This is why later meetings with school comrades are often so boring. After the magic of school days has disappeared banality takes the place of words that formerly created community. You find that you have nothing to say to each other.[6] The same is

---

[6] Cf. Erich Kästner's poem "Klassenzusammenkunft" ("Class Reunion") in *Lyrische Hausapotheke*.

true of the comradeship we have with persons with whom we work. Frequently, comradeships of soldiers facing death together at the front can generate communication and may also include the being of the persons involved; these, however, are on the borderline of a completely different kind of personal relationship.

So there are good reasons why in our definition we did not speak of the urge to "community" or "fellowship," but rather of the urge to "union." For even etymologically the suffix "-ship" denotes a state, condition, or quality, whereas the suffix "-ion" denotes an act or process and thus the fleeting character of that which is striven for. The soldier on leave or a summer visitor who picks up a "date" is not interested in "community" (indeed, he may even *fear* it as threatening marriage!). What he is interested in is the fleeting moment of "union."

But this inconstancy of the mere urge applies not only to the relationship of the two partners to each other, so that the extreme fluctuation in the sex urge, which we spoke of earlier, prevails in their relationship; it also has the effect of making the partnership itself almost unlimitedly interchangeable. For the farther we remove ourselves from the realm of the personal and the more we move into the realm of purely physical and psychic reactions the more we remove ourselves from the dimension of the "once-for-all" and move into the dimension of the general and interchangeable.

One can therefore set up the following proportion: the more an individual's life is determined by his urges the more he falls into promiscuity and the more exchangeable he regards his partner. All that is required is that the other person fulfill certain functional conditions; he must satisfy the most elementary requirements of health and normality in order to be utilizable. The strength of the sex urge is by no means the thing that determines this attitude. The strength of the sex urge by itself is not what produces this kind of "polygamy," this constant change of partners. An extremely strong sex urge can also be present in those who, as Christians, subject their sexuality to the discipline of obedience and reverence for one's neighbor. It is rather merely a question of whether and to what extent my *existence* is determined by instinct and impulse (to what extent these gain *exousia* over me, I Cor. 6:12, 10:23), instead of the urge itself becoming a personal function, i.e., a means of expressing a personal relationship which is capable of persisting even apart from this expression of it. If this possibility that the sexual expression of personal community can disappear did not exist, we would not be able to understand how aged married couples can still be happily married.

We have said that the more we are determined by instinct the more "polygamous" we are. But we can also say that the more we are determined by instinct the less we seek the "once-for-all" and nonexchangeable Thou of the other person and the more we regard him as a mere specimen, a mere "representative" of the other sex, whose individual conformation is a matter of indifference, but whose instrumental significance is therefore all the more important.

This may also explain why a uniform has such a strange attraction for a girl. This attraction may lie less in the handsomeness of the uniform (the modern military is exercising more and more restraint with regard to the trappings of war), than the fact that it tends to provide a general evidence of a certain masculinity and virility, even though it contains only a cook or a company clerk. It has the significance of a general (not individual) representation of the masculine. Analogous on the feminine side is what is admired in the way of uniform character, standard hair-do, make-up, and stereotyped physiognomy. Its "general" character is, so to speak, further potentiated by the fact that it tends to be constructed on the pattern of movie idols and ideals, which are themselves a representation of the unconscious general ideal and even owe their success to this circumstance. The copy of a copy, the representation of a representation—this is what the extreme absorption of personal individuality into the *genus masculinum* or *femininum* turns out to be.

We have already said that prostitution provides the extreme example of the degree to which pure instinctuality seeks only the instrumental value of the representative of the *genus*. This thought is further supplemented in a way that is important for anthropology by the fact that we find a corresponding attitude in the prostitute who is "used" in this way, except with this shade of difference: what is for the person who uses the prostitute for purely physical purposes a negative, an ethical deficiency (that is, the fact that he is seeking merely the function and not the person, desiring union and not community) is for the prostitute a positive element in her "professional ethics." A certain self-respect, which is found even in these circles, requires that the prostitute must not give herself as a "per-

son," must not share in her professional acts, but only exercise instrumental functions. She distinguishes very precisely between her business
activity and her personal love (possibly for her *souteneur*) in which she
participates and also invests her person. Therefore when a woman de-
scends to the level of prostitution a strange reversal of ethical standards
occurs (and it would be pharisaical not to recognize that there are *ethical
standards* even on this level): the dissociation of the person from the union
becomes a virtue, a requirement demanded by self-respect, whereas for
the same reason the partner of a prostitute must see himself regarded with
contempt as morally delinquent. In the pastoral care of prostitutes, regard
for this strange inversion of ethical structure cannot be a matter of indifference. One who does not address the prostitute at the point of her self-
respect is not addressing her in a Christian way but rather moralistically
and therefore is not addressing her at all. Here, too, the gospel—unlike
moralism—gives us the freedom to make a fellow human approach
(John 8:7).

Important material illustrative of what we have described as an inversion of the ethical structure is given by Siegfried Borelli and Willy Starck
in their book on prostitution as a psychological problem.[7]

On the "professional ethos" of prostitutes this comment is made: "For
a definite fee they provide a clearly defined service. . . . They claim the
virtue of honesty, because the other women (that is, those who have sexual intercourse with frequently changed partners, but do not have a police
license for prostitution) engage in the same activity as they do, but will
not admit it or do not like to be labeled as 'public prostitutes,' for the
'P.P.'s' (*puellae publicae*) are conscious of the discrimination this term implies."[8] Interviews with prostitutes show that this kind of "professional
ethos," and even an otherwise respectable existence, including being the
mother of a family, is possible only if prostitution is practiced without
any personal involvement whatsoever, and also completely without any
expression of libido, as a purely business matter.[9] As a rule the public
prostitutes are not motivated by physical desire. On the other hand, it
turns out that erotically sensitive, and therefore participative, women, possibly by nature possessed of a definite ethical attitude, are more likely to
become completely demoralized, becoming hetaerae or courtesans with
constantly changing partners, and yet persistently refusing to go the way
of prostitution. Thus one such completely destitute courtesan said, "The
only thing wrong is that I like love too much." "She would really rather

[7] *Die Prostitution als psychologisches Problem* (1957).
[8] *Ibid.*, p. 31, 249.
[9] *Ibid.*, pp. 199 f.

live the 'life of a beggar' than become a prostitute." That which one participates in—even by means of such a perverted "love"—cannot be treated in a businesss way and as a means of earning money.[10]

Thus even in the distorting mirror of prostitution and hetaerism we see again this fundamental thesis that *eros* is permeated with the personal element. If this *eros* is a reality, then prostitution would mean that one was selling "one's self." Hence, this way is avoided by all those who possess a certain modicum of ethical self-regard. The typical prostitute, however, who does not participate in the act with her *eros* (but for obvious reasons merely pretends to do so), puts only her genital apparatus at her partner's disposal, while she "herself" is elsewhere.

We have used prostitution as an illustration of how person and libido, community and union, are related to each other for two reasons. First, because this borderline case provides unusually characteristic expressions of this relationship, and second, because it reveals a basic fact which is significant for ethics. And that fact is that definitions of relationship, such as that of person and libido, can never be framed in general and abstract terms, but must always be seen in the light of a concrete situation: to one who visits a house of prostitution the separation of the person from the libido function has a different ethical meaning from that which it has for the prostitute. Ethics cannot be formulated by subsuming cases under principles, but only by seeking—with a knowledge of these principles—to see cases "from the inside." Then these cases take on a completely different aspect. But to see cases "from the inside" means nothing less than meeting with understanding the human beings who are involved in these cases. It is in this sense that the gospel teaches us to approach "cases"; it teaches us to enter *into* them. But then they cease to be merely "cases" and become situations in which human beings are living out their own unique relationship to God, their own peculiar responsibility, and their own personal crises, which therefore can be understood only in terms of this individual. Thus Jesus does not deal with the "case" of adultery; rather he addresses himself to the adulteress. He see the case "from the inside" and allows it to become a model, in which others too must recognize themselves (John 8:1 ff.; Luke 7:36 ff).[11]

We may sum up and round off what we have said about the nature of the libido and its relation to the person as follows.

First, the libido drives at fleeting union, while all personal engagement seeks community. Accordingly, personal fellowships grow

---

[10] *Ibid.*, pp. 239, 240.

[11] On prostitution cf. the analysis of the character of the prostitute Sonia in Dostoevski's *Crime and Punishment, ThE II,* 1, §1027 ff.

deeper to the degree that the partners grow deeper; but functional pleasure relationships evaporate. Often it is only this consequence of a deepening or an evaporating relationship that indicates the innermost motives with which two people have entered the relationship. For at the moment of entrance desire is often taken for love and sexual function is taken for self-giving of the person. The reason for this is that vitality—even purely physical vitality—possesses a creative power, a kind of expressionistic vision that imparts idealized personal features to the other person and transforms him from a poor little rivulet into a majestic stream, while in reality it was only the rushing sound of one's own blood that produced these optical and acoustical illusions.[12]

Second, the libido, even though it is directed toward another, seeks *self-fulfillment*, and it does so in two senses: first, in the negative sense of desiring to put an end to the pain of sheer passion in pleasurable fulfillment, that is, the orgasm, and second, in the positive sense of striving to transcend one's own self in the ecstasy. For along with the libido and its satisfaction there goes an extraordinary enhancement of vital consciousness: the experience of creative, generative power, the joy of being able to please another person and be desired by him, the proof of youth and "infinite potentialities," and finally a psychophysical upswing that proves to the harried soul that he is still something more than a mere labor machine, a mere brain, a humdrum vegetator, that he can transcend himself and get "outside of himself."

The anthropological significance of carnival and Shrovetide celebrations probably lies here too; not only because they are an outstanding arena for the exercise of *eros*, but above all because here the power inherent in *eros* to transcend oneself seems to come into play. Dressing oneself in costume and becoming someone else is a form of this self-transcendence, of getting outside of oneself and out of bounds. Here one loses one's identity and possibilities which remain unrecognized in normal life are opened up. Here the diminishment of possibilities that comes with growing older is halted for a few moments. Therefore carnival celebra-

---

[12] Therein may lie the validity of the frequently given counsel that those who are in love or think they are in love should separate for a time in order to allow distance to show whether their relationship may not be based upon an illusion of the libido.

tions are not only an "opportunity" for the ever-ready libido; they also share with it a common structure, namely, the ecstatic mode of being, self-transcendence, the experience of enhancing and surpassing one's own potential.

## 2. THE HUMAN INTEGRATION OF THE SEX IMPULSE

### a. Libido and Serving Devotion

The egoism which we have observed in the libido is therefore by no means related only to the sex organs themselves, but rather to the whole self and its self-fulfillment. The term "egoism," however, is not adequate to express fully the drive of the sex impulse toward self-enhancement and self-fulfillment. Note well that here we are not saying that sexuality *as such* is nothing more than pure egoism. This should be self-evident; for sexuality (even from the *eros* point of view) exhibits personal features beyond the functional, and even *agape* has a place and a mission in it. What we are saying is that even the physical sex impulse—and therefore only one factor *within* sexuality—is not exclusively egoistic, but that it too is directed to the *other partner* in the sense of self-surrender and self-bestowal and thus exhibits some essentially altruistic features. In any case, this is true of the healthy sex impulse.

Since so much depends upon our understanding and substantiating this thought, we must define it more precisely. We need to recognize that we must *not* think of this altruistic tendency in one's attitude toward the sexual partner in such a way as to regard the impulse as being by nature exclusively egoistic, and therefore directed solely at self-fulfillment, while the so-called *"higher," personal constituents* of the self (such as the spirit, conscience, etc.), are opposed to this selfish tendency of the impulse. We must see very clearly that we must not picture the situation in the self as being only a struggle between will and impulse, spirit and sensuality, and then conclude that it is the task of these "higher" personal constituents of the self to see to it that, despite the impulse, a deeper, "human" community emerges and thus that the impulse may be domesticated as much as possible and made subservient to the higher *personal* end.

Precisely because this *Idealistic* interpretation of sexuality has been so widely accepted since Kant so radically separated the *mundus sensibilis* (world of sense) from the *mundus intelligibilis* (world of mind),[13] everything depends upon our addressing ourselves very carefully to this conception and as far as possible breaking it down. This conception is based primarily on the assumption that there is a mutually exclusive opposition between the impulse and the will, and therefore it operates with antagonisms which break apart the total unity of bios and person. This assumption is in turn based upon an anthropology which views man as being built up in stories, in such a way that the higher apartments of the mental and moral are placed above a lower floor of the sensual and instinctive.

It is certainly a fundamental contribution of Christianity to anthropology that it rejects this partition and stratification of man and teaches us that man is a psychophysical unity, in which even the body is a "temple of the Holy Spirit" (I Cor. 6:19; cf. 3:16 f.) and therefore loses that inferiority which attaches to it in the Hellenistic tradition.[14] But if the body is regarded as a mode of being-one's-self—as "I myself" in a particular relation—and not merely an inferior part of this being-one's-self, then one may also regard the physical libido as a mode of this being-one's-self and not merely as the possibly "demonic" antagonist of this self. It is true that in the New Testament view the self can be destroyed by the rebellion of the libido; that is to say, it can become subject to the flesh, the *sarx* (Eph. 5:5; I Cor. 6:9 ff.).[15] But the self can also be destroyed by the rebellious *spirit*. What Paul means, for example, by "the wisdom of the world" (I Cor. 1:18 ff.) is for him the ideological form in which the rebellious, unbridled spirit of man expresses itself. So, according to this, both flesh and spirit have demonic possibilities. But they are not by nature demonic. Rather each in its own way represents the whole self, and therefore they cannot be partitioned into alleged higher and alleged inferior constituents of the self.

[13] Cf. on Kant and Schiller, *ThE* I, §228 ff., 1612.
[14] Cf. the corresponding examination of Paul's anthropology, especially the terms *soma, psyche, sarx,* etc., in Bultmann's article on "Paul" in *Religion in Geschichte und Gegenwart* (*RGG*), (2 ed.), IV, 1032 ff.
[15] Cf. *ThE* I, §336 ff.

Now, if we keep in view this unity of man (it is the unity of body and soul before God), then this means that we must ask to what extent the libido *itself* (and not merely that "higher self" which really does not exist at all) moves toward real communication, toward serving the other person, and hence to what extent it seeks much more than mere "self"-satisfaction.

This, in our opinion, not only brings us to some new ways of looking at theological anthropology; our purpose is also to mitigate a rigid and apprehensive attitude toward what is frequently thought to be a Christian conception of sex, but above all to get rid of sterile moralistic categories.

In order to appreciate this human integration of the libido we must make the following observations.

To begin with a very trivial statement, the sex impulse is never confined to the person who is driven by the urge, but rather seeks the partner. But it does not do so (except under destructive conditions) with the sole purpose of "using" the other person merely as an object with which to stimulate and satisfy itself. Rather, as we have already indicated, there is something in the structure of the libido itself that points to a two-way communication, in any case to the rudiments of such a possibility; for the prerequisite for the fulfillment of the pleasure is that the other person give himself to it, that he participate. But this giving of oneself cannot mean that he merely puts himself "at the disposal" of the other person merely as an object to perform certain functions. Rather it implies that he must feel that he is being "carried along" and is himself excited, that he is responding to the other's wishes, and doing so spontaneously, that is to say, on the basis of his *own* aroused libido. Thus the other person should not be a passive object upon which one's own urge is simply "abreacted." If he is, then the sexual intercourse degenerates into a kind of disguised masturbation and accordingly remains unfulfilled.[16] Only the crudest physical side of the libido can be subdued for a moment in this way; but, instead of the "peace" of satisfaction, what is achieved is at most a brief truce with the libido. The thirst is, as it were, quenched with salt

---

[16] Thus even prostitutes, who allow themselves to be used as a passive object of an abreaction, at least simulate participation; cf. Borelli and Starck, *op. cit.*

water, and therefore not quenched at all. The libido arrives at real satisfaction only by entering into the other person's libido. The sex partner cannot desire only himself. And if we were to express it epigrammatically, we might say that out of egoism he must be altruistic in order to gain the other person's response to himself.

There are in the structure of the human urge some astonishing indications of this fact which is fundamental to sexuality. The most important of them may well lie in the curve of excitation in man and woman. It is well known that the man's curve of excitation rises steeply and falls equally precipitously. In the woman, however, the rise and fall are slower and more prolonged. The woman's curve spans longer stages of foreplay and postlude, of "erotic atmosphere." If each of the two partners were to think only of himself, he would inevitably leave the other person in solitude and to that extent unsatisfied. But the resulting incongruence would react upon himself; for he would get out of step with the rhythm of the process and lose the co-operation of the other partner.

One who has at his disposal only physiological categories with which to assess these incongruences in the structure of the sex impulse in man and woman must arrive at the conclusion that this is an imperfection of nature, an ultimate disharmony. For in this way it actually becomes possible that one partner (as a rule it will be the woman) will not "keep pace," and not only will the orgasms not be synchronized, but one partner may possibly be left out in the cold completely, feeling that he has been left behind. Fire and ashes, excitement and sleep may find themselves in tormenting proximity.

The positive consequence of this for the theological problem of sex is that the difference between the sexual nature of man and woman does not allow human beings merely to follow the impulse in blind, animal fashion, if the urge is to be satisfied. (Here in the midst of the physical realm itself we find a fundamental difference between human and animal sexuality.) This difference rather confronts us with a *task*, which challenges us to transcend the purely natural. The creatureliness of the body is something more and something different from its naturalness. Creaturehood implies that man is challenged at every moment to transcend nature—including his physical moments. The body along with its libido is the representative of the man himself. And just as man is created for communication, just as he exists in relationship to the other, just as he must serve and allow himself to be served, so he is also in the realm in which his body represents him. Hence, for its own sake (not for the sake of "higher duties") the difference in the nature of the sexes prohibits the human being from merely "letting himself go." On the contrary, it compels "challenge and response" (to use Arnold Toynbee's phrase); it is a provocation, something that literally "calls him out" of determination by natural laws. It exposes him to failure and success, and in all this it confronts him with the theme of human communication instead of mere animal copulation.

So all this appears on the level of the impulse itself and not only on the level of higher reflection or even the level of conscience, which deals with conscious decisions and the categorical imperative.

And this is what we mean by the human integration of the libido. It is "human" not only insofar as it is directed by reason and conscience; it is already "human" in the way it directs itself. The human libido cannot desire *only* itself when it desires itself; it must take the other person into account. It must affirm the other person and it cannot only desire him. The libido must have in it a "diaconic" element, an element of serving love, if it is not to be left by itself and cheated of its own goal. The incongruence between the male and female sex structure may be a defect in the ontological, natural sense. But this is precisely what gives it the chance to be human—even in the physical realm. Here the automatism of the animal instinct is transcended.

What is observable here in the physical realm has the character of a *sign* of humanity. Hence what is indicated here as being specifically human demands expression in the other realms of human existence too. This means that what in the physical realm is largely left to instinctive action (remembering, however, that this is specifically *human* instinctive action), demands in the totality of communication to become a *motive,* which in turn reflects back into the physical realm. For every human sex community, such as marriage (and specifically marriage!), becomes a reality only as the partners give themselves to each other, only as one desires to bring sexual joy to the other and thus desires to serve him. If one first seeks to help the other person to achieve his optimum, then one's own optimum will be added unto him. Satisfaction—in any case in this optimal sense—can never be had directly, but rather diminishes when it is sought in this way.

Here we see how *agape* makes its presence felt in the medium of sex community and the way in which it is used. Its characteristic is that it does not "seek its own" (*ou zetei ta eautes,* I Cor. 13:5) and yet receives all things "as well." *Agape* takes hold of a tendency which is built into the creaturely sex nature of man in the form of a sign, a challenge, and transforms it into a motive. It gives meaning and purpose to what instinct may do ignorantly and relates it to the whole of human existence and community for which man was created. In this way the sex community which is determined by *agape* also has its effect upon the physical elements of the relationship.

True, even the libido which is operative within the human being as such does not seek *only* its own; it does not do so because of the cunning of the instinct. And an *ars amandi* (art of loving) can be highly developed in which this instinctive action is elaborately refined and this tactical "altruism" is carried to extreme limits. But where *agape* permeates the sex community the happiness of the other person is sought in the whole breadth of common existence, and therefore can also become operative in the physical realm. The *ars amandi* is thus enclosed in a new context of meaning.

It is important that we see this close interconnection of *eros* and *agape* in a theologically conceived anthropology. For this prevents the physical side of sex life from being left to its own autonomy—which in fact does not even exist—and it also prevents us from reserving *agape* and all the specifically human motives for communication to the supposedly "higher" dimensions of existence. This segregation of higher and lower leads either to indifference to the elemental realm or to its demonization. Both have been amply evident in the history of Christianity. And it is a great pity that the term "heresy" has been reserved only for dogmatic deviations and not applied also to false ethical constructions. For this construction of anthropology by virtue of which the realm of physical sexuality has been left without theological guidance or put in a false light is a genuine and massive heresy. Therefore it is of central importance that the sphere of the libido is not only included in the realm of the human (*humanum*) but also that its affinity to *agape* be recognized; and conversely, that *agape* should be seen as that which helps, and liberates and fulfills even in the realm of the libido.

This orientation toward the other person, this element of mutual self-giving and stimulation, becomes concrete and practical at two points, which need only to be indicated. They are primarily important in the application of these anthropological considerations in pastoral care.

First, numerous marital crises fall into the area which we have just discussed. This is most often the case when the crisis has its roots in the area of sex and one of the partners of the marriage makes it understood (within the broad scale of possible statements in question here) that he "gets no value for his money" from the other person, that he can find no understanding or appreciation in the realm of intimate relations. Every marriage counselor knows how frequently these complaining accusations are expressed. In not a few cases the therapy here will hardly consist in the recommendation of certain techniques (possibly of the kind given by van de Velde), though this is by no means to call in question the validity of these instructions. In most cases the solution will rather be sought in a totally different direction, namely, in the challenge to face the task of human communication, the challenge of *agape*. We now know that this attitude is not alien to sex and why it is not alien, and we also know that we are doing an injustice to the elemental physical self if we think of it as being regimented by the "higher," "ethical" self. On the contrary, the nature of the libido does not work against the ethos of this challenge, but is rather in accord with it. Because man is an ethical being, the ethos is an ingredient that belongs *in* his *ars amandi*; it is by no means in a heteronomous relation to it.

Concretely, and thus in terms of therapeutic counsel, this means that he who is primarily interested in "getting his money's worth" is the very one who does not get it. It is not unreasonable in a situation like this to refer to Jesus' words, "Whoever would save his life will lose it" (Matt. 16:25, 10:39). This applies to sexual life too. But he who thinks of the other person and wants to give him sexual gratification also gains it for himself. A stricken marriage—especially the marriage which is stricken at the physical level—will very often *not* be regenerated by physical means, but can be restored only by achieving the human quality of "devotion" and therefore only if something happens in a totally different dimension of existence. And yet, is it really such a different dimension? Do not both point to each other again in the next moment? And is not the term "devotion" for this integration of the one into the other indicative in itself, since it can be a sexual *terminus technicus* as well as an ethical term? Human sex community is so "human" that without humanity it disappears, even on the physical level. What is important in marital pastoral care, however, is that this must not be "legalistically" stated, but rather that the person must be helped to realize that the ethical task of communicating sexual gratification to the other person is a task that is inherent in, and demanded by, the physical realm itself.

Second, another point at which the actualization of this relationship of *eros* and *agape* becomes acute is at the *beginning* of the sex community. Here we are thinking of the consummation of marriage.

Anybody who knows anything about life knows how many marital crises are set off by the first sexual encounters, even though at first these crises remain latent. The reason for this false start and the consequent emergence of fear of sex instead of enjoyment lies precisely in this relation of *eros* and *agape* to which we have called attention. That is to say, the awakening of the two sexes to sexual consciousness is not synchronized, any more than are the curves of sexual excitement which we mentioned above. Whereas masculine sexuality is already awake, the woman's sexuality—in any case that of the untouched woman—is in a state of slumber and requires to be awakened. More precisely, she requires a *process* of awakening, which takes place in stages over a longer or shorter time. This awakening naturally cannot simply be an unconcerned pursuit of the male sex entelechy, but rather requires self-denial, self-control, and "selfless" compliance. Thus what we have called *agape*, namely, self-giving, serving love, which therefore also serves to awaken the other person, manifests itself again as an integrating force in the sex community, which breaks down when it is completely absent. And conversely, the sex community achieves its fullness only where there is a devotion that is willing to renounce self and seek the other person; one might say quite simply, only where there is love.

In all this we can hardly escape the impression that this knowledge of the *agape* factor gained from the gospel is not only a knowledge that is "obedient" and submissive to God, but also an insight that is in accord with reality. Even apart from everything else, the gospel is a valid interpretation of reality. To this extent it has a side which is related to wisdom literature. From this point of view it gives us to understand that all knowledge that seeks to know things—in this case the physiological laws of sexuality—*directly* remains blind or becomes deluded, and thus misses the point of the things. The mystery of sexuality reveals itself only when the mystery of humanity and what it is intended to be is revealed and only when love—in this fullest sense of the word—is perceived to be the very theme of life itself. Only when this is taken into account can there be such a thing as realistic sexuality. For the real is not simply identical with what one encounters in a person. He who sees only what he meets with in a person (his outward appearance, his intellectual and technical ability, his functions) has by no means seen the reality of that person. Reality, especially that of a human being, discloses itself only as one sees its destiny, what it was intended to be. Therefore he who interprets the reality of human sexuality only on the basis of what he meets with—say, the physical processes—is precisely the one who misses its real theme. The person who likes to act as if he were a realist in matters sexual and for whom nothing human around the love-bed seems to be alien may be the very person to whom the really human is alien. Therefore he is delivered over to irrationality, even if he is conversant with all the artful dodges of the *ars amandi*. Knowledge and skill of this kind which are alien to actual reality will therefore cause him to fail at the task of establishing real communication (and thus also to miss sexual fulfillment), because he takes the part for the whole and this illusionism must be paid for.

### b. The Rhythm of Oestrus Seasons and the Omnipresence of Eros

We shall attempt here to track down in the realm of the sex impulse still further human characteristics which distinguish man from merely animal existence and indicate an inner urge toward the personal or permeation by personal elements.

In the animal the sex act is completely automatic in character.[17] The encounter of the male with the female in oestrus does not present him with decision; rather there is something compulsive in it. In the same way the rhythm of the rutting seasons is automatically regulated. If this automatically evoked instinctive act is forcibly interrupted by some external interference, this produces an outbreak of anger or some other disturbance. But never does any compensatory action take place in which the instinctual energy is sublimated or shifted to another area.[18]

---

[17] It is well known that a housebreaker cannot bring a watchdog to heel with a piece of meat, but that he can do so with a bitch in heat.

[18] Cf. T. Bovet, *Die Ehe, ihre Krise und Neuwerdung* (4 ed.), p. 16.

This automatism is clearly lacking in the human being. In the normal human there is no simple "compulsive" instinctual action. And one basic reason for this is that the human being has no oestrus seasons—with the exception of certain seasonally conditioned hormonal reactions which are manifested in an intensified urge and make the month of May, for example, a month of erotic delight or sorrow. Because of this absence of any real oestrus season man is exempt from the time cycle in this realm of instinct.

Incidentally, this observation contains some interesting allusions to the myths and their cyclic concept of time based upon the changing times of the day and year. The myths see man as embedded in nature and its rhythm, whereas postmythical, "historical" time no longer regards man as being determined by nature, but rather as a being who goes beyond nature, a "historical" being who must accept himself as a bearer of decisions.[19]

At first glance this exemption from the rhythm of nature, this immunity from the rhythm of oestrus periods, like the incongruity of the masculine and feminine curves of excitement, may appear to be a *loss*, an alpha privative, so to speak, with which man as a natural being is burdened. Can we really say that this nondetermination by a natural rhythm implies a surpassing of nature? Must it not rather be regarded as a falling short of nature, that is, as an outbreak of uncertainty in instinct, a loss of the natural sureness of instinctive control? The question increases in urgency when we see that man is a being who can fail and go wrong and in doing so wreck himself. In contrast to man, the animal cannot fail, go wrong, and wreck itself, unless it be a young animal that is still without experience and not adjusted to its environment.[20] Apart from this, however, the animal does not go wrong, whereas man does go wrong. His surpassing of nature is identical with a loss of instinctive control and to this extent with a reduction, a stunting, of his instinct.

This privative factor, this deficiency, is, however, not *merely* a

---

[19] Cf. Friedrich Gogarten, "Theologie und Geschichte," in *Zeitschrift für Theologie und Kirche* (1953), 3, pp. 339 ff.

[20] If we observe an animal committing an error, we find that the cause lies either in some organic injury or that it has been momentarily deceived by its environment (as in the case of a caged bird flying against a windowpane). Cf. S. Bally, *Vom Ursprung und von den Grenzen der Freiheit* (1945).

negative quality; it is rather a sign of greatness. One can learn from folk wisdom that to err is human. This implies, first, that to be human means that there are extenuating circumstances, that there is reason why his conduct must be condoned. After all, we are "only" human and we lack the sure guidance of instinct. But in this phrase there is also the implication that man is distinctive and that this distinctiveness exposes him to risk, to the possibility of failure. The Prodigal Son in the New Testament has a certain human dignity by reason of the fact that in his failure he nevertheless remains a person who decides, a "historical" figure, whereas the elder son who stayed at home remained in the grip of his environment, and thus under the control of that which is analogous to nature. We do not quite believe that he is capable of breaking away from his environment and therefore of taking the risk of making the wrong decision to go into the far country, and therefore we also take no pleasure in his unbroken, pedestrian uprightness. But the Father, who is God, loves the man who takes a risk, the man who is himself a being created by God's taking a risk, and as such is capable of failing, and in his very failure learns to understand that he lives by grace.[21]

So here, exactly as in the case of the differing curves of excitement, we can see that it is man's exclusion from the natural realm of instinct that provides the *chance* for him to become a human being. The diminution of his potency as a natural being is the very thing that contains his human potentiality. For now the ordering of his life, because it is not simply a given, but is rather subject to a risk, becomes a task and a responsibility: he must seek for meaning, find values, and make decisions. Thus the ability to err becomes a precondition of the fact that man is set down between possible alternatives of potential being, that he himself "is" a possibility.

This means that the realm of instinct is constantly projecting itself into the personal realm in that now man can be addressed as a responsible being, which means that he must think of himself as a subject who makes decisions. And here an intentional or indifferent, a forced or careless ignoring of a situation requiring decision is itself a

---

[21] Cf. Pascal, *Pensées,* "Of the Necessity of the Wager" (New York: Modern Library, 1941), pp. 64 ff.

decision. For example, a man who "forgets" himself with regard to a woman—which means that he is evading a decision or not thinking about it or not admitting it—can be said to have decided against the situation in which he must make a human decision and therefore against the specifically human status of sexuality. In other words, he has forgotten that he is a human being dealing with a human being. We see, therefore, that the absence of the oestrus seasons with their automatism in the realm of the libido is actually a "humanizing" factor.

The fact that the human sex impulse is not subject to the rhythm of the oestrus seasons entails the fact that *eros* is constantly present, that in every moment I am a sexual being and that only the strength of the impulse is subject to fluctuation. This does not mean simply that the human being is superior to the rhythm. Rather, as the idea of risk has already suggested, it exposes his sexual existence to greater danger. Paul goes so far as to say that, though discontinuance of sexual intercourse for a limited time may be in accord with spiritual, and thus also human, existence (that is to say, fasting, *nesteia,* and prayer, *proseuche*), indefinite abstention and consequently a radical departure from sexual nature leads to satanic temptations (I Cor. 7:5). Translated into psychological terms, this would mean that radical abstention leads to a "damming up" which can produce such an intensification of the urge that its inevitable explosion and abreaction will be similar to the automatism of the oestrus season and therefore to an irruption of animalism. But when animalism takes control in human life this is "demonic," perverse, diabolical confusion (*diaballein*). The fact is that man cannot become purely "bestial." If he could, this would mean that he could escape in a sphere beyond good and evil and divest himself of his humanity. Then flight from culpability would really be possible and we could actually "take the wings of the morning" (Ps. 139:9; Jonah 1:3) and fly to the uttermost parts of the sea—the Elysian fields of animality—where the commandments of God are no longer binding and therefore can no longer become the law that accuses us. But right here is where the "right hand" of God would "hold me" and the covering darkness of animal night would be made light (Ps. 139:10-12). Therefore we should speak here, not of bestialization, but rather—*cum grano salis*—of dehumanization.

### c. The Possibility of Sublimation

In human beings the sex relationship can be divided into individual stages and degrees. There are erotic relationships which are content with simply enjoying the presence of the other person and do not require even the simpler degrees of physical caresses. There is a kind of relationship, like that of Goethe to Charlotte von Stein, which finds its human greatness—the emphasis is upon the word "human"! —precisely in sacrificing and forgoing these physical contacts, but still remains altogether erotic. It is also possible for there to be such a thing as engagement, a waiting period before fulfillment. All this would be inconceivable if the personal relationships, love in the narrower sense, did not project itself into the realm of instinct and "express" itself in the medium of the erotic, that is, if it made this erotic expression not an automatic process, an end in itself, but rather a servant and only an expression.

In the case of Goethe and Frau von Stein the personal element is quite obviously not merely a negative restraining force that steps in and simply obstructs the primary sexual attraction. On the contrary, the psychophysical attraction is so strong that it might also express itself in the sphere of *eros,* but does not *need* to express itself here—at least in the full sense—and therefore can persist even without this form of expression. Here we see the *personal* element of human *eros* manifesting itself simply in the phenomenology of the erotic. There are a great many such manifestations—love at a distance, for example—which we would not be able to understand at all, and such forms of love would not even be possible, if the immediately sexual were not merely a means of expressing the personal and therefore a secondary factor.

A further consequence of the absence of automatism in the human sex act and hence the fact that the act of copulation does not occupy the center of the erotic is that *eros* can disengage itself from the sexual process (in the narrow sense) and become transformed. It can, for example, be sublimated, and the potential passion inherent in it can be shifted into other channels and be made creative there. Thus we can raise the question (which, of course, cannot be answered with any precision): What effect did Goethe's love for Frau von Stein have upon his creative power as a poet? We should also have to point out that the purpose of the Roman Catholic practice of requiring celibacy of its priests is by no means merely the negative one of mere abstinence and thus "repression"; but rather that here we have a very carefully thought out pedagogy of sublimation, which strives, as it were, to transform the sexual energies into religious energies. The Roman Catholic practice of meditation—in the form, for example, of mystical love and perhaps also the veneration of Mary— is hardly conceivable without this background of sublimated *eros*. Here again we have evidence of the personal element breaking into the sphere of purely instinctive determination. This it does in two ways:

First. In animals the automatism of the sexual approach cannot be interrupted by the animal itself, but only by some forcible external intervention, such as an experiment, whereas the human being has control of the shaping of his sexuality and when he allows his sexuality to get out of hand we say that he has forgotten himself. Here again, seen purely from the point of view of the philosophy of language, we find expression of the fact that the "self" cannot be reduced to sexuality, but rather remains aloof *from* it in the relationship of a subject: whenever I think only of my sexuality I forget my "self." Hence this self is something other than my sexual being. To be able to forget one's "self" in thinking of one's sexuality is the same as to forget the *whole* of the self in the *part* of the self, to forget duration in preoccupation with the moment, and in obsession with time to forget eternity, when it is only *sub specie aeternitatis* that my self exists.

Second. When the automatic sex process is interrupted in an animal this leads to manifestations of aggression, whereas the human being is capable of creative transformation. He is able, so to speak, to retract the sexual expression of the personal relationship into this relationship. Thus he is able to fill relationships other than sexual with these sublimated energies (for example, in teaching or in the diaconate); he can also form relationships which remain basically erotic in tone—such as that between Goethe and Charlotte von Stein—but he can shape them in a direction other than the sexual.

Related to this is what Bovet calls the cultivation of the "erotic atmosphere."[22] Whereas the animal presses directly toward the act of copulation as the goal of the instinct in order to return to a state of repose in which it completely dispenses with sex for a period of time, the human being—especially the woman—yearns for a continuing erotic atmosphere, for personal intimacy, and for many small proofs of solidarity which give tone to the atmosphere and do not merely flash through it like a stroke of ecstasy. This is true when no sexual union at all takes place and possibly is not even sought as well as when it has taken place, but unlike that of the animal, is not ended, but rather continues in the erotic atmosphere.

The institutional form which is designed to maintain this atmosphere is found in *marriage*. And—even from a one-sided sexual point of view—it possesses this constancy only because sexuality does not come to full expression in the curve of sexual excitement and the automatic course of the impulse, but precisely in this erotic atmosphere which remains even when the sexual encounters themselves cease to take place (as, for example, in old age). In young marriages this atmosphere frequently condenses in the tempest of sexual encounter; it builds up into stormy concentrations and discharges, but the atmosphere itself is more than what occurs within it. The atmosphere itself is not the storm; the storm takes place in it.

In concluding our discussion of the sex impulse, the above metaphor may illustrate how the libido in its human form always points to the personal element (it requires concern for one's partner and a like concern on the part of the partner) and also how it is not subject to the law of automatism, but is rather embedded in personal structures (it exposes one to the risk of self-forgetfulness; it is possible to sublimate it; and it broadens out into an erotic atmosphere which deepens and fulfills the relationship).

[22] Theodor Bovet, *Love, Skill and Mystery*, p. 59.

## Excursis I: The Plasticity of Human Sexual Behavior

The term "plasticity," as employed by Arnold Gehlen and Helmut Schelsky in their sociological analyses, has the same meaning as that which we have discussed in connection with the question whether man, who has become "historical," surpasses nature or sinks below it. That is to say, plasticity signifies that human behavior, indeed the sex structure itself, is subject to human control and is capable of being molded and transformed. Expressed in negative terms, it means that man is not determined by nature. Thus Schelsky, too, speaks of the peril and the opportunity of human sexuality.

The peril for man as a biological being lies in the fact that man's discernible loss of instinctive control, or more precisely, his lack of a fixed quota of sexuality set by instinct, can entail a tendency to pansexuality and promiscuity.[23]

And yet, according to Schelsky, therein lies the opportunity to become human, indeed the chance for the development of culture as a whole. "Since man has escaped the constraint of bondage to his environment and the rigidity of instinct, he is capable of controlling his impulses in conscious actions. Consequently, he must cast about for norms and values in the name of which he can direct and order his chaotic, vagabond instincts. In the place of the natural ordering which has fallen away he must put something in the nature of a conscious and structured cultural order."

This plasticity also expresses itself in the fact that manhood and womanhood, the fundamental polar structure of sexuality itself, is not a constant, biologically fixed thing, but rather can be varied considerably, at least in its functions. This is particularly apparent in the division of labor according to sex differentiation. To be sure, W. G. Sumner's statement that only the woman bears children and not the man is still true, however banal and trivial it may sound.[24] But this also seems to be the only constant. Almost everything else is variable. This is all the more astonishing with respect to the division of labor between the sexes, since here physical constitution certainly plays a part and it is obvious that motherhood and menstruation limit the capability of woman. One might therefore be inclined to conclude that the woman is more fitted for the quieter, domestic tasks while the man is more capable of dealing with the combative task of facing the "hostile" world. The biological constant of sex would suggest

[23] H. Schelsky, "Die sozialen Formen der sexuellen Beziehungen," in *Die Sexualitat des Menschen. Handbuch der mediz. Sexualforschung,* ed. H. Giese (1954), p. 242.

[24] "No amount of reasoning, complaining or protesting can alter the fact that woman bears children and man does not." Quoted in Schelsky, *ibid.*, p. 247.

a certain constant in the division of labor between the two. But empirical observation does not confirm this at all.

"Thus among primitive peoples the woman generally bears the burden of tilling the soil . . . whereas in European and Asiatic cultures this position is reversed. Even in occupations generally considered to be peculiarly masculine, such as hunting and waging war, or conversely, that of cooking and keeping house, which is regarded as being specifically feminine, there are plenty of socially conditioned exceptions. Among the Tasmanians the difficult hunting of seals is carried on by the women: 'They swam out to the seal rocks, crept up to the animals, and clubbed them to death; the Tasmanian women also hunted the opossum, which required them to climb up high trees' (R. Linton, *The Study of Man* [1936], p. 117). Famous in ethnology is the extremely bellicose and cruel bodyguard of the King of Dahomey which was made up of women. On the other hand, we find this outcry in Athenaeus, a Greek writer of the third century: 'Who ever heard of a woman who cooks!' (O. Klineberg, *Social Psychology* [1940])."[25]

The sex character of men and women is therefore not an absolute. And it is its obvious plasticity that contains the challenge to give structure to human sexuality and responsibly choose the goal and purpose of this structuring. One could also say that, paradoxically, the fact that sexuality and the relationship of the sexes is not determined by the constraint of nature means that there is a constraint toward humanization. The transition from the constraint of nature into conscious and responsible actions is both an ability and a compulsion.

## EXCURSIS II: LITERARY STATEMENTS (JACOBSEN AND SAINT-EXUPÉRY

We may conclude our discussion of the character of animal and human sexuality with a consideration of several literary statements. In literary expressions the interpenetration of *agape* and *eros*, the interplay of personal *humanitas* and elemental *bios*, can be stated with a kind of concision and compactness which theoretical analysis seems incapable of attaining. This is also the reason why modern philosophizing is carried on by means of interpretations of literary works (in Heidegger, for example).

We shall use for our purpose a quotation from Jens Peter Jacobsen's novel, *Niels Lyhne,* a book which meant a great deal to Rilke. In this quotation it will be noted that the sexual encounter, even at the climax of the act, the moment of ecstasy, is not merely a convulsion of the libido,

[25] Schelsky, *ibid.,* p. 248.

but rather that it raises the question of the mystery of personality. For Erich the beloved Fennimore must be more than what she means in the moment of sexual encounter, even at the farthest point of growth beyond herself; for even beyond this she stands in a totally different relationship which is inaccessible to him. If we were to express this relationship in religious terms, we would say that the other person belongs to God; she has received from God her own individual destiny, her own ultimate loneliness, and also her responsibility. This ultimate region is inaccessible.

Because of the other person's "alien dignity"—for in the last analysis this is what it is—he always retains an ultimate remainder of his own being, which I must respect even in the most intimate and loving encounters as something that is withheld from me and which I dare not lay hands upon even in the extreme of ecstasy. In other words, since the other person still stands in his own individual relationship to God, he can never be completely reduced to his relationship to me. Therefore I can never wholly "possess" the other person. If I try to do this nevertheless and ignore his self-sovereignty, he would be destroyed at the center of his being. And this is precisely what Jacobsen shows. He does it in a completely non-Christian way and yet, curiously enough, in such a way that the religious interpretation can be applied unbroken.

"She loved him with her whole soul, with the hot, tremulous passion born of fear. He was to her much more than a god, much nearer—he was an idol, whom she worshipped without reason and without reserve.

"His love was strong as hers, but it lacked the fine, manly tenderness that protects the loved woman against herself and watches over her dignity. Dimly he felt it as a duty, which called him sometimes in a faint, low voice, but he would not hear. She was too alluring in her blind love; her beauty, which had the provocative luxuriance and the humble seductiveness of the female slave, incited him to a passion that knew neither bounds nor mercy.

"In the old myth about Amor is it not told somewhere that he puts his hands over Psyche's eyes before they fly away, rapturously, into the glowing night?

"Poor Fennimore! If she could have been consumed by the fire of her own heart, he who should have guarded her would have fanned the flames; for he was like that drunken monarch who swung the incendiary torch, shouting with joy to see his imperial city burn, intoxicating himself with the sight of the leaping flames, until the ashes made him sober. . . .

"Poor Fennimore! . . . She did not know that the intoxication which uplifts today takes its strength from the wings of tomorrow, and when at length sobriety dawned, gray and heavy, she realized tremblingly that they had loved themselves down to a sweet contempt for themselves and each other—a sweet contempt which day by day lessened in sweetness and became, at last, utterly bitter."[26]

In this description of the disenchantment, the "hang-over" that follows the rapture of love, we have a picture of how love is spoiled when *eros* becomes autonomous. It becomes autonomous when it sweeps the lovers into the polar tension of mere physical attraction and robs the man of that "manly tenderness that protects the loved woman against herself and watches over her dignity," in other words, the tenderness which recognizes that in her which dare never be lost in the communication of the encounter. The vehemence of excess causes the poles to leap unchecked into flames, but it is the drunken monarch who flings the torch into his imperial city. The very word "polarity," which suggests itself here, is significant; for, being a term in physics, it calls attention to the threat of depersonalization in the process. Once the spark has leaped from pole to pole and the explosion has taken place, charred points are left behind. Therefore those who truly love each other dare not treat each other *only* as poles. Human communication has a quality fundamentally different from polarity. This is made clear in the myth of Amor and Psyche. The lover is not merely a captor who flings the torch; he is also the protector who guards the beloved from herself, and by putting "his hands over Psyche's eyes" is not trying to prevent her from seeing and participating with her eyes, but rather symbolically setting bounds to the province in which she herself must properly belong and in which is contained that which she must not include in her surrender. In speaking of this inviolable reserve, it is difficult for the Christian not to think of that "alien dignity" which incorporates man into relationship with God and therefore sets limits to all human relationships, even the most intimate and ecstatic, commanding an ultimate kind of possession, which is "to have as though one had not" (I Cor. 9:20 ff.). And just because this is so, violence, wickedness, the torch in the imperial city, can exist. This is apparent in Erich's attitude toward Fennimore. The Christian possibly sees the mystery of a literary figure in a way different from the author himself. And the reason for this is that the author is saying more than he realizes. To this extent his function is prophetic.

The *eros*, which strives to take possession of its object, therefore reaches its limit, since it is impossible to express the partnership of love in terms of "the conqueror" and "the conquered," or more sharply, and then with depth of meaning which Jacobsen is approaching, "the possessor" and "the possessed." Thus if we call Fennimore "the possessed," then even our language expresses something of the ambiguity that hangs over

<hr/>

[26] J. P. Jacobsen, *Niels Lyhne,* trans. by Hanna Astrup Larsen (New York: The American Scandinavian Foundation, 1919), pp. 196 f.

the process of "being-taken-possession-of" *and* that change in substance that results when to seize possession of another is *everything*. This change in substance means the intrusion of something that is alien to the human, a possession, a slavery, which from Erich's point of view is rape and from Fennimore's self-surrender. Thus at the end of the fire of passion come the sobering ashes.

A passage in Antoine de Saint-Exupéry's *The Wisdom of the Sands* refers even more directly to this human quality that transcends sex, and here there is probably a conscious reference to the "alien dignity" of which we have spoken.

"True, O Lord, when I watch a young wife sleeping in her sweet nakedness, pleasant it is for me to feast my eyes on her beauty . . . and why should I not have my joy of her? But I have understood Thy truth. It is for me to ensure that she who now is sleeping . . . shall not be like a blind wall against which I knock my head, but a portal opening on another world; and that I do not disintegrate her, seeking for an impossible treasure amongst the fragments, but bind her together in oneness, a tight-drawn knot, in the silence of my love.

"Thus with my sleeping wife, did I appraise her for herself alone, soon would I grow weary and quest elsewhere. For it may well be that she is shrewish; or, even though she be perfection's self to look on, that she sounds not that sweet bell note on which my heart is set. . . .

"But sleep untroubled for your imperfection, imperfect wife. I do not knock my head against a blind wall, for though you be not a fulfillment, a reward, a jewel venerated for itself—of which I soon would be weary— you are a vehicle, a pathway, and a portage. And I shall not grow weary of becoming."[27]

Here we have a direct reference to this unknown quantity which does not and must not dissolve in the communication, but rather "stands outside" of it. My purpose must be "not to disintegrate" the beloved, but rather to "bind her together . . . in the silence of my love." This means that I cannot have the body without the heart. I cannot split off sexuality from the person. But as I face the indivisible totality of a human being I participate in the relationship in which this person is enclosed. For he is not a walled-in entelechy, against which I knock my head, a circumscribed physical body who can permit me only to stand beside and outside of him. He is rather a "person-in-relationship"—in relationship to the "Lord" to whom these words are addressed. And therefore he points beyond himself, he becomes "a vehicle, a pathway, and a portage." But

[27] Antoine de Saint-Exupéry, *The Wisdom of the Sands,* trans. by Stuart Gilbert from the French *Citadelle* (New York: Harcourt, Brace and Company, 1950), p. 312.

I "have" this totality of the other person—this is the second point—only if he is not merely "a fulfillment, a reward, a jewel venerated for itself"; in other words, not merely the bearer of certain values (such as beauty, character, culture, intellect). For if I center my interest only in his immanent value I would immediately relativize him, because his possession of these values may pass away, or he may become the prey of time and become boring and unattractive, or because I shall compare him with other bearers of values and he may not stand the test of competition. Exupéry alludes to this possibility of "questing elsewhere" for others who are better. But here the "alien dignity" manifests itself in the sleeping wife, putting her in a higher relationship and under a higher protection, which places her beyond all these relativities. "I have understood Thy truth," says Exupéry.

### d. The Sense of Shame and the Knowledge of Sex

*i) The Knowledge of Sex.* Because sexuality is a dimension of human existence itself, it is a mystery in the same sense that man himself is a mystery. In the terminology of a current philosophy it might be said that man is a mystery because he is not objectifiable, because he is not something that is (*Seiendes*) among other things that are, but rather an existence (*Dasein*). In theological terms, "mystery" would mean here that man is an object of faith, since he cannot be seen. For the visible part of him, that which can be established empirically does not reflect his real being. The ground, goal, and meaning of his existence, which contain this authentic being of man, consist in his relation to God. This is what man "is," and this can only be believed or denied. In this sense man is a mystery which cannot be "seen." And his sexuality participates in this mystery. His body (*soma*) is a symbol of this mystery. But the mystery resists disclosure.

We have already referred both to the fact and to the reason why it was that in earlier times people were reticent about the mystery of sex and, on the other hand, to the depotentiation of this secret, intimate realm that resulted when the psychoanalytical style of speech permitted us to objectify this intimate matter and break its taboo by drawing it into our ordinary conversation.

The mystery, the "taboo," is always a sign that something vulnerable is to be protected. Since sexuality was put under the protection of taboo this meant that it was considered to be a point of existential vulnerability. Here man is in great danger of losing himself. Here he can surrender himself and be "possessed." But the "nakedness" or weak spot—more in the metaphysical than in the physical sense of the word—must be concealed.[28]

In connection with this vulnerability of man, it should be noted that the taboos vary in different places; the vulnerability or "nakedness" is localized at different points. Today many people no longer feel they are vulnerable at the point of sex. They do not feel any threat to their "existence" here. As soon as sexuality becomes merely an impersonal, glandular process—say, in the sense of the "glass of water theory"—its taboo also disappears. Today perhaps the taboo has shifted from sex to *death*, i.e., to our existence in finitude. In earlier times death was not taboo. The oft-repeated *memento mori* made it the subject of public knowledge that was constantly kept in view. Today, however, death has become a taboo: nobody must tell the dying man that he must die,[29] and funeral cosmetics put the mask of life on the corpse.[30] For us the natural processes of decay have been just as shocking as the natural processes of copulation and birth were a century ago. "Our great-grandparents said that babies were found under cabbage leaves or were brought by the stork. Our children will probably say that those 'who have passed away' are changed into flowers or sleeping somewhere in a lovely garden."[31] The sign of vulnerability that reveals itself in this taboo of death could perhaps be reduced to the following formula: Man can no longer cope with his finitude. He no longer knows how to fill this finitude with meaning and therefore he must comfort himself with the pretense of a living corpse, the illusion of deathlessness; he is compelled to prolong an existence that has remained unfulfilled. He tries to rub out the boundary line of death with lipstick. Certain forms of make-up (by no means all!) are also to be explained in this way; when we fail to come to terms with finitude we are forced to disavow time. This leads, therefore, to a protest against growing old and the wrinkled faces are plastered with the mask of youth, the deceptive symbol of a *praesens aeternum*.

And yet there is still a lower level of loss of meaning than that which

---

[28] Cf. from this point of view the meaning of clothing, G. van der Leeuw, *Der Mensch und die Religion* (1941), pp. 23 ff.

[29] Cf. the chapter on the physician's telling the truth in *ThE II*, 1, §567 ff.

[30] Cf. Evelyn Waugh's novel, *The Loved One*, and Geoffrey Gorer on the relationship between prudery and pornography in "The Pornography of Death," *Die Welt*, May 5, 1956.

[31] Geoffrey Gorer, *ibid.*

manifests itself in the elimination of the boundary of death. This level is reached when people go further and abandon this modern taboo of death just as the taboo of sexuality was abandoned. When this happens it would indicate that one no longer considers existence vulnerable, simply because one no longer has any existence. For what one no longer has can no longer be wounded. One no longer suffers from the meaninglessness of finitude because the question of meaning is no longer raised at all. This depotentiation of the taboo of death is apparent, for example, when death is regarded as being merely the physiological extinction of the individual. Such an extinction ceases to be a mystery the moment we lose our sense of the unrepeatable, once-for-all character of life, our sense of individuality (which is connected with the loss of meaning). Forms of this attitude are discernible in economic and biological materialism, which in various ways reduce man to his function.[32]

The connection between the dissolution of the mystery and the loss of meaning as it becomes apparent with respect to death is described by Bruce Marshall in his novel, *The Fair Bride,* the scene of which is laid in the Spanish Civil War:

"Down in the street the municipal hearse flashed by on one of its many daily journeys to the cemetery. From the high window the naked corpse lying in the unlidded coffin looked like a doll in a cardboard box. There were no mourners and no priest. There was no hope, no despair, no mystery. Everything was simple and clear: life meant something only because it meant nothing."[33]

It would seem that it is no accident that in our discussion of the mystery of man we should encounter this connection between *eros* and finitude, between love and death. We may be reminded that our folk songs and love songs are full of references to this connection.

The mystery of sex, with which we are here concerned, cannot possibly be explained by any objectifying method—the scientific method, for example. That mystery is unveiled in the temple of love, but not in the laboratory. Sexual knowledge is qualitatively different from knowledge about sex.

Therefore a very special kind of knowing goes with sexual knowledge. The Old Testament actually describes sexual intercourse itself as a process of "knowing" (*yada'*): Adam "knew" Eve his wife (Gen. 4:1). But the same can be said of the woman with respect to

[32] Cf. Helmut Thielicke, *Tod und Leben* (1946), pp. 62 ff.
[33] Bruce Marshall, *The Fair Bride* (Boston: Houghton Mifflin Company, 1953), p. 97.

man: of Lot's daughters in Sodom it is said that they had "not known man" (Gen. 19:8). Both together, not to have known a man and not to have been known by a man, can be equated with virginity (Gen. 24:16). Even if we were obliged to assume that the term "to know" is used as a mere code word for euphemistic reasons (just as the word "feet" is used to designate the genitals in Isa. 6:2), we should still have to ask why this particular code word was chosen. If the sex act had been regarded merely as a physical process, it surely would have been more natural to choose a physical symbol. (One need only to think of the various phallic cults and their symbolisms.) Obviously, there must be an inner affinity between the act of sexual union and the act of knowing the other partner. We shall therefore take some pains to understand the encounter with the mystery of sex as a mode of "knowing."

Unlike objectifying knowledge, which sees a thing "from the outside," this is a kind of knowing "from the inside." It is co-ordinated with the processes which are to be known, so that the knowledge of them becomes accessible only in the course of these processes. Here again death presents itself as an analogue of the *eros* realm. It is true that dying and death can be known from the outside, in terms of its physiological laws. But what dying "is," I know only as one who is dying; and what finitude is, I know only insofar as I myself am in "being-toward-death." Because I see that others die, it is true that I can say that "one dies" and thus "level" dying to a mere "occurrence,"[34] but I am not relating it to my own dying.[35] Here adequate knowledge can be attained from the inside. And the same applies to the "experience of life,"[36] which likewise cannot be known from the outside and therefore cannot be had *before* we have passed through the school of life. The object of faith is also one of the realms which can be experienced only "from the inside," in the actual living out of a believing existence. Only he who "is" of the truth hears the voice

---

[34] Martin Heidegger, *Being and Time*, trans. by John Macquarrie and Edward Robinson (New York: Harper & Row, 1962), pp. 296 ff.

[35] Cf. Leo Tolstoi's *The Death of Ivan Ilyich,* in which the inward and outward way of experiencing death is dealt with. Discussed in *ThE II*, 1, §625.

[36] Cf. Eduard Spranger's essay, *Lebensführung* (n.d.).

(John 18:37).[37] It was in this sense that Kierkegaard distinguished objective truth, as it is used in the natural sciences,[38] from the "truth of the relationship" in which the existing thinker relates himself to his object. This kind of truth, which is only existential and is accessible only "from the inside," is therefore not simply communicable; it is determined by the particular and peculiar condition [the *Jemeinigkeit*] of my own experience; it can be summoned only to put itself in the place and in the relationship where it is released. *Outside* the situation in which it is released, this kind of knowledge remains alone and noncommunicable.

Now, this nonobjectifiable knowledge "from the inside" is also related to sexual experience in the sense conveyed by the Hebrew term *yada'*. In the sexual encounter I know the mystery of the other person is here represented by the knowledge of his body. It relates, not primarily to his nakedness (which, as art shows, can be thoroughly nonsexual), but rather to the ability of the body to express the person and his emotions and thus to be symbolical. And just as it is certain that the sexual encounter runs the whole gamut of human forms of expression—from intentional self-control to ecstatic moments beyond all control of the will, that is, to being completely oneself—so it is equally certain that it has in it a *special* experience, a special knowledge of the other person which has a quality that is *different* from all other forms of knowing. It is likewise fundamentally different from a physician's knowledge of a person whom he is treating in sexual matters.

All knowledge "from the inside," from existential experience, therefore always has two sides: it never relates only to the other person or to the situation in question (the danger of death, for example), but also to myself. *In it I learn who I am.* So in the longing for borderline experiences, felt especially by the masculine temperament (the craving to engage in hazardous mountain-climbing exploits, to endure the extreme risks of war, and to skirt the edge of death), there is at least along with many other motives the fundamental drive

---

[37] On the concept of existential knowledge, cf. Helmut Thielicke, *Was ist Wahrheit?* (1954); *Tod und Leben* (1946); *ThE II*, 1, § 342 ff., 571 ff.

[38] *Reflexionen über Christentum und Naturwissenschaft,* in Hirsch edition of Kierkegaard's works, Abtl. 17, pp. 123 ff.

to experience "one's self" and thus learn "who one is."[39] We speak of "proving oneself," and what we mean is: This is the way I act in the face of death or extreme hardship; this is what I can accomplish by force of will, or this is the limit of my endurance.

The same applies to sexual knowledge: here I experience myself at the extreme of my potential. I experience something of "the wholly other person" within me, which is nevertheless "me"; and thus I experience my self. And here again we are reminded of folk songs and love songs: Love and death tell most about myself and therefore about the mysteries of existence.

Only as we appreciate this aspect of sexual knowledge shall we be able to understand certain factors in sexuality which must be familiar to anyone who is in one of the professions dedicated to helping people (the physician, the pastor, the teacher, the youth leader). We illustrate it with the sex problem of *youth*.

*ii*) *The Elucidation of Sex.* As far as young people are concerned, their sexual problem is less a physiological problem than one of knowledge. In making this statement, we are not unaware of the perils and the resulting challenges which are inherent in the *physiological* problem, which is that the young person must cope with his sexually awakened body without having the option of sexual intercourse, or having it only by running into new problems. The real crises in these earlier stages, however, are the result of a problem of knowing, or more precisely, the state of waiting before the doors of knowledge. And here is where a certain aporia manifests itself in sex education, a perplexity about what to say, where to begin, and where to stop, at least as laying down specific methods is concerned. That is to say, whereas the physiological problem can be dealt with (for example, by means of physical exercise and athletics, the structuring of a healthy environment, and the utilizing of possibilities of sublimation), we try to counteract the desire for sexual knowledge by explaining it.

But is the information about sexual things which is imparted by ex-

---

[39] It is clear—and this is what makes this type of literature so fascinating—that this search for the self lies behind the life of action *and* the writing of such men as Colonel T. E. Lawrence, Ernest Jünger, Antoine de Saint-Exupéry, and Winston Churchill.

planation, by sex education, identical with what the biblical term *yada'* means by sexual *knowledge*? Before we discuss this easily recognized difference, let us also briefly consider the *connection* between knowledge of sex based on information about it and sexual knowledge itself.

We are familiar with the question: "How shall I tell it to my child?" This question is usually uttered with a sigh, which indicates that giving this information is painful and embarrassing to the parents. At the same time the same embarrassment and reserve in the attitude of young people toward their parents manifests itself as soon as questions of sex are raised —even in situations where there is otherwise a good relationship of trust between them and the parents. The question "How shall I tell it to my child?" is matched by the question "How can I keep it secret from my father?" So the way out is chosen in accord with the law of least resistance and the child or teenager is given a pamphlet, or the instruction is left to the school, and here again possibly to a doctor called in for the purpose, or if necessary a biology teacher.

A theological ethics cannot make this statement merely to criticize certain methods and make suitable pedagogical recommendations. Theological ethics is rather interested in an *anthropological* problem, which can be stated in the form of a question: What is the "existential" motive behind this tendency to give sexual enlightenment from a safe distance? Or, to put it more precisely, what attitude toward sexual knowledge betrays itself in this tendency? This question becomes the more urgent when we remember that the analogous situation is present in the young person himself. He secures his information secretly from an encyclopedia or from the books which his father has carefully stowed away *behind* the respectable volumes in the front of the bookcase (without suspecting, of course, that this symbolical arrangement of putting these books in the background is the very thing that increases the fascination of the mystery); or he gets his information from his comrades, where it is usually acquired in the code language of smut and derision.

In this tendency toward objectivity (information secured through a physician or encyclopedia) as well as the tendency to assume a derisively superior attitude in the inner circle of youngsters, there is a need to keep one's distance, which at the same time indicates the reason why the parents are inhibited from giving instruction, why the subterfuge of the stork story is resorted to, and why they withdraw into the zone of silence during the decisive years of puberty. That inhibition is caused by something they remember: the parents know from their own past that a young person is not yet capable of understanding the sex act as the "expression" of ultimate human communication, and that therefore at his first acquaintance with it he will think of it as something indecent, something of which he would never imagine his parents capable. This inability to credit parents with such behavior and at the same time to assure themselves that it is not really true tends to produce profound emotional disturbances and to bring on the first phobia with regard to sex (except perhaps among children in the country who have grown up with a more natural attitude toward these matters and also reflect upon them less). This crisis of mutual confidence as well as the shame of being connected with an act which their children would not think them capable of, causes the parents to shy away from taking the initiative in giving instruction.

It is therefore essential to define very precisely the reason for this inhibition. It is not rooted in any superficial squeamishness and prudery (otherwise fathers who are quite able to hold their own at a stag party would not suddenly shrink in old-maidish shame), but rather in the essential structure of sexuality itself. In other words, it is integrated in the human, personal nature of man and this integration is something which cannot be understood and therefore cannot be communicated in childhood and in the first stages of maturity. Consequently, the sexual act, which is the very thing the youngster wants to get in the clear about, can be conceived only as something animal, which—for some puzzling reason —the parents engage in despite the fact that they are loved and respected human beings. And with instinctive insight the youngster concludes quite correctly that, if this is the kind of animality which he has already observed in domestic animals and thought was funny or strange, then it would be a "great sin." It is precisely the unsheltered youngster who knows that bestiality—and this is exactly what he thinks he is witnessing!—would mean brutalization in man, and that this must mean sinfulness. And here are his parents engaging in this dark, secret thing!

At this point and from this perspective we come very close to the significance of sexual knowledge in the sense of the biblical term *yada'*. It is true that the youngster can gain some knowledge about sexual matters through instruction, but he cannot know the *mystery* of sexuality. The two things are in completely different dimensions. And this is why a higher degree of "information" about the processes (when the youngster not only knows how we get children but even how not to get them) basically leads nowhere. As long as he does not know the mystery and is incapable of understanding the connection between sexuality, humanity, and communication, sex remains for him an area of ill fame. And it remains so all the more if he first encounters sex as something which is in itself forbidden, something which in *his* world results in guilt, and which he cannot resist and is always defeating him. It is therefore understandable that parents should shrink from putting themselves as persons into this realm of fantasy in their own children. But at the same time this presents a challenge to overcome this inhibition on the part of the parents if the fear of this loss of trust is not to become the *cause* of this loss.

Not that the knowledge of sex in the sense of *yada'* can be attained by way of imparting information or that the combination of the physical and the personal is something that can be stated in words. But as the child sees this combination being *lived* by his parents and at the same time notes their attitude toward the question of sex (an attitude of obvious good conscience which is manifestly different from the furtiveness of his companions), he cannot, to be sure, "know" this combination of the physical and the personal, but he can "believe" it. It can, so to speak, be present in the anticipation of trust.

So, added to these two forms of encounter with sexuality, namely, learning about sexual matters and sexual knowledge itself (in the sense of *yada'*), there is a *third* form: it is that of trust, which as yet does not see and is not yet sure of its basis either intellectually or existentially and yet carries certainty within itself.

It hardly needs to be pointed out that this trust presupposes a special kind of instruction. The test of the correctness of the form of instruction is whether later on in the child's own experience there is a loss of trust in his parents or whether he finds that this trust has been justified. If the parents choose the subterfuge of the stork story, this loss of trust is sure to ensue, because the growing child cannot reconcile it with his experience of sex and thus learns that it was a deception. On the other hand, the continuity of the child's own experience with the parents' explanation is not dependent upon the child's learning the "correct biological facts" right from the beginning. Truth is not always identical with objective correctness. There are entirely "legendary" paraphrases for young children which nevertheless tell the truth about where man comes from and where he is going, about love and birth, and take into account the fact that here truth is something that grows.[40]

[40] On the historicity of a "growing" truth, as distinguished from a timeless intellectual truth which can be recalled at any time, cf. *ThE* II, 1, §569 ff.

The inner ability of the parents to intervene helpfully even in these areas and be available for enlightenment then depends in turn upon whether and to what extent they themselves have found their way through to the essential mystery of sexuality. In marriages where there is no real personal relationship, but only an animal relationship, and also in marriages in which sex is surrounded with anxiety or constraint or is atrophied, the initiative toward sexual education will hardly be taken. The truth of existence, which, after all, is related to the truth of sexuality, is always bound up with the existing person; it is a part of his "confession" of his real attitude toward life. Since it cannot be transmitted, but only "witnessed," since it can appeal only to trust, the precondition of it is the credibility and trustworthiness of the witness. This kind of truth, unlike the objectifiable truth of mathematics, cannot be separated from the person who utters it; the person must invest himself in it in order to be able to represent it. Therefore the way in which it is represented or not represented is very revealing of the person. The practice of giving sexual instruction or the omission of it is a mirror of the marriage itself and frequently enough a judgment upon it. Hence the same statement applies here which we made with regard to the physician's obligation to enlighten and tell the truth to a dying person. The physician's question "How shall I tell my patient?" recoils back upon himself in the form of this reflection, "Who am I that I should be authorized to speak here?"[41]

Thus in reflecting on the problem of sexual education we have at the same time thrown more light upon the concept of sexual knowledge. It was precisely this problem of knowledge that led us to the question whether it could be solved by education and thus by communicating information. The question was an urgent one because we were obliged to say that the sex problem of youth is a problem of knowledge. Meanwhile we have seen that sexuality is a "mystery" and therefore resists an objectifying transmission. Like all genuine mystery, it is, as Rudolf Otto would say, a *mysterium tremendum et fascinosum*.

The mystery is *tremendum* [terrible] in that it is surrounded by

[41] Cf. *ThE* II, 1, §602.

the kind of awe which in the area of sex is called shame. People who are unsophisticated do not speak about it lightly, at least not without using euphemistic or cryptic language. Often people seek counsel about a difficulty by speaking of the case as being not their own but that of a third person. The *tremendum* invests itself with the seclusiveness of the taboo. But the mystery is at the same time *fascinosum* [fascinating]; like everything mysterious, it keeps tempting one to unveil it. And this unveiling of the mystery is *not* accomplished by sex education. Sex education merely describes the shadows on the inner wall of the Platonic cave, but never brings into view the thing itself that casts the shadows. One cannot be instructed concerning the mystery; one can only "undergo" it and by undergoing it, experience it.

Here again we encounter the mystical component in the sex urge, which exists alongside of the physiologically determined libido: the mystery can be unveiled along with another person. And while the physiological libido can be controlled by means of self-discipline, this mystical component is beyond the sphere of the will. This is the reason why sexuality—contrary to what is commonly thought—does not merely split man into flesh and spirit, but rather divides the spirit within itself. The spirit is not merely opposed to the "fleshly" urge; it is, at least partially, on the side of the flesh, because it is lured by the mystery and the desire to unveil it. The will is not merely the opponent of the impulse. The will itself becomes an exponent of the "flesh" (Rom. 7:7 ff.).

Therefore moral appeals to the will, particularly in this area, are of very limited effectiveness: the Law proves to be powerless in a very significant way. Even the available will power proves to be anything but decisive. The problem by no means lies in whether the potential of the will is equal to the potential of the urge. (Therefore the saying "A man can control himself if only he wants to" is clearly a moralistic illusion.) The problem lies rather in whether the will can be brought to "will" at all, whether the will is under man's control at all. Most admissions of powerlessness, if they were precisely formulated, would not read: My will is too weak; but rather: I am too weak to allow my will to exert itself; in reality I do not "will" at all (to keep my distance from the mystery); and the fact is I cannot will to do so. My trouble is not that my will is subject to the impulse, but rather that it is bound up with it and I cannot break this connection. If I could just bring myself to will it, I could probably win out. But the way things are now, the forces of my will are beaten before they ever reach the front and never come into action at all.

There could be no worse misunderstanding of the statements we have just made than to regard them as psychological. We have not been describing the autonomy of psychic processes, but rather observing the structure of sex mystery as it is reflected in its psychological effects. Because the mystery of sex does *not* consist in the stimulation of the impulse (in that case it would not be a mystery at all, but merely a calculable play of psychosomatic forces), but rather because it addresses the total man, physically, psychically, spiritually, and volitionally, the mystery cannot be thought of as a lower urge that is opposed to the will; it is rather secretly on the side of the mystery; it becomes its advocate and "wills" it.

Only when we see this do we arrive at the ethical problem, which therefore lies on a level completely different from the moral level. Consequently, young persons may *perhaps* be influenced in other areas of life by appeals to the will, but most certainly not in the face of sexual temptation. On the contrary, since the will is exposed to the lure of wanting to know, it can be influenced only through trust in adults who for the time being vicariously guard this mystery for the youngster, in whom, therefore, he knows that it is present and so possesses it indirectly.

This observation is the adumbration of a *theological* fact. As we have seen, I cannot cope with the lure of the mystery of sex by means of my will, because, after all, the will is on the side of the mystery. So we also find that the terms "flesh" and "spirit" can no longer be used as designations of "parts" of man. On the contrary, they always represent the whole man. It is not something "in" man that comes into conflict with something else "in" him; rather the whole man is involved in a contest as to whether he wants to belong to *sarx* or to *pneuma*, to "God" or to "this world." This is how Paul sees this contest within man in Romans 7:14 ff. Therefore I can cope with the lure of the sex mystery, not through the initiative of my will, but only by gaining another *bond* to which my existence is tied, which in turn will replace the mere desire with another kind of mindset, another kind of seeking (*phronein*). For the *phronein* depends upon an *einai*, an existing thing to which my existence is related, whether it be of the flesh or of the spirit (Rom. 8:5 ff.)[42] The ultimate relationship in which I am thus determined in my *einai* also determines my *phronein* in sexuality. If I am related simply and solely to sexuality, then I fall into the relation of *sarx* and am at the mercy of its *exousia*. If as a young person I live (in the sense of *einai*) in trust and love toward my parents (who, according to Luther, are "masks" of God himself), then out of this there comes a different *phronein*. In any case, this seeking, this striving for a goal, depends decisively upon the relation that determines me.

*iii*) *The Veiling of Sex.* The mystery of sex evidences itself in still other signs. One of these signs is the concealment or veiling of sex. In this veiling of sex modesty (or shame) discloses itself. It would be wrong to associate shame only with sexual delinquencies, such as the fact that a "fallen" girl feels shame before her parents or a boy anxiously conceals his sexual excursions. Shame is rather inherent in sexuality *itself* and not merely in its divagations. Thus one can say that where there is concealment and thus modesty or shame, there as a rule sexuality is involved. This statement can be illustrated by means of a number of symptoms.

1. The fact that nudity in art—the Greek statues, for example— is sexless and that it evokes in the spectator what Kant in *The Critique of Judgment* called the essence of the aesthetic attitude, that is, "disinterested delight"—in this case, delight in which libido plays no part. Nudity in art is sexless because it is without mystery. In any case, however, in the area of sexuality nudity is therefore regarded as being an unveiling, a violation, or an act of betraying the mystery only when the mystery is a part of a process and not of a state (such as nakedness). Hence in northern countries where bathing in the nude is practiced, nudity, being such a "state," is nonsexual (also in the sense that it is not exhibitionistic).

2. A second symptom of the unveiling of the mystery of sex is the obscene word or joke, which as a rule has the structure of a double meaning. The double meaning is intended to exercise its fascination by being spoken in mere hints, indirectly, and thus in a veiled way— but yet the veil is transparent, so that what is meant is nevertheless clear. The double entendre functions in much the same way as the

[42] Cf. the important exposition in Ernst Gaugler, *Der Brief an die Römer* (1945), pp. 264 ff.

Socratic or maieutic act of bringing thoughts to birth, the intention being to arouse the hearer's lasciviousness and provoke it to action. One could even say that there is an analogy between the story or remark with a double meaning and the act of undressing. The direct, unveiled telling of a downright dirty story would be quite as unsexual as the unveiled nudity of a statue—except that it would be unaesthetic. The story with a double meaning, however, provides the opportunity to "undress" and in this symbolic analogy to act sexually, even though only in imagination. The lasciviousness of this symbolic act of undressing lies in the fact that only transparent veils need to be removed and the point is already evident.

3. The third symptom that shame and concealment are integral to the mystery of sex is the appeal to the libido by means of exhibiting the half-clothed.

Only the morals policemen seem to operate on the assumption that the last wisp of clothing worn by a cabaret dancer represents the fig leaf of morality, while everybody who knows regards this practice with the knowing smile of the initiate, for they are well aware that this is precisely the thing that expresses the ultimate artifice of sex appeal. The mystery which is still veiled but allowed, as it were, to show through, expressing itself in hints and allusions, is definitely sexual in nature. And the cash-conscious show directors therefore have an interest in seeing to it that the last vestige of clothing is *not* removed, because this would mean taking a step toward the far less attractive and lucrative realm of the aesthetic.

There is therefore a certain wisdom in the regulations of the British Board of Censorship, which is regarded as being unusually conservative and somewhat prudish, permitting nudity on the stage, but only in the form of motionless, statuelike, and therefore aesthetic, nudity. The fact that this permission is very rarely taken advantage of would seem to show how important sex appeal is to the organizers and the extent to which they understand the relation between sex and concealment and therefore the mystery of sexuality.

At the same time we see here the real nature of sacrilege. It does not consist merely in denial of the holy; this would mean in the area of sex: it does not consist in ignoring the sexual, as is done, for example, in the statuelike nudity mentioned above. The sacrilege consists rather in *playing* with the mystery, or one might say the psychologizing of the mystery, the sole interest of which is not to preserve the thing itself, but merely to exploit its physical effects.[43]

Connected with all of this is the fact that Christianity too has certain views with respect to clothing and make-up. When one thinks of the standard terms "modesty" and "soberness" (I Tim. 2:9), there can be no doubt that the motive for this lies in the realization that sex is a mystery. And this means that the mystery must be preserved and not allowed to degenerate into a mere psychological effect. It should manifest itself veiled with modesty and not enticement. Unfortunately, Christianity—at least in many of its circles—tends again to discredit this motive that underlies the preservation of the sex mystery and which leads it to some definite attitudes with regard to the question of dress. Many Christians think that a sack equipped with sleeves is peculiarly pleasing to God and that well-creased trousers are a sure sign that the wearer has sold out to the prince of this world, and the only task of the children of God is to exorcise him. In reality, however, what matters in this aeon is the struggle between God and Satan and the sovereign freedom of the children of God, who stand on the side of the Victor and therefore receive the gift of an almost unlimited open-mindedness (I Cor. 3:22; 6:12) and *therefore* a receptiveness to culture. Schleiermacher expressed the fear (in the open letter to Lücke) that a degenerate Christianity would no longer consort with culture but rather with barbarism. In any case, it can be an ethical (if not a dogmatic) denial of its Lord if Christians, presented with a choice between looking decent or like frumps, choose the principle of seediness as the supposed banner of humility. What happens when this *"kerygma"* of shabbiness is proclaimed is ultimately something worse than the mere suspicion of regard for the body and for beauty which it provokes and which raises soul-destroying barriers for people, who are unfortunate enough to be endowed with the charism of taste, even before they get to hear the gospel. It goes beyond this and confuses the rejection of the purely psychic effect of the mystery of sex (which we quite rightly reject when it takes the form of sex appeal for its own sake) with the equally wrong attitude which ignores sex altogether and identifies Christianity with sexlessness.

---

[43] An example of such "play," which is no longer concerned with the sex mystery itself but only its libido effects, may possibly be found in the erotic method of "petting" (cf. Geoffrey Gorer, *American People, A Study in National Character* [New York: W. W. Norton & Co., 1948]), as well as "flirting" as an end in itself.

# C. The Realization of the Sex Nature

## 1. BECOMING ONE'S SELF

The meeting of two persons under the influence of *eros* momentarily throws them both off their usual track. Like two colliding billiard balls they are deflected from their previous course. This is exactly what Margaret is referring to as she sings at the spinning wheel:

> My thought is lost,
> My senses mazed.[1]
> Is racked and crazed;
> My poor weak head
>
> My peace is gone,
> My heart is sore:
> I never shall find it,
> Ah, nevermore!

Ecstasy in the sense of being beside oneself also means being thrown off the track. This leads us to ask whether this is really a matter of being blindly shifted away from one's self or whether it is rather knowingly coming to one's self. The question could also be framed in this way: Is what happens in the *eros* encounter a "transformation" [*Umformung*] of one's essential nature or is it a forming of the self from within of itself [*Herausformung*]? In line with the verse on love in Goethe's *Orphic Sayings* we should have to say that it is

---

[1] Goethe, *Faust,* I, 16, trans. by Bayard Taylor (New York: Modern Library, 1950), p. 129.

the latter.[2] In other words, the solitary Robinson Crusoe does not, strictly speaking, come to himself.

Here again we come to the mystery of sexuality: just as the mystery of the person is enclosed in the husk of sexuality, so this person comes to himself only *in* sexuality and also becomes the object of its self-knowledge. But since on the other hand sexuality points beyond its physical ingredients, we may say that *mutatis mutandis* this coming to oneself takes place not only in the erotic encounter but also in the *agape* encounter with other people (in diaconic love, for example, and many other sublimations into which the structure of love can change). We have intentionally said *mutatis mutandis,* for naturally in both kinds of relationship a self is formed in each case with a different center of gravity, and the one without the other generally leads to an actual self that has imperfect contours (even though some very significant exceptions do occur). It is as if a photographic plate with its still invisible picture were immersed in each case in a different developer containing different reagents, which then have their effect in the different way in which the picture "turns out." Therefore the real image of man emerges only in love of God, the magnitude which encompasses all I-Thou relationships. And connected with this is the fact that a living Christian is freed through his encounter with God to become an "original" person and that in the succession of more original—because they are closer to the Origin—Christians there actually are those persons whom we call "originals," because they are different from mere copies of everybody else (*das Man*) and functions of the *Zeitgeist.*

A woman reveals her essential image, as it "comes out" in the sexual encounter, more than does a man. The reason for this is that the

---

[2] (The relevant passage, in prose translation, reads: "Many a heart floats about in the General, but the noblest gives itself to the One." Goethe's own comment on this verse [pp. 420 f., *Select Minor Poems . . . of Goethe and Schiller,* by John S. Dwight (Boston, 1839)] includes the following: "Two souls must fit themselves to one body, two bodies to one soul. . . . The body, consisting of so many members, by its earthly fate grows sick in some of its parts; instead of enjoying itself in the whole, it suffers in details, and yet, in spite of that, is such a relation found to be as desirable as it is necessary." Trans.)

Cf. Martin Buber, *I and Thou,* 2 ed., trans. by Ronald Gregor Smith (New York: Charles Scribner's Sons, 1958).

woman is identified with her sexuality quite differently from the man. It is, so to speak, the "vocation" of the woman to be lover, companion, and mother. And even the unmarried woman fulfills her calling in accord with the essential image of herself only when these fundamental characteristics, which are designed for wifehood and motherhood, undergo a sublimating transformation, but still remain discernible, that is to say, when love and motherliness are the sustaining forces in her vocation.

The man, on the other hand, invests a much smaller quantum of the substance of his being in the sex community. He has totally different tasks and aims beyond the sex relationship, which cause him, to be sure, to come back home to his companion, but only in the sense that he returns home from an outside world that claims a far larger part of his time. The peculiar nature of the man tends to emerge less exclusively in his sexuality; it comes out more strongly in confrontation with what Schiller called "hostile life," in which he must struggle, take risks, scheme, and hunt.[3]

Therefore the wife gives her "self" when she gives herself sexually. She holds nothing back and precisely in doing this she comes to her self-realization. She gives away her mystery (and even—how powerfully symbolic this is!—her maiden name), whereas the husband brings in only a part, a very substantial, but still only a part, of himself. The consequence of this nontotality of the man's sexuality is that the man is not nearly so deeply stamped and molded by his sexual experience as is the case with the woman. And related to this again are three basic features which show the difference between the sexu-

---

[3] We are aware that such statements in terms of ideal types can be made only in a very generalizing way. But this generalized indication of the main characteristics of the man and the woman is unavoidable, even though the actual instances almost never coincide with this outline of the ideal type. This incongruity, which appears in countless exceptions, applies not only to individual cases, but acquires a certain general significance when the social structure is such that it largely neutralizes the polarity of the sexes in the world of labor. In the case of a man working in a factory with a highly socialized structure or in many office jobs one could hardly describe his vocation as "struggle, taking risks, scheming, and hunting." "Industrial-bureaucratic conditions of production have themselves created a large number of sexually neutral jobs and professions and thus have become a contributing cause of the modern tendency toward assimilation in the role of the sexes." H. Schelsky, "Die sozialen Formen der sexuellen Beziehungen" in H. Giese, *op. cit.*, p. 248.

ality of the man and that of the woman.

First: We speak characteristically of the seduction of a girl, but not —at least in the same sense and certainly not with the same seriousness—of the seduction of a man.[4] The meaning that underlies this usage is probably clear enough after what we have said: to seduce a girl[5] means to bring her to self-abandonment; it means to characterize, to stamp her by sexual intercourse and thus to release her from a bond which was decisively constitutive of her essential image. In this way the seduction works against the self-realization which the sex community is meant to bring about.

This can be seen in the tragedy of Margaret in *Faust*: it is not Faust who is ruined because of the seduction, but Margaret. It becomes a tragedy of Faust only very indirectly, since Faust has wronged another person. Faust must come to ruin because he caused the ruin of Margaret and because—and here again the mystery of the person appears—the man is bound to the personal fate of another person and thus is indirectly subjected to his own fate.

This fact that the woman must abandon herself when she gives herself sexually[6] explains why it is that the term "harlot" is actually applied only to a woman and that we have no parallel term for a man even though we take into account the term "gigolo" [*Strichjunge*]. When a man who lives a promiscuous life is called a gay dog, a Casanova, a philanderer, or any other of the terms available in popular speech, even the most drastic of them have a different quality from that of the word "harlot." For while the term "harlot" is actually meant to express the real nature of a female individual,[7] in the case of a man people tend at most to speak of an unfortunate "sector" of

---

[4] The only exception, which, however, does not essentially alter the usage, is the seduction of a young boy.

[5] Cf. "The Diary of the Seducer" in Kierkegaard, *Either/Or*, Vol. I (New York: Doubleday & Company, 1959, Anchor Books), pp. 297 ff.

[6] We have already seen in our interpretation of the selection from Jacobsen's *Niels Lyhne*—remember the reference to Amor and Psyche—that in the woman too there is a limit beyond which the giving of the self must not go, that there is a limit which cannot be ignored with impunity, that she is "marked" by it, and indirectly—but only indirectly!—marks the man by doing so.

[7] This is true at any rate on the "human" level, which, typically, is left behind when Jesus preaches the good news to the harlots and sees in them the violated sister; cf. John 8:3 ff.; Luke 7:4 ff.; John 4:1 ff.

his life. We are capable of speaking of a weak "spot" in an otherwise serious life and of merely saying that a man's "private life" is questionable in order to set it apart from his professional and public activity. In the historians' books such references are usually relegated to the footnotes. Over against this the great hetaerae who have entered into history, from Cleopatra to Madame de Pompadour, are characterized, not primarily by what they actually accomplished, but rather by the fact that they acquired historical significance through being hetaerae.

Naturally, this phenomenological observation cannot mean that we attribute to it the normative force of a fact. And yet even though we hold that this general normative attitude and its evaluations are highly questionable and unjust, we cannot fail to recognize that underneath this Pharisaism which puts an unjust burden upon the woman there are certain characterizations which bring out the difference between the sex nature of man and woman.

Second: Connected with this difference is also the phenomenon of the so-called "double standard of morality." This means that general normative public opinion expects of the woman before marriage an abstention from sex in an altogether different way from what is expected of a man, and that the man, even though he himself may live by other standards, not infrequently demands virginity of his future wife. Perhaps we may say that this disparate evaluation of virginity in man and woman, in other words, this "double standard of morality," does have some basis—which we would not wish to be understood as a legitimation of it!—in the physiological structure of the sex organs: whereas the woman receives something into herself, the male sex organ is directed outward, away from himself; it discharges. The *receiving* of something is contrasted with being *relieved* of something. From a purely physiological point of view, the woman receives something from the sexual encounter (and the medical men point out that this is important even though conception does not take place), whereas the man discharges and thus rids himself of something. The extraordinary force of the symbolism of this disparate physical structure can hardly be evaded.

Thus if we make the physiological element normative we do in fact arrive at the double standard. However, we have already been sufficiently warned to see the dubiousness of this absolutizing of the merely partial, physiological side and to know that it is untenable even in the realm of the purely sexual. In connection with the problem of monogamy we shall have to find out at what place the critical point and therefore the theological problem is to be sought.

Third: Connected with this basic physical structure is the fact that there is in the man a polygamous tendency but in the woman a monogamous.

In the light of our foregoing investigations we can no longer doubt the fact that woman is oriented monogamously and the reason why this is so: the woman, because she is the one who receives, the one who gives herself and participates with her whole being, is profoundly stamped by the sexual encounter. To this extent she is marked by the first man who "possesses" her. One must go even further and say that even the first meeting with this first man possesses the faculty of engraving and marking the woman's being, that it has, as it were, the character of a *monos* and thus tends toward monogamy. Kierkegaard was alluding to this when he said that it would matter nothing to him to betray the whole world, but that he would shrink from betraying a pure maiden; for this would mean that one was violating the "self" of this maiden.

Numerous psychopathological symptoms are determined by this structure of feminine sexuality, which in turn bear witness to this structure. Thus a woman's frigidity as well as the vampire insatiability of the strumpet can be caused by a similar experience in youth (violation or brutality in her first sexual encounter). A case of frigidity with this provenience must then be interpreted psychologically: it can be unconsciously willed and used as a defensive weapon by means of which the woman shuts herself off from further invasions and, so to speak, "plays dead."

Here again the *way* in which such a defense occurs is characteristic of the interrelationship of the physical and the personal. We see this clearly when we observe the corresponding masculine parallel. We have such a case when a man is, for whatever reasons, a chronic antifeminist—like Schopenhauer, for example. Sexually, this results in his continuing—for simple physiological reasons—to make use of sexual intercourse, but the emphasis here is on "use." Thus Schopenhauer, with all his contempt for women, made use of prostitutes. Thus one refuses ever to allow the woman to enter the personal realm of one's own self in such a way that might result in real community or human partnership, but permits her only to come into the physical forefield of the self by using her for the purpose of an instinctive abreaction. It is therefore significant that the male nature *can* interpret, or rather misinterpret, the physical realm as this kind of forefield and thus is capable of interpreting sex as a mere accident of the person but not as something which is itself *permeated* with the personal. This indicates how the man is able to escape from being stamped and characterized by the sexual encounter and that it does not touch him at the core of his personality—or *seem*s not to touch him. On the other hand, if the woman is determined by an anti-male attitude (for which there may be reasons other than those mentioned above), she defends herself against the invasion of sex by resorting to frigidity, in other words, to sexual anaesthesia. Accordingly, she does not think of the physical as a forefield in which she might receive at least a physical satisfaction. Rather in her the physical is so interfused and amalgamated with the personal that she can no longer experience orgasm and resists even the very idea of the physical. If she is married, she may tolerate cohabitation as a duty, but then she not only suffers it as something alien to her person which she must put up with, but also she merely endures it physically.

In the light of this peculiar integration of the physical and the personal in the woman and the consequent formative power of the first sexual encounter, we begin to understand why there is an innate tendency toward monogamy: out of the center of her nature the woman strives to make totality of her experience correspond to her total submission to the man. Her goal is to make not only the physical side of the man her own, not merely once or temporarily, but rather to own the man's very self. The motive of monogamy lies essentially in the very nature of feminine sexuality. It lies in the urge toward self-realization; whereas without this *monos*-bond she is threatened with being delivered up to a deep contradiction of her own nature, namely, the cleavage of that which in her is integrated and which as a unity she cannot give up without suffering a trauma at the center of her being. In her the incapability of separating the physical from the personal and ignoring the "person" of the man would promote loss of selfhood rather than effect the sought-for self-realization.

## 2. MONOGAMY—POLYGAMY

In what light, then, does this put what we have called the polygamous character of the man? The difference which we have observed between the sexual nature of the man and that of the woman has already indicated the basis of this polygamous tendency, namely, the relative ability of the man to isolate the physiological realm and thus treat it as accidental. But a partnership which is merely physiologically determined can be exchanged at will, because the phenomena of nature are general,[8] while the person is unique and nonrecurrent. However, if we are not mistaken, what comes out of this sex nature of the man is by no means only a physiologically determined urge to change partners, but also what might be called a general "life urge" to exploit the stimulative value of every kind of change (whether it be a change of scene or a change of activity). Thus in this trend toward change there can be a motive that reaches out for what is human, even personal. This is quite clear in the case of Faust. The man Faust seeks the "eternal feminine." But—to interpret Goethe through David Friedrich Strauss—the Idea "does not love to pour all its fulness into *one* specimen," but rather reveals itself in an infinite abundance of finite forms. For Faust's *eros* this would mean that the eternal feminine is not exhausted in Margaret, any more than the Idea of truth is exhausted in an individual discipline of knowledge.[9]

Because the erotic encounter may have been a relatively super-

---

[8] This is why Wilhelm Windelband calls natural science "nomothetic" and history "idiographic." Similarly, H. Rickert speaks of a "generalizing" tendency in natural science and an "individualizing" tendency in history. Cf. H. Rickert, *Die Grenze der naturwissenschaftlichen Begriffsbildung* (5 ed., 1929), pp. 191 ff.

[9] Faust himself says, "I've studied now philosophy and jurisprudence, medicine—and even, alas! theology,—from end to end, with labor keen," *Faust* I, 1 (Modern Library, p. 15).

ficial thing, he finds it relatively easy to get over his experience with the individual form (Margaret) and experience in many different forms the eternal feminine, the Ur-phenomenon.

Here we begin to see the metaphysical background of what we have called the polygamous character of the man. And at the same time we see difficulty involved in this polygamy. Even for Faust the encounter with Margaret ultimately meant a profound invasion upon his destiny and he had to pay for it by sharing in her ruin. Faust did not reckon with the "once-for-allness" of Gretchen the person; as it turned out, she did *not* allow herself to be treated as an interchangeable symbol of an Idea, a mere specimen of the eternal feminine. He did not grasp that Margaret was—in Christian terminology—an *imago Dei,* possessing an unexchangeable human dignity. Therefore the man Faust cannot exchange women in the name of the eternal feminine as he exchanges faculties in the name of truth and "the inmost force which binds the world and guides its course." Interfaculty study is qualitatively different from interfeminine love!

Therefore the Faustean wanderer, whose progress is normally not only "torment and joy" but also fulfillment of the meaning of existence, encounters guilt at this point, for here he turns his back upon a person, the meaning of whose existence he then destroys. He may traverse and experience the whole world in his quest, for its transitory forms are parables, and in that the wanderer passes through all things finite he comes close to the ground of all things. All except the person he meets, the person who gives herself in community and is marked by that community—she is something more than a symbolic bit of finitude, something more than a mere experience to be passed through on the quest. She calls a halt and demands a quite un-Faustean sacrifice.

Certainly we dare not moralize the guilt of Faust. It has a definite tragic quality. The tragedy, of which he is the executor in the tragedy of Margaret, lies in the fact that Faust's entelechy compels him to keep on questing and that, beyond this, his entelechy is a microcosmic reflection of Being itself, which manifests itself in finite, constantly moving forms. He is merely obeying the "law according to which he started out" when he continues his quest and thus "developing" as he lives the "minted form" with which he was stamped from the beginning.[10] Margaret's entelechy, however, is not the "eternal feminine," but merely to be finitely feminine, to be a woman who gives and pours out "herself" in the sexual encounter and therefore must remain hidden in this encounter. She can exist and be herself only as long as the other person, who has become the one and only for her, preserves the bond in which she has invested her being. It is tragic in the strict sense of the word that these two entelechies contradict each other and that they subject the participants to the conflict of deciding whether to hold to the other and become unfaithful to oneself or to serve the law of their own being and sacrifice the other person. But however true it may be that here we are confronted with a profound contradiction in the structure of the world, which must be borne by men who must vicariously endure this conflict, the fact remains that it is wrong and involves guilt. "Thou guiltless of this murder, thou! Who dares such thought avow?" says the chorus in Aeschylus' *Agamemnon*.[11] In other words, "Yours is the deed, and no judgment will ever absolve you of murder"; and the chorus says this even though it is fully aware of the fate, of which human guilt is only the symptom, the place where it erupts.

Having said this, we have already seen something of the questionable side of masculine polygamy (which may be a banal or perhaps a deeper and more significant form of "wandering"). Our basic question is this: Is there a conceivably adequate form of this masculine polygamy?

If it were possible to conceive of the masculine in isolation, which, of course, can be done only by some devious experiment of thought, the question could be answered in the affirmative. Physiologically, at any rate, there would be nothing at all to prevent this form of living; and as far as the personal dimension is concerned, the sex experience could possibly be relegated to the periphery, leaving the core of personality untouched (in the way Schopenhauer, for example, tried to live). But this is merely talking in terms of an artificial abstraction.

---

[10] The allusions in quotation marks are from Goethe's *Orphic Sayings*, "Destiny." (Trans.)

[11] Trans. by E. D. A. Morehead. (Trans.)

For the fact is that the man "exists" as such only because there is such a thing as "woman"; that is to say, he simply cannot leave out of consideration her existence and therefore her sex nature. And since the woman cannot live polygamously without damage to the very substance of her nature, the man cannot do so either.

The reason for this inability is something deeper than a merely moral reason. By "moral" we would mean that the man did not give way to his polygamous tendency merely out of altruistic considerations. The fact is, however, that because of the totality of sexuality *itself* he cannot give way to polygamy without suffering loss of his own substance. As we have already said, he wants an intact wife for himself; he wants this on the assumption that she alone is able to give him the ultimate sexually, since she has not been "marked" by another man and therefore has no zone within herself which is reserved for someone else. But he can demand the two at the same time—namely, sexual freedom for himself and sexual integrity in his partner—only at the cost of an ethical inconsistency, a profound and hypocritical self-contradiction, which he and society in his name seek to justify with the phrase "double standard of morality."

So monogamy is in the last analysis grounded in the personhood of man, inasmuch as this personhood cannot be separated from the physical realm of sex. Since this separation is seemingly possible in the man, but obviously impossible in the woman,[12] monogamy is based primarily upon the wholeness of feminine selfhood. We can speak of masculine polygamy only indirectly and *cum grano salis,* because, after all, masculinity is a relational term, that is, because it cannot be defined apart from feminine existence (I Cor. 11:11). Therefore one should guard oneself against saying that polygamy is "natural" for the man. For this would be an illegitimate restriction of the term "natural" to the animal. Rather what is "natural" for the man is his manliness, and this means his relationship to the woman. But this means that he cannot define and exercise his own sexuality apart from that of the woman without denying his own manhood. Therefore what is "natural" for the man is not that form of

---

[12] In these statements we are leaving out of account special cases such as prostitution, for example.

sexuality which is in accord with the man as such, with man in his isolation as an entelechy; this cannot be so, if only because such an artificial "man as such" would be a physical monstrosity. What is "natural" is rather that form of sexuality which is in accord with his relatedness to the woman. Hence polygamy, when it is seen from the point of view of the polar wholeness of the sex mystery, is not in conformity with the masculine nature, but rather a denial of it.

We recall in this connection our discussion of the pastoral side of the problem. Sexual fulfillment is to be found only in entering into the sex nature of the other person and not in blind pursuit of one's own sex entelechy. Marital crises of this kind therefore require an appeal to the kind of mutual compliance which is not merely a response to the demands of the *libido* but also to those of human communication. This kind of mutual compliance is equally related to both *eros* and *agape*. The limitation put upon the man's polygamous sex entelechy by its relatedness to the woman's sex entelechy is also a mode of this mutual compliance. It belongs, as we saw, to the masculine nature, as soon as it is seen that the masculine nature exists in relationship to the feminine nature. So what *agape* demands—namely, to exist for the other person and to relate one's own life to him—is not confined to the spiritual or personal sector, which actually does not exist as a sector anyhow, but is related to the whole "nature" of the other person. *Agape* is at the same time the deepest interpretation of the totality of the human being.

Once we see that Christian *agape* regards this "existence-for-the-other-person" as the foundation of all fellow humanity, and that it regards man as being determined by his neighbor, it becomes apparent that under the gospel there is a clear trend toward monogamy. Because the wife is a "neighbor," the husband cannot live out his own sex nature without existing for her sex nature and without respecting the unique importance which he himself must have for the physical and personal wholeness of the feminine sex nature. We have already seen that this postulate of *agape* does not mean that the sexual is merely to be lifted to a higher ethical plane and thus subjected to regulation from the outside and from above, but rather that it is already in fundamental accord with the law of "mutual compliance" *within* the realm of the libido and thus is really in accord with nature itself. But in spite of this clear affinity of monogamy with the gospel, we have intentionally spoken of a *trend* toward monogamy that comes with the gospel. What we mean to express by the use of this term, which appears to be a qualification, is that monogamy is not simply "given" when one becomes a Christian, but rather that it "becomes" the sole form of relationship.

Here it is characteristic that the Bible contains no references to this connection which can be quoted in so many words. The Old Testament does not, since it recognizes polygamy. In the New Testament —except with respect to bishops (I Tim. 3:2; Titus 1:6-7)—the problem is not mentioned at all. So we cannot speak of there being a "law" that demands monogamy. All the more, then, are we prompted to ask how it was that Christianity arrived at the completely unambiguous decision to give monogamy the prerogative of being *the* Christian form of marriage.

The solution of this question, which has been strangely neglected and hardly mentioned in the literature,[13] requires some thinking which will have to make up for the lack of historical documentation by making some conjectures, though they will have to be theological in nature.

If our statement that the masculine sex entelechy, in contrast to that of the woman, has a polygamous tendency is correct, then the autonomy of *eros* within a society which is determined by the primacy of the man would lead us to expect a trend toward polygamy. And since long periods of history, including church history, are characterized by the primacy of the man,[14] it is surprising that Christian-

---

[13] Even the current books on ethics do not deal with it. Emil Brunner operates with some peculiar speculations on the order of creation in providing an argument for monogamy (*The Divine Imperative*, pp. 342 ff.). Otto Piper reminds us of one covenant God in the Old Testament who declares that Israel's whoring after other gods is adultery and by doing so points to monogamy, just as does the Epistle to the Ephesians with its analogy between the relationship of Christ and his church and the relationship of man and wife. "From the preference of the Old and New Testaments for the metaphor of marriage as a description of the God-relationship one may conclude that the bond is the closest of all bonds, and accordingly we may conclude from the mutual exclusiveness of the relation that true marriage also demands exclusiveness" (*Die Geschlechter, Ihr Sinn und ihr Geheimnis in bibl. Sicht* [1954], pp. 241 f.). [It should be noted that this statement does not appear in this form in the two English versions of Piper's books, *The Christian Interpretation of Sex* (1941), and *The Biblical View of Sex and Marriage* (1960). Trans.]

[14] Cf. the section on equality of the sexes, pp. 145 ff.

ity very emphatically allowed no room, not even the slightest, for this expected tendency.[15]

This Christian decision in favor of monogamy is certainly not to be explained as a conclusion of a "natural theology." For as a rule, natural theology tends to regard what is given and desired as natural, so that one can easily figure out what a male-dominated society would have produced in the way of a "natural theology" on this subject. Since direct biblical injunctions also were not the basis for the formation of definitely monogamous customs, we must suppose that quite different motives were at work. These can be found only in the new Christian orientation of personal community—and thus the marriage relationship too—upon *agape*. Even in primitive Christianity the undisputed primacy of the man in society and the family was limited by the requirement that the man should love his wife (*agapan*).[16] But *agape* in its New Testament sense means to exist for the other person and enter into his life in a very realistic (not primarily emotional) way. If this is not to be thought of as being merely a universally human, diluted, and abstract attitude of mind—and what could be farther from the New Testament!—then it implies, as we have said, an acceptance of our actual neighbor as he is and therefore of his sex nature too. If for the woman not to be the sole wife of her husband means to wound her, then *agape* demands that this wound must not be inflicted upon her.

Hence we have here a classic instance of how theologically and anthropologically determined ends are intertwined, how grace and nature work together unmixed and unseparated (without necessarily leading to an *analogia entis*!). That is to say, *agape*, which accepts the other person, would not really be "seeing" the other person as he is if it regarded him merely as a human being in general (*humanum generale*) and did not approach him as the particular person that he is, with his own particular and individual nature. Therefore *agape*, which is understood as being "bodily" and personal and not Docetic, possesses an infinite variety of possible forms: in the realm of *eros* it

[15] A few special cases affecting princes primarily, in one of which even Luther was involved, can hardly be regarded as a counterargument.
[16] Eph. 5:28; cf. the exegetical comments in the section on marriage.

has a tone which is different from what it has in loving service (*diakonia*); it is one thing in the fellowship of the workaday world and another between parents and children. And yet in all these areas it is the same.

The only explanation of Christianity's decision in favor of monogamy which seems reasonable to us lies here and here alone: The appeal to *agape,* which demands the full acceptance of the other person, causes the husband to deal with his wife as a unique, individual person and thus checks his own tendency toward polygamy. Love in the sense of *agape* teaches us to understand; it also teaches us to understand the other person's sex nature and then in the light of that understanding to "be there," to "exist," for him.

Implicit in these statements is the negative assertion that monogamy cannot be explained simply on the basis of the autonomy of *eros* itself. Not that *eros* in itself is altogether without a tendency in this direction. As we have already seen, the compliance with the other person which is required by the *ars amandi* is in itself one of the indications of this tendency. But, as history shows, these tendencies in *eros* are not sufficient to establish monogamy. Only a large number of analyses of actual situations in polygamous societies could show the sociological and psychological reasons that block the road to monogamy or make it seem—in the erotic sense—unnecessary. In any case, *eros* itself does not have in it an inherent trend toward monogamy, although certain "secular" philosophers have tried to find a basis for monogamy in arguments which appeal to the autonomy of *eros.*

The central argument that is usually advanced here is that basically there is only *one* person who fits another, in other words, that it is the uniqueness, the singularity of the partner, that constitutes the basis of marriage and leads to its monogamous form. The argument for this unique affinity may employ mythological concepts, like Plato's spherical man which we mentioned above, namely, that the reason that two lovers fit each other perfectly is that originally they were one in a pre-existent unity; and therefore love is two halves, which are specifically suited to each other, finding each other again. The same idea of two highly differentiated individuals belonging together can also be argued quite unmythologically on the basis of the laws of sexual complementarity. This argument asserts that every human being has in him an M (man) component and a W (woman) component, and in each case in differing proportions. The formal relationship of mutual completion, which Plato already regarded as the goal of *eros,* thus comes into being through one's discovering the corresponding M-W proportion in the other.[17] Therefore in the ideal case, i.e., if the partner is to be the "one and only," the total sum of M and W must always equal 200.[18]

Now, it is probably beyond all doubt that this harmonizing with each other is the *conditio sine qua non* of all real life relationships which are based upon *eros.* We have already made it clear that *agape* does not take the place of *eros,* but rather takes it into its service and leads me to love the other person in the milieu of the erotic and in an erotic way just as I love him in other areas of life in another way. In this context, then, this would mean that *eros* and the law of complementarity and mutual conformity which it demands is not the thing that forms the foundation of marriage but only that which conditions it.

If, however, the marriage is founded exclusively upon this erotic principle,[19] then it will be subject to a permanent crisis, for it will be repeatedly compelled to ask: Is the other person really the "right one" for me; in other words, does he represent the optimum of complementarity? This recurring question is prompted by three motives:

First, once the empirical diagnosis (which is often nothing more than a prognosis!) that this particular person is the optimum complement for me, it demands constant re-examination and possibly revision. For, in the first place, we are both beings with a history and therefore we change. What may have been, or only appeared to be, complementarity at the moment when the union was entered into can change or turn out to be a mistake. Self-love (*amor sui*), which is in-

---

[17] If the man has 60 per cent M and 40 per cent W, the woman must have 60 per cent W and 40 per cent M in order to harmonize with him. If a man has a proportion of half M and half W or even a preponderance of the W-component, then no woman but only a partner of the same sex will suit him.

[18] Thus Weininger, *op. cit.*

[19] Cf. the section on the development of the concept of the individual *eros,* especially since the period of romanticism: "Historical Changes in Our Understanding of Eros," pp. 295 ff.

herent in *eros,* brings up the question in the interest of self-preservation and self-development. And then, too, during the course of my life I meet other representatives of the opposite sex who provoke comparisons and thus likewise appeal to my tendency to make revisions in my original estimate.

Second, the *eros* which is isolated to itself makes not only the *being* of the other person, but also his *functions,* the criterion of his complementarity. For, after all, it is precisely in the erotic realm that a person's being is actualized in specific functions, that is to say, in the *ars amandi.* This results in something like a permanent compulsion to keep on the watch to see whether the other person is still capable of functioning. Here again the historical character of our existence is at work: we know that in the course of time the ability to function changes, and that this change is not synchronized in the two partners (one ages faster than the other) and that this must inevitably result in strains and disharmonies. In this historical sense the functions are far more variable than the being of the two individuals.

Third, a further cause of this compulsion to keep watching arises from the rhythmical character of *eros* itself: The ecstasy of the moment is followed by phases of indifference or even repulsion, in which the question (which often becomes a neurosis) whether the complementarity still exists, gains a foothold. Thus often enough in the merely erotic, the merely "romantic," marriage the honeymoon is followed by crisis. With a deadly certainty the moment comes in such marriages when the comparison of one's own partner with other and especially younger representatives of his or her sex turns out to his or her disadvantage, and then the half solution (like infidelity) or the radical solution (like divorce) is sought for. After all, the progressive instability of the kind of marriage which has appeared since the rise of individual *eros* is notorious in history. The old saying that love will come with marriage has proved to be right, at any rate as far as the solidity of the marriages so undertaken is concerned, over against the postromantic notion that love (meaning *eros*) must be the foundation of marriage and therefore must precede it. This observation cannot mean that the development can be reversed and that we can go back behind romanticism and recover that patriarchal form of marriage or even that we should do so. Its only intent is to show us the underlying problem of a marriage that is based only upon *eros*.

It is therefore strange to observe how both the *eros* line and the *agape* line point to the uniqueness of the sex partner. In both cases this uniqueness becomes a basic consideration. (This is not altered by the fact that we were obliged to conclude that in the realm of *eros* that uniqueness is desired but "in the long run" never attained). *Eros* postulates this uniqueness by its insistence upon a highly specified complementarity. *Agape* has it as its goal, because the indissoluble bond between the physical and the personal (especially in the woman) implies a single partnership and therefore tends toward monogamy.

With a view to controverting the idea that this uniqueness can be grounded only upon *eros,* we state in conclusion the Christian antithesis to it: *Not uniqueness establishes marriage, but marriage establishes uniqueness.*

The negative portion of this statement we have just discussed: the uniqueness of the sex partner demanded by *eros* cannot establish marriage because it must necessarily remain subject to constant reexamination and revision. Thus strictly speaking, the partner's uniqueness is such only "at the moment," or at most "for a time," but never for life "until death us do part."

With respect to the positive portion of the statement, namely, that it is the marriage that establishes the uniqueness, we have also said the most important thing already: the sexual encounter that takes place in the marriage and certainly the children who issue from it "mark" the two partners and make them the "one and only" for each other, so that they exist for each other and become a part of each other's destiny. Through it the wife especially—and indirectly through her the husband—acquires a *character indelebilis* in the sense of belonging to each other permanently. And this is exactly what is meant by the uniqueness which comes into being in the marriage *itself*. As we have seen, the wife who surrenders herself invests her whole self in the community of love. She even gives up her name. And since we were compelled to conclude that this is connected with the congruence of sexuality and personhood, especially in the case of the wife, the uniqueness that arises in love cannot have its source only in *eros*, but must be grounded essentially in *agape*, which qualifies *eros* and gives it meaning and purpose. For only *agape*, the sole attitude in which the other person is really seen, in which he is seen as one who is dearly purchased, as a "person before God," and as a "neighbor," takes into account this congruence. And thus it also takes into account the characterizing character of sexuality and causes one to respect that uniqueness which comes into being in the sexual encounter.

In view of this uniqueness that comes into being in marriage (it is really something that "happens" and not a timeless, arithmetical assumption), it is therefore not going too far to speak of the *creativeness* of married love. This creative side is the gift of *agape*. Luther once defined the love of God as contrasted with human *eros* in this way: "The love of God does not find that which is worthy of his love, but rather creates it for himself; but the love of man comes into being through the lovableness which it finds."[20] Human love, that is, *eros*, is dependent upon what is worth loving in the other person, that is to say, upon such immanent values as beauty, character, intellect, and harmonious complementarity. It is therefore dependent upon what is transient and unstable and is therefore subject to revision. Hence it is based upon what is perhaps a highly sublimated self-love; for, after all, this kind of love is directed, not to the other person's values "as such," but rather to his value "for me." Thus it has within it the question—and this makes it "questionable" in the strict sense of the word—of what the other person means to *me* and whether he *still* has any value for me. But the love of *God*, which we imitate in *agape*, is not based upon the calculable value of the other person for me. For God does not love us because we are so valuable; rather we are valuable because God loves us. Because the other person is valuable to God, he compels me to show reverence. Therefore my love is no longer addressed to an unstable function, to what in any given moment I can or cannot find to be "valuable for me" in the other person. The continuing faithfulness of God with which he is surrounded also makes my relationship to him a continuing one.

[20] "*Amor Dei non invenit, sed creat suum diligibile, amor hominum fit a suo diligibili*" (WA 1, 354, 35).

*Agape* therefore penetrates beyond the superficialities of the momentary adequacy or inadequacy of the other person and addresses itself to his ultimate mystery. And this is precisely what makes it creative: the other person knows that he is being addressed and respected at the core of his being, at that point of human dignity which is unconditioned by, and independent of, what he is in actuality and which has its own hidden history with God. In this way *agape* brings out, "loves" out, as it were, the real person within the other human being. This is why all those who came into contact with Jesus—and especially the dubious characters, the harlots and publicans, the outcasts, the outsiders, the insulted and injured—were dignified by his *agape* and grew up into that dignity. They did not first have to qualify themselves in order to become worthy of this love; rather they were qualified by this love; and if this is not misunderstood in the sense of idealistic philosophy, one might even say that under the warmth of this love they grew to be something beyond themselves. This love addressed itself to the child of God within them, and therefore it also liberated that child of God within them. It was a creative breath that blew upon them. Therefore it is not mere romanticism to dare to say that one can tell by looking at many older married folks that they have been much loved. Qualities have been released within them, "loved out of them," which their own entelechy would never have brought out. This, too, is part of the law of "forming the self" which genuine love carries into effect.

Thus all love in the sense of *agape* and *eros* which has been transformed by *agape* is like a reproduction of that divine creativity which Luther ascribed to the love of God. It is in the light of this creative love that we are to understand the statement that married love creates uniqueness and does not itself arise from uniqueness.[21]

[21] On the problem of monogamy and polygamy cf. also the problem encountered on the mission field, dealt with in our discussion of the question of divorce in polygamous marriages, pp. 178 ff.

# III   THE ORDER
## OF
## MARRIAGE

# A. The Biblical Interpretation of Marriage

## 1. The Theological Significance of the Biblical Statements

The biblical statements concerning marriage are not aimed directly at what is usually called the "modern problem of marriage." This does not mean that we regard them as having only relative value, but merely affirms the necessity—which we encounter at every step in ethics—of taking seriously the task of hermeneutics when we deal with these statements. And for the purpose of preparing ourselves for this task right from the beginning, the following points of view commend themselves as useful for interrogating the biblical texts.

The first point of view is concerned with the theological character of the "order" which is represented in the institution of marriage and our question is: In what relationship does it stand to the creation of man and the purpose of that creation? The second point of view, which interests us especially with respect to the Old Testament, relates to the question whether and to what extent the Bible presupposes such a thing as individual *eros,* and further, whether and to what extent we can discern any lines that run back and forth between the evaluation of *eros* and the regulations that govern monogamy and polygamy.

NOTE: Problems of the family related to the theme of marriage, especially the relationship of parents and children, are discussed in connection with other themes in *ThE.* Cf., e.g., the chapter on parental law (II, 2, §1697 ff.), the family in society (III, still unpublished), artificial insemination (pp. 248 ff.), etc.

It is obvious that the latter question is aimed in a *special* way at the modern problem of marriage. We know that in the period before Romanticism marriage regulations were largely determined by the fact that the marriage contract was the responsibility of the family, that it was the family that acted in the matter, and that the candidates for marriage were largely under its control. Even though this cannot mean that these arrangements were governed only by rational, economic, and similar considerations, but rather that we must assume that parental instinct also played its part and that the question whether the children were suited to each other was by no means left out of consideration; nevertheless it cannot be denied that it was not until modern times (in this case beginning with Romanticism) that the individual *eros* was introduced as a standard criterion for determining whether two persons are "created for each other" and should enter into marriage with each other.

Not that the individual *eros* did not exist previous to this time! Ever since primeval times and probably in all places it has been the theme of narratives, songs, and philosophical reflection—we need only to recall the Platonic myth of the spherical man or the minnesongs of the Middle Ages (to limit ourselves only to our own civilization). In modern times, however, this individual *eros* has in the public mind come to be the only condition, indeed, the only basis, of any possible *marriage* relationship (and not only of a friendship or a nonmarital love relationship). Expressing it in rather generalized terms, we might venture to formulate it in this way: *Before* the period of Romanticism people married (or were married) and looked forward to the individual love that would arise *within* this bond. *After* the period of Romanticism people married on the basis of love already experienced.

Personal love as a consequence or as a precondition: this in somewhat oversimplified fashion sums up the transvaluation that took place with regard to individual *eros* in marriage. Naturally, we cannot get back of this historical caesura—any more than we get behind nature in order to recover direct contact with the biblical message. The course of history, once taken, is irreversible.

Therefore the problem of a theological ethics is to bring the biblical kerygma into the co-ordinate system of changed understanding of the world and the self and interpret its statements in the context of the new situation. This is why it has been so important right from the beginning to deal with the changed relationship of *eros* to marriage in the modern mind. For it is this change in attitude that presents the real problem in our task of interpretation. The problem is: what does the message concerning the theological character of the order of marriage look like on the other side of the historical caesura? To what extent is it at work in the new feeling about life that is now presumed to exist? Is its purpose to break down this new attitude? Does it change it? Here we encounter very considerable difficulties which, even more than in other areas, make it impossible simply to "quote" Bible passages.

Some of the problems indicated have already been explored in connection with our discussion of the relation of *eros* and *agape*. There it became apparent that the *eros* tone of the relationship of the sexes—even when it is interpreted positively and made fundamental to marriage as it is in the modern mind—cannot become autonomous, either in pursuance of "nature" or under the rule of "grace," without corrupting the humanity of man. Because *eros* binds together persons who are "neighbors," it is drawn into the sphere of laws of communication which are determined by the concept held by these persons of what a neighbor is. For Christians this concept or image of what a neighbor is has well-defined contours. But the reverse is also true: *agape* realizes itself in this realm by permeating the given—and necessarily given—*eros* relationship. There can be no love relationship between the sexes which is interested only in *agape,* with no regard for *eros*.

It is clear that this original pattern of sex relationship, insofar as it is determined by this mutual interfusion of *eros* and *agape,* cannot be affected at its core by the change in attitude which occurred in history, but rather persists. We may therefore presume that the institutionalization of the sex relationship in *marriage* contains within it essential components which remain unaffected by that historical change, however greatly our concept of marriage may have changed. We can assume that features can be recognized here which not only persist but also have a continuing *kerygmatic* significance for the many different kinds of possible marriage relationships, for example, for marriage in modern cultures, which is based essentially upon *eros,* as well as for the polygamous structures which the biblical message encounters in the mission field.

In the discussion that follows, as we attempt to set forth the basic features of the biblical view of marriage, we shall keep in mind this kerygmatic core which persists in the midst of all marriage customs as they change with the times. This core is determined primarily by the fact that marriage rests upon a primeval order of creation and is at the same time incorporated in the order of salvation, in the sense that it has symbolical or parabolical force and is capable of representing the relation between God and his people, between Christ and his church.

## 2. Marriage in the Old Testament

We turn our attention first to the Old Testament view of marriage, to the extent that we have not dealt with it in our previous discussion of the "duality" of man.

Because marriage is grounded in the primeval relationship of the sexes it is a constituent part of the things that were created and is therefore an order of creation. In earlier volumes of this work on theological ethics we have had repeated occasion to deal with the concept of orders and the disastrous misuse of the term "order of *creation.*"[2] Our reservations with regard to this term were based upon the conclusion that the orders of history (for example, the order of the state and of the law) have been stamped by the fallen world along with everything else and that their meaning and purpose is that of a God-ordained structure for the preservation of the world[3] as well as a self-objectification of this aeon and its *sacro egoismo.* Therefore, because of their broken, fallen character, these orders cannot be a direct representation of the Creator's will, but rather bear the marks of human "hardness of heart" (Matt. 19:8), which, in the form they now have, cannot be regarded as having legitimacy "from creation" (*ap' arche*).

But marriage, which is an order of creation in the *real* sense, transcends

[2] Cf. *ThE* I, §2144 ff.; II, 1, §655 f.; II, 2, §3086-3103.
[3] Cf. the Noachic covenant, Gen. 9:1-17.

these orders of history. This reveals itself even in the fact that marriage is located in the original state; in other words, it is an order "before the Fall," even though the actual form it took was drawn into the Fall, just as the *total* status of man was affected by the Fall (Gen. 3:16 f.). In its original intention its status was to be that of a partnership between man and woman (Gen. 2:18), a state of being created for each other (2:21-22), and of recognizing themselves in each other (2:23). The original identity —represented by the simile of the rib—which divides itself into the man-woman polarity, is an "ante form" of individual *eros,* in which one recognizes himself in the other person and at the same time a complement of himself.

In this concept there is obviously a certain resemblance to the Platonic myth of the spherical man.[4] The analogy, however, is only partial, for the Old Testament does not draw the conclusion which Plato draws from the original identity of the sexes, namely, that now the two parts seek each other in order to fulfill themselves in an individually harmonized complementary relationship. On the contrary, the meaning given to the relationship of the sexes in the creation story is hardly discernible in the Israelite laws with respect to marriage. For here the patriarchal supremacy of the man is obvious and evidences itself primarily in three ways: first, the man has the freedom to have more than one wife; second, he has the right to dismiss his wife (whereas the wife cannot dissolve the marriage); third, and most important, the wife is the object of a legal transaction in the sense of a "Munt"-marriage [*Munt* being ownership or guardianship acquired by purchase]. The suitor pays to the father of the girl or to her brother as a representative of the father a "bride-price" (*mohar,* cf. Gen. 34:11 f.; Deut. 22:29, etc.). The wife thereby passes into the power of the husband. Thus she has no part in this transaction as an independent individual under the law.

Certainly this legal position of the woman is not in line with the relationship of the sexes in the creation story, and, naturally, it is also not in accord with the Platonic conception of the spherical man. Rather this is clearly an infiltration of Arabian influences, which are still discernible in modern Islam.[5] Nothing is more characteristic of this position of woman as a mere object than the fact that the man is called the lord (*ba'al*) and the woman is called property (*be'ulah*). Equally significant is the fact that the law regarding the seduction of a virgin who is not betrothed appears in the catalogue of crimes against property rights (Exod. 22:15 ff.; Deut. 22:28 f). The seducer must pay as compensation for this property damage (and significantly, damage done to the *father's* property) an amount

---

[4] Plato, *Symposium,* 189 ff.; in Jowett, *op. cit.,* pp. 558 ff.
[5] J. Wellhausen, *op. cit.*

equivalent to what the father could have claimed if his daughter were regularly married.

There are two points, however, that show that this position of woman as a mere object was limited and that the relationship of the sexes reflected in the creation story nevertheless remained in the background as a kind of corrective. First, the husband's position of dominance was limited by the fact that the wife had some backing from her family, though naturally this would vary in effectiveness with the prestige of the family. Second, the husband's ownership of the wife was also not absolute; she was never merely a "thing," a mere "labor unit"; on the contrary, she was distinguished by the fact that she provided the tribe with its most valuable asset: its sons. Furthermore, the husband's right of possession actually consisted only in the wife's being required to live with him and bear children for him; he was not, however, the master of her person, since he could not sell her (as he could sell her daughter).

Finally, we must not overlook the fact that the laws regulating marriage in the Old Testament do not by any means set forth the *pleroma*, the full picture. They do not capture the reality of marriage any more than do our civil statutes today. The personal sense of belonging to each, which is evident in the order of creation, is constantly breaking into the general tendency to regard the wife as an object, as a mere piece of property. One might even say that the *humanum*, the human element, repeatedly asserts itself and transcends the legal ordinance. This is especially evident in the Old Testament accounts in which the individual *eros*—for which the laws make no provision whatsoever—breaks through and asserts itself in the courtship as well as in the marriage itself. It is true, of course, that even this manifestation of *eros* does not annul the legal procedures (purchase and sale of the woman) or alter the legal status of the man and the wife; and yet it is quite clear that it can definitely determine the real and human relationship of the couple. One need think only of Jacob's courtship of Rachel (Gen. 29), the relationship of Shechem to Dinah (Gen. 34:1-4), and the marriage of Paltiel to Michal (I Sam. 18:20 ff.; 25:44; II Sam. 3:15 f.). The individual tone of married love is also clear in Malachi 2:15, "Take heed to yourselves, and let none be faithless to the wife of his youth." The term "wife of his youth," with its remembrance of the "days of youth" spent together, clearly alludes to happiness personally shared with each other.[6]

To be sure, this is only a certain "tone" that is given to married life, not something that constitutes the foundation of the marriage. The foundation is and continues to remain the order and the convention. This is apparent not only in the legal statutes but can also be seen in the actual

[6] Ludwig Köhler, *op. cit.*, p. 80.

practice of life, particularly in two phenomena:

1. Whereas the prevalence of individual *eros* not only entails individual choice of partner but also makes it possible to refrain from marrying, in Israel practically *everybody* was married. The Old Testament has no word for "bachelor" at all, whereas the Arabs have the term, but only in the ironical, pitying form of the word *azab*, forlorn, lonely, forsaken.[7] So universal and accepted as a matter of course was the institution of marriage that we do not know whether there were any unmarried people in Israel. Though we today can never again go back to the time before the individual *eros* asserted itself, we can nevertheless say—with this Israelite order of marriage specifically in mind—that this form of *eros* has not only enriched and deepened marriage but also jeopardized it and exposed it to instability and uncertainty. Ludwig Köhler is certainly right when he says, "Wherever in a community everyone marries and is married, many tensions are absent."[8]

There is no mention whatsoever in the Old Testament of the tragedy of separated lovers, or of unhappy marriages in which the partners are afflicted with an "unconquerable aversion" to each other. Because the order relieved one of all individual decisions, it gave stability to those who lived under the order: this is the way things are done; one does not take oneself and one's feelings too seriously. This tendency is further fortified by the fact that in the marriage not only two individuals but rather two tribes enter into relations with each other. Here again the unstable emotions of *eros* are provided with a suprapersonal counterbalance that gives permanence to the relationship.

2. Among these stabilizing factors provided by the prevalence of the idea of order is also the practice of *polygamy*, even though at first one might not expect this to be so. The basis for this practice (which again was legally regulated) was probably the fact that in the original conditions in which people lived very close together it seemed better that "every marriageable woman be in proper relationship to some man."[9] In this way not only the problem of childless women (and thus the problem of women whose lives, according to the view then prevalent, were unfulfilled) but also the tragedy of homeless, illegitimate children was avoided. Beyond this we do not know how common such polygamous marriages were and how many wives were involved. The accounts of a number of kings having a relatively large number of wives (II Sam. 3:2-5; I Kings 11:1-8; II Chron. 13:21) must not lead us to draw exaggerated conclusions. Courts naturally occupy a special position.

[7] *Ibid.*, p. 76.
[8] *Ibid.*, p. 76.
[9] *Ibid.*, p. 78.

In conclusion we may say that, though Israel's law governing marriage clearly manifests a predominance of the institutional over the individual, it does not fully express the whole of its understanding of marriage and married life. The factor which is missing in the legal picture expresses itself not only in the breakthrough of what we have called the individual *eros* but above all in two theological characteristics which transcend all merely statutory fixations of the marriage ordinance. The first is to be found in the relationship of man and woman in creation, which makes them equal in status, goal, and grace under God and before God. And the second is the fact that marriage is capable of being used as a simile for the relationship of God to his people, as it was later for the relationship of Christ to his church (Isa. 50:1; Jer. 2:1 f., 3:1 ff.; Ezek. 16:23, and above all Hos. 1-3; in the New Testament: I Cor. 11:3; Eph. 5:22 ff.).

The order of creation and the order of redemption converge in the symbol of marriage. While the legal regulations are discernibly affected by contemporary historical influences, primarily by the ethnical customs of neighboring nations, these factors which transcend the law are aimed at the kerygmatic core upon which later and different (and thus also *modern*) interpretations of marriage must be oriented, if they are to lay claim to being Christian interpretations of the meaning of marriage and the relationship of the sexes.

### 3. Marriage, Divorce, and the Remarriage of Divorced Persons in the New Testament

The New Testament witness concerning marriage can be properly viewed only against this Old Testament background. Here already we see the beginning of the struggle with the contemporary, and therefore relative, legal ordinance of marriage, and how this is done in the name of that kerygmatic core which we have called the essence of the factors which transcend the law. In this process the kerygmatic core undergoes a transformation similar to that which prophecy undergoes when it is fulfilled and that which the Old Testament *nomos* undergoes when it is radicalized by the Sermon on the Mount.

Thus we see that the New Testament interpretation of marriage differs from that of the Old Testament in a number of respects:

In the dialogue on divorce with the Pharisees (Matt. 19:3 ff.; Mark 10:2 ff.; cf. Matt. 5:31 f.) Jesus begins with the order of creation: God, who "from the beginning made them male and female"

(Matt. 19:4), made them *one* flesh. "What therefore God has joined together, let no man put asunder" (v. 6). The Creator has made this bond even stronger than the bond to father and mother (v. 5: cf. Gen. 2:24). If, in spite of this, there is the possibility of receiving a "certificate of divorce," this is not the "original" and real will of God (*ap' arches de ou gegonen outos*, v. 8), but rather God has condescended to make a concession to your hardness of heart.

Thus here explicit reference is made to the *arche* of creation and hence to the order that provides the standard for marriage. It is made the standard for the essential *nature* of marriage and at the same time a criterion for the relative rank of the *divorce* statute. It follows from this that divorce, even though God has conceded it in special cases, does not correspond with the will of God in the same sense as does marriage itself. Here it is clear that the legal ordinance of divorce is a mark of "this aeon"; it is definitely *not* an order of creation, but rather—like all law—a regulation of necessity (*Notverordnung*) for the fallen world in the sense of the Noachic covenant.[10]

For that very reason, however, it would be entirely wrong to turn around and again interpret Jesus' reference to the order of marriage in creation legalistically and think of it as a new, purified law which has been restored to its original meaning.

Rather the marriage law remains fundamentally *below* the level of the original institution of marriage. And yet it needs this reference back to the original institution in order that we may be constantly aware of how relative and provisional the marriage laws are. Only in this way will we be preserved from thinking that the marriage laws contain evidences of the fundamental nature of man, of what he was meant to be, and hence *also* of the nature of marriage. This is just not so. Rather the laws define only the "man in revolt." In order that this man may be disclosed in his state of depravity and then also learn to see that this is what he is, it is necessary that the *real* standard of what man (and his marriage!) was meant to be in creation be clearly set forth, that it may relegate the law of this aeon to the rank of a mere regulation of necessity.

[10] Cf. the discussion of the logical foundation of law in another part of *ThE,* still unpublished.

He who does not see this corrective—as the Pharisees with whom Jesus was speaking did not see it—falls victim to the perilous illusion that he is capable of satisfying the law and is therefore quite "in order," whereas when he sees this corrective he realizes that not only he himself but also the ordinances of this aeon are questionable. *Therefore when Jesus criticizes the "certificate of divorce" he is not setting up a new ordinance, but is rather recalling to mind the standard of all ordinances.* Consequently, he is not concerned to proclaim a putative law of creation (this would be a contradiction in itself!); he is rather uttering a call to repentance, which sets man down before the ultimate court of appeal, whereas man following his own inclinations seeks that fatal security which he gains when he takes his standard from the penultimate courts of appeal.

In terms of Luther's theology we might say that here Jesus is not *annulling* the "kingdom on the left hand" in the name of the order of creation, but is rather setting the order of creation under the *light* of the "kingdom on the right hand." Naturally, this cannot remain a process that occurs only in the dimension of thought; it will rather radiate into all the processes of life: the person who knows this will regard marriage and his marriage partner differently from the person who does not know it and who merely asks whether he is acting "correctly" in accordance with the law. He will also see the question of divorce in a new and different way.

The radicalization brought about by this appeal to the order of creation, however, not only results in making the legal ordinances relative, but also calls in question the correct behavior of the individual. For now even the person who keeps the marriage law externally—and therefore "correctly"!—can become an adulterer by looking "at a woman lustfully" (Matt. 5:28). This is only the consequence of the relativization of the law. For as long as the law alone is what counts, only concrete acts are relevant in making a judgment. "Nobody can be hanged for thinking." But the moment a man sees that he is confronted with God himself, the Author of the order of creation, then his heart and his thoughts become important. For, after all, we belong to God totally, whereas we belong to the law and the earthly judge only partially, that is, only as we *act* and *exteriorize* ourselves. The judgment of the "God who knows the heart" (Acts 15:8) strikes not only the heart but also our "thoughts." We stand before his bar not only in our acts but in our whole being.

Connected with this radicalization is also the prohibition of the remarriage of divorced persons (Matt. 5:32b; Matt. 19:9; Mark 10: 11 f.), which likewise cannot be interpreted as being a new law and therefore applied legalistically. This again is to be understood as a call to repentance addressed to the law and to those who participate in it. Behind the prohibition of remarriage of divorced persons (which in the Jewish legal structure affected primarily the responsibility of the *man*) is again the remembrance of the order of creation: this order, by virtue of which man and woman are ordained for each other in a general way, is also applied to the individual relationship of "this" man to "this" woman. It is a sign of the "hardheartedness" of man and the corruption of creation when an individual marriage is no longer congruent with the original plan, i.e., in this case, when the finality of that which is once entered into is not observed. The assumption on which this view is based is that a marriage once entered into continues to exist, that even though a divorce may affect the actual practice of marital cohabitation, it cannot affect its ontic foundation. Because this foundation remains, entrance into a new marriage becomes "ontologically" impossible.

As we have already indicated, it is of course more than doubtful whether this affirmation can be translated into a provision in a legally established order of marriage. Our insistence that here we are dealing not with a legal ordinance but rather with a call to repentance has already warned us against drawing too hasty conclusions in this direction. If it is a "call to repentance," it will be addressed primarily to certain social attitudes, conditions, and practices with respect to entering into marriage, which allow young people, for example, to slip carelessly into a marriage which one can hardly assume that *God* has joined together, and hence that it actually possesses this ontic foundation. (We are thinking, for example, of the marriages by proxy that took place during the Second World War and similar hasty marriages in times of crisis which are psychologically understandable but exceedingly questionable.) The call to repentance will apply chiefly to those who are responsible for bringing about such conditions, but certainly also to those who hide from the seriousness of marriage in the turbulence or the carelessness of the times.

But when what is thus "outwardly" constituted as a marriage breaks down, this is not simply a mere nothing, as if it had not existed at all. On the contrary, it contains an offense against God's order of creation. In such cases one would appeal least of all to the order of creation to justify the annulment of a marriage or the remarriage of the divorced. It may be true that such outward unions, which have the character of a marriage only because of their legal status, are in certain cases nothing more than "nullities"; nevertheless the very fact that something must be declared a nullity, which at the moment it was effected faced the claim of the order of creation without carrying that claim into effect, is an offense. Because the call to repentance makes this clear, it leads to something more than understanding; it acts as a warning and a preservative.

The fact that the Gospels can countenance an "annulment" of an existing marriage, despite the fact that a marriage once contracted possesses ontic continuance, is based upon the single exception which can justify divorce, namely, unchastity (*porneia*) on the part of the wife (Matt. 5:32, 19:9). With regard to the bindingness of this exception, which probably was not recognized by Jesus himself, we shall have something to say presently. If we interpret it merely on the basis of the text, we should have to say this:

There is obviously one obstacle to the marriage relationship (here consisting in *porneia*) which, even though it does not dissolve the ontic bond between man and wife established by the order of creation, even in the *individual* case, nevertheless constitutes a *de facto* disavowal of the other person. In this case the disavowal is not consummated by means of a certificate of divorce, but only confirmed as having taken place. How little the ontic relationship is affected by this is shown by the above-mentioned prohibition of the remarriage of divorced persons. As we have said, this prohibition makes sense only if the once established marital relationship has an indelible character. In this case it has the significance of an exceedingly demonstrative interpretation of this indelible character of marriage. For in a society in which practically all its members are married (see above), the demand required by this prohibition that one remain single constitutes an almost intolerable exception to the general rule, which would undoubtedly bring about a psychic friction. Since remarriage as a way out of this friction is barred, the only recourse is restoration of the broken marriage. In a case where the husband has dismissed the wife on the basis of his right as the "master" to exercise his arbitrary power, this restoration, according to the view then prevalent, would be no problem. (This certainly cannot be quite that easily said of modern man with his concept of the individual *eros* and his exceedingly different I-thou relationships.) In the case where the woman is dismissed because of her *porneia* the Gospel may have in view a restoration of the marriage which would result from willingness to forgive (John 8:7). The very fact that here divorce and remarriage appear in the context of a call to repentance and not that of marriage legislation—a fact that cannot be sufficiently emphasized!—will compel one to see that the prohibition of remarriage is asking this critical question: "Are you not running away from your marriage because of selfish reasons, because of dubious 'thoughts of the heart'? That's why there must be a barrier to your flight. But if you flee in spite of this warning, then you will have to bear the friction that must inevitably arise from your remaining unmarried in a society made up of married people. Then you must be prepared to endure this friction as a sign that you have dissociated yourself from the order of creation. Then by your very status of being unmarried you must acknowledge your hardheartedness. And this, despite the broken status of a divorced person, would be at least an indirect glorification of that order which was 'from the beginning'; it would be as it were your praise in a negative mode. So if through your divorce you inflict a wound upon the order of creation, then at least this wound must be kept open by abstaining from remarriage; then you must put your abstention from a second marriage into that wound as you would gauze to prevent it from healing and giving you the illusion that everything is in order."

In this sense, then, the prohibition of remarriage has demonstrative and interpretative significance for the nature of divorce. And this divorce in turn has demonstrative and interpretative significance for the import of order of creation "from the beginning," that is, for the *real* will of God, in the light of which we see that a certificate of divorce is only a concession of God to man's hardheartedness.

The continuance of the original order of creation, which remains in force despite all the attacks of men upon it, can be illustrated by the example of the *atheist*. After all, by denying the existence of God the atheist does not annul His existence. God remains God, quite independent of whether He is recognized or denied. And what is more, He remains so not only for believers, the nonatheists, but also for the atheist himself, seeking, troubling, keeping the door open, and omnipotently disposing all things, even though the atheist does not know it or refuses to recognize it. In the same way the validity of the order of creation remains untouched by human attacks upon it. Man may violate it individually by dissolving his marriage; he may also set up superindividual legal regulations in which marriage is regarded merely as an institution that can be manipulated at will; but all these attacks and all this refusal to accept the order of creation does not cancel its existence and its continuing claim upon him. The prohibition of remarriage is the most symbolically strong interpretation of this continuance.

With regard to the variations in the texts which are apparent in the statements of the Gospels concerning divorce and remarriage the following comments should be made:

The fact that divorce is understood to be a reprehensible adultery or breaking of the marriage is variously expressed in the relevant texts. Matthew 5:32 assumes for contemporary social reasons that the wife who has been dismissed (either because of *porneia* or innocently) will marry again, since as a divorced and single person she would remain without protection and a home. But this second marriage would, for the reasons set forth, constitute an adultery, for which the husband who had dismissed the wife is perhaps not solely but yet chiefly to blame.

In contrast to the other texts (Luke 16:18; Mark 10:9-12), the Matthew logia regard the husband as exonerated if *porneia* on the part of the wife is the cause of the divorce. Neither Mark nor Luke mention this exception, nor does Paul even though in I Corinthians 7:10 f. he explicitly cites Jesus' prohibition of divorce. From this the exegetes have repeatedly concluded that this was an addition by Matthew who was influenced, as is discernible elsewhere, by the nomistic casuistry prevalent in Judaistic circles. Whether this addition accords with Jesus' call to repentance can hardly be proved directly; and how it is to be interpreted according to the mind of Jesus likewise remains an open question. Just as surely as marriage is broken by *porneia,* so on the other hand the question must remain open whether in the mind of Jesus it cannot be restored. The pericopes of the Woman Who Was a Sinner and the Woman Taken in Adultery (Luke 7:36 ff.; John 8:3 ff.) undoubtedly leave room for forgiveness; and the husband in question may also not be excluded from this room for forgiveness.

The exegetes' dispute over whether this interpolation in Matthew is right or wrong is fundamentally a question of substance and not a problem of textual criticism. This question of substance related to the problem of whether the radical and unconditioned character of Jesus' call to repentance is not destroyed by introducing casuistical exceptions to its validity. Do we not have here an expression of an alien point of view which is concerned with legalities and juridical practicability, whereas the very thing that the Sermon on the Mount does in its great protological and eschatological declarations is to pass beyond the broken relationships of this aeon and by this very means shows that this present world structure is only a regulation of necessity which is to be clearly distinguished from the original order of creation? Does not this again open the door to giving sanction to "man in revolt"?

Legitimate as this anxious question may be, it is not permissible to answer it with a simple yes and interpret the Matthean interpolation as a twisting of the original intent of the text. It is characteristic of the radicalisms in Jesus' preaching that they are not simply formulated as theses, but rather as antitheses, that they are always set over against the Mosaic *nomos* by the use of the phrase, "But I say to you" (Matt. 5:22, 28, 32, 34, 39, 44). The radicalisms require, so to speak, this dialectical reference to the "normal" of this aeon. They can be heard only as protests. And only so does it become clear that they are not timeless, universally accepted truths, but rather that they come as something new [*novum*], that they have a very definite place in the history of the Kingdom of God and inaugurate new stages in that history. Likewise, only this protesting reference back to the *nomos* can make it clear that what he is saying "now" is not merely a quantitative tightening of the existing law, but rather something qualitatively different, and hence that here a completely new level is being entered. For the radical demands of the Sermon on the Mount cannot be simply put into practice in the same way as the Mosaic *nomos,* which takes into account the hardheartedness of men. They are not accommodated to the existing form of reality and adapted to it with a view to their possible realization. On the contrary, they call into question this form of reality with all its structures and ordinances. As we said in the first volume of the *Theological Ethics*,[11] they demand of us that we live as if we were "still" living in the original state and as if the Kingdom of God had "already" come. They take away from this aeon and its structure of reality the "normative power of the factual" and transform it into an interim. Therefore they can never become anything like constitutional principles for "this world" or moral directions for life. They cannot be "juridified" or moralized; they are rather the corrective that calls in question, relativizes, and de-ideologizes all law and all morals. But in order to be this, these radicalisms need always to be referred back to the facticities—the facticities of "this aeon" which are indispensable and therefore must be conceded, because of the hardheartedness of men.

Now, exactly the same thing happens when Jesus proclaims the radical demand of the order of creation in marriage. He exemplifies this demand precisely by showing that it is different from the reduced demands of earthly legislation. These laws can never be anything in the nature of a reflection of the order of creation in natural law,[12] because they are faulty in principle since they must take into account the hardheartedness of men. And among these factors of hardheartedness which determine all laws is undoubtedly the factor of *porneia* as an expression of selfish libido.

Reference to the way things are in actual fact[13] therefore helps us to understand the relativity of all legal ordinances in this aeon—and thus also helps us to understand the "otherness" of the order of creation existing "from the beginning." Therefore we believe that when Matthew interpolates the seemingly casuistical element of an exception for *porneia,* this is not a matter of compromising between Jesus' radicality and the *de facto* provision of the law, but that this is simply a matter of giving a concrete illustration of the difference between the two. Then, however, it still must remain an open question whether this is an interpolation at all or whether we have before us here an original saying of Jesus himself. To be sure, a weighty theological problem is not involved here.

In conclusion we can summarize the statements of the Gospels concerning divorce and remarriage as follows (keeping in view the fact that they are not to be understood as directions which are ends

---

[11] *ThE* I, §204, *passim.*

[12] *ThE* I, §2014 ff.

[13] This is a free translation of the author's use of a Heideggerian phrase, *faktisches Da-sein,* which has been translated, not very helpfully, "factical being-there"; cf. the glossary in Martin Heidegger, *Being and Time,* trans. by John Macquarrie and Edward Robinson (New York: Harper & Row, 1962). (Trans.)

in themselves but rather as negative commentaries on the nature of marriage as an order of creation):

1. The *woman* violates the order of creation in marriage when she breaks it through *porneia* and thus provokes the divorce.[14]

2. The *husband* violates the order of creation:

a) if he arbitrarily dismisses his wife. Here Jesus differs sharply from the Old Testament, using the phrase "But I say to you." For in the Old Testament unilateral divorce is taken for granted as customary (Deut. 24:7 ff.). The sole ground for divorce mentioned here is "some indecency in her" not further specified.[15]

b) The husband violates the order of creation if he marries a divorced woman. This applies in both of the cases mentioned in the Gospels:

First, in case he marries a woman who has been divorced because of *porneia;* in this case he is sanctioning the adultery of the woman and possibly—if he himself was a partner in her *porneia*—his own adultery.

Second, in case he marries an innocently divorced woman, for in this case he is sanctioning the guilty act of the husband who divorced her, in that by his marriage he is declaring that this arbitrary act of divorce is actually capable of legitimately ending the earlier marriage and thus opening the way for a new marriage. Only from this point of view do we understand what otherwise must seem cruel and legalistically harsh, namely, that the innocently divorced wife is delivered up to insecurity and deprived of recourse to a new marriage. The concern here is not merely to uphold the "principle" of the prohibi-

---

[14] Although according to Matthew and Luke the divorce originates with the husband—whether it be arbitrarily unjustified or justified by reason of *porneia* —in Mark provision is also made for the case in which the wife deserts her husband (Mark 10:12). This would then constitute a further possibility of guilt on the part of the wife. As a matter of fact, Judaism was familiar with this legally sanctionable form of divorce initiated by the wife. Cf. Strack-Billerbeck, *Kommentar zum Neuen Testament aus Talmud und Midrasch,* I, 318, 3a.

[15] The arbitrary power of the husband is, of course, not unlimited in the Deuteronomic law. For the wife there are certain safeguards against abuse of the right to divorce, mistreatment, slander, etc. in that the husband can be punished by imposition of fines, loss of the right to divorce, and compulsory marriage. This, however, does not really abate the unilateral character of the right to divorce which the New Testament broke down.

tion, but rather that an offense against the order of creation dare not be sanctioned.

In thus systematizing the statements of the Gospels on divorce and remarriage it becomes apparent how very thin the line is that separates them from a legalistic, casuistical interpretation. The very setting down of these possible cases in this form makes them appear to be casuistical; they seem to be bases for prohibitions justified in such and such a way and thus to project into the sphere of law. But this would be the very worst kind of misunderstanding. It would also be disastrous inasmuch as such legalistically understood prohibitions would not only have been problematical at the time it was uttered (for it would have been a juridical perversion of Jesus' radicalisms), but also since their transference to a changed era like our own would inevitably lead to even worse distortions and intolerable anachronisms. The fact is, of course, that this legalistic understanding has repeatedly gained a foothold and produced humanly and spiritually destructive results.

Therefore it is important at this particular point to state very precisely the intention of Jesus' words and thus define the radius in which the explanatory details are applicable. This can be done by means of the following theses:

1. The words of Jesus concerning marriage appear in the context of a call to repentance which measures the realities of this aeon by the standard of the original order of creation.

2. The realities of this aeon include not only actual sins (concrete instances of adultery, etc.), but also the legal ordinances of this aeon, which are made to fit the fact of sin and must necessarily take realistic account of it in order to be able to fulfill their ordering function at all.[16]

3. The actual realities of this aeon are not meant to be abolished by being thus called into question in the name of the order of creation, but rather put into their relative position of importance: they are seen to be regulations of necessity for this aeon. These realities therefore cannot become the determinative norm for man; they are not the real judgment before which he might be able to know himself,

[16] Cf. the section on the doctrine of the orders in *ThE* I, § 1852 ff.

rather these realities themselves are under judgment.[17]

4. In this context the prohibition of the remarriage of divorced persons must not be understood as an independent legal direction; it rather serves to interpret the divorce: Since man cannot put asunder what God has joined together in his order of creation, he dare not in the form of a remarriage act as if he *had* put it asunder.

5. On its part again the prohibition of divorce serves to interpret the marriage itself; it expresses the fact that the sexes belong together by God's institution and therefore that this does not rest upon the human will (a contract, for example) and hence that its dissolution cannot be left to man's arbitrary discretion.

This *interpretative* significance of the examples—and they are really nothing more than examples!—of divorce and remarriage must be firmly retained, because this is what allows us the freedom in a changed historical situation to take seriously the claim of the order of creation in forms and in ways that are different from those which were required among the Jewish people at the time of Jesus. He who keeps in mind that these statements have the character of a call to repentance will always have to consider also the battlefronts against which the polemic of the call to repentance is directed. Among these battlefronts there are certainly some that are unchanging and permanent, such as the selfishness of the human heart and the libido of mind and body. But there are also other battlefronts which are subject to the change of the times. Today, for example, Jesus' call to repentance could be directed less one-sidedly to the husband—simply because at the present time in civilized countries the hegemony of the husband with the volume of responsibility inherent in it no longer exists. Furthermore, the broad acceptance of the equality of the sexes would cause people to feel that it would be "double morality" to regard the *porneia* of the wife as a possible ground for divorce while the *porneia* of the husband was not considered equally condemnable.

This distortion of Jesus' saying would be inevitable if one were to

[17] Any form of a doctrine of the two kingdoms must be connected with this non-abolition, this relativizing, of the realities of this aeon. At this point too lies the generative principle that leads to the establishment of such a doctrine. Cf. *ThE* I, §1783, ff.

regard it as a legal dictum which was laid down once and for all as an apodictically binding law apart from its concrete purpose, which was to exemplify God's order of creation over against a specific, historically conditioned system of laws. In our later systematic discussions of divorce we shall have to examine whether the claim of the order of creation does not have a quite different thrust today.

For example, with the increasing ascendancy of the individual *eros,* which in turn has its roots in profound psychical changes in men, marriage has become less a "family concern" and more a matter of individual, personal decision. In this process it is being subjected, in a way quite different from that of ancient times, to the diffuse influence of the emotions and their instability, which diminishes the sense of conscientious responsibility in the moment of passion. Hence, it may be that under these changed conditions the meaning and our assessment of divorce should be changed and that possibly the fault may not lie in the divorce itself, but rather in careless entrance into a marriage, which was not a marriage from the beginning, so that the divorce could be an honest admission of this confusion. This is suggested merely as an example of a case which illustrates the task presented by the changed form in which Jesus' word comes to us today and also the impossibility of an apodictic, legalistic interpretation of these words of Jesus.

Another way in which the New Testament understanding of marriage differs from that of the Old Testament follows from the fact that just as marriage is dignified by the order of creation so it is relativized *by the order of redemption.* In a community in which all were married this point of view has the effect of being revolutionary. Jesus himself was unmarried. He also demanded of his disciples the renunciation of family ties. Though (naturally!) he did not ask that they be "divorced," he nevertheless demanded that the bond to him and his mission take precedence over all human ties (Matt. 10:37; Luke 14:26). Those who made this sacrifice were given the promise that they would gain far more than they gave up (Matt. 10:20 f., 19:28; Luke 18:29 f.). The expectation that the end of the world was near and the exceptional existence which this demanded of those who had a special call to the Kingdom of God and served it directly undoubt-

edly played a part in this. They were already living, as it were pro-
leptically, under the commandments of the new world. For in the
Kingdom of God one neither marries nor is given in marriage (Matt.
22:30; Mark 12:15; Luke 20:35 f.). From this point of view and
measured by this standard, marriage—despite the high honor given
to it in the name of the order of creation—appears to be merely earthly
and provisional.

What is thus an eschatologically conditioned exceptional possibility
in Jesus' words becomes in *Paul* a dominant motive (I Cor. 7:1 ff.; cf.
I Thess. 4:3 f.), though he repeatedly qualifies his teaching on this
subject by saying that here he is stating his personal opinion and cannot appeal to a word of the Lord (I Cor. 7:12, 25); on the other hand
in the tables of household duties he makes no mention whatsoever of
the advantage of the unmarried state which he normally advocates
(Eph. 5:22-6:9; Col. 3:18-4:1).

In I Corinthians 7, which is the most detailed presentation of his
teaching on marriage, it is clear that marriage as an order of creation
appears only in the shadowy background, whereas preparation for the
end and its distresses (7:26, 28) makes it expedient to remain unmarried (7:1, 8, 26, 38).

1. So far as *theological* motives are concerned, the basis for this
recommendation is twofold. First, the concern that marriage and love
will bind men to human beings and thus relate them to the world instead of to the Lord (7:33 f.). Only the unmarried person has his
mind free for the Lord and is concerned to please him and not the
other person (7:32). Second, the unmarried person will go through
the distresses of the imminent time of the end more easily (7:29, 31)
and will be spared many tribulations (v. 28), which he would have to
endure if he were bound to another person. Therefore the disciple
must no longer belong to the world. If he is already married, he
should not, to be sure, seek to be free (v. 27). But all these things we
must have as if we had them not, we must live aloof and in freedom
from all these things, without any passion for them (7:29 f.). One
who belongs to the Lord is no longer *engage*; he is without any concern that might agitate him.

Many, of course, cannot make this renunciation. Then it is better if they marry rather than to be "aflame with passion" (*purousthai,* 7:9). In view of the threat of *porneia,* it is *then* better that "each man should have his own wife" (7:2).

2. This already indicates the *personal* motives: where Paul speaks personally, not citing a word of the Lord but speaking for himself, marriage as an order of creation hardly enters in at all, but is rather an emergency institution [*Not-Institut*] for fallen man, who is on the one hand in danger of being seduced by sexual libido and on the other is not sufficiently gripped by the coming Kingdom of God that the dominion of God may triumph over the dominion of this libido and the subjection to this world which it implies.

Undoubtedly, for anybody who allows the main emphases of Paul's statements to have their effect upon him and, what is more, catches the intermediate tones, the Pauline understanding of marriage is not decisively oriented upon the order of creation, but is almost exclusively located in the correlation of sin and redemption. Stating it somewhat pointedly, it might be said that while in the Gospels divorce is conceded by God only on account of our hardheartedness, in Paul marriage itself is an institution which was established in view of this hardheartedness, this devotion of man to his libido instead of to the Lord. When Paul—in a way that is really inconsistent with the main thrust of his statements—takes over Jesus' prohibition of divorce (7:10 f.) and even advocates the fulfillment of conjugal duties (7:5), this strikes us as being curiously weak and almost as a reluctant concession. In this extraordinary reinterpretation of marriage—for what we have here is nothing less than that—there is undoubtedly an expression of a certain nonaffinity of Paul with the realm of *eros* and *sexus.* But certainly only such an affinity is capable of understanding the created order of the sexes more than merely rationally and appreciating it for reasons other than merely its authoritarian claim. We probably shall not go wrong in assuming that here we have a preformation of what later led to monastic asceticism.[18]

---

[18] "Accordingly, Paul would have been affected, at least in his personal feelings, by that rejection of sexual intercourse which later led to monasticism, even though he would not have made of it a universally binding doctrine. (Büchsel, *op. cit.,* 120.) This view was still having its effect upon Luther at the time when he was capable of calling marriage—regarding it like the state as being an order *post lapsum*—a "*remedium peccati*" (a remedy against sin), a "hospital for the sick." (Cf. Løgstrup, *op. cit.,* 326.) In Luther, of course,

It is true, of course, that these statements are characterized as personal opinions and therefore are not endowed with apostolic authority. Apart from the explicit references to the fact that it is not the Lord but he, Paul, who is speaking here, this qualification is also expressed in his insistence that he does not wish to impose any burden of conscience or "lay any restraint" upon those he is addressing (7:35). Hence he leaves room for freedom to make other decisions and for different convictions. The criterion for making these decisions is, of course, universally binding and "apostolic"; it consists in the question which is addressed to every act we perform in freedom, namely, "Does this enslave me?" (I Cor. 6:12). Only I can determine *what* enslaves me, since this may differ in every case and resistance to such enslavements is dependent upon individual differences in degree of spiritual maturity (cf. Rom. 14:4 f. 22 f.; I Cor. 8:7 ff., 9:18 f.). This criterion here constitutes what above we called the "kerygmatic core," from which alone we gain orientation in *our* situation.

What Paul says about marriage as an emergency institution is therefore—judged according to its kerygmatic rank—nothing more than an individual, extremely personal exemplification of this criterion applied to his own life and is therefore conditioned by the time and place in which it was uttered and the constitution of the man who is speaking. Hence they can no more be understood "legalistically" and transferred just as they are to other situations and other constitutions than can the words of Jesus concerning divorce and remarriage in the context of his call to repentance.

In other situations other ways of obedience will emerge from the kerygmatic center. Paul avowed *his* way of being obedient; and undoubtedly he did not do this in order to put his own individuality into the foreground, but rather because he believed that his own personal situation had a certain prototypic significance for other Christians, at least for his contemporaries in that they were living with him in the

---

there are humane correctives of this theoretical judgment on marriage, which show that his personal experience of love and marriage overrides this negatively critical evaluation and which is in any case not adequately expressed by it. Such indications are not to be found at all in Paul. And this is precisely what prompts us to express the opinion that the personal and psychical constitution of the Apostle (*horribile dictu!*) was not without influence in the formation of his theological statements.

"short span of time before the end."[19] Nevertheless, as his own qualifying of his view shows, he too considers that it is possible for another person to make a different decision.

Here more than anywhere else in the New Testament it becomes clear where the stable and the variable sides of a commandment lie, where the substance is and where is the illustration of the substance which is conditioned by the time and the constitution of the person involved, and how disastrous it is, in view of the nomistic dangers, when the illustrative, variable side of such statements is carried over without interpretation and therefore without transformation into other situations. This is where theological ethics has an essential contribution to make to basic hermeneutical questions.

A final difference between the New Testament doctrine of marriage and that of the Old Testament becomes evident in the way in which the status of the wife is changed. We have already dealt with this in the section of the duality of man and shall content ourselves here with mentioning only the main points.

In the table of household duties in Colossians 3:18-4:1 the subordination of the wife is assumed as before, and yet here it is given a new meaning in that both the wife and the husband are characterized by their being-in-the-Lord (Col. 3:18). So here the social hierarchy can no longer determine the nature of the wife. The nature of the woman comes rather from the order of creation and redemption, which brings her into the freedom of those who receive equal grace in this order. Correspondingly, the husband too is not determined by his prestige in the social order, and therefore his relation to the wife is not determined by domination but rather by *agape* (Eph. 5:21 ff.). Since the subordination of the wife to the husband is compared with the subordination of the church (the Body of Christ) to its Head, the wife is given to understand that her salvation is not affected and therefore not diminished by this subordination; for, after all, she too is incorporated in this Body. The husband, however, is given to understand that his analogy to the headship of Christ brings with it the claim upon his self-sacrifice in the spirit of *agape* (cf. also I Pet. 3:7).

---

[19] *o kairos sunestalmenos estin,* 7:29.

# B. The Sacramental and the "Worldly" Interpretations of Marriage. Controversial Theological Considerations[1]

## 1. THE SACRAMENTAL VIEW OF MARRIAGE IN CATHOLIC THEOLOGY

In the preceding section on the interpretation of marriage in the New Testament it became clear that the marital union of husband and wife is a transparency which has behind it a spiritual reality which shines through it and fills it with meaning. This reality that shines through can be the order of creation as well as the order of redemption, the relation of Christ as head to his church as body. On the basis of this "symbolic" character of marriage, Ephesians 5:32 speaks of a "mystery" (*musterion;* in the Vulgate translation, *sacramentum*). In the New Testament the term "mystery" is always used in the sense that a visible, earthly reality or process becomes a similitude of the transcendent sphere of salvation, that "nature" thus points to the "supernatural" (to use, with some reservations, this scholastic terminology). This kind of pointing or reference is called a "mystery" because it cloaks and reveals at the same time: the mystery reveals itself to faith, whereas unbelief cannot understand it; "to him who has, will more be given . . ., but from him who has not, even what he

[1] The term used here is the adjectival form of the word *Kontroverstheologie,* the branch of theology which deals with teachings and usages in controversy with other confessions. (Trans.)

125

has will be taken away" (Matt. 13:12). The parables of Jesus are therefore a kind of prototype of what the New Testament calls "mystery"; for they have in eminent degree this characteristic of revealing and concealing (Matt. 13:10 ff.; Mark 4:11 ff.).[2]

Because marriage points to the order of creation and redemption it is a similitude of this kind and it also exhibits the same double meaning: for those who stand in faith within the order of redemption it *has* this symbolic character, whereas for others it can be merely a contract, a biological phenomenon, or at most a human bond. This is why the letter to the Ephesians calls it a "mystery."

Nevertheless it is completely out of the question to say that marriage in its character as a sign also *mediates* grace and *establishes* connection with the order of redemption. It "bears witness" in parable form to the order of redemption (though, as we have seen, it does this very indirectly, and the Christological analogy rather more illuminates the relationship of man and wife than the other way around, in which this relationship would cast light upon the Christological fact). But in no case does it incorporate the spouses in the order of redemption or bestow the faith that binds us to grace. The assertion that nature, to which marriage belongs as a part of the order of creation, is simply open to the supernatural and that there is an analogy between nature and the supernatural is, for reasons which we have discussed earlier, not in accord with New Testament thought.[3] It is probably this idea of analogy that constitutes the presupposition for the fact that Catholic dogmatics was able to view marriage as being endowed with that special affinity with the order of redemption and construe it as a sacrament (having equal rank with baptism and the eucharist!). The exegetical impulse for this was provided by the term *"musterion"* in the letter to the Ephesians, which in the Vulgate translation *"sacramentum"* may have been peculiarly suggestive of this association.[4]

[2] Cf. the foreword "To the Reader" of my book, *The Waiting Father,* trans. by John W. Doberstein (New York: Harper & Row, 1959), pp. 11 ff. On the paraphrasing of the term "mystery" cf. Prov. 3:32; Amos 3:7; Rom. 11:25; Eph. 1:9, 3:3; II Thess. 2:7; I Tim. 3:16.

[3] Cf. the chapter on natural law in *ThE* I, especially the correlation of nature and supernatural, and also the doctrine of the *imago Dei,* especially §2014 ff.

[4] Luther certainly quite correctly said of this exegetical argument that it betrays "great shallowness and a negligent and thoughtless reading of Scripture" (*magnae oscitantiae et indiligentis inconsultaeque lectionis*) *WA* 6, 551. On the argument itself cf. Diekamp, *op. cit.,* p. 383.

What, then, is meant by the sacramental character of marriage?

The nature of a sacrament requires not only that it be a sign but also that it have an effect: "A sacrament is a sign of a holy thing, insofar as it sanctifies man."[5] The sanctification which it effects consists in the impartation of supernatural gifts. Because marriage is understood as being sacramental in this way, it is among those goods which effect salvation, and in this case it does so by embedding the supernatural purposes in the medium of the natural.

Among those natural purposes is the procreation of children and the mutual spiritual and physical helpfulness of the spouses. Both of these fundamental purposes are inseparable from the supernatural purposes; for the procreation of children is bound up with the obligation to rear them not only to natural perfection but also to supernatural perfection. The mutual helpfulness of the spouses is likewise oriented toward this *perfectus status*, "that the one may bring the other with him to heaven." The orientation toward this supernatural perfection effected by the sacramental of marriage is not affected when a part of its natural basis drops out, e.g., the *commixtio carnalis*, which the couple may vow to forgo. This nonfulfillment of the purpose of marriage to procreate children does not impugn the substance of the marriage. This abstinence not only plays a role in the practice of life but the declaration of the principle of its possibility also makes it possible to interpret the relationship of the parents of Jesus as a fully valid marriage.[6]

The sacramental structure of marriage becomes evident also in the fact that even the *form* of the sacrament is actualized in it with respect both to *form* and to *matter*: while the priest [*priesterliche Spender*] ordinarily sets the *form* of the sacrament, in marriage it is the bridal couple who administer the sacrament to each other. The *mutuus consensus*, the acceptance expressed in the form of a mutual agreement, is the effective cause of the sacrament of matrimony[7] and includes both its *form* and its *matter*.[8]

Generally—though this is not undisputed dogmatically—this summary co-ordination of form and matter is further defined by saying that the matter signifies the mutual surrender (*traditio*) of the object of the con-

---

[5] Thomas Aquinas, "Sacramentum est signum rei sacrae, inquantum est sanctificans homines" (*De sacramentis in communi*, 3 q. 60 a. 2).

[6] Augustine in his treatise against Julian of Eclanum, *De nupt. et conc.*, I, 11, 12; C. Jul., V, 12, 46 ff.

[7] *Decr. pro Armenis*, Denzinger 702.

[8] Thomas Aquinas, 3 q. 84 a. 1 ad 1; Suppl. q. 42 a. 1 ad 1 and 2.

tract, namely, the *jus in corpus,* while the form expresses "its mutual acceptance" (*acceptio*).[9]

Since the bridal couple themselves are the ministers of the sacrament, the words of the participating priest do not have effective character but only declaratory character.

This peripheral importance of the priest has raised the question whether *every* marriage of baptized persons, whether entered into by Protestants or Catholics or by confessionally mixed couples, is *eo ipso* a sacrament. This question is actually answered in the affirmative in many parts of the tradition.[10] The conclusion that really follows from this position, namely, that even confessionally *mixed marriages* possess sacramental character at least "in the broader sense"[11] and—despite all their undesirability— should be recognized in principle by the Catholic Church, may well have been a factor in the raising of a bar here and allowing this sacramental character to be at least disputed. This can be done only by calling in question the marriage agreement which forms the basis of the sacrament. And this is in fact what Michael Schmaus does when he argues that the marriage agreement entered into by partners of different confessions "violates the form which the Catholic Church can prescribe for all who belong to it and in its opinion all who are baptized. Therefore the baptized can establish the sacramental sign of marriage only if they adhere to the form of agreement prescribed by the Church for Catholic marriage. Otherwise the agreement and thus the sacrament does not come into being."[12] Here we need not go into the complex interpretations of non-Catholic marriages on the basis of earlier statements in the tradition and the variation represented by Schmaus.

Also inherent in the sacramental character of marriage is the fact that its administration is effectual *ex opere operato.* This puts the marriage in the realm of "objective" operation, which makes its existence largely independent of subjective elements such as feeling and the growth or diminishing of *eros* attachments, at least so far as the continuance of the marriage and its validity are concerned.

[9] Diekamp, *op. cit.,* p. 386.
[10] Thus the Council of Trent, *Sess. 24, can 1,* Denzinger 990. Also Pius IX, Denzinger 1640, cf. 1766 and 1773, and Leo XIII in the *Encyclical "Arcanum,"* Denzinger 1854.
[11] Diekamp, *op. cit.,* p. 378.
[12] *Deutsches Pfarrerblatt* (1962), 12, pp. 272 ff.

This subjectivity plays a part in the validity of the sacrament only at the moment of its administration, and it does so on the part of the minister in the sense that he must intend and do what the church intends and does, and on the part of the recipient in the sense that he does not deny the reception of the sacrament. (In the sacrament of matrimony the bridal couple in personal union are both minister and recipient.) Failing this, a bar (*obex*) prevents the grace which is given *ex opere operato* from coming to these persons. Apart from this the validity of the sacrament remains unaffected by subjective factors. Thus there is no mention of "marital love" as a condition in the definition of the sacrament of matrimony. Indeed, the presence or absence of love is of no importance for the canonical continuance of a marriage entered into in this sacramental sense— though on the other hand the married partners are pledged to treat each other with love and respect.[13]

The *ex-opere-operato* effect of the sacrament also brings it about that a *divorce* is impossible and that now more than ever the subjective factors, which are irrelevant in the sacramental sense (such as estrangement, mental cruelty, etc.), cannot constitute grounds for a possible divorce. In fairness it must be said, however, that this does not mean that the importance of a marriage which is imbued with subjective factors is denied. The persons concerned should seriously ask themselves whether they are equal to such a marriage *before* they enter into the sacramental union and not after the bond has been accepted, when it is too late and when, moreover, the danger arises that the continuance of this God-given union will be dependent upon the highly unstable conditions of the *eros* and other emotions. The pastoral thought with which they seek to overcome the rigor (not to say rigidity) of the theological-sacramental principle runs as follows: One will examine oneself far more seriously before entering a marriage in which there can be no divorce than when one marries as it were conditionally in order to try out this compatibility in consummating the marriage, viewing it as a more or less nonbinding experiment which can be broken off at any time if it turns out negatively.

Even though Reformation theology opposes the sacramental interpretation of marriage, it would be unfair to combat it with the argument that Catholic dogmatics simply ignores the human problems of

---

[13] Cf. the *Encyclical Casti Connubii* of Pius XI, Act. Ap. S., 1930, 542, 548, 549.

marriage by appealing to a rigid dogmatic principle. On the contrary, one might wish that the Protestant doctrine and practice of marriage had somewhat *more* "rigidity," or rather, continuity and consistency and that it were less affected by certain marriage reformers—even though *this* kind of steadiness can never be bought at the price of a sacramental fixation of marriage.

The pastoral and humane consideration with which Catholic theology accompanies its sacramental principle of marriage (namely, that the decision to marry must be made more difficult in view of its sacramental character and its indissolubility and that therefore people must be made aware of their responsibility) is also acceptable to evangelical ethics and is in many respects exemplary. The question is, however, whether the emphasis on responsibility at the beginning of marriage cannot be made by theological means other than a sacramental interpretation. To be sure, this would necessarily mean a greater degree of elasticity—precisely in judging whether a marriage is endurable and thus whether a divorce may be permitted; for a radical insistence upon the unconditional character of the prohibition of divorce can be cemented only by a sacramental principle, whereas, as we have seen, it has so support in the New Testament statements and could be achieved only by subjecting it to a legalistic misinterpretation.

This is why at this point we are already saying in a precautionary way that not the *whole* responsibility, but rather the *main emphasis* upon responsibility for a marriage, entered into before God for life and secured by a vow, must be placed at the beginning and divorce made correspondingly difficult. In any case the core of our doctrinal discussion of the Catholic theology of marriage cannot consist in practical, humane considerations; it must come to grips with the sacramental principle.

## 2. Luther's Objection To The Sacramental Interpretation Of Marriage

In this study of Luther's opposition to the sacramental interpretation of marriage we are not concerned with that side of the question which has to do with church history. Therefore we shall pass over the development of his thinking on this subject, the unresolved tensions that appeared between his monastic origin and his new reformatory insights,[14] and also the questionable forms his action took, which in some cases can hardly be reconciled with a theological substantiation of marriage.[15] We shall rather make use of Luther's polemic only insofar as it makes a contribution toward overcoming the sacramental concept of marriage and contains the beginnings of a reorientation of the interpretation of marriage which accords with Reformation theology.

### a. The Negation of the Sacramental Argument[16]

In *The Babylonian Captivity* Luther sets forth three main objections to the elevation of marriage into a sacrament, a theological, a phenomenological, and an exegetical argument.[17]

1. The *theological* argument states first that marriage contains no peculiar sign (which is constitutive of the sacrament), even though the sign alone cannot make a sacrament. It is true that marriage may have a side which is signlike;[18] but it shares this quality with all other things which can be interpreted as types and figures of invisible things.[19] Consequently, one cannot take the statement that a sign is an essential part of a sacrament and turn it around by saying that where there is a sign there is a sacrament. This would lead, if we pushed Luther's thought to its furthest extreme, to the total sacramentalization of reality (*res visibiles*).

The theological argument states in the second place that marriage

---

[14] On this cf. Elert, *op. cit.,* pp. 80 ff.

[15] Cf., e.g., the counsel given in *The Babylonian Captivity* that a wife married to an impotent husband should with his consent seek sexual satisfaction elsewhere. *WA* 6, 558; also 10, 2, 278.

[16] The most important sources are "Von Ehesachen" in "Unterricht der Visitatoren" (*WA* 26, 225); "Traubüchlein für die einfältigen Pfarrherrn" (*WA* 30, 3, 43); and above all the section "De matrimonio" in "De captivitate babylonica" (*WA* 6, 489; *CL* I, 426).

[17] *WA* 6, 550 ff.

[18] Presumably Luther is thinking of the analogy between the man-wife relationship and the relationship of Christ to the church in Eph. 5:23 ff.

[19] ". . . licet omnia, quae visibiliter geruntur, possint intelligi figurae et allegoriae rerum invisibilium." *CL* I, 486, 39.

lacks any sacramental character whatsoever because, not only does it lack a peculiar sign, but also the "effect" which is constitutive of a sacrament. For nobody is promised that when he marries a wife he thereby receives the grace of God. Nowhere in Scripture is marriage given any such redemptive significance.[20]

2. The *phenomenological* argument says that marriage existed before Christ and also among the heathen. To interpret the marriage of baptized persons as a sacrament would be to depreciate pre-Christian and non-Christian marriage and reduce them to nonmarriages.[21] Luther's reference to the ancients (*patres*) suggests that he was thinking of the patriarchs of the Old Testament and thus may have been pointing to the order of creation. But this order embraces all men, Christians *and* Israelites *and* the heathen. Therefore true marriage is not a monopoly of the baptized,[22] but is rather (we may say, interpreting Luther's words) a worldly institution within the world created and preserved by God. He who says otherwise would then have to go on and assert that temporal power[23] exists only in the church, whereas it is simply a fact that the heathen and the Turks—just because they are exposed to the alternation of Law and Gospel and employ only their political reason, thus acting in a purely worldly way—often have better governments than Christians who are tempted by theocratic illusions.[24] It is just this analogy between rejection of a Christian monopoly of marriage and a Christian monopoly of the state that is characteristic of Luther's pioneering "worldly" interpretations of marriage.

3. The *exegetical* argument says, as already discussed above, that the Vulgate translation of the New Testament word *musterion* as *sacramentum* does not provide the slightest basis for speaking of a sacrament in the theological sense, either with respect to marriage or the other implications of the *musterion*. For, in contrast with the word "sacrament," the term *musterion* signifies, wherever it occurs, not the

---

[20] *"Nusquam autem legitur, aliquid gratiae* (this probably must be translated: 'not even a trace of grace') *accepturum, quisquis uxorem duxerit." CL* I, 486, 35.

[21] These marriages too are "sacred" and "true" marriages. *CL* I, 487, 6.

[22] *CL* I, 487, 10.

[23] *"imperium temporale." CL* I, 487, 11.

[24] On this cf. *ThE* II, 2, §111 and the surrounding text.

outwards sign of a sacred thing, but rather the thing itself.[25] The content of the "mystery," the *res sacrae,* is accordingly Christ *himself* as well as his church, for which, it is true, marriage serves as an earthly allegory,[26] though this does not qualify it to be a sacrament. Otherwise the sun, which serves as a type of Christ, and the waters, which symbolize the peoples, would also have to be sacraments, whereas they all lack the very thing that constitutes a sacrament, namely, divine institution and the promise of God.[27]

Consequently, when men call something a sacrament which owes its dignity, not to divine institution, but rather to human invention (*ab hominibus in ecclesia inventum*), they are being carried away by an ignorance of the thing itself as well as of the word that interprets it.:[28] of the *thing,* because they conclude that since a thing is signlike it has a sacramental quality, without considering that it lacks divine institution and the assurance of a salvatory meaning (*promissio gratiae*); of the *word,* because, led astray by the Vulgate translation, they simply misunderstand the literal meaning of the term *musterion.* Even ignorance, says Luther, can be charitably borne with, since it does not conflict with the faith (*fidei nihil obsit*). But here the *foundations* of faith are falsified, and we are exposed to ridicule if we accept this sacramentalism which is not only not contained in the Scriptures but is actually contrary to them. Indeed, to do this would be to destroy the authority of the Scriptures.[29]

Marriage having thus been stripped of its sacramental character, the liturgical form employed by the church in marriage also had to be changed. For Luther the rite of marriage is a worldly (civil) act for which the church has no constitutive importance—simply because by reason of the order of creation marriage is an institution for all men and not only for Christians. Where the church nevertheless performs

[25] *Ubique enim significat non signum rei sacrae, sed rem sacram, secretam et absconditam." CL* I, 487, 22.
[26] ". . . *figurari quidem per matrimonium ceu reali quadam allegoria." CL* I, 488, 31.
[27] ". . . *deest et institutio et promissio divina, quae integrant sacramentum." CL* I, 488, 35.
[28] ". . . *ab hominibus . . . inventum, ignorantia tam rei quam verbi abductis." CL* I, 489, 28.
[29] ". . . *ludibrio nostram fidem exponamus . . . scripturae sanctae autoritatem elevemus." CL* I, 489, 35.

the marriage it is not acting on its own authority but rather as a "mandatory of the civil government." Its real mandate is only to bless the marriage which has already been contracted. But for a church of the Word this again cannot be done in the traditional nuptial mass (*missa pro sponsis*), but only by way of the proclamation of the Word, the uniting in marriage, and the blessing of the couple.[30]

This kind of ecclesiastical co-operation is expressed ceremonially in the fact that the act of marriage is divided into two consecutive parts: first, the marriage before the church or in the home,[31] and second, the ceremony at the altar, which originally consisted in a nuptial mass and was then changed into a "benediction" by the Reformation.

As far as form was concerned, this order in the ceremony was not a radical break with the tradition since this division of the act of marriage in both the Roman church and the Reformation was based upon ancient German law.[32] The only thing that is new is that now this division takes on a theological significance which it could *not* have had in a sacramental interpretation of marriage. For whereas the sacramental interpretation must inevitably have the tendency to make the performance of the marriage itself an ecclesiastical institution[33]

[30] A form for this is contained in Luther's *Traubüchlein für die einfältigen Pfarrherrn* ("A Marriage Booklet for Simple Pastors"), *Works of Martin Luther*, Vol. VI, pp. 225 ff.

[31] Up to the tenth century marriages were performed by laymen in the home and in the two succeeding centuries in front of the church; only later did marriage gradually pass into the hands of the priests, but it was still performed before the doors of the church. Cf. the order for marriage stemming from this tradition in use at the beginning of the Reformation period in Jordan, *op. cit.*, pp. 75 ff.

[32] R. Sohm, *op. cit.;* also *Theol. Stud. u. Krit.* (1874), p. 731—"It is true, of course, that Luther said that marriage is a wordly thing [a civil affair]; but this was not his real Reformation insight [at least not so far as the civil *form* was concerned, but certainly the theological interpretation was his!]; it was understood in this way throughout the Middle Ages, and despite the development of the sacrament of marriage was so taught by the Catholic Church up to the Council of Trent." F. K. Schumann, "Zur system. Erwägung der Frage des Eheschliessungsrechts," in H. A. Dombois, *Familienrechtsreform* (1955), p. 154.

[33] This holds true even though the bridal couple as laymen are the ministers of the sacrament. They are such, however, as baptized persons and thus by reason of their relationship to the church. Since the ministration of the sacrament effects the marriage, there must necessarily be a tendency to reduce the civil character of the marriage or (later!) not to allow it regain its place. There is also a certain consistency with this tendency evidenced in Schmaus's

and thus to do away with the division in the ceremony, Luther's understanding of marriage would inevitably have had to *lead* to this division even if it had not already been present in the tradition. If marriage as a true marriage (*verum matrimonium*) belongs not only to Christians but to *all* men as an order of creation, then marriage becomes a "legal transaction which belongs to the family and not the church; then the church is excluded from it; attendance at the church [*Kirchgang*] *follows* the marriage; the actual ecclesiastical rite (*in* the church) does not contract the marriage but rather presupposes it."[34]

Luther's own marriage on June 13, 1525, was carried in accord with this conception and this ceremonial pattern.[35] It is important here that Luther's marriage took place in his home (not in the church!). The fact that a minister, that is, Bugenhagen, the Wittenberg parish pastor, performed the marriage does not mean that this was an ecclesiastical act. Rather, since the fourteenth century it had been a fixed tradition that the copulation was performed by a clergyman. The benediction in the church had nothing to do either with the copulation or with the public announcement that Martin and Katie were now man and wife. This announcement rather occurred through the procession to the church and back again. As the letters show, this action that took place *before* and *outside* of the church was more important for the marriage itself than that which took place *in* the church. For the copulation as a legal act is not dependent upon its being blessed by the church, but rather upon this public demonstration, "because by this means the new marriage was made known to the public, indeed, actually 'confirmed.' Thus in our territory as late as the seventeenth century (passport of Magdeburg in the year 1674), the city councils, instead of furnishing a marriage certificate, gave the young couple a certificate to the effect that the man had publicly conducted the woman 'in chaplet and ribands and also with string music to the church and through the streets.' "[36] On this line it becomes quite obvious that civil marriage, which was later so hotly contested, has its altogether legitimate place, indeed, that where it is not obligatory and never or hardly ever practiced (as in Sweden), marriage by the church can be performed

---

(*loc. cit.*) insistence that the presence of the priest at the ministration of the sacrament of matrimony is constitutive. "The bridal couple *and* the priest together establish the sacramental sign. For the latter must be actively present."

[34] Sohm, *op. cit.*

[35] Cf. *W. BR* III, Nr. 890, p. 531; Nr. 894, p. 534; Nr. 898, p. 539. Description in Böhmer, *op cit.* p. 40, and Jordan, *op. cit,* p. 73.

[36] Böhmer, *op. cit.*, p. 50.

only by mandate, as representing the state. If one wishes to speak of this as a secularization of marriage, then one should not object to seeing the theological meaning of this secularization also. The doctrine of the two kingdoms, which is already apparent in germ in the interpretation of marriage here set forth, is in fact aimed at a certain form of secularization. Hence this is a legitimate daughter and not a degenerate variant of the Reformation. And as Gogarten has pointed out, it is also to be distinguished from so-called "secularism."[37]

While Luther very soon gave form to his new theological insight in the ceremonial of marriage, his understanding of marriage itself continued for a long time to waver between the scholastic tradition and a revaluation of marriage. Undoubtedly it was the continuing influence of his past that prompted him, in dependence upon Paul, to call "chastity a nobler gift than marriage,"[38] or to regard marriage as a "hospital for the sick," or even to state in the Augsburg Confession that marriage was instituted "to aid human infirmity and prevent unchastity."[39] On the other hand a new understanding began increasingly to emerge from his own experience of marriage, evidenced sometimes in spontaneous expressions (for example, in speaking about his Katie; in the relevant letters the overtones are also important!), and sometimes in statements of principle, so that what appears is not merely a negative interpretation of marriage (as a *remedium adversas vagas libidines*) but rather a positive one, such as an *amoenus hortus, ex quo plantae societatis humanae sumuntur.*[40] Luther is also capable of saying that "pleasure and love" are the content and presupposition of the married state.[41] Sometimes he can speak of the joys of married life quite apart from its procreative purpose, calling them a gift of God.[42] Paul Althaus cites an almost hymnlike statement of this kind, even though it be granted that the concluding passage of it shows that this hymn of praise actually refers more to Adam and Eve before the Fall and that it fits very well in the theological setting which Luther gives to the married state in his more rigorous statements: "Above all this [namely, the natural love between parents, children, and brothers and sisters] is married love. This is a bridal love that burns like fire and seeks nothing else but the married partner. It says: I do not want what is yours, I want neither gold nor silver, neither this nor that; I want only you yourself; I want it all or nothing. All other love seeks something other than the one it loves; this love alone wants the beloved himself. And if Adam had

---

[37] Gogarten, "Theol. u. Gesch.," in *ZThK* (1953), pp. 339 ff.; cf. *ThE* II, 2, §3894 and index under "Säkularisation."

[38] Elert, *op. cit.*, p. 82.

[39] Augsburg Confession, Article XXIII.

[40] *WA* 42, 354, 23; 43, 321; cf. Elert, *ibid.*, p. 83.

[41] *WA* 24, 518, 533; 2, 167; 17, 2, 351; 43, 630.

[42] *WA* 43, 454.

not fallen, the loveliest of all things would have been bride and bride-groom."[43]

### b. The Theological Implications of the "Worldly" Interpretation of Marriage

The way in which Luther is capable of stressing the worldliness of marriage and at the same time declaring that it is a divine institution, that marriage must therefore be lived before God, and that the Christian should not begin it without the benediction of this God, has repeatedly caused confusion in the minds of many. Secularist and liturgical interpreters choose one or the other pole of this arc, either a worldly marriage freed from all clericalism, for whose "de-Christianization" Luther paved the way;[44] or a "spiritual" interpretation of the marriage estate which makes it possible in the name of Luther to push the ecclesiastical marriage ceremony to the verge of sacramentalism. The historians also have been disturbed by this tension and have tried to explain it biographically on the basis of an unresolved transition from monastic life to a new "worldly" existence.

Moreover, how can we reconcile the fact that in many variations he says that "the wedding and the marriage estate are a worldly affair"[45] and then in the same breath and also in other connections he can say that "even though it is a worldly estate, it nevertheless has God's Word for it, and was not invented or instituted by men";[46] or that the estate of matrimony is "the most spiritual" estate;[47] or *"matrimonium institutum a Deo"*?[48]

In reality these statements contain essentially co-ordinate terms which are complementary to one another and are not even to be regarded as paradoxes. They can seem to be "antithetical" only to one who has failed to understand the relation between spiritual and worldly in Luther's theology, or one might say the structural inter-

---

[43] *WA* 2, 167 f.; Paul Althaus, "Luthers Wort v. d. Ehe" in Th. Heckel, *Ehe-u. Fam.-recht* (1959), p. 8.
[44] This is in line with the interpretation of Luther given by A. Deutelmoser which he applies primarily to Luther's political ethics, *Luther, Staat und Glaube* (1937).
[45] *CL* IV, 100, 3.
[46] *CL, ibid.,* 26.
[47] *EA* 51, 18.
[48] *WA* 27, 24, 25.

relationship of the "two kingdoms."[49] After all, when something is designated as "worldly," belonging to the kingdom on the left hand, and hence assigned to the sphere of reason, and thus excluded from the government of faith,[50] this does not mean that it no longer has any spiritual relevance and is emancipated from the rule of God. On the contrary, the kingdom of the world is included within the scope of God's sovereignty and to that extent is structurally related to the kingdom on the right hand.[51]

When marriage is understood as a "worldly" estate in this sense, then it has actually been instituted as such by *God*. This objective theological relationship has a corresponding subjective theological relationship in that the Christian, who lives in the "world" and has himself been placed in this world by *God,* cannot be indifferent to that relationship and has been commanded to interpret and respect the dignity of marriage as a divine institution and to accept it from the hand of God.

Marriage, however, is by no means confined only to those in whom the objective and the subjective relationship are present *together;* this, after all, could be so only in the case of Christians; but marriage is in no way only a Christian institution. On the contrary, the objective relationship—that is, that marriage is an order of creation instituted by God—remains in force quite independent of the question whether it is recognized and accepted in faith. This means that even those who know nothing about this divine institution or deny it can satisfy the order. For by establishing the order of preservation (Gen. 8:21 f., 9:1-7, 13 f.) "for the whole world," God makes it known that he is also the God of those who do not know him. He is not only the God of those who know and acknowledge him; he is not only the God of his partisans, and he certainly does not become God only as there are men who elevate him to this rank.[52]

[49] This criticism does not apply, however, to B. Jordan (*op. cit.,* p. 87), though here he rather loosely uses the term "antitheses."

[50] Cf. B. Lohse, *Ratio und Fides. Eine Unters. üb. d. Ratio i. d. Theol. Luthers* (1958).

[51] Cf. *ThE* I, §1825 ff., 1837 ff.

[52] This is evident in the Old Testament, for example, where God's sovereignty is by no means confined to Israel as his people, but rather includes the heathen nations, even though they themselves do not know it: Ps. 22:28, 72:11, 102:16; Isa. 5:26, 42:1, 60:3, 65:1; Ezek. 36:23; Jonah 4:2; Hag. 2:7; Mal. 1:11, etc.

So God is the Author of orders which are in force and can be observed even without knowledge of the Author. Among these orders is not only the order of creation in marriage but also the order of necessity (*Notverordnung*) embodied in the state. This is the reason why in the dogmatic tradition the *political* use of the Law (*usus politicus legis*) is the only use of the law in which the Author of the Law remains anonymous: it proves itself before the bar of reason and is therefore in force also *extra ecclesiam*.[53] In this respect the order of marriage has the same structure.

Therefore what is said in Rietschel-Graff[54] is really inaccurate: "When Luther speaks of marriage as the right, heavenly, spiritual estate in all these passages he does not have in mind the external institution of marriage itself. As such it belongs to the worldly and earthly sphere. In all these passages he is speaking of the sanctification of the estate of marriage through faith." No; this estate is not made holy only through faith; it is hallowed as such, just as it is in its worldliness, through its quality of being divinely instituted, and this is true whether or not there is a faith that acknowledges this fact. What faith brings into this relationship is solely the fact that the Christian reverences the estate of marriage for this quality it possesses as a hallowed ordinance, that he accepts it from the hand of its Author and begins, continues, and ends it in His name.

Thus when we speak of the "worldliness" of the estate of marriage the following points are enunciated:

1. It is asserted that the estate of marriage is not constituted by the fact that it is entered into by persons who are aware of its theological implications and who therefore, since they know the Creator and Redeemer, know it also in its affinity to the order of creation and redemption.

2. It is asserted that marriage has no redemptive significance and that one is not "saved" through it. We are not saved through an ordinance with which we are in conformity, but only through *faith*. This point was developed in the discussion of the sacramental interpretation of marriage

3. It is asserted that as an order of creation marriage is an institu-

---

[53] Hollaz, *Examen* 1021; Apology 16, 7; cf. *ThE* I, §1232 ff.
[54] G. Rietschel, *Lehrbuch der Liturgik*, 2. ed. von P. Graff bearb. (1952), p. 703; quoted in Jordan, *op. cit.*, p. 88.

tion established for "all men" and which can also be observed by "all men," that is, independently of faith.

4. And finally it is asserted that marriage is instituted as an order of preservation for "the whole world." In a way parallel to that in which for Luther the state constitutes the *social* basis for life itself and prevents the world from sinking into chaos,[55] so marriage establishes the *biological*[56] prerequisite for life. Both orders are required for the preservation of a world which is to be kept in being for its salvation, preserved for the chance of the day of salvation (*kairos,* II Cor. 6:2).[57] They do not themselves *mediate* salvation, but they do *preserve* for salvation. We are preserved because we must have the chance to be called.

This at the same time indicates the point at which the order of creation, the necessary order of preservation, flows into the realm of redemption. The world is not preserved through the order of creation and the emergency order of the state merely for its own sake, nor does it *produce* these orders by means of its own instinct for self-preservation. It is rather preserved by God's patience (I Pet. 3:20) for an *end*: "that he may have mercy upon all" (Rom. 11:32; I Tim. 2:4; II Pet. 3:9; Ezek. 18:23). Purely physical existence on the biological and social side is therefore not understood as an end in itself, but rather as the precondition for the chance of salvation.[58]

Here is where the objective theological relationship of the estate of marriage emerges with all the clarity that could be desired. It is both positively and negatively determined by the *"solus Christus,"* positively, because in its quality as an order of creation instituted by God

---

[55] The state—similar to marriage—is thought of as a "necessary remedy for corrupted nature." "For it is necessary that the sinful desires be bound by laws and penalties in order that they may not run wild." *WA* 42, 79, 7 ff.; *ThE* II, 2, §104 ff.

[56] Here something should also be said concerning the social and political importance of marriage. Cf. the passage quoted above concerning marriage as an *amoenus hortus,* a pleasant garden, a nursery of human society. *WA* 42, 354, 23.

[57] *ThE* I, §2160.

[58] Jordan is therefore certainly right when he says: "In the light of the 'solus Christus' it becomes clear that it is for the sake of Christ that the institution of marriage has its reality in the framework of the world's preservation and that this is precisely the reason why it belongs to the whole world." Jordan, *op. cit.,* p. 89.

it preserves the world for the chance of its redemption;[59] negatively, because in view of this *"solus Christus"* it possesses no redemptive significance whatsoever but is only one of the institutional *chances* for salvation.

Viewed from this positive and negative perspective the meaning of the *worldliness* of marriage also emerges. The positive point of view says that what is involved here is the preservation of the *whole* world for its *kairos,* not only the Christian but also the pagan, not only the religious but also the atheistic world, not only the parental homes with their sons who stayed at home but also the far country with its lost sons (Luke 15:11 ff). The negative point of view says that entrance into a legitimate marriage, a *verum matrimonium,* is open to "everyone,"[60] and therefore is not dependent either upon baptism or a sacramental act that presupposes baptism.

So we arrive at the surprising result that it is precisely the axiom of the doctrine of justification, namely, the *"solus Christus,"* that makes it possible for the Christian to assert the pure worldliness of marriage and to differentiate it from sacramentalism but also from any kind of general religious glorification of *eros.*[61] Only faith can be completely worldly, precisely because it does not overvalue and glorify the world. Only faith can be completely objective and matter-of-fact, because it rightly estimates the value and rank of facts. Only faith can be completely reasonable, because it sees the limits of reason over against that "which passes all understanding" (Phil. 4:7).

Precisely because faith sees something more and something else in marriage than does reason, it gives to reason and the worldliness allied to it the place it deserves. For because faith understands reason

---

[59] This thought contains a further problem which cannot be gone into here, namely, the question whether and to what extent redemption applies not only to the *fallen* creation but also to the created world itself insofar as it is elevated and perfected through redemption. On this cf. the concluding chapter in my book *Geschichte und Existenz. Grundlegung einer christl. Gesch.-Theol.* (1935). I still stand by this passage in this work of my youth.

[60] This, naturally, applies only on condition that the legal qualification for marriage is met. But this itself is again a concept that is taken from our natural being-in-the-world.

[61] On the latter point cf. Walter Schubart, *op. cit.,* p. 237. Religion and the glorification of *eros* have the same aim; they propose to redeem and transform men. Also Ellen Key, *op. cit.*

better than it understands itself,[62] it can also find its way in reason's radius of action better than reason itself. It also reacts more sensitively than reason to transgressions of its limits and equally, of course, to situations in which reason does not exercise its full competence. Faith knows the *causa efficiens* and the *causa finalis* of the estate of marriage, its origin in the order of creation, and its goal as an institution of preservation for the order of redemption. It knows the theological implications of marriage and therefore it knows that marriage is really the "most spiritual estate." Faith also knows that marriage is a similitude of "heavenly things." But just because this is so, it gives it its due as a worldly thing and does not make its legitimacy and its being a true marriage dependent upon this knowledge.

Because faith trusts the ordering will of God (*voluntas ordinans Dei*) even where it is not recognized, it can see the leavening power of this will at work even where man does not comply with it or acts contrary to it. Faith calmly observes God's institutions remaining in force even where the ultimate meaning remains hidden; it sees how capable they are of dispensing with man's co-operation. But whenever the believer deals with this worldly "thing," the estate of marriage, he cannot do otherwise than actualize its spiritual implications and allow them to exert their formative influence upon his entering, continuing, and fulfilling the estate of marriage. Then he cannot do otherwise than think of him who instituted this order as the one who is calling him into this order and who in doing so is making use of reason and *eros*, of natural law and natural love. Faith allows God to emerge from his anonymity and sets him forth, not only as the Author of the order, but also as the Thou who stands over against him and in whose sight the estate of marriage is entered, continued, and fulfilled. Therefore he will desire the blessing of its beginning, and therefore this benediction is obligatory for him, even though it does not establish the estate, but rather brings to mind the already *established* estate and its blessing.[63] In the blessing of the marriage which is already contracted, the new understanding of the estate of marriage that comes

---

[62] Cf. my "theological critique of reason" in *ThE* II, 1, §1321 ff.

[63] In the forms of marriage in common use today this finds expression in the fact that the minister already addresses the woman with her new name as a wife.

through faith finds expression. Hence it has no "efficient" significance, but only "noetic" importance.

This is why Luther makes two seemingly completely different statements about this ecclesiastical blessing of the couple, which will inevitably be regarded as contradictions—and actually are so regarded—as long as the co-ordination of "spiritual" and "worldly" which we have just discussed is not understood. Thus on the one hand Luther can say that one *may* desire the blessing of a marriage for whose legal performance the civil government ("the lords and the council") has exclusive competence.[64] Here it would appear that the blessing belongs almost in the realm of adiaphora; in any case it is facultative, even though recommended. As a divine institution marriage should be accounted "a hundred times more spiritual" than estates invented by men such as that of monks and nuns.[65] Moreover, it is well "the young people should learn to regard this estate seriously and honor it as a divine creation and command,"[66] that is, to be reminded by this benediction of the theological meaning of the estate of marriage (in the noetic respect mentioned above). In any case, where this benediction is desired, one may be sure that the young people do not look upon a wedding as "a laughing matter or a heathenish monkey business."[67] On the other hand he can say that he who scorns this benediction relapses into bestiality—probably in the sense that then the marriage becomes an animalistic coupling: *"Si qui autem nullam benedictionem habere voluerit, maneant bestiae multis legibus vel ordine indigentes." "Wollen sie jha bestien seyn, wollen wyr yn auch darzu helffen"* (["If you want to be beasts, all right, we'll help you"]).[68]

The two statements must doubtless be seen together:

The insistence upon the facultative character of the benediction is certainly based upon his cautiousness with regard to marriage as a sacrament which is constitutive of marriage. The benediction is something that is added to marriage, not something that establishes it. Therefore the lack of it does not subtract from the legitimacy of the marriage, however much it is to be recommended.

The other statement, which regards the benediction as obligatory, views the same question from another angle: If in a Christian community the spiritual implication of the "worldly business," marriage, is recognized on principle, then omission of the benediction would mean scorn of him who instituted the estate of marriage. But to scorn the spiritual meaning

---

[64] *Traubüchlein, CL* IV, 100, 11; 101, 13. (See note 30 above.)
[65] *Ibid.,* 100, 28.
[66] *Ibid.,* 101, 3.
[67] *Ibid.,* 101, 11.
[68] *WA* 27, 411; cf. Jordan, *op. cit.,* p. 87.

of marriage brings about a state of being which is different from that which obtains among those who know nothing about this spiritual meaning. It is true that marriage is a worldly thing and can be entered into as a *verum matrimonium* by all people of the world. But he who knows the spiritual implication of marriage and has the opportunity to receive the benediction which brings it home to him and then consciously refrains from entering before the face of God is not simply undertaking a subtraction which leaves him with nothing but the purely worldly thing called "marriage," but is denying a claim which he can never again evade. Then for him even the worldly thing has been perverted. Putting it in modern terms, we may say that post-Christian paganism is something qualitatively different from pre-Christian and extra-Christian paganism.

This perversion of the worldly thing called marriage in the face of its spiritual claim does not annul the legality of a marriage so contracted; but it does deprive it of its legitimacy. The subtraction of the Christian element from it does not leave a remainder which is the unbroken *humanum* but rather—and this is stated very sharply and emphatically—something that comes close to the animal. Perhaps this somewhat problematical emphasis arises from the fact that Luther had in mind certain degraded contemporary wedding customs which here prompted him to speak of "bestiality." If this is the case, then we must not overinterpret the contrast of *christianus* and *bestia*.

# C. The Changed Position of Woman in the Family and in Society (The Problem of the Equality of the Sexes)

Along with the awakening of the individual *eros* nothing has so deeply affected the relationship of the sexes as the changed position of woman in the family and society. The ancient marriage, in which the husband had a property right in the woman (*Munt-Ehe*), with its clear subordination of the wife and incorporation of marriage in the supraindividual entities of family and tribe, made the marriage bond considerably less complicated than that which obtains in a time in which a relationship of the spouses which is more that of partnership and equal rights is commonly accepted.

To be sure, profound sociological changes promoted this process of transformation; and we shall discuss these presently. But this transformation, the straight course it took, and its co-ordination with certain historical epochs would hardly be explicable if we did not include among its incentives as well as its aims the conviction that "individuality" as a form of existence is a privilege and title of humanity that belongs also to the *woman*. The idea of partnership can take root only where equals are involved. Therefore it is very characteristic that the movement toward partnership is, as it were, "synchronized" with the awakening and growth of the consciousness of individuality and that it is bound up with certain other symptoms (such as woman's political right to vote).

Therefore when we cast a glance at the contributory sociological factors we should not overestimate their importance. Their significance is more that of occasions and sociotechnical preconditions which made possible the breakthrough; its real motive, however, lies in the anthropological background.[1]

The historical development can be described in the familiar statement that "for the woman the legal development is a history of increasing freedom."[2] At least this is true of her formal, legal equality with the man, which need not necessarily mean a corresponding *de facto* gain in prestige, but rather in many areas may also mean a loss of moral—not, of course, justiciable—authority which she formerly enjoyed.[3] The formal legal principle of "equality before the law" has now been recognized and anchored in the constitutions of many modern civilized states.[4]

For the Federal Republic of Germany the law says: "All men are equal before the law. Men and women have equal rights" (GG [basic law], Art. 3, par. 2). On April 1, 1953, this definition in the basic law became actual law.

The constitution of the Soviet Union (December 5, 1936) says in ble, paragraph 2, proclaims this principle: "The law guarantees the woman in all areas the same rights as the man." There is, however, no concrete legislation respecting the equality of husband and wife in family law.[5]

The constitution of the Soviet Union (December 5, 1936) says in Article 122: "In the U.S.S.R. the woman is granted in all areas of economic, civic, cultural, and sociopolitical life the same rights as the man. The possibility of realizing these rights is guaranteed to the woman by equal status with the man in the right to work, remuneration for work, vacations, social security and education, by state protection of the interests of mother and child, by allowance for leave of absence for pregnancy with full pay, etc." The reform of 1944 brought no changes in this area.

---

[1] It is one of the curiosities of church history but yet a good illustration of the long road that had to be traveled to get to the principle of equal rights that in the sixth century it was possible to raise the question whether a woman was a "human being" in the full sense (even though it was answered affirmatively). According to Gregory of Tours VIII, 20 (*SS. rer. Merov.* II, 1; *edd.* Krusch/Levison, p. 386), at the National Council of Macon in the year 585 one of the bishops expressed the opinion that *"mulierem hominem non posse vocitare"* ["It is not possible to call women human beings."] though he received no support for it.

[2] Schwab, *op. cit.*, p. 59.

[3] Cf. *ThE* II, 1, §2073.

[4] Cf. Dölle, *op. cit.*, pp. 19 ff.

[5] *Ibid.*, p. 25.

On the contrary, it is to be noted that in practice the principle of equal rights is being carried out even more consistently than compliance with the literal terms of the constitution would seem to demand.[6] Similar provisions obtain in the Peoples' Republic of China.

This may be a sufficient enumeration of symptoms to indicate the extent to which the formally legal equality of the sexes has prevailed in the civilized countries. The list could be enlarged almost indefinitely; but it would reveal only differences which are never more than nuances and for the most part are confined to legislation for family affairs [*Familienrecht*].

As we have already indicated, the external opening and impetus for this line of development which led to the present situation was provided by the changes that took place in the sociological structure, while Romanticism, with its higher estimate of woman and the irrational element it represented, created certain *inner* presuppositions for this development. The sociologically conditioned changes are characterized by the following factors:

1. Technological industrialization very largely broke down the old patriarchal structure of society mainly by shifting the man's work from the home, so that the home and the place where a man works (factories, offices, etc.) were more or less widely separated. The father thereby lost his influence upon the family and the rearing of the children. Correspondingly, the woman gained ascendancy in all concerns within the family.

2. Technological industrialization had its effect, however, not only upon the home, but also in the world of labor: most of the labor functions formerly performed by men can also be performed by women. This applies especially—but by no means only—to the area of unskilled labor. In the Federal Republic of Germany almost half of the women of working age have a job; a considerable percentage of them are married women.

3. Industrialization also led to a larger degree of freedom of movement for the woman. Very many domestic functions which were formerly a part of the woman's task (spinning, butchering, preserving, or even brewing beer as Katie Luther did) have been shifted to the province outside the home. Thus unmarried "aunts" were no longer so necessary for the life of the family as they were before. The "aunts" have largely changed from appendages to the family to independent workers. Further, whereas in the preindustrial age the household was not only a consuming but a producing community and thus required the domestic services of the women, it has now become almost exclusively a consuming community.

4. Women working in industry, because of their special situation, also need a correspondingly special social protection. This applies, for exam-

6 *Ibid.*, p. 21.

ple, to the period of pregnancy and to children who need to be cared for during working hours. This resulted in the demand for protection and the ability to compete with men and this had to be answered with appropriate social legislation. This is another evidence of the tendency toward equalization of the rights of men and women.

5. The participation of women in the labor process inevitably focused attention upon the value of the work they performed. The question arose whether it was really true that only the value of *professional* labor could be expressed in figures and not *also* the contribution to the support of the family through domestic work by helping in family business concerns. Thus the equality of man and woman automatically involved the question of the equality of the working woman and the housewife. Both performed labor which could be expressed in terms of wage scales and money values, and this had to lead to the point where the values of the contribution to the social product or to the family property had to be credited to the individual participants, as between the working woman and the housewife on the one hand and the husband and wife on the other. The result was the tendency toward a revision of marital property laws to govern the coadministration by the wife of the property she has brought into the marriage or earned as well as the division of this property after the ending of the marriage by divorce or death. The details of these regulations and the different ways in which they are dealt with in individual countries is less important for our concern than the fact that here again we have evidence of a very clear trend in the direction of equal partnership for the woman. To that extent these reforms are important to our theme. Here again we have a structural change in the social position of woman. The law of marital property rights is likewise determined by the tendency toward equal rights.

We have already dealt exegetically and systematically with the main points in the theological attitude toward the equality of the sexes.[7] We have also supplied historical materials and discussion of the awakening of individuality and the changed sociological structure insofar as these were involved. For our particular subject it still remains to deal with the question of how far the principle of equality is to be carried from the point of view of a theological ethics, the question whether it leads to a total leveling of the sexes, or whether in some areas such as the family various competences and perhaps also hierarchical gradations of man and woman should be recognized.

---

[7] See the sections on "The Duality of Man" and "The Biblical Interpretation of Marriage" above.

This question becomes a very practical one when the legislator is obliged to translate into concrete laws what the constitutions normally set forth as principles and therefore only in a very general way.

The whole subject of the equality of the sexes must be discussed under two heads: first, insofar as it affects the position of man and woman in society—especially in the world of labor—and second, insofar as it affects the rights and duties of both within the family, that is, in their relation as spouses to each other and to the children.

Whereas the first of these areas (their position in society) has no special theological relevance,[8] the legal definition of the relationship of the sexes in the family has a very considerable theological significance, because the family is not just "any" *social ordinance* which can be changed at will, but rather because, through the original relationship of parents and children which it embraces, it is an *order of creation*. As such it is not in its basic structure at the disposal of human manipulation. Moreover, it lies in the province of immediate human relations and is therefore subject in a special way to the commandment of *agape*. Because here people are responsible for the temporal and eternal welfare of the other person—as could not be otherwise in a community of life and education—the kingdom on the left hand can hardly be distinguished from the kingdom on the right. Here one's "neighbor" becomes a responsibility that carries with it a heightened degree of urgency. It is therefore obvious that every legal ordinance that affects this intimate zone of neighborly love and fellow-human responsibility has theological and spiritual relevance.

Here the theological and the legal problems run parallel for some

---

[8] Nor is it possible to object to this statement by citing I Cor. 14:34, "The women should keep silence in the churches" [meaning, in public], and I Tim. 2:12. In the first place, what is meant here is speaking publicly in the *ekklesia*. Naturally, there is also behind this the opinion that the public appearance of women outside the church is not to be allowed either. This is so self-evident that it need not even be mentioned. But neither is this the point at issue here. The motive which here prompts Paul to make this statement is the very serious theological concern lest justification, that is, the fact that men and women are equally recipients of grace, be used as an argument to equalize the position of both within the earthly orders too. So here in Paul there is in the background an argument which Luther later directed against the rebellious peasants who were revolting against contemporary ordinances, such as serfdom, etc., in the name of Christian liberty. Second, reference is being made here to a contemporary social ordinance which has no kerygmatic authority for other times.

distance. For the question of how far equality of the sexes within the family should go cannot be answered without reference to the criterion by which equality of rights is to be defined. This is primarily a problem of formal definition of terms. We have to state what "equal rights" really means.

And here we have two fundamentally different criteria with which to operate, criteria which since Aristotle wrote his *Nicomachean Ethics* have been known as arithmetical and geometrical justice. *Arithmetical* justice judges from the point of view of the absolute equality of the parties within the area in which it is applicable. Every individual has, as it were, the value of "1" in legal structure. *Geometrical* justice, however, judges from the point of view that men are different and therefore does not attribute to each the same but rather a different *suum,* namely, that which is *"his* peculiar due." Now, since the postulate that the sexes have equal rights is asserted in the name of *justice* and hence declares that any differences in rights are unjust, this distinction made by Aristotle between the two forms of justice must immediately become acute and evoke the question which of the two forms is here the proper one for defining the equality of rights.

If one says that the *arithmetical* form of justice is the proper criterion the consequence is a radically formal, or as we often say, a "mechanical" equality of the sexes. The advocates of this solution reject any moderation of the principle of absolute equality, fearing that any concession must immediately lead to an unforeseen proliferation of differentiations.

The sole exception to this mechanically interpreted principle of equality is dictated purely by the elementary biological difference between the sexes. Thus there must naturally be laws for the protection of motherhood (social regulations for the time of pregnancy), for which, naturally, there can be no equivalent on the other side (in the form of laws protecting fatherhood).[9] Characteristic of the repeatedly manifested limitations of this mechanically applied principle is the fact that in the constitutional reforms undertaken in the United States it can be seen that the intent is to interpret the laws in such a way "that no present or future rights, assistances, and exceptions to which persons of the female sex are entitled shall be infringed upon in any way."[10] What that means, after all, is this:

[9] Cf. Schwab, *op. cit.,* p. 50.
[10] Dölle, *op. cit.,* pp. 26 f.

The mechanical principle of equality is advocated on behalf of the *woman* (and accordingly with particular vigor by women's organizations and suffragettes) because it is the most radical principle.

It now turns out that social legislation on the basis of the principle of equality has succeeded at various points in achieving *positive* gains for the woman and securing her privileges over against the man. But now if that principle is applied mechanically, its consequences militate *against* the woman and again deprive her of her privileges. So the mechanical principle is advocated only as long as it is a question of restricting the rights of the man. When the opposite case arises, this principle is regarded with reservation, in order that the appeal may not be made to the slogan "Equal rights, equal duties" and thus the woman lose the protected positions "which have hitherto been granted to her because of her constitutional [that is, physically constitutional] peculiarity."[11] E. Kaufmann therefore speaks of the task of protecting those who are socially weaker in order that the principle of equality may not work against them rather than for them.[12]

The length to which this mechanical principle can be pushed is evident, for example, in the discussions of the legislation for equal rights in West Germany, in which the argument was put forward that the drafting of men only for compulsory military service is a violation of Article 3, Section 2 of the basic law and therefore could not be enacted without changing the constitution.

It is typical of the materialistic, mechanistic structure of communistic thought that here the mechanical principle is interpreted and applied with logical, abstract consistency. According to Section 8 of the draft of the law governing family concerns in the DDR (German Democratic Republic) "the spouses are entitled to live apart, if their education or work requires it." Section 9 even grants to the wife "the right to make her own decision with respect to learning or training for a profession or a social occupation without taking into consideration the attitude of the husband."[13] Thus the spouses are no longer seen in the organic bond of the family, but rather as individual, isolated molecules in the collective. So here equality of rights does not issue from the conviction that the wife is an independent person who is an equal partner with the husband, but rather from the principle of sociofunctional equality. Here it is not the woman struggling to gain her rights who is employing this mechanistic principle of equality, but rather a pragmatic-minded *society*. It orients the equality not upon the person but upon the function. Moreover, the tactical

[11] *Ibid.,* p. 27.
[12] Kaufmann, *op. cit.,* p. 18.
[13] Schwab, *op. cit.,* p. 55.

idea behind it is that parents who are working and possibly also living apart are compelled to leave the rearing of their children to state institutions.

If, on the other hand, one says that the *geometrical* form of justice is the proper one by which to determine the form and the extent of equality, then one will not define equality *mechanically* but rather *organically*. In this case the legal concept of the equality of man and wife will not regard them both as isolated individuals whose individual rights are to be assigned to them in much the same way that a hat-check girl is required to treat each individual exactly alike, that is, according to his position in the queue. Such an understanding of equality would be appropriate only if marriage were understood as a contract, that is, if it were the product of an act of will on the part of two individuals. If, however, marriage is understood as an institution which is *given* to the two individuals, and thus into which they are called,[14] then the law governing family affairs can no longer treat the two spouses as isolated individuals, but must see them "organically," that is, as persons "who are joined together in a higher fellowship, within which each of them has an organic function in accord with the biological, psychical, and social characteristics of his genus, and in the structuring of which regard is to be paid to the individual and also to the community as a whole."[15] With this "organic" understanding of equality it becomes possible to apportion duties, responsibilities, and rights within marriage and the family according to the special disposition which the husband or the wife brings to them. Moreover, in this setting it would also be consistent (as it is not consistent with the mechanically understood principle of equality) to grant to the wife the safeguards and considerations which she needs because of her biological particularity.

There can be no doubt that only the second alternative, namely, the "organic" understanding of equality, is in accord with the order of creation in marriage as well as with the apostolic instructions. In both,

---

[14] This is the case, for example, when marriage is understood as an order of creation; but this givenness of marriage (as something above and beyond a contract) may also be accepted outside the realm of Christian thought in the narrower sense, for example in marriage legislation.

[15] Dölle, *op. cit.*, p. 27.

the particularity of the sexes is clearly distinguished. Their mutual dependence (Gen. 3:16 f.), their being equal recipients of grace (I Pet. 3:7), and thus their solidarity in the vertical dimension, is matched by differentiation in the horizontal dimension. Many of these differentiations may be determined by contemporary sociological factors; but certainly not the assumption that the man is the stronger and the woman is the weaker sex (I Pet. 3:7.). It is precisely upon this ontological foundation that the man is admonished to support the weaker partner through *agape* (Eph. 5:25, 33), and on it is based also the special consideration given to the woman in modern social legislation which is intended to protect her from the negative consequences of the principle of equality.

This basic theological decision in favor of the "organic" understanding of equality provides leeway for many possible individual interpretations and ways of working out this understanding in concrete legislation. Here it will be largely a matter of practical, objective decisions conditioned by the situation, which have no theological relevance, but are rather left to the judgment of reason. There may, of course, be exceptions.

In order to find the limit of this freedom of judgment we must distinguish the jurisdictions in which the principle of equal rights is actually applied, at least as far as the competence of laws affecting the family is concerned. (For reasons stated above we exclude from theological consideration the question of equal rights in society, especially in the world of labor.) In the area of family law the concrete applications occur chiefly in connection with the question of the wife's practice of a vocation and the choice of domicile on the one hand and the question of mutual responsibility for the rearing of the children.[16]

The first problem, that of the wife's working and the choice of domicile, is essentially in the province of rational judgment. And yet some more precise definitions are necessary here, and this is what prompts us to indicate a limitation by using the word "essentially." It is a matter of the applicability of a judgment related to the situation

[16] Properly speaking, the concrete application of the principle of equality in the area of property rights should be included here too. We may content ourselves, however, with the reference made to this at the close of our historical survey.

primarily because theology can have no interest in insisting that the patriarchal social order is binding and ignoring the changes that have taken place. In an age which grants full political rights to woman and also the same level of education and professional training as that of the man, the church cannot identify itself with the husband's exclusive power of decision in those areas where the extent of the wife's independence in matters connected with her vocation is concerned. This applies also to the choice of a vocation.[17]

However, on the basis of our position that marriage is an ordinance which is *given* to the individual, this freedom of decision granted to the wife, which frees her from the one-sided authority of the husband, cannot mean that the wife can make her decision in the name of her own individuality and its untrammeled development. On the contrary, she is bound to bring her work and the choice of her domicile into harmony with the primary obligation which is laid upon her by responsibility as a wife and mother. In this case her equality of rights can mean only that the husband cannot settle the question of the wife's working and domicile on his own authority, but rather that the wife makes this decision on her own responsibility.

This cannot mean, however, that this decision can be made just as she pleases; on the contrary, it means that the wife has the responsibility of determining whether and to what extent she is meeting the criterion which will make her decision a legitimate one, in other words, whether she is fulfilling her "main office" as a wife and mother. It lies in the very essence of the matter that this question cannot be solved unless the wife seeks to gain the consent and approval of the husband. For a failure to obtain this approval would in itself be a breaking of the marital fellowship.

The freedom granted to the wife by the principle of equal rights therefore cannot mean an emancipation from the marriage and the obligation to seek the building of a common will on the part of the

[17] "The Evangelical Church has no grounds for identifying itself with the support of the husband's *universal power of decision*. Inasmuch as today the present law is frequently branded as patriarchal, it must be pointed out that the Evangelical Church also has no grounds to desire the continuance of this relative patriarchalism as such." Bishop Otto Dibelius, speaking for the Council of the Evangelical Church in Germany, in a letter, March 22, 1952, to Secretary of the Interior Dehler, *FR*, p. 12.

spouses. Rather this freedom can mean only that this common will cannot be one-sidedly dictated by the husband, but must be achieved in partnership. The *agape,* which Paul requires of the husband and which he understood as yielding to and accepting the wife (since the wife had no legal claims upon him), is now required in a higher degree of the wife too (since now the husband is no longer in the one-sided position to make certain legal demands).

As far as the appropriate legislation is concerned, both partners in the marriage should be required to make these decisions in mutual responsibility and thus in mutual agreement, so that "the intentional omission of such an effort" would in itself represent an abuse of the power to make the decision.[18]

These problems naturally come to a critical point in the borderline cases. What happens when a meeting of minds does not take place? What happens, for example, when the spouses make different decisions about two possible places to domicile? The very simplicity of such a banal situation makes the problem peculiarly clear. In this case two legislative solutions present themselves, for which there is no clear theological criterion, but which nevertheless touch the understanding of marriage indirectly and at least suggest a discretionary theological judgment (for this too can exist!).

One possibility is that the lawmaker may simply waive the possibility of making a legal decision on this point. (This is what happened in the German Federal Republic through the striking out of Section 1354, *Bürgerliches Gesetzbuch*). By so doing he refrains from interfering in marriage and leaves it to its self-regulation. The insoluble conflict which may then arise because of dissenting choices of different domiciles may perhaps then have to be resolved by divorce.

The other possibility is that the state would assume the burden of providing "marital aid," either by "judging" the case of conflict or by "arbitrating" it, that is, by leaving it to the discretion of the judge whether to resolve the lack of consensus by a judicial decision or to resign himself to the first possibility and leave the marriage to itself and possibly its dissolution. The possibility that this resignation would occur is unavoidable, since in the area of intimate relationships there will always be decisions which are not justiciable. So here too dependence upon the tact and discretion of the judge would be necessary.

---

[18] Dibelius, *ibid.,* p. 13. Cf. the "Position of the Commission on Marriage Law of the Evangelical Church in Germany" with respect to the draft of a law governing family affairs (1952), *FR* pp. 17 ff., especially p. 21.

It is in the very nature of the discretionary theological judgment, to which we referred above, that it may arrive at different conclusions and that at any rate it cannot be dogmatically unequivocal. As a matter of fact, it is precisely in this area that it tends to arrive at different conclusions. If we incline to the opinion that the first of the two possibilities mentioned is to be preferred in the light of this discretionary theological judgment, our reasons for this are as follows:

First, it would mean a fundamentally destructive interference in the intimate relationship of man and wife, which is based upon trust, if an extramarital court of appeal were called upon to make a judgment which was anything more than counsel requested by both parties. But this destructive interference is present in any kind of legal intervention. Second, the fact that these nonjusticiable factors exist and hence that dependence upon the tact of the judge is inevitable would mean to put an excessive demand upon the legal judgment. This legal decision cannot be made dependent upon the individual qualities of a judge—his human maturity, his empathy, and his "musicality" in a range of tones which is largely irrational. And finally, a general trend of the times, which tends to break down personal responsibility and thus human substance generally, leads to a growing inclination to allow the courts to intervene. This is apparent not only in the realm of marriage but also in education (where administrative courts are expected to review pedagogical and disciplinary decisions of the schools) and in politics (where constitutional courts are expected to promote or obstruct political decisions). The church must not aid and abet this trend in order to help make possible the continuance (and in most cases only an outward continuance) of a marriage.

The second problem, the *rearing of the children,* makes far more difficult and in this case more theologically relevant demands upon the interpretation and administration of the principle of equal rights. In this case too the problem becomes more acute in the borderline cases, namely, when united educational authority of the parents is jeopardized by differences of opinion between the married partners. In addition to the problems of vocation and choice of domicile, two other complications arise here.

First, this is not only a question of the responsibility of both partners for their marriage and each other, but of responsibility for a third party, namely, the children, who besides play no part in the origin and the solution of the conflict through their own power of decision and responsibility. This correspondingly increases the responsibility of those who are vested with the rights and duties of education. Second, in this area decisions *must* be made when there are conflicts. And this raises the question who is to make the decision here.

The urgency of this question becomes apparent as soon as one thinks of exemplary cases in which a decision with regard to the children *must* be made. Who shall make the decision, for example, when a father desires that his daughter shall have advanced education and university study, while the mother wants her to have practical training? Or who shall make the decision when a child is critically ill and one physician says that an operation is absolutely necessary, while another doctor (or a healer) just as urgently counsels against it and the parents make correspondingly different decisions?

With a mechanically interpreted principle of equal rights it is perfectly clear how the conflict must be solved. (But it is precisely this theologically unacceptable interpretation which renders such a solution suspect from the start.) In other words, absolute equality of both parents makes it inevitable that in such cases an extramarital court of appeal will be called upon to decide the issue. As a rule the domestic relations court [*Vormundschaftsgericht*] is recommended for this purpose.

This alien intervention in the internal affairs of the family is subject to the same scruples expressed above.[19] It destroys the relationship of trust and the direct interpersonal responsibility by which a sound marriage lives. Connected with this ethicopsychological point of view there is also an "ontological" aspect, namely, that marriage and the family are antecedent to the state and that therefore it is improper that the primary ordinance should be regimented by a secondary institution.[20]

Added to this scruple about recommending appeal to a domestic relations court are still others:[21]

First, there is the consideration that precisely in the borderline cases which suggest this intervention no "easy" solution is possible

[19] As early as 1889, O. von Gierke wrote: "No one who still desires a healthy family life will concur with the proposal that the domestic relations court should decide." Schwab, *op. cit.*, p. 61.

[20] We have dealt with this side of the problem in the chapter on parental law, *ThE* II, 2, §1697 ff., especially §1793 ff.

[21] Cf. the "Position of the Commission on Marriage Law . . .," *FR*, p. 21.

and also cannot be expected of a domestic relations court. (Cf. the cases cited as examples!) At best such a solution would be possible only if there were an obvious abuse of discretion, gross prejudice, or a selfish motive on the part of one of the parents. Second, we must reckon with the fact that the court too can make a wrong decision. Indeed, according to the Commission the danger "that the judges of the domestic relations court will make their decisions in thoughtless and routine fashion is greater than it was among our forefathers."[22] And finally, the state totalitarianism which has hardly been fully overcome makes it dubious, especially in Germany, whether family life should be subjected to the constant pressure of the possibility that whenever there is disagreement between the partners the authority of the state will be called in. This would kill the desired total responsibility for each other in marriage at the very outset.

The question then is how the parental power of decision is to be regulated if we adopt not the mechanical but the organic interpretation of the principle of equality. In the "normal" cases it would be a matter of the parents arriving at a common agreement through discussion. In the "borderline" cases, where there is disagreement, however, it would be inevitable that one of the parents should have the right to make the final decision, if for the reasons stated above it is at all possible to keep an extramarital court out of the picture—at any rate insofar as its legal power to decide is concerned. At this point where a choice simply *has* to be made and where the exceptional character of a borderline situation prevails, a theological ethics cannot abstain from declaring, in line with the tradition of Christendom based upon the Holy Scriptures, that the father holds the final decision. Though it is true that the New Testament does not recognize any spiritual subordination of the wife to the husband (Gal. 3:28; Eph. 5:23; I Pet. 3:1),[23] it nevertheless upholds this subordination in the earthly affairs of marriage.[24] To be sure, this is embedded in contemporary judgments which are partially determined by the social order of the time. But the fundamental hierarchical order of powers

---

[22] *Ibid.*, p. 21.
[23] Dibelius, *op. cit.*, p. 13.
[24] Cf. E. Kähler on the "subordination" of woman in the New Testament in *ZEE* (1959), I, pp. 1 ff., especially p. 11.

in marriage itself is independent of this factor, however much it may likewise be subject to variations conditioned by present-day mores and however much it should be abolished, if possible altogether, outside of marriage. The frictions to which a marriage is necessarily exposed when it has come to this borderline situation where the final decision has to be made by the father will at any rate be less than the tensions that result from outside interventions.

It is true that the unity of a family can be broken whenever *any* will is arbitrarily imposed upon it, whether from the outside or from within the family itself. And yet we must not overlook the differing chances of success in these alternatives; for the very knowledge that this borderline situation must be settled within the family itself will strengthen the inclination of both partners to arrive at a consensus and render the borderline situation less likely to arise than if the way were always open to resort to an extramarital court. And even if it does come to the point where the borderline situation exists, and the father exercises his right to make the final decision, it is important that the responsible person is one who is constantly aware of the other person in the marriage itself and must accept the consequences of his decision while continuing to live with the other partner. The road on which these consequences arise is one that has many stations of a further life together, at which there may still be subsequent opportunities—in view perhaps of consequences which clarify the decision—to secure the other partner's agreement or to admit that he or she was right; in short, stations at which a reconciliation is possible and where in any case the mutual effort to achieve this remains an obligation.

The settlement of this borderline situation has an ethical and a legal side:

The *ethical* side is that the authorization of the husband to make the final decision does not entitle him to exercise his primacy dictatorially. Even in a social order which had no conception of the principle of equal rights, Christian ethics did not make this decision, but rather required that the husband accept the wife and take her into account in love (*agapan*).[25] What is variable may be simply the form which this acceptance takes.

[25] *Ibid.*, p. 11.

In an age when the wife lacked social rights and the education that goes with them, this acceptance may have consisted in a husband's not necessarily sharing with the wife his right to make the decisions, but seeking to gain her understanding through explanation and thus not treating her as a mere object which is expected only to note accomplished facts or take orders. In what else would that *agapan* demanded by Paul consist—that *agapan* which meant the recognition of the wife as a person and which was a complete exception in the ancient world?

In a time in which woman has "come of age" and become a partner with equal rights in marriage, this acceptance in love will find far more distinctive forms, in which the wife will participate in the formation of a common will and be heard and taken seriously even in the borderline situation where the father makes the final decision. Precisely because the principle of equal rights is by no means merely a legal principle, but is rather only a legal *formulation* of a changed anthropological situation, it implies, on the ethical side, that the full rights (*Mündigkeit*) and thus also the joint responsibility of the other person—in this case, the wife—must be taken seriously. What in a time when woman had not "come of age" may have been a legitimate practice (namely, that paternal authority justified the making of "solitary decisions"), becomes in other times, when the principle of equal rights legitimately expresses the wife's partnership, an affront to her person and her conscience in which she accepts joint responsibility. Thus along with the ethical side of equal rights there goes an ethical—and by no means merely juristic!—form of wronging the other person.

Then, secondly, there is a *legal* side to the settlement of the borderline case. The right of the father to make the final decision is something that can be juridically fixed. It is equally possible to bind the father legally to give constant consideration to the mother's opinion and thus to prevent him—in the borderline case of disagreement—from making dictatorial "solitary decisions."[26] Naturally, the father's right to make the final decision must not be allowed to put an intolerable strain upon the principle of equal rights, as would be the case

[26] The law of the German Federal Republic makes this provision: §1627, *BGB*.

if the father misuses his authority as the head of the family. In this extreme case—and here its character as being the extreme exceptional case is important!—it must be possible for the mother to appeal to the domestic relations court for the sake of the children and the risk of jeopardizing the marriage, which this entails, must be faced. And here it would seem to be a wise and proper solution if the court would not simply decide the disputed case, which the father has clearly and demonstrably failed to settle, but rather authorize the mother to make this decision and thus confine its intervention to the indispensable minimum.[27] Thus, despite all our scruples against interventions from the outside, we cannot absolutely rule out the possibility of permitting the courts to act in intrafamily affairs. In view of the primacy of marriage as an order of creation over the state as an "order of necessity,"[28] however, everything depends upon our seeing to it that this intervention of the state does not become a constantly available routine but remains a highly specialized exceptional case.

This exceptional case should be recognized as such only on the basis of a whole chain of conditions: 1. It should not apply to a marriage in which the children do not need to be taken into account in the spouses' problems of vocation and domicile. 2. An exceptional case when an insurmountable disagreement between the parents on a question which is vital to the life of the children arises and thus makes it necessary for the father to exercise his right of final decision. 3. The father must have demonstrably and grossly failed in the exercise of his right to make the final decision. These conditions may provide the necessary measure of certainty that marriage as a community of responsibility may be allowed to remain as autonomous as possible and that the necessary tribute will be paid to the organically understood principle of equal rights.

In taking this position, we believe that we have followed quite generally the line laid down by the Commission on Marriage Law of the Evangelical Church in Germany: "The commission cannot . . . relinquish the father's right of decision with respect to the children, as in extreme cases it can relinquish the husband's right of decision

---

[27] This is the procedure in the German Federal Republic according to §1628, sec. 2, *BGB*.

[28] Cf. *ThE* I, §692; II, 1, §655 ff; II, 2, §1552 f., etc.

with respect to the wife. The ascertainable relationship of the parents to the children, the principle of the welfare of the child, the desirability of a decision made within the family, these factors are available to legislation . . . and have already been extensively tested in the courts. . . . Resort to the decision of a domestic relations court carries with it the danger of flight from the father's responsibility before God. . . . Nevertheless, the right of appeal to the domestic relations court against an improper decision of the father should by no means be precluded. . . . An abuse of the father's right of decision would be present if he has failed to make an earnest effort to reach a mutual agreement and persistently fails in his duty to take into account the opinion of the mother.[29]

In view of the possibility of such exceptional cases—but certainly not *only* these!—there should be places where people can receive marital and educational counseling (which can also be helpful in less critical cases) before the legal decisions are made. Since such counseling centers would have only an advisory function, they could not go beyond an appeal to the parents' and spouses' sense of responsibility and a clarification of the question in dispute. But they would render legitimate "marital aid" since they would not take the responsible decision away from, or impose it upon, the marriage. Unlike the law, which must necessarily be general in character, they could also take into account the individual case and even the difficult intimate problems. So along with the endeavor to keep the created order of marriage as far away as possible from intervention by the state there should be the proviso that the court can be appealed to only if marital counseling institutes, pastoral care, or similar agencies have been consulted first. This would also apply to divorce.

[29] *FR,* pp. 21 f.

# D. Divorce and the Remarriage of Divorced Persons

## 1. DIVORCE

We have already dealt with the problem of divorce from the exegetical and the historical point of view. We dealt with the *exegetical* point of view insofar as the New Testament in stating its attitude toward divorce and its reasons for reserve with regard to it indirectly expresses essential features of its understanding of marriage. We dealt with the historical aspect of the question of divorce insofar as the problem was affected by certain anthropological changes, particularly a changed understanding of human individuality and the individual *eros*. We shall therefore assemble the results we have already arrived at in order to evaluate them systematically and develop the essential points.

1. Jesus declares that marriage in the sense of God's original order of creation is indissoluble and describes entrance into a new marriage as adultery (Mark 10:1 ff.; Matt. 5:32, 19:1 ff.; Luke 16:18).

2. This position taken by Jesus is maintained in the tradition of the primitive church. Only narrowly restricted exceptions justify a divorce: the *porneia* of the wife[1] and a mixed marriage in which the pagan partner demands or carries out the divorce (thus Paul in I Cor. 7:15).

3. These two statements have been repeatedly regarded as being

[1] The relevant terms are as a rule those which come from the authorship of Matthew (5:32; 19:9).

contradictory. The second—conditioned freedom to divorce—was felt to be a softening of the first, and this was explained by saying, for example,[2] that in making his unconditional demand Jesus was proclaiming the new aeon in which "God's original will again became the law for all," while the primitive church faced "a new situation because of the delay of the *parousia* and had to adjust itself to the realities. This explanation, however, is improbable,[3] since the proclamation of an order of marriage for the new aeon is out of the question, if only because there is no marrying or giving in marriage at all in the Kingdom of God (Mark 12:25) and because a radical acceptance of the new aeon does not involve a new order of marriage, but may rather require the sacrifice of remaining unmarried (Matt. 19:12). Both statements—the indissolubility of marriage in principle and divorce as a possible exception—must rather be taken together. We say:

4. Jesus' reminder that marriage is an order of creation dare not be interpreted legalistically in the sense that he proposed to abolish the law of this aeon and put in its place the radical law of the new world. His challenge is rather a call to repentance addressed to those who are subject to the legal ordinances of this aeon.

5. This call to repentance implies that man must not think of himself in terms of his legal ordinances. If he does this, he is fooling himself in the illusion that he is intact, in possession of integrity. For he may, indeed, be able to satisfy the demands of the law. But the fact that he can meet the requirements of the law is owing only to the fact that it was written to suit him—fallen man, the *homo inordinatus*—and that it has been accommodated to him as he actually is. For the law, including the law of divorce, is adapted to fit man's "hardheartedness." Hence, if man takes the law as the standard of his understanding of himself, he would not be orienting himself upon the will of God; he would be in a very dubious way overlooking the fact that he does not satisfy God's will and that God says no to his life as it is. Therefore Jesus' call to repentance is a calling to remembrance of God's "real" order of creation; it startles man out of his self-chosen

[2] J. Jeremias, quoted in G. Bornkamm, *op. cit.*, p. 284.
[3] Thus also Bornkamm.

defenses and testifies to the *broken* relationship of this aeon and its
ordinances to the will of God. The call to repentance means that the
ordinances of this aeon appear not as the order of creation, but rather
as an "order of necessity" because of man's sinfulness and therefore
cannot be interpreted as being synonymous with the *real* will of
God.

6. But then the proclamation of the original will of God (*ap'
arches*) over against the legal ordinances of this aeon cannot mean
that it is to take the *place* of these legal ordinances, or better, that it
is now to constitute a *new* law, a *new* code. This would be a completely wrong conception if only because a new law in the sense of a
possible set of statutes simply cannot be derived from the radicaliza-
tions of the Mosaic *nomos* in the Sermon on the Mount. These are
simply not justiciable (Matt. 5:21 ff., 5:27 ff., 5:33 ff., 5:38 ff.,
5:43 ff.). The meaning and purpose of the call to repentance and the
summons back to the order of creation is not to eliminate but to
relativize the legal structures of this aeon.

7. Consequently, the "contradiction" between the conditional allowance of divorce and the radicalism of the order of creation is only
a symptom of the deeper "contradiction" between this aeon and the
original will of God, in which the legal ordinances of this aeon are
also involved. It is thus at the same time a variant of the "contradiction" that exists between the original command of God in creation
(Gen. 1:28) and the Noachic reconstitution of the world after the
Flood (Gen. 9:1 ff.).[4]

8. Since this contradiction is retained and made the very foundation of the call to repentance, the "additions" in Matt. 5:32 and 19:9
(if indeed we are to assume that they are additions) are a "practical
and proper [*sachgemässe*] interpretation of Jesus' injunction in the
sphere of law."[5] This interpretation is proper in that it expresses
how the original will of God is refracted when it passes through the
medium of this aeon and thus does two things: first, it testifies to the
majesty of this will of God precisely by pointing out how estranged
from it man has become, and second, it sets up the original will of

---

[4] *ThE* I, §692; II, 1, §655; II, 2, §3023.
[5] Bornkamm, *op. cit.*, p. 284.

God as the real standard and protests against the false identification of it with the legal norm.

9. Because this conditional allowance of divorce is thus a proper interpretation of Jesus' injunction, it declares that the indissolubility of marriage is the "real" will of God (*voluntas propria*). But if this is so, then it is impossible to think of the legality of an accomplished divorce as being at the same time legitimate. On the contrary, then the law can no longer be a cloak to cover the wrong that is *always* inherent in a broken marriage and in *every* case is expressed in its divorce.

10. In the New Testament the reason given for exceptional divorce is "hardheartedness," that is, the *de facto* condition of man between the Fall and the Last Judgment. It is therefore based upon an order of necessity, in which God—without calling in question the normative character of his real intention in the order of creation—takes into account the real condition of man and the real world in which he lives. This taking into account of the concrete reality of things in God's dealings with man is what also gave us the right to see the anthropological changes in our understanding of individuality and the human *eros* in the context of their theological affinity, that is, in the context of the concrete reality of things, of *which* God takes account.

At this point it becomes apparent then that the individual *eros* can make an enormous contribution to the bond of marriage when both partners complement each other in the way symbolized by the Platonic myth of the spherical man. But at the same time it is also true that it is an outstanding cause of difficulties. It becomes this in three ways:

First, because the ecstasy of *eros* can conceal the incompatibility of two human constitutions insofar as its effect is "blinding." So-called "love at first sight," which would bid the moment to remain and make it be the whole of a life relationship, is by no means always possessed of prophetic insight, but has just as often proved that love also makes one blind.

Second, individual *eros* becomes a cause of difficulties in that its emotional character subjects it to the rhythm of attraction and repulsion as well as of passion and indifference. Consequently, to the degree that *eros* is made the criterion of the worth or worthlessness of the marriage it is subjected to phases of unusual instability which can jeopardize the continuance of the marriage itself.

And finally, not only a crass disharmony between the two constitutions but even small differences between them lead to tensions which, depending on the degree of refinement of the individuality and the sensitivity that increases with it, can become a shattering burden.

Thus the positive potentialities for binding two persons together which are inherent in individual *eros* are accompanied by a corresponding number of increased possibilities of wounding and being wounded by each other. In view of the close human relationship which marriage represents, however, this means a corresponding degree of potential or real injustice and wrong that can be inflicted upon each other. This goes to such lengths that it appears impossible to found a marriage exclusively upon *eros*, even when one deliberately and rightly avoids regarding *eros* as being colored only by sex. Here Christian ethics can only protest emphatically against the domination of an idolatrized *eros* and make it clear that *eros* not only unlocks men's hearts but also hardens them and that therefore the rise of the individual *eros* also leads at the same time to a new and very modern variant of hardheartedness.

This association between *eros* and hardheartedness certainly justifies us in saying that a complete breakdown of *eros* in a marriage, that is, a disagreement between the two constitutions which has become a torment and is manifesting itself in complete disorganization, can be subsumed under that criterion of hardheartedness which may determine whether an exception exists for granting a divorce. This would certainly be possible only in borderline situations, which is certainly not the case in the "normal" fluctuations in the rhythm of *eros* —and most certainly only when every effort of an understanding, forgiving, and seeking *agape* has failed of its goal. Even in this case the admission that hardheartedness plays a part in the marital crisis —and not only the hardheartedness of the *other* partner!—will be concerned that this kind of breakdown be not interpreted naturalistically, simply attributed to, and covered up with, the cloak of the so-called law of *eros,* and thus withdrawn from the demands of God's commandment. The fact that the individual *eros* plays a part in the situation only produces new variations of the relationship set forth in the New Testament between the "real" and the "strange" will of God, the *voluntas Dei propria* and *aliena,* but it does not do away with this understanding of God's will, it does not annul it in the name of the supposedly completely new situations in which the much touted "modern man" finds himself.

We must remain true to our constant purpose of bringing historically changed situations, which cannot be found in direct form in the Bible, into relationship with the biblical *kerygma* even when—as in the case of the individual *eros*—this results in an aggravated problem. Here too we must deal seriously with the realization that fundamentally there are no exceptional "new situations," but despite the unquestioned profound changes that have taken place, only variations on the old theme that man who was created for God goes on seeking his own selfish ends, while God nevertheless bears with him in patience and seeks him wherever he is to be found. The medium in which and with the aid of which man seeks himself and practices his *amor sui* can change. It can be the Jews' desire for a sign and the Greeks' wisdom (I Cor. 1:22), but it can also be the individual *eros.* In any case, however, it is always a gift and a talent, and thus a *chance* that he is given, on which man breaks down and goes wrong. *Eros* too is a gift, a talent committed to us, a chance. He who rejects, devilizes, and relegates it on principle to a pseudo-Christian catalogue of vices simply because it is abused has failed to give it its Christian interpretation and turned himself into a catchpole of a non-Christian philosopheme.

11. The fact that the new situation in the history of *eros* still remains under the claim and the judgment of the order of creation becomes clear from another point of view. We said that divorce as a regulation of necessity [*Notordnung*] arises when in an individual case the indissoluble "one-flesh" relationship of man and wife (Gen. 2:24) is not congruent with the order of creation on which this oneness is founded. It can turn out, therefore, that it was obviously *not God* who joined these two together, but rather that it was Moira

(fate) and Tyche (fortune) who were involved here, causing the corresponding errors and confusions. Nevertheless, this admission cannot mean that the order of creation does not apply to such cases and that this individual case falls outside of its province. On the contrary, the possibly justified conclusion that God did not join these two together can mean only that a marriage so entered into was not in accord with the order of creation, not only as it proceeded, but right from the start, and that therefore the unfulfilled demand of the order of creation becomes a judgment. So even from this point of view divorce is always wrong, not, indeed, because the wrong lies in the act of divorce itself and therefore would become less heinous or not occur at all if the act were left undone, but rather because the act of divorce is only a symptom of the condition of the marriage itself. In other words, by admitting their mistake the participants cannot imply that they were outside the order of creation and therefore immune to the commandments of God, that they were acting, as it were, in a realm beyond good and evil and hence that their case was only "psychoanalytically" relevant, falling within the competence of the "physician" (who, of course, can never be a judge!) rather than that of the "priest."

No; even that which one may call simple human error and not necessarily willful carelessness or even blameworthy infatuation does not exonerate from the charge of having failed to satisfy the claim of the order of creation (even though there are naturally many different degrees of culpability). For those who stand before God (*coram Deo*) the consciousness of guilt also becomes more intense as a marriage, which had in it the seeds of ruin from the beginning, quite apart from the fact that it is breaking down as an institution, leads to ever-increasing wrongdoing to each other, to tormenting and bullying each other. Here again Jesus' reference to the order of creation, which calls in question all concrete law and everything that is justified by the law—including a justified divorce—and does not allow it to be used as a means of self-justification, makes it impossible ever to regard the breakdown of a marriage as a merely psychological and thus an ethically neutral problem. *Thus the injunction of Jesus is immediate to every age; only the way it is applied and the form of its competency varies in different times.*

12. The fact that a marriage which is breaking and was headed for breakdown from the beginning is subject to the demand and judgment of the order of creation and thus constitutes guilt implies a theological concept of guilt which cannot be adequately expressed in legal terms and is not justiciable in the sense of our being able to formulate it in a possible divorce law. This difficulty of formulating a legal concept of guilt,[6] especially in connection with the divorce law, expresses itself particularly in the way in which the law is obliged to bring the factor of guilt into play.

One way in which the law may introduce the factor of guilt is by interpreting the special situation in which the marriage was entered into as a kind of exonerating misfortune and thus accepting a form of incompatibility [*Zerrüttung*] or nullity in the marriage which at bottom has no affinity with the question of guilt. An extreme example of such exceptional situations which practically prevent the legal question of guilt from rising at all would be the "marriages by proxy" [*Ferntrauungen*] which were possible during World War II.[7] In the extraordinary situation caused by the war couples entered into marriage when they had hardly learned to know each other personally and the question whether they were suited to each other undoubtedly could not be explored with the due amount of care. Even the act of marriage itself could be executed at a distance. Here the questionableness of a marriage so entered into need not be seen only in the fact that financial benefits or other security motives may possibly have been the controlling factor. The peculiarly intensive desire for security, warmth, and solidarity that is felt in the face of death and destruction may well have been the motive. In the realm of law the divorce of a marriage of this kind which under later normal conditions of life turns out to be a mistake can no more be regarded from the point of view of guilt than a divorce which proves to be unavoidable because of "estrangement" after years of imprisonment as a prisoner of war. In this case for the judge the amoral factors of fate must so greatly outweigh those of possible guilt that the question of legal guilt becomes almost irrelevant. In order to avoid misunderstanding, it should be explicitly stated that it is also quite impossible to define theologically the "guilt before God" which is operative here and it certainly cannot be stated in generalized terms. Here there will be a whole gamut of forms of

---

[6] Cf. the chapter on law in the forthcoming volume of *ThE*.
[7] Dölle, *op. cit.*, pp. 10 ff.

guilt which can hardly be defined by the persons themselves much less by someone on the outside and of which the Christian involved can speak only in the form of the petition that God may reveal even his "hidden faults," which actually are hidden until the Day of Judgment (Ps. 19:13, 130:3; Job 9:3).

But the law may also introduce the guilt angle by weighing up the guilt of the one against the other in the marriage and dissolving the marriage by deciding that one is guilty and the other innocent. It is true, of course, that there will be cases in which it will be possible to ascertain that the guilt lies preponderantly or even wholly in one of the partners. And yet this endeavor to calculate the guilt has a very definite limitation, the theological significance of which is immediately discernible, but which must evoke certain legal reflections:

Even if the legally definable guilt of the one partner is clearly established—say on the ground of willful desertion of the family or proved permanent adultery—there is still the ethical—and therefore largely nonjudiciable!—question whether this proved desertion of the marriage may not be a reaction to a deeper insufficiency in the other partner—his incapability to be erotically attractive or to create a homelike atmosphere or to provide certain nonrational conditions for communication.

The pastor who is given an insight into the intimate sphere of a marriage can therefore arrive at a completely different point of view with regard to the guilt involved from that of the judge who must necessarily seek to focus his judgment upon the external facts. For the same reason the examination of divorce papers, which is often requested when divorced persons come for remarriage by the church, convey no real clarity with regard to the question of guilt (quite apart from the fact that often the recorded grounds for divorce have for pragmatic reasons been obscured, retouched, and sometimes attributed to one of the partners with the collusion of both). As a general rule the person who looks deeper will find that in every case *both* are involved in the guilt of a broken marriage and that the outwardly innocent or less guilty party is more at fault in the breakdown of the marriage than the other. The general impossibility of defining marital guilt in legal terms becomes even more hopeless as the partners involved are more differentiated and the stronger the irrational factors become in highly developed individualities.

This is not to say that the juristic concept of guilt is simply to be ruled out and set aside in favor of the mere principle of incompatibility. If we are rather inclined to let it stand, subject to the necessary limitations, this is not because it cannot bring out the actual guilt—to say nothing of the theological guilt which is on principle nonjusticiable—but only because to give up in principle the concept of guilt would mean that marriage could be manipulated at will, with all the unforeseeable consequences this would entail. Then it would be possible for the partners to separate simply because they no longer like each other and then after a suitable interval make application for divorce on account of incompatibility. It is obvious that marriage, even from the legal point of view, is of too high a value to be left to this degree of arbitrary manipulation. Therefore the juristic guilt concept—and this is precisely its limitation within the marriage law—has less a diagnostic than a prophylactic importance: its significance is that of a deterrent and it safeguards the weaker or "more innocent" party against flagrant arbitrariness on the part of the other person.

And yet this implies a certain depreciation of the juristic use of the guilt concept and a certain preference for a stronger consideration of the point of view which emphasizes the brokenness or incompatibility of the marriage. To find this stated in a theological ethics may occasion surprise and perhaps resentment, since theology seems to require a stronger emphasis upon the idea of guilt. And as a matter of fact it does; except that it denies that its radical understanding of guilt can ever be adequately expressed, or even expressed in remote analogies, in terms of law. On the contrary, its pastoral experience reinforces its thesis that one-sided emphasis of the divorce law upon the guilt concept must inevitably lead to hypocrisy and, what is more, to more than shameful prying and spying. The question of guilt in the full sense of the word does not lie in the competence of the law, but rather in that of the pastor, who is concerned with the healing of a collapsing marriage from the point of view of the Law and the Gospel. (To be sure, there are also certain humanistic counterparts of the office of the pastor!) Here too the guilt question emerges within the framework of a call to repentance, which responds *in* the sphere of the law, but which can never be institutionalized by the law.

The question how the law can handle this limiting concept of guilt in detail goes beyond the competence of a theological ethics. We may, however, suggest as an example one wrong way which obviously transgresses the limits of the legal concept of guilt and which has been, and to some extent still is, controversial in the course of the efforts to revise the laws concerning the family in the German Federal Republic.

This wrong way expresses itself in the provision that a marriage may be divorced in exceptional cases because of incompatibility, but that "if the fault for the incompatibility rests upon one of the spouses or predominantly upon one of them, only the other spouse can sue for divorce."[8] In this case the prejudicated question of guilt would already determine the

---

[8] Dölle, *op. cit.*, pp. 26 f., 32 f.

possibility of the action itself. Besides, whether the guilt lay on one side or predominantly on one side could undoubtedly—if it were thus accepted as settled in advance—be understood only in the sense of crass marital delinquencies. Since these would disqualify persons from initiating divorce proceedings, there can be no possibility, in the proceedings which are thus estopped, of determining whether and to what extent these marital delinquencies may not have arisen from the conditions which are to be laid, possibly wholly or partially, to the charge of the *other* partner. It is, of course, apparent what the legislation intends to accomplish by this possible refusal of the right to bring suit. It is seeking to prevent the abuse of Section 55 of the marriage law, according to which either partner can appeal for divorce if the domestic relationship has been dissolved for three years and there is not hope of restoring a relationship in accord with the nature of marriage because of a deep, irreparable breakdown of the marital relationship. If this provision were taken by itself, it would be possible for one of the partners simply to desert the other in order to sue for divorce after three years. But this would mean that the very existence of marriage could be manipulated arbitrarily and at will and that this would give way to a practice which we said would not do justice to marriage as a legal entity [*Rechtsgut*]. But in order to prevent this abuse, is the legislator's only recourse this questionable device of granting the right to sue only to the innocent, or possibly only seemingly innocent, party? The law provides other possible ways of preventing willful and culpable manipulation of marriage. In order that the guilty or predominantly guilty party may not break up the marriage by means of the three-year separation clause, the other party can contest the divorce, if the plaintiff has been wholly or at least essentially to blame for the breakdown of the marriage (though this is something which could be shown with *relative* clarity only in a court action!).

In order that the question of guilt which here comes into play may not in turn be manipulated and made a means of tactical exploitation (by way, for example, of the other party contesting the divorce merely from spite, desiring to make a new life impossible for the partner, and instructing his counsel to play upon the guilt theme), the legislation provides the possibility that this objection on the part of the accused and less guilty partner may be disregarded if "in the light of a proper evaluation of the nature of marriage and the whole relationship of the couple there is no moral justification for upholding the marriage" (Sec. 48, par. 2). It must be granted that here the minimal legal requirements for the consideration of the question of guilt are fulfilled and also that they have not been overstepped. It must also be granted that this upholds the "nature" of marriage over against the concept which makes it an arbitrary and therefore manipulable contract. Accordingly, the rights of the relatively innocent party, insofar as secular law can deal with this task, remain safeguarded as far as is at all possible.

On the other hand it is a theologically unjustifiable curtailment of the concept of incompatibility [*Zerrüttungsgesichtspunkt*], and one that goes in the direction of legalizing (in the theological sense) marriage as an institution, when the revision of Section 48 declares that the accused party's contesting of the divorce shall *always* be determinative—except when it is shown to be a "misuse of the law." By means of this nuance the outward appearance of what is really a broken marriage can be maintained almost at will and thus the door is opened to the decadent phenomena which are familiar in countries where no divorce whatsoever is allowed (nonlegalized second marriages with the corresponding consequences for the children who are born of such illegal "marriages").

Here a Catholic view of marriage, which may be granted tolerance within its limitations, may have been carried over into the sphere of secular law. Where this legally codified view is not confronted with another denominational view which compels it to make adjustments it must inevitably lead to bad conscience and institutional falsehood.

The technical legal possibility, which could theoretically avoid this difficulty of conscience in individual cases—in which the plea is shown to be a "misuse of the law" and therefore becomes null and void—can hardly be realized in practice. What is most disastrous, however, is that the question of a real marriage is left out of account in the divorce problem and thus the marriage which is artificially maintained and formally recognized becomes just as much a lie as, say, the newly entered marriage which is not legally valid and even punishable by the law and therefore must inevitably take on dishonest forms of hypocrisy.

Apart from the difficulty of applying the ordinary legal concept of guilt to the personal relationship of marriage, marriage exhibits other peculiar features of a legal kind which are almost without analogy. Thus it is true that marriage has the legal status of a contract. This contract, however, does not specify mutual rights and obligations, as other contracts do, but rather contains a legal personal relationship, which, of course, implies rights and obligations. The act of marriage touches upon the sphere of law with respect to its form and its content.

It touches upon the sphere of law with respect to its *form* insofar as every contract, which relates to the regulating of real things or property and not to the mutual relations of the persons themselves, contains clauses which formulate the conditions under which the contract remains valid and failing which the contract expires or is altered. In a marriage, however, the nuptialities do not swear their loyalty in this conditional sense.

That is to say it would be unthinkable that the marriage contract should contain a clause providing that it was valid only as long as neither of the two committed adultery or committed some other grave act contrary to the marriage. It is true that this possibility is dealt with in the divorce laws. But it is not taken into account in the marriage contract itself. A contingent cause for divorce is not dealt with as a possibility and hence the corresponding consequences are not defined in the contract. This indicates that divorce is not a possibility that lies in the nature of marriage itself and that therefore it cannot be provided for in the marriage contract, although in other contracts every conceivable contingency is anticipated and usually explicitly stated. In this form, without conditions, the marriage contract touches upon the sphere of law.

It touches upon the sphere of law also with respect to its content, at least so far as the Christian understanding of it is concerned. For the peculiarly distinctive thing that happens in the marriage contract is that "God himself is also at work in this act of creating community in that he causes man and wife to become one flesh."[9] Only because this concept is reflected in our secular marriage law, only because it is present as a memory, a tradition, or an immediately present universal norm of law, is marriage even in present-day forms of law granted privileges which could never have been derived from its mere contractual character and its similarity to all other kinds of contract. Perhaps this is the only way to make it clear that the marriage contract is simply not subject to recall— even by consent of both partners—and that it contains no conditions whatsoever on the basis of which it could be terminated.

This exceptional position of the marriage contract on the borderline of the sphere of law is owing to the fact that a third party who is beyond our control is thought of as participating in the community of the contracting parties: God. Normally, he is not officially mentioned by name in this connection. He may appear, however, in many different ciphers or symbols (such as the moral point of view, the general consciousness of standard, the norm of tradition, the common sense of Western culture, etc.). He is always present, however, as the representative of that which is beyond our control.

Therefore one may perhaps also say that the divorce decree handed down by the judge does not have the significance of an efficient action (as if he or anybody else could ever dissolve a marriage!), but rather that it has declaratory significance. Thus it can only purport to say: What has happened here is the extreme exceptional case of what can happen in a fallen world: a marriage has collapsed, it has been wrecked by one or both of the partners, and both have therefore divorced themselves. A marriage

⁹ Dombois, *Materialdienst* (1962), 1, p. 2.

can be dissolved only by those who entered into it in the first place. (In both instances the name of God is connected with the decree in a different way: in one case it is the Lord of the order of creation, in the other it is the Lord of "order of necessity.") The judge merely declares and legalizes the fact that the divorce exists (or he denies it). But he himself is not the ontic "divorcer."

13. The reasons why the co-operation of the church is desirable in the divorce of a marriage which it has solemnized we have discussed in connection with the problem and the modalities of civil marriage.[10] This could be only a pastoral form of co-operation. The spouses cannot evade the fact that they requested and received the blessing of God upon their marriage vows. The "court" which pronounced this blessing in the name of God should be able to appeal to them on this basis, bind them by virtue of this blessing, and by instruction and counsel leave nothing undone to keep persons who are having marital difficulties within the sphere of this blessing. In the remarriage of divorced persons, where the church faces the difficult question whether it can properly pronounce this blessing once more and declare this second marriage one that is joined before God, this pastoral co-operation in the divorce of the first marriage can provide a safeguard against the idea that the church is not taking its own blessing seriously and is simply repeating it arbitrarily and uncritically.

## EXCURSUS 1: THE DIVORCE OF MINISTERS

In parentheses as it were, we mention the special problem of the divorce of a bearer of the ministerial office. Since the ministerial office has no special "character" within the universal priesthood, the bearer cannot be subject to special stipulations from that point of view. The fact that he is nevertheless subject to a special demand in this particular area can be justified only on the ground that his message and especially his performance of marriage services threaten to become unworthy of belief coming from his mouth, if his own marriage is broken. To hear the words ". . . till death us do part" spoken as a vow by one who himself could not or did not satisfy that obligation can provoke offense and seriously in-

[10] Cf. also Schlatter, *op. cit.,* p. 400.

crease the already threatening danger that the church's blessing will be misunderstood as a mere conventional ceremony. If, however, the pastor has been guilty of a breakdown in his marriage in a way that is discernible and reprehensible to men, then not only the possibility of creating this personal offense but also the respect of the church for the institution of marriage demands that it no longer permit him to exercise his office in its name. In this as in every other conceivable case it must examine and decide such questions in a disciplinary action which must not be merely a formal legal trial but also a matter of pastoral concern and responsibility.

But even in the case where from the legal point of view the minister is the "innocent" party in the divorce, the continuation of his office presents him and the church which has commissioned him with problems whose gravity dare not be underestimated. For quite apart from the theological questionability of this juristic concept of innocence (which we dealt with above), it is legitimate in the case of the bearer of a public office to take into account the "outward point of view." This is far more than a matter of dressing up outward appearances. The bearer of a public office is not in a position to make his motives plausible and, what is more, reveal the background of his intimate personal life. On the contrary, he is in a position where the facts as they are now known to the public (as in the case of a divorce) are at the mercy of whatever interpretation the public may put upon them and he has no possibility of controlling the judgments people make before or after the fact and preventing them from casting doubt upon the credibility of his office and his message.

On the other hand it would be a spiritually intolerable form of legalism if a minister who is living in a broken marriage were to be compelled, unlike all other Christians, to maintain the appearance of a marriage for the sake of his office. In this case legalism would lead to a degree of hypocrisy and duplicity which would really jeopardize the credibility of his message, even if nobody takes notice of this jeopardy.

Therefore in every case—including cases where the minister is declared "innocent" in civil law—it is obvious that the minister must give up his office and should be urged to do so. If, for whatever reasons, this conclusion is not drawn, then at least a transfer is unavoidable, since in a new environment where the case is not known there will be no occasion for uncontrollable and scandal-begetting speculations. In no case, however, dare a bearer of the ministerial office who is divorced without any fault which is discernible and reprehensible to men and who gives up his office for the sake of the dignity of the ministry be defamed by his church and considered unfit to become an office-bearer in some other area of the church's work.

## EXCURSUS 2: THE DIVORCE OF POLYGAMOUS MARRIAGES[11]

On the mission field the question repeatedly arises of what is to be done with regard to the baptism of those who are living in polygamous marriages, especially men (chieftains, etc.) who have a "harem." As far as we know, this question has—curiously—never been made the subject of explicitly theological reflection. It appears to have been left to improvisation or to a dogmatical legalism which makes the reduction of polygamy to monogamy a requirement for baptism. In the face of this obvious aporia, a systematic theological ethics cannot claim the competence to say the last word on this subject. To do so would require—apart from everything else—a thoroughgoing, detailed empirical knowledge, which would probably lead us to differentiations determined by place and time. We are here presented with a very considerable task in the scientific study of missions. We can mention only a number of theological criteria which would have to be determinative in the solution of the problem.

First, however, we may take our bearings upon three observations made by Walter Freytag in a book which (at least theologically) is not yet outdated.[12]

1. Everywhere polygamy is abandoned very soon after Christianization. Even in cases which are more complicated and in which an invasion of the structure of ancient customs is subject to special difficulties the trend toward monogamy prevails. The reason for this is the position it gives to the woman as a person. *Agape* as a bond of fidelity tallies with monogamy.

2. The personal nature of the bond manifests itself also in the fact that after Christianization the purchase price for the bride is abandoned. Often in the first period after conversion the bridegroom's gift or the bride price is retained;[13] and the custom is obviously tolerated by the church because it can be a kind of guarantee of the stability of the marriage. For since the tribe of the bridegroom supplies the bride price and the tribe of the bride receives it, it constitutes a sign that the marriage is not merely the coupling of two individuals, but rather that the two tribes are the contracting parties. Thus there is inherent in the marriage something objective which goes beyond likes and dislikes and certainly beyond the inconstancy

---

[11] Cf. Section on "Monogamy-Polygamy," pp. 86 ff.
[12] Walter Freytag, *Die junge Christenheit im Umbruch des Ostens* (1938).
[13] *Ibid.*, pp. 240 ff.

of fluctuating emotions. The marriage thus rests upon the basis of supra-personal communities.

It is exceedingly significant, however, that in no case does the custom of the bride price continue *permanently* after Christianization, but is gradually abolished. There are two reasons for this. First, because the bride price is a selfish thing and cannot be conceived of in personal terms; for it gives the larger right to the one who has the most money. The man is accordingly not a partner because of his person but rather as a bearer of property. Thus he can *also* regard his wife only as a piece of property, as something to be acquired, and therefore as an object. Second, after conversion there is a regard for the personhood of the partner and thus a bond of fidelity which makes it possible to do away with the guarantee of the tribe as a kind of additional legal safeguard. So here, too, the Law "came in," to use a phrase of Paul's (Rom. 5:20; Gal. 3:19), until the Gospel itself made them free, i.e., made possible a free relationship of two persons based upon *agape*. It is tolerated as Law by the mission churches only as long as the Gospel of personhood has not been sufficiently developed to provide the basis of a new existence. As soon as the Gospel is in force, it is no longer the clan or the tribe that assumes responsibility for the marriage and its maintenance, but rather the Community, the fellowship of persons which is engrafted in the body of Christ.

The handling of the bride price is significant for our theme, the question of the divorce of polygamous marriages upon entrance into Christianity. It shows that the question of the bride price was not dealt with legalistically and in abrupt doctrinaire fashion, but rather allowed to mature and solve itself through experience under the Gospel, so that it became a task to be worked out in responsible freedom. We shall keep in view this reference to our problem.

3. Just as the younger Christian churches turn away from the old polygamous or nonpersonal tribal ties on the basis of the personhood bestowed by Christ, so they also recognize the opposite threat to marriage which presses in upon them from the secularized West. An educated Batak reports[14] that the young Christian church is not only turning against the nonpersonal pre-Christian forms of marriage, which he characteristically calls the "cinema marriage," and which is turning the heads of many young people in the congregations. Eroticism, this Batak says, is not the foundation of marriage. Christian marriage is based upon something deeper: upon fidelity. Thus he plays off the personal element as it emerges under Christ's dominion of the conscience not only against the old tribal customs, against polygamy, etc., but just as strongly against the eroticism

[14] Freytag, *ibid.*, p. 242.

of the West. And when he says in this connection, "We Bataks still need the support of the old ties," this surely can be understood only in the sense that in situations where the young seedlings of faith have not yet grown sufficiently strong to guarantee the personal relationship the law of the pre-Christian tribal ties must be called upon to help keep out the neo-pagan lawlessness of complete nonpersonalism. The old ties to gods and tribe are better than the nihilistic eroticism of secularism; for they at least contain a preservative *nomos,* whereas "cinema love" is subject to the instability of emotions and egotism. Here again there is evidence of a willingness to allow something to grow or to wither away under the power of the Gospel, but not to resort to legalism and command it into or out of existence. The new life—and also the new order—must arise out of the freedom of the children of God; otherwise what grows out of it will be, not children, but slaves. And then it could turn out that even the most Christian order would not be expressing the new fellowship between God and man but would rather infringe upon it and destroy it from within.

We proceed, then, to draw from this the consequences which would have to govern the handling of the question of monogamy and polygamy on the mission field.

1. It should be said right from the beginning that monogamy arises not under the Law, but rather under the Gospel. The tendency toward monogamy grows in proportion as men grow into Christ and thus into *agape* and thus again into loving understanding.[15]

2. If this conception is correct, it has very considerable importance for the position to be taken with regard to the polygamy of candidates for baptism. Because monogamy cannot be interpreted as "Law" and also is not to be found in the Bible as an express command, because it is rather only a Christian custom (though indeed a spiritually grounded one), it dare not be made a *conditio sine qua non* for becoming a Christian. (This must at all events be said with respect to the special exceptional situations the possible continuance of which we cannot judge.)

The fact that monogamy arises not under the Law, but under the Gospel, means that it must grow as a "fruit"; it must arise out of the *agape* which is determined by the Gospel.[16] The task of the mission is not to preach monogamy, but rather the Gospel—though, of course, in the expectation that then monogamy too will come into being. If in its preaching of the Gospel the problem of monogamy should appear—and why should it not be allowed to be mentioned?—it will appear only as an

---

[15] On this idea of growth cf. Eph. 4:15; II Pet. 3:18; also *ThE* I, § 1097 ff.; R. Hermann, *Luthers These "Gerecht und Sünder zugleich"* (1930), pp. 234 ff.

[16] On the significance of this "growth" see *ThE* I, §254 ff.

illustration that demonstrates in concrete terms what *agape* means and what its consequences are.

3. If monogamy follows only as a kind of by-product from the preaching of the Gospel and in this way becomes an essential part of a Christian existence, then it must be understood as a goal of a growth. But if it is made a condition of entrance into Christianity and bound up with the act of baptism, it acquires the character of the Law. And in this case, too, the Law kills, because it destroys the old order instead of leaving room for the trust that under the Gospel something new will grow and thus also develop "organically." It is well known how destructive have been the effects of certain missionary measures which have been carried out without distinguishing between Law and Gospel and therefore have all too often identified European customs with Christianity itself. This kind of illegitimate and unchristian violence done to native customs usually has to be paid for in the rebellion that comes in the second and third generations.[17]

4. Monogamy which is thus wrongly and unjustly raised to the level of Law also does violence to *agape* and robs it of its normative character. This is evident in the fact that when monogamy is put under the rule of Law its meaning and intent is reversed. That is to say, whereas monogamy can be motivated and determined only by *agape* (in the sense of accepting and entering into the monogamous sex nature of the wife), under the rule of a Law which is not guided and "prepared for" by the Gospel (in the sense of the third use of the Law)[18] it becomes a destructive force which breaks down the existing relationships and responsibilities.

This finds concrete illustration on the mission field. When monogamy is made a prerequisite of baptism this means that a candidate for baptism who is living in a polygamous marriage must abandon all his wives except one. Quite apart from the temptation for him to retain only the youngest and disown the older ones, this demand would work a cruel hardship upon the wives who are dismissed. In most of the existing tribal structures they would be left without any ties or protection whatsoever and in most cases delivered over to prostitution. Moreover, it would sever inner ties which can develop with a polygamous marriage despite its questionable character.

5. Therefore the only possible general rule would seem to be that existing polygamous marriages may be allowed to continue when a person is baptized and that it must be left to the freedom of the candidate

[17] Cf. Søe, *op. cit.*, pp. 294 f.
[18] Cf. *ThE* I, §552 ff., 624 ff.; W. Joest, *Gesetz und Freiheit* (1956), pp. 21 ff.

whether and to what extent he can justify the dissolution of his polygamous marriage. It would perhaps be in line with the law of growth
which is operative under the Gospel that only the unmarried candidate
for baptism would be obligated by the order not to enter a polygamous
marriage. This presupposes that the preaching of the Gospel goes along
with the baptism and that it will "result" in an understanding of the
meaning of monogamy, all the more since it may appear as an illustration
of the Christian concept of personhood which is rooted in *agape*.

In conclusion we may at least mention an objection which could be
raised against the conception which we have here set forth by an ethno-
logically oriented anthropology. It would be possible to call in question
the validity of our assertion that the two sexes have different tendencies,
one polygamous, the other monogamous—which constitutes the foundation of our conception—by pointing to empirical facts. These facts undoubtedly show that there is great variability and plasticity in the nature
and behavior of both sexes.[19] After all, there is such a thing as polyandry
too! The answer to these objections would be that distinctiveness of the
two sexes, especially the female sex, which we have characterized in
something that flows only from a particular concept of personhood. Until
individuality has developed there can hardly be a personal tie to another
individuality, any more than there can be a doctrine of individual im-
mortality where there is no concept of the individual.[20] It is true that
this concept of individuality can arise outside of Christianity, but there is
no doubt at all that it does arise under the norm of *agape* as a realization of man's *dignitas aliena,* or as Adolf von Harnack put it, the "infinite
value of the human soul."

## 2. THE REMARRIAGE OF DIVORCED PERSONS

Whether the church can approve the remarriage of divorced persons and thus grant its blessing to a second marriage depends in the
first place upon whether it even recognizes the possibility of divorce as
a borderline case in the sense of a regulation of necessity, whether, for
example, it recognizes that there can be a case in which it was *not*
God who joined the couple together, but rather that it was the persons

[19] Cf. the section "Eros and Agape" above; also Margaret Mead, *Sex and
Temperament in Three Primitive Societies* (New York: William Morrow & Co.,
1955); W. G. Sumner, *The Science of Society* (New Haven: Yale University
Press, 1927), Vol. I.
[20] Cf. W. Baetke, *Art und Glaube der Germanen* (Hamburg, 1934).

themselves who wrongly or carelessly, mistakenly or blindly, but in any case contrary to the order of creation, joined themselves together. We have endeavored to justify this possibility as a borderline case.

Second, the church's approval of the remarriage of divorced persons depends upon whether it can overcome the no which was spoken by Jesus or the primitive church on this question. In the exegetical sections of this chapter we pointed out the intention the Gospel is pursuing when it forbids marriage to a woman who has been divorced by her husband (only this kind of divorce had relevance at that time in history). If a man marries a woman who has been divorced because of her *porneia,* he is by his marriage sanctioning what she has done. If he marries a woman who has been arbitrarily divorced, he is thereby approving an illegitimate situation. And to recognize an adultery is itself adultery.

The sin of such a remarriage is therefore not based upon the fact that it is in itself inconsistent with the order of creation. On the contrary, this question does not arise at all. The sin of a remarriage consists rather in the fact that it sanctions another sin, namely, the breaking of the order of creation through *porneia* which destroys marriage or through arbitrary dismissal of the wife.

It follows from this that the bindingness of the prohibition of remarriage depends upon whether, under completely changed conditions, that is, in view of an entirely altered divorce law, a remarriage is subject to the same verdict of sanctioning the sinful breakdown of a previous marriage. This alone is the legitimate theological question. In any case, it rules out any "legalistic" interpretation of the rule which obtained in the primitive church and which was partly stamped by the particular conditions of the time and was intended for a special purpose.[21] And it also rules out the acceptance of a theologically unjustified ontology of marriage which would inevitably lead to legalism.[22]

It is not necessary here to examine whether and to what extent the

---

[21] "Can the church today in particular situations and in certain cases allow a second marriage, which the primitive church obviously did not permit? In principle the answer must be yes; for the precept of the primitive church cannot be elevated to the status of a law established once and for all, any more than the primitive church itself converted the words of Jesus into such a law." G. Bornkamm, *op. cit.,* p. 285.

[22] F. K. Schumann, *RGG* II, col. 338.

right granted by the law of the state to divorced persons to enter into a new marriage can morally sanction the divorce that precedes it— even if it was the result of a *guilty* breaking of the marriage. As long as the law continues to accept, however imperfectly and minimally, the relevance of the guilt concept and thus reserves to itself the right to designate guilty divorced persons as such, it continues to erect in the sphere of law certain barriers against the notion that divorce or anything that is contrary to marriage is sanctioned and that divorce is simply a restoration of a *tabula rasa.* A legal divorce does not contain within itself the ethical legitimation of the divorce. A certain reserve which society entertains with regard to divorced persons—unjust or Pharisaic as it may be in some cases—is a symptom of the fact that a distinction is being made between the two.

The question whether the law is morally sanctioning the divorce of a previous marriage and the guilt that caused it by permitting remarriage is therefore not to be answered with a simple yes.

But this is not the real question at all. The question is rather whether the *church* can associate itself with such a second marriage as being a marriage that is permitted by God, entered into in his sight, and one that is to be blessed in his name, and, in case it does see its way clear to do this, what it can do to combat the cheapening of this "repetition" of its blessing.

The answer to this question depends upon whether the blessing of the marriage of divorced persons in the sense of an act which condemned by the New Testament must have the effect of "sanctioning" the divorce which preceded it and whether the church is therefore simply acting on the basis of questionable facts.

This question is relatively easy to answer in theory, but very difficult in practice. It is easy to answer theoretically, since in principle the church, through the *preaching* which accompanies its act, has it in its power to prevent the assumption that it is sanctioning the divorce and to set the previous divorce under the judgment of the order of creation.

Wolfgang Trillhaas[23] would dispute this argument. It is true that he grants "the inevitability of dissolving marriages which have become un-

[23] *Op. cit.,* p. 269.

tenable in concrete individual cases." Nor "can the remarriage of divorced persons be denied." Trillhaas, however, desires that such marriages should not have the church's "approbation . . . as if they were marriages according to the Christian rule and in the Christian sense." Such marriages can only be tolerated without granting to them a Christian wedding. In support of this position Trillhaas presents, in addition to exegetical reasons (which, however, have not been thought through hermeneutically), the main argument that, since marriage is indissoluble, the only thing that exists is a "separation" within the marriage which continues to exist even if it has been dissolved by law.[24] He is therefore pleading, though of course with different reasons, for the Catholic distinction between "divorce" and "separation." In this way the possibility of a reconciliation remains open. But such a reconciliation "is fundamentally and permanently excluded once a divorced person marries another person."[25] Thus the remarriage of divorced persons makes the separation a divorce in the strict sense. This fact must prevent the church from approving the second marriage because it would be identical with sanctioning of an irreversible divorce. Undoubtedly correct as Trillhaas is in his statement that remarriage puts the seal of finality upon the preceding divorce, yet it seems unrealistic to assume that without this seal the possibility of reconciliation and hence the resumption or renewal (after a legal divorce) of the earlier marriage actually exists.

It is self-evident that the church can have the freedom to give its "approbation" only if it is convinced that the previous marriage is "irreparably" broken. It is true that there are cases in which it is impossible to determine this with ultimate certainty, but there can be no doubt that there are also cases in which this certainty does exist. This is true, for example, in the very numerous cases in which the marriage has been destroyed by the interference of a third party, resulting in another marriage. Shall the remaining "innocent" divorced person be prevented once and for all from entering into a new marriage even in this case in which the question of reconciliation has become baseless and in which Trillhaas' basic argument against remarriage has broken down?

We mention this possible kind of case not for the sake of subtle casuistry but because this case must inevitably compel Trillhaas to show his theological colors. That is to say, in the way in which he would teach us how to decide this case it would inevitably appear whether it was really only the intention to secure a possible reconciliation which was preventing him from approving a second marriage of divorced persons (in which

[24] *Ibid.*, p. 268.
[25] *Ibid.*, p. 269.

case he could grant approbation, since, after all, reconciliation is now out of the question), or whether underlying his position there is a certain "ontology of marriage" in the sense formulated by F. K. Schumann—an ontology, by the way, which we have sought to prove exegetically questionable.

Thus, while theoretically we believe that through its preaching and pastoral care the church has the possibility of preventing the scandalous impression that it is giving a "cheap" approbation when it blesses the marriage of divorced persons and thus denying the claim of the order of creation, it must be admitted that the practical realization of this possibility gives rise to many questions and that it is difficult to incorporate it into general regulations of church law.

The determination of this question must begin with the premise (discussed above) that as a rule the blame for the breakdown of the preceding marriage lies with *both* partners. Consequently, only in rare cases are men capable of defining even approximately the proportion of fault between them or of assigning the blame only upon one of the two partners. Likewise, the statements of the divorce court concerning guilt or innocence can give us no true information concerning the backgrounds of the breakdown. Aside from relatively rare exceptions in which we have before us a request for marriage from a divorced person who from an ethical (and therefore more than merely legal) point of view was "innocently" divorced, the church will always have to start with the guilt of both parties, and therefore it cannot make the legal divorce decree the basis of its own decisions, even when it assigns the guilt to only one of the partners.[26]

But if the church starts with this assumption in making its decision

---

[26] As instances of such relatively clear cases of innocence, which prevent no particular problem for the blessing of a second marriage, the *"Entwurf für eine neue Trauungsagende"* ("Draft of a New Order for Marriage," *5. Ev. Landeskirchentag Württ., Beilage 14,* Nov., 1955, cited hereinafter as *AG;* p. 95) mentions the following: ". . . if a war-bride becomes unfaithful to her husband, who has been subject to long imprisonment as a prisoner of war, and secures a divorce, and the returning husband is thus innocent of breaking the marriage and now desires to enter a new marriage. Or if a husband has wilfully deserted his family and vanished from the country and the deserted wife desires to give her children a better provider and parent. Or if a minor girl is forced by her parents into a marriage with an older man and the relationship goes to pieces because of his selfishness. Or if a marriage can no longer be realized because of the incurable mental illness of one of the partners."

whether it can bless the marriage, then it cannot, without making its blessing and thus its approbation incredible, simply pass over the offense of the fact that a marriage has failed to meet the claim of God's order of creation and that the blessing pronounced upon the previous marriage broke down upon human sin. How can this offense be overcome?

In the studies which have been made on this question,[27] there has been a tendency to recommend a definite ecclesiastical regulation, which on the one hand would provide for a pastoral interview with the couple to awaken a discernment and repentant willingness to accept responsibility for the fault in the first marriage, but would nevertheless withdraw from the pastor the responsibility for making the sole decision with regard to the church's approbation of remarriage. The very earnest reason for this latter provision is that for the sake of integrity of the desired blessing of the marriage every appearance must be avoided that such a matter can be arranged "personally" or by having "connections" or that in any case it can be left to the discretion of the individual instead of being placed in the responsibility of the church which is here acting. Besides this danger of giving a misleading impression, we may also point to the human weakness with which the pastor may be threatened in a situation which can expose him to considerable moral or social pressure but also to the temptation to yield to "human-all-too-human" sympathy.

Because the blessing of a marriage is an institutional act of "the" church, in cases like these, which can obscure the fact that this act is an act of the church as well as the fact that it is bound to the Law and the Gospel, it is most necessary that the decision should not be left to one person, but rather symbolically distinguished as the decision of the church, the congregation of Jesus Christ. The question *how* this can be done, whether a committee of the congregational church council or a superior church office should participate in granting the ap-

---

[27] Besides those in *AG* and numerous similar documents, these studies are to be found primarily in the *"Ordnung des kirchlichen Lebens von christlicher Ehe und kirchlicher Trauung,"* adopted by the General Synod of the United Evangelical Lutheran Church in Germany (VELKD), 1953, and accepted by the Conference of Lutheran Bishops in the same year (*Informationsdienst d. VELKD*, May, 1953, pp. 63 f.). Cf. also *Lutherischer Rundblick*, 1954, 6/7, pp. 79 ff.

proval, is a secondary question of order and not a matter of fundamental principle.

While the direction which the pastoral interview should take and the participation of the church in the decision whether approbation is to be granted are matters which are theologically evident, the question whether the prayer for forgiveness of guilt in the previous marriage, the confession of this guilt, and the granting of absolution require a special liturgical act is one that presents greater difficulties.[28] The difficulty here is that any form which is used must necessarily be general in character and therefore will be only very limitedly appropriate to this kind of highly differentiated case. But any confession of sin, which is to be really serious and not degenerate into a farce or do violence to conscience, can be only general (in which case it is possible in the service of the congregation where it is left to the individual to apply the general statements to his own particular condition) or it can be only special, exposing one's personal life (in which case it belongs to private confession and is under the seal of confession). A hybrid, which is the inevitable result in a form that is drafted for a special case but does not take account of its exceedingly variable individuality, must be wrong in principle.[29] The fact is that the liturgical experiments which have been made in this direction and incorporated in the formularies are thoroughly discouraging examples.

Accordingly, the only thing which can be made an obligatory condition of the church's giving of its blessing to the remarriage of divorced persons is the outcome of the pastoral interview which must be approved by another church authority—without, however, breaking the seal of confession. This approval of the outcome of the pastoral interview could be given only if the couple which desire the blessing are willing to include the breakdown of the previous marriage in their confession of sin and receive forgiveness. The personal character of this pastoral interview, which takes place under the seal of confession and is therefore different from the ordinary premarital interview in which three persons are involved, makes possible a situation in which

---

[28] *AG* presents a form for this, p. 98.

[29] The author must confess that in none of the cases of this kind with which he has been concerned has he been able to use the proposed form.

confession and absolution will not remain at the level of a noncommittal generality.

A symbolical expression of this settling with the past and the possibility of a new beginning under forgiveness would be participation in the Lord's Supper before the remarriage, in which the couple could then relate the general form of confession to their own special form of sin which has been made explicit in the pastoral interview, having been expressly called upon to make this connection. It must be remembered, however, that in the very nature of participation in the Lord's Supper it cannot be made obligatory but can be only a matter of counsel.

Though it is of utmost importance to the church that the blessing of such a second marriage must not impugn the veracity of its teaching concerning marriage and therefore can be granted only under certain demonstrated conditions, it is not possible—as might be desirable in itself—to require that evidence of fulfillment of these conditions must be given publicly to the congregation, but must rather be confined to symbolical acts. Announcements with comments made in church concerning specific cases of this kind and using them to make reference to the essential indissolubility of marriage are undoubtedly impossible in a national church [*Volkskirche*]. For it is more than questionable "whether the condition of our congregations would permit us to presuppose the kind of mature spiritual understanding which would be necessary here in order not actually to provoke Pharisaic pride."[30]

There is one determinative declaration in the Lutheran statement on marriage which is extremely questionable, not only with respect to its use of Scripture (it makes no distinction between seeking a divorce and suffering a divorce, as even Paul does in I Cor. 7:12 ff. when he says that the one who suffers the divorce "is not bound," v. 15), but also with respect to the ontology of marriage which obviously underlies it and evokes the same question which was addressed to Trillhaas above. The statement reads: "The church . . . must bear witness to the fact that the Holy Scriptures require that divorced persons either return to their marriage or remain unmarried. Therefore denial of marriage of divorced persons by the church must be the rule." In any case, this statement cannot appeal

[30] *AG*, p. 97.

to the tradition of the Lutheran Church. We recall the statement in the *Treatise on the Power and Primacy of the Pope*: "Unjust is the tradition which forbids an innocent person to marry after divorce."[31] Schumann quite properly argues from this passage: "If it is 'unjust' to forbid a second marriage to one who is innocently divorced, then one cannot fundamentally deny him the church's blessing upon the second marriage."[32] In any case, this statement is true under the conditions which we have elaborated. Luther expressed himself similarly in his "Christian epithalamium" (an exposition of the seventh chapter of I Corinthians which he wrote in 1523 for the Hereditary Marshal of Saxony Hans Löser and his bride Ursula Portzig): ". . . in these cases in which one spouse forces the other to live unchristianly or deserts him, he is not bound to remain with him. But if he is not bound, he is free. And if he is free, he may take another, just as if his spouse had died."[33] Similarly in his treatise *On Matrimonial Matters,* 1530: "Accordingly, when a spouse breaks the marriage and this can be publicly proved, I could not and would not forbid the other party to have the freedom to be divorced and marry another person. . . ."[34]

Instructive for a practice in the remarriage of divorced persons which was wise both legally and ecclesiastically is the Prussian Common Law and the procedures of the Prussian Church authorities.[35] According to Prussian Common Law, the guilty as well as the innocent party could be remarried without any special permission.[36] The guilty party, however, was not allowed to marry the person on account of whom he had been divorced. And yet by Order of Council, March 15, 1803, it was decreed that the consistories should exercise "wise clemency" in these cases and be guided by the consideration "whether a dispensation might not prevent further immorality."[37] The important thing here is that the general line was established by law and the granting of exceptions was not allowed to soften it but was based upon a special dispensation of the consistories. Here we must recognize as a legitimate legal point of view that the law must keep in mind the question of order and therefore its intention must be that of curbing the threat of immorality even when it must depart

---

[31] *The Book of Concord, The Confessions of the Evangelical Lutheran Church* (Philadelphia: Muhlenberg Press, 1959), p. 333.

[32] *Op. cit.,* col. 338.

[33] *WA* 12, 123.

[34] *WA* 30, 3, 241.

[35] On this see Anneliese Sprengler, *op. cit.,* II.

[36] *Preuss, Landr., Tit.* 1 Tl. II, 732.

[37] P. 270. The text of this Order in Council is printed in P. J. Vogt, *Kirchen-und Eherecht der Katholiken u. Evangelischen i. d. Königl. Preuss. Staaten* (2 Tl., 1857), pp. 20 f.

from its general line by exceptional acts of grace.[38]

The church regulations which set forth pastoral and instructional standards for guidance in dealing with this problem also move within the framework of these legal provisions. Thus the circular order of the Evangelical High Consistory of Berlin, February 11, 1856, says that one cannot suddenly go back to the divorce practice of the sixteenth century. It is a matter of taking careful educational steps in which the present moral conditions—deplorable as they may be—are taken into account. "In any case, the course to be taken is not that of setting up an abstract norm, but rather the practical treatment of concrete individual cases for the healing of a disease which has been developing for centuries."[39] Here we must observe the prudence of a gradual process of education, as is always advisable when a dogmatic problem is carried over into the realm of ethics.[40] Even more precisely in line with this basic principle is the circular order issued to the consistories on February 15, 1895.[41] It speaks first of the "strict line" which appeals to the Holy Scriptures and will admit only adultery and malicious desertion as grounds for divorce. And yet "we have been faced with another line, which also submits in obedience to the Word of God, but finds in it not a law but a principle which is to be applied to the relationships of life with wisdom and gentleness not only for the preservation of the sanctity of marriage, but also for the saving of persons and the upholding of the law. After long and earnest deliberation and in view of the course of history and present conditions in the state and the church, we are convinced that we must take the latter of these two fundamental points of view."

Today we would certainly express what is meant here in more "guarded" theological terms, since we have had some rather bad experiences with the appeal to the "course of history" and similar arguments of natural theology. Nevertheless, anybody who is willing to listen and to see through the theological terminology of that day will very clearly perceive that what is being enunciated here is the theme of "Law and Gospel" and that what they are saying is that in the name of disciplined freedom the procedures of ecclesiastical law must be motivated by pastoral intention.

It is certainly not the political point of view which pursues the "art of the possible" that dictates this gradual procedure, but rather the recog-

---

[38] Cf. the section on the absolutizing of law in the chapter on law elsewhere in the *Theological Ethics*.

[39] In *Aktenstücke aus der Verwaltung des Ev. OKRs,* Bd. 3, 1, pp. 69 ff., Sprengler, *op. cit.,* p. 277.

[40] Cf. *ThE* II, 2, §4341 ff.

[41] Sprengler, *op. cit.,* p. 278.

nition of man's hardness of heart. To be sure, this recognition also has a political side, even a side that affects the policy of the church.

## 3. POSTSCRIPT ON A SPECIAL CASE: MIXED MARRIAGES[42]

Both churches warn against confessional mixed marriages and point out their dangers. It certainly cannot be said without reservations that the main concern is that the parent who belongs to one's own particular denomination may be lost to the church along with the children. In any case, insofar as this motive plays a part it need not be dismissed as mere "propaganda." For this must not be interpreted merely sociologically or in terms of power politics, as if all that the churches cared about was the maintenance and growth of their own denomination. Rather we may doubtless understand it as an expression of the concern to hold the members who are entrusted to their care to the "truth."

It is altogether certain, however, that this is not the sole motive behind this warning against mixed marriages. Probably much stronger is the concern about the inner homogeneity (and thus the stability!) of the marriage which grows out of an unbroken fellowship of faith, and also the concern about a Christian family life and the sharing of a common faith with the children whose education and upbringing should not be distracted and robbed of its clear normative guidance by a difference of faith on the part of the parents or by the compliant indifference of one of the parents.

In *our* situation the problem of mixed marriages is practically the problem of marriage between Protestants and Catholics. And here the problem presents a peculiar difficulty in that here we are confronted with a divergent interpretation of marriage which becomes especially acute in the case of mixed marriages. We have already defined the basic lines of this dissent in our discussion of the Catholic-sacramental view of marriage and the Reformation-"worldly" view. Now we are concerned only with the question of how this dissent becomes actualized at its most neuralgic point, namely, where it must be carried out

[42] Cf. what has been said above in the section on the sacramental interpretation of marriage.

in the face of and within a specific marriage, that is, in a mixed marriage.

What is the view of the Roman Catholic Church with regard to mixed marriages? That is, what consequence does it see as being inherent in its sacramental understanding of marriage for a marriage in which both parties are baptized but only one belongs to the Roman Catholic Church? (We must confine ourselves here to this one focal point of the problem.)

Up to the promulgation of the Code of Canon Law at Pentecost 1918 a marriage between a (Catholic) Christian and a "heretic" was regarded as sacramentally valid. At Pentecost 1918 this was suddenly changed: a mixed marriage not performed by the Catholic Church was decreed to be a nonmarriage, which can be distinguished from concubinage only insofar as, unlike concubinage, its intention is that of marriage and therefore presents at least the appearance of being a "marriage-like" relationship (Schmaus).

The argument for this denial of the sacramental character to such marriages is not simple, since the participants themselves are the ministers of the sacrament and on this basis at any rate it would require no ecclesiastical co-operation for the sacrament to take place. Hence the denial can be substantiated only by declaring by means of *canon law* that the presence of the priest and the ecclesiastical benediction are a *conditio sine qua non* of the full validity of the marriage. According to Roman Catholic theological understanding, canon law is not simply a "human addition" which is supplied for reasons of order, but is rather a structural element of the visible, institutional church which is to a certain degree a part of its divine institution. Hence the thesis that, though the supervention of the priest and the ecclesiastical benediction are not constitutive or even co-constitutive of the sacrament of matrimony, both are nevertheless necessary for the full validity of the marriage. For precisely because marriage has sacramental character it is of immediate concern to the church; it represents its oneness with Christ the Head of the Church.[43] Therefore the church is not only competent but obligated to regulate marriage.

With respect to the status of canonical regulations this means that this regulation is more than an external mode according to which the sacrament is administered. The regulation is itself a *conditio sine qua non* of validity which belongs to the thing which is regulated. An ultimate lack of clarity in the doctrine of the sacraments, which is evident here and which did *not* exist for the sacrament of matrimony *before* the promulga-

---

[43] Cf. G. Reidick, *op. cit.*

tion of the Code of Canon Law, is obviously being accepted here in order to gain a stronger dogmatic means of combating the spread of mixed marriages.

This lack of clarity may be formulated as follows: the co-operation of the priest and the ecclesiastical benediction do not have any constitutive, "effective" character for the sacrament of matrimony, but only a declaratory significance. But by virtue of the canonical ordinance this declaration regains its constitutive significance, because without it there can be no ecclesiastically recognized marriage. For in the strict sense a marriage exists only insofar as the church "ratifies" the marriage contract which is established by the sacramental consent and makes it a *matrimonium ratum;* whereas a valid marriage between non-Christians—and hence also the confessionally mixed marriage—is a *matrimonium legitimum.* But according to the Catholic view which has largely prevailed since 1918, a *matrimonium legitimum* is no longer a fully valid marriage in the Catholic sense.

The break in the tradition which is evident in this revision is unmistakable. It suggests—if an interpretation is allowed—that pragmatic considerations may have played a part in its formulation. At any rate for Thomas Aquinas this canonical reservation with respect to a sacramentally valid marriage does not exist: *"Si aliquis fidelis cum haeretica baptizata matrimonium contrahit, verum* est matrimonium, *quamvis peccet contrahendo si sciat eam haereticam*: non *tamen propter hoc matrimonium* dirimeretur."[44]

Likewise Pius XI says in the encyclical *Casti Connubii* (1930) that "the nature of the sacrament is so intimately bound up with Christian marriage that no true matrimony can exist between baptized persons 'unless by that very fact it be a sacrament.' "[45]

It is obvious that this declaring of non-Catholic marriages to be nonmarriages entails enormous practical consequences, which presumably were intentional (though fairness forbids us to regard certain vulgar-Catholic practices—zealous priests who interfere in mixed marriages and seek to break them up—as being included in that intention). Although the dissolution of a mixed marriage, as provided for in the Code of Canon Law,[46] leans heavily upon I Corinthians

---

[44] "If anyone of the faithful contracts marriage with one baptized heretically, it is truly matrimony, although he sins by contracting it if he knows the other party to be a heretic; yet on this account the marriage is not nullified." *Comm. in IV libr. Sent., d. 39q. 1 art. 1;* italics not in original

[45] Denzinger, 2237.

[46] Canons 1120 f.

7:12-15 and is therefore referred to by the term "Pauline privilege," it is obvious that this theological defamation of mixed marriages (this is not a polemical remark, but just an objective finding) at least does not place any checks on certain vulgar tendencies which take the value judgment "nonmarriage" and turn it into the fact "annulled marriage." And if these practices are to be interpreted as misunderstandings, we must say that they are certainly very *natural* misunderstandings. Beyond this clear statement we shall forgo any further documentation in order not to encumber unnecessarily the confessional controversy which we have no interest in exacerbating.

Even apart from the question of truth, the discussion of mixed marriages, which, at least among the theologians of both confessions, has happily not been broken off, is a part of the *pastoral* duty of the Roman Catholic as well as of the Protestant Church; for it is a burden upon the souls of individuals, families, and even children.

In any case, there are two things which are *not* in dispute between the two confessions. First is our common principle of reserve with regard to mixed marriages. We have given the reasons for this (without, however, being able to say that therefore there can be no such thing as a God-pleasing mixed marriage!). Second, it is not disputed that the church must have the right to give its blessing only to those couples who satisfy its requirements. Among these requirements would be the obligation to rear the children in the faith of the church whose blessing is desired by the parents. In any case, however, a regularly contracted marriage between persons of different faiths is a *fully valid* marriage. Also any possible measures of church discipline which may be imposed upon a couple whose marriage has been solemnized or blessed in their own church—what we are referring to is doubtless clear!—dare not detract in any way from the recognized validity of the marriage as a *matrimonium verum*. It is almost unbearable to deal with the problem of mixed marriage without having cleared up this elementary premise. The fact that here Roman Catholic theology is not confronted with an invincible difficulty is shown by its tradition before the introduction of the Code of Canon Law.[47]

[47] On the whole question of mixed marriages cf. Sucker, Lell, Nitschke, *Die Mischehe. Handbuch für die evangelische Seelsorge* (Göttingen, 1959).

# IV    BORDERLINE
# SITUATIONS

# Introduction

In the following section we shall be dealing with borderline cases. The purpose they are meant to serve within the whole system is not merely that of including for the sake of completeness the exceptions which are difficult or impossible to fit into the system. Nor do we advert to them because of a casuistical interest in penetrating into some especially intricate or problem-filled marginal areas in which the reader might feel more need for the counsel of a book of ethics (and which he often seeks for in vain in the indexes of such books). On the contrary, we are following the point of view which has been tested and abundantly practiced throughout the *Theological Ethics,* namely, that the "border line is the truly propitious place for acquiring knowledge."[1]

Our method, then, is to take the borderline situations, which compel us to seek the whys and wherefores, and allow them to make us look for the normative and thus interpret the center of a subject by starting from its periphery. Thus the problem of birth control leads us to examine the nature of marriage, the interruption of pregnancy to the nature of life, homosexuality to the nature of the polarity of sex, and artificial insemination to the nature of parenthood.

[1] Paul Tillich, *Religiöse Verwirklichung. ThE* II, 1, deals almost wholly with borderline situations, as does *ThE* II, 2, Part C.

# A. Birth Control (The Problem of Optional Sterility)

The problem of birth control presents itself in the concrete relationship of the sexes. That is to say, it arises less from the systematic study of the problem of marriage than from some very definite individual and historical situations. It arises from certain definite "causes" that make it urgent. It is a problem which presents itself in an atmosphere of friction and conflict. This is the reason why the discussion of it is not pursued with a merely *theoretical* passion. Accordingly, theological reflection too must always take into account this background of concrete causes and occasions.

This is important so far as our methodology is concerned, for since the interpretation of situations requires a judgment of opinion, it is to be expected that the close connection of the problem to these situations will bring out very sharply the dialectical tension between dogmatic judgments and judgments of opinion.

The historical causes which provoke this question in an atmosphere of conflicting judgments are primarily three: (1) premarital and extramarital sexual intercourse, (2) the social and health situation of the wife or (potential) mother, (3) the rapid increase of the population of the earth, especially in the developed countries. In line with the "ontic" way in which the problem arises we shall deal with it "noetically" by starting out from these situations. This is methodologically possible only because we have already thought through the positive systematics of sex and marriage. Failing this, we should have to be afraid that by beginning with the situation we were choosing an exceedingly unstable and slippery starting point.

## 1. PREMARITAL AND EXTRAMARITAL SEXUAL INTERCOURSE

If we leave out of account the "tragic" borderline cases in which there is a deeper, marriagelike relationship between a couple, but one which is not (or *cannot* be made) legal, and consider instead the "usual" situation, the question looks somewhat as follows: since premarital and extramarital sexual intercourse is sought mostly for pleasure and relaxation of tension, as satisfaction of libido, those indulging in it are generally little inclined to make the corresponding sacrifices and accept the responsibilities that go with it. To this extent there is here a denial of one of the essential purposes of sexuality, namely, a personal relationship designed to be permanent and the willingness to accept the office of parenthood. This unwillingness ceases to exist to the degree that one regards the union as being merely temporary and therefore as a momentary pleasure, consequently and to the degree that one excludes the element of responsibility and thus of personhood. Since in the human realm the libido always tends to build up an "ideological superstructure" (here the term really fits!), the result in persons who are not altogether primitive in nature is almost always a physiologically induced illusion that there are deeper affections or even some personal elements in the relationship. The libido is such that it generates such wish-images, partly because it achieves the maximum of its ecstatic potentialities when it is directed, not merely partially to the body (or merely to certain zones of the body) but rather to the *totality* of the other person, and partly because the elemental tendency of man is toward the communication of this kind of make-believe. In any case, a relationship within the realm of sex which does not aim at permanence invites this self-critical question.

Sexuality loses its essential nature when it is practiced outside of marriage with no respect for the personhood of the other partner (thus failing to be "love" in the full sense) and refuses to accept parenthood. This loss of the essential nature of sexuality would indicate that the contraception practiced under these circumstances is only a symptom of a far deeper problem. Therefore it cannot be dealt with here as a problem which can be isolated from a larger context.

## 2. THE SOCIAL AND MEDICAL INDICATION FOR PREVENTION OF PREGNANCY

The real theological and ethical relevance of the problem arises, for the reasons we have stated, out of *marriage*. In order to gain the proper starting point for dealing with it, we need to recall certain conclusions which we arrived at in thinking through the problem of marriage.

We stated that the family,[2] by which we mean the marriage relationship as well as the relationship of parents and children, is an *order of creation*.[3] We must not, of course, overlook the fact that the order of creation asserts its claim in a *fallen* world, in this world (*aion houtos*), and that here it undergoes certain alterations, at least insofar as its concrete realization is concerned (but not insofar as the continuance of the claim itself is concerned). The relationship of creation and history is one of "tension." It is of the long-suffering patience of God that he does not abandon history to its brokenness, but rather—as we have seen—remains faithful to it in the "regulations of necessity" of the Noachic covenant.[4] The alteration of the command of creation in history after the Fall (*post lapsum*) appears, for example, in the exceptional possibility of divorce which is granted

---

[2] Cf. also the section on the family in the chapter on society in the still unpublished Vol. III of *ThE*.

[3] It is beyond our understanding how Karl Barth can say that the order of creation expressed in the command "Be fruitful and multiply" (Gen. 1:28) has "ceased to be an unconditional demand *post Christum natum*" (*Church Dogmatics* III, 4, p. 268; cf. pp. 142 ff.). Such a statement is possible only if Barth abandons the distinction between a command of creation and a law of creation. (On this necessary distinction cf. *ThE* I, §691 ff.). Only so can he then proceed also to interpret the status of parenthood, which he no longer views as being a command of creation, as a law which has been abolished in the new aeon. At this point our argument with Barth would center upon the concept of the original state of man. (Cf. on this the controversy with Barth on the distinction between Law and Gospel, *ThE* I, §554 .)

[4] Cf. *ThE* II, 1, §642 ff.

to man "because of his hardness of heart," but which still remains something that is "out of order" and not in accord with God's real will. This tension between creation and history, between the command of God and the situation which is inadequate to the command, also has a bearing upon the problem of contraception. For here the command of creation "Be fruitful and multiply" is confronted with concrete situations which resist its realization and *can* alter it in its application to concrete circumstances, especially since these situations are largely beyond the ability of the individual to change them. Among these circumstances are certain exceptional cases in life: "severe illness of the mother, numerous births accompanied by weak health or difficult living conditions, severe hereditary affliction, or economic circumstances which will not permit the rearing of another child even with the greatest frugality,"[5] early marriages, among students for example, which delay the establishment of a larger family, housing difficulties, job situations, etc.

In any case, when Jesus takes into account man's "hardheartedness" in the application of the order of creation, there exists this point of comparison between this consideration and the consideration of the above-mentioned exceptional situations: it is always the concrete situation of the person involved that renders difficult the full enforcement of the order of creation and brings it about that a person is unable to live in this aeon "in the name" of the order of creation but, faced with its claim, can live only "in the name" of the forgiving *patience of God.*

We could probably go even further and say that the point of comparison between Jesus' consideration of man's hardheartedness and our consideration of these exceptional situations is not confined only to the given "concrete situations." We may ask: In the last analysis does not this hardheartedness of man also lie behind these concrete situations of sickness and social misery? Can the disorders of this aeon be interpreted in any way except in their relationship to original sin?[6]

---

[5] Bovet, *Die Ehe,* p. 161.
[6] Cf. my book *Tod und Leben. Studien zur christlichen Anthropologie* (1946), Excursus pp. 213 ff.

This rhetorical question does not mean that our consideration of these situations should make the reality of the situation the standard of judgment and thus pragmatically distort the order of creation, but rather that it can be exercised only under the claim and under the judgment of the order of creation. If, for example, our willingness to exercise this consideration should lead to the conclusion that contraception is permissible, this will certainly not be because we argue that "such is life" (*c'est la vie*), but rather because we know that in this situation—and we are purposely phrasing this guardedly—the begetting of children is fulfilling only *one* side of the created [*schöpfungsmässige*] relationship of marriage and that this introduces a *conflict* in the order of creation which it did not have "from the beginning" (Matt. 19:8). Here something is being "put asunder" which God has "joined together." By expressing it in this way we respect the claim of the order of creation and allow it to continue to be a dam against the inevitable degeneration that must result as soon as the alleged realities are made the standard of judgment instead of being themselves subjected to judgment.[7]

In particular there are two theological criteria for dealing with the question: first, the nature of marriage, and second, the permissibility or nonpermissibility of interfering in nature.

First, the order of creation in marriage combines both the companionship of the spouses and their parenthood.

To that extent we would agree with the Encyclical *Casti Connubii,* of Pius XI: "The mutual interior formation of husband and wife, this constant zeal for bringing each other to perfection, in a very true sense, as the Roman Catechism teaches, can be said to be the very first reason and purpose of matrimony; if, however, matrimony be not accepted too narrowly as instituted for the proper procreation and education of children, but more broadly as the mutual participation in all life, companionship, and association."[8] This would mean, therefore, that the Encyclical does not simply co-ordinate the fellowship of the spouses and parenthood as two different purposes, but rather defines *fellowship* as the fundamental purpose of marriage and includes in it the procreation of children only *insofar* as parenthood makes possible the *pleroma* of this fellowship (and

[7] Cf. *ThE* II, 2, §692 ff. and the preceding sections.
[8] Denzinger 2232.

indeed, the *pleroma* which the Creator *willed* that it should have). Consequently, the procreation of children is only a partial component of marriage, which is subsumed under, and derived from, its main purpose, namely, "the mutual interior formation of husband and wife."

According to this, the obligatory character of the procreation of children as a purpose of marriage is not derived from an isolated command of creation, but is rather regarded as obligatory only insofar as the main purpose of marital fellowship cannot be fulfilled without the *conditio sine qua non* of willingness to have children. It would appear to us that in this order (if we are interpreting it correctly) there are possibilities of arriving at a position with regard to contraception which is quite different from that which rejects it for other reasons. With reference to this "rift," E. Michel may be right when he deplores the lack of an "inner connection of responsibility" that should exist between responsibility for the marital fellowship and responsibility for the procreation of children.[9] The question of this inner connection arises when the two purposes—the main purpose and the partial purpose—come into conflict with each other and the situation arises where the procreation of children does not perfect the marital fellowship (as is intended by the order of creation) but rather threatens it (as it can in some concrete exceptional situations).

If there is a conflict between the two sides of the purpose of the order of creation, that is, if the situation occurs in which the procreation of a child would not perfect the marital fellowship but rather burden or threaten it, then the question must be asked whether the marital fellowship even *apart* from the willingness to have children has any sustaining intrinsic value.

Certainly this question cannot be answered simply in the negative. This is evident in the very fact that nobody impugns the purpose of a marriage which remains involuntarily childless. Therefore, more precisely stated, the question is this: (1) If the absence of children does not in principle call in question the full meaning and purpose of a marriage, is it nevertheless called in question if the *willingness* to have children is lacking and moreover *always* instead of *temporarily* lacking? (2) Must it necessarily be a lack of willingness if the outward and inward conditions of a specific situation make it very difficult or impossible to assume the responsibility for a child? Cannot the force of circumstances other than biological permit us in certain cases

[9] E. Michel, *op. cit.*, p. 189.

to speak of "involuntary" childlessness? Is it not, for example, a form of involuntariness not to be allowed to want something, though one would like to have it?

As far as the first part of the question is concerned, there can be no doubt that a willful and permanent refusal to have children on principle constitutes a reduction of the purpose of marriage in the order of creation, a sundering of what God has joined together, and therefore something that is not in accord with the proper will of God (*voluntas Dei propria*).[10] This makes all the more urgent the problems stated in the second part of the question, namely, whether involved in this fundamental and permanent refusal to have children there may not be obstacles which may rightly be called involuntary, or whether the motives behind it stem from selfishness (such as desire for comfort, fear of responsibility, or the desire for a higher standard of living).

It requires no further argument for us to say that this second motivation for refraining from having children constitutes an offense against the order of creation. In the first case the ethical question is more difficult and cannot be decided by generalizing.

That is to say, if we grant the possibility that the pressure of circumstances can reach such a pitch that causes the refusal to have children to become an *involuntary* decision, it becomes impossible to uphold absolutely the distinction between a temporary and a persistent refusal. For in this form of involuntariness it is not within the power of the person concerned to remove the hindrances in the situation (illness of the mother, social misery, etc.) or to foresee when they will be ended. If such discernible or positively predictable hindrances are present *before* the marriage is entered into, then it is impossible to escape the question whether under these circumstances it is justifiable to enter into marriage. Certainly there would have to be very individual and very grave reasons to permit one to disregard this kind of deliberation. Since the emotional and thus "irrelevant" side of situations in which such questions arise is so immense, it

---

[10] Catholic moral theology positively forbids continuing contraception even when it is achieved by observing the seasons of sterility (*observatio temporum*) and in this case labels it as conjugal onanism (*onanismus conjugalis*). Jos. Mayer, *op. cit.;* Stelzenberger, *op. cit.,* p. 232.

would seem wise in these and similar cases to recommend that someone outside, who is not emotionally involved—perhaps a pastor—should participate in the deliberation.

In this problem of fundamental refusal to have children we dare not overlook a definitely "modern" factor which undoubtedly complicates the question. We refer to the situation of the working wife, which may make it impossible to do justice to the task of rearing children—but then, logically, may also not permit the bringing of children into the world. If this working at a job or profession serves for pleasure, if it is only a favorite occupation, or its purpose is only to provide a certain material comfort or social prestige, it falls under the same verdict which we have had to lay upon the selfishly motivated refusal to have children. Undoubtedly the case is different when the work has the substance of a "calling," in the sense in which we set forth as possible in the chapter on the working wife. But in this case too the question arises whether entering into marriage is justified. (Therefore it is also not without significance that the problem of the working wife emerged in connection with discussion of the unmarried state.) Certainly it cannot be decided in advance whether this kind of a working wife must absolutely refrain from a marriage, if for her the precondition is fundamental abstention from having children. Can a marital existence have broader meaning and purpose on this level too?

If this is possible, then we are again faced with the question whether the order of creation must not remain indivisible, whether, in other words, we can on principle and voluntarily leave out a part of it, or whether—if things as they stand [*rebus sic stantibus*] are simply unavoidable—*abstention* is not incumbent upon them.

Certainly this question whether the order of creation may possibly be "divided" cannot be answered without determining in what *sense* it is to be divided. We have already rejected one of these possibilities of dividing it. This is the possibility of insisting upon having the fatherhood or the motherhood inherent in the order of creation by itself through the begetting of an illegitimate child (as might be the wish of an unmarried working woman). Corresponding to this partially realized order of creation would be the *opposite* form of dividing it, namely, that of a person who wants to be a wife or a husband but not a mother or a father. It is clear that these two forms of division do not stand on the same ethical level. The situation of the illegitimate child is a completely different problem from that of the situation of parents who are childless (voluntarily or because of need, though not of "necessity").

The question whether situational conditions can exist which are so elemental that voluntary childlessness would be based not upon willfulness but rather upon lack of freedom of will depends upon the other question whether what Kant calls a "moral necessity"—insofar as the conscience regards itself as inescapably forced to this decision —can have the same degree of coerciveness as the "natural necessity" that exists, say, in biological sterility.

The fact that it *does* exist we believe we can demonstrate in the next section of "the permissibility of intervention in the processes of nature." The only thing that makes it possible for us to continue this discussion at all is the fact that we regard the personal relationship of marriage to be the central emphasis of the order of creation and thus attribute to it an intrinsic value which exists even apart from the pro-creation of children and the function of marriage to channelize the libido. We have already given detailed reasons to substantiate this intrinsic value in the chapter on marriage. Despite the fact that the whole of the order of creation embraces both parents *and* children, this intrinsic value must be retained as its focal emphasis. After all, it is one thing to assert that there is a focal emphasis within a totality and quite another thing to say that this totality can be divided as one pleases. The necessity for seeking a focal point is brought about by the fact that concrete situations over which our individual will has no control can introduce a conflict in the order of creation. Such a conflict exists, for example, when it is a question whether this is a childless marriage because of necessity or because of need. Even Catholic moral theology, which can never pose the question of possible childlessness in the way we do here, is compelled—and *Casti Connubii* shows it!—to elaborate this focal point. It does so by insisting that a marriage which is childless by reason of sterility still has meaning and consistency. But this already establishes indirectly this focal point of

personal relationship.[11] In any case, this focal point becomes important as a means of orientation when we are faced with the problem
that in certain situations children can jeopardize a marriage (understood in the sense of its focal point) rather than perfect it.

The second theological criterion is the permissibility of interfering
in nature. The order of creation, which embraces both marriage and
the blessing of children but accentuates as its focal point the personal
relationship, is not simply identical with the natural biological order,
in which the sexual relationship and parenthood are likewise joined
together. Such an identification is illicit simply because man in creation is not merely another natural being, but unlike the other natural
being is in a relationship of responsibility to God. As we said above,
he is not simply the passive result of God's "Let there be," but rather
a personal being vis-à-vis the Creator who addresses him in promise
and command and calls him to act in responsible freedom.[12]

I move in the direction of the order of creation, not simply by following the order of nature in a functional way, but rather only as I
make the decision of obedience before my Creator and thus forsake
determination by nature. Hence the claim of the order of creation
transcends the order of nature and therefore does not permit any
identification of the two.

[11] It is not quite clear to us how the position taken by Pius XII in his
address of October 29, 1951 (*Herder-Korrespondenz* VI, 117), relates to this
indirect establishment of the focal point and beyond this to the wording of
*Casti Connubii*: "Now it is true that marriage as a natural institution does not
have as its first and innermost purpose the personal perfection of the
spouses as is the will of the Creator, but rather the awakening and rearing
of new life. However much the other purposes are intended by nature, they
still do not stand on the same level (!) as the first, and still less are they set
above it; they are rather essentially subordinate to it. This applies to every
marriage, even if it is unfruitful." Instead of the last sentence it would seem
that the proper conclusion would be that a childless marriage is not a
marriage because it has failed of its foremost purpose. (But this, of course,
would bring the Roman Catholic position into rather dubious proximity to,
of all people, Bertrand Russell, who—though he is speaking from a sociological point of view—treats the childless marriage as a nonmarriage: "In a
rational ethic, marriage would not count as such in the absence of children.
A sterile marriage should be easily dissoluble, for it is through it alone that
sexual relations become of importance to society, and worthy to be taken
cognizance of by a legal institution." *Marriage and Morals*, p. 125.) There
would seem to be some inconsistencies here which have not been reconciled.

[12] Cf. *ThE*, I, § 706 ff., 776 ff.; II, 1, § 1247 ff.

As a matter of fact, even where the claim of the order of creation is not taken into account human existence is always understood in this sense of transcending nature. It is axiomatic in every ethic that human existence consists not in *compliance* with nature but rather in *assertion* over against nature. In my very refusal to yield to my hunger, thirst, or sex urge I transcend nature. But only in the relation of the sexes in marriage is there any obvious controversy about this question.

That is to say, here there is dispute over the question whether man is permitted to intervene in the connection between cohabitation and the procreation of new life. Then, if the order of nature and the order of creation are identified, this can lead to the false postulate that in the matter of procreation everything must be left to chance, which generally is then glorified "in religious terms as 'leaving it to Providence,' "[13] But this "letting things go as they come" would not be the responding and responsible attitude appropriate to the claim of the order of creation, but only "a bondage to nature camouflaged by religion."

The conclusion to be drawn from this is that when we recognize within this world conditions which in our human judgment present insurmountable hindrances to the procreation of children, then the claim of the order of creation cannot simply be interpreted in doctrinaire fashion in the sense that it brushes aside these conditions of existence and "stubbornly" insists upon the oneness of wedlock and parenthood, and therefore that it dictates that we must "let things go as they come" as they do in the order of nature (regardless of losses!). Here the claim of the order of creation must rather be heard as a summons to responsibility *over against* the order of nature.

Theologically, this variation of the direction of the claim of the order of creation is connected with the fact that since the Fall, in this aeon of "hardheartedness," it is possible for two integral elements of the order of creation to come into conflict with each other. In other words there can be a conflict between the oneness of wedlock and parenthood on the one hand and responsibility to procreate life on the other. In the unbroken world as it was in its original state (*ap'*

---

[13] E. Michel, *op. cit.*, p. 189.

*arches*!) it was *not* so. There the intention of creation and responsibility still coincided. But he who overlooks the fallenness of this aeon, in the sense of taking over untransposed the law of the original state into this aeon,[14] is acting "fanatically" in the same sense as one who takes the radical claims of the "new world"—say in the form of the demands of the Sermon on the Mount—and sets them up as ethical and legal norms in this aeon. It is possible to be fanatical in the protological as well as the eschatological sense!

Therefore we must see the possibility that the sound order of creation has been wounded by the unsound world and that the Mosaic bill of divorce is an evidence of that wound in its integrity. We must see that in this aeon its elements are in conflict.

A fanatical denial of this conflict in the sense of insisting without reservation upon the oneness of wedlock and parenthood in this aeon leads, not to obedience to the order of creation—which one may honestly desire—but rather to bondage to the order of nature, which one must then, as E. Michel says, "glorify religiously."

Therefore it is legitimate to ask the question in the here and now of our aeon: Can I responsibly receive the blessing of children as things are now [*rebus sic stantibus*]? (In consciously using the term "blessing" of children, we are expressing the fact that this question can be asked legitimately only if the child is regarded as a blessing and not from the outset as a burden or even as a curse; in other words, if there is the fundamental willingness that is assumed to be present when a gift is understood to be a blessing.) And in exactly the same way the opposite question must be asked: Can I, as things now stand, responsibly refuse to have children?

The responsibility referred to here is twofold. First, it is responsibility with regard to the bringing of children into the world. There can be exceptional situations—we have enumerated them according to certain types—which may lay an undue burden upon a child and which may make impossible or intolerably difficult the rearing of the child which is included in the purpose of marriage in the order of creation. Second, it is responsibility with respect to the marriage itself. It may be possible that the personal relationship of marriage will

---

[14] Similar problems occur in connection with natural law; cf. *ThE* I.

not bear the additional "burden" of a child, or another child, or that it would mean a real threat to the health of the mother.

It is therefore conceivable, and, of course, this actually happens repeatedly, that certain situations make it seem irresponsible to bring children into the world. In this case a decision may have to be made —not merely a decision "against" the order of creation, but one that is made in the name of its demand for responsibility in the face of "things as they stand"—a decision that evokes that "moral necessity" of which Kant spoke. This "moral necessity" militates against mere compliance with nature and against *its* necessity. I cannot allow myself simply to be driven by its laws and "let things come as they may." As one who transcends nature I am also called upon to transcend it by an act of will. And then in the second place this "moral necessity" militates against the making of an arbitrary decision; rather the "ought" points me in a very definite direction and does not leave me free to act as I please but rather binds my freedom.

Not until we get this clear in our minds can we see that a decision of "moral necessity" made under the pressure of a very definite exceptional situation can be called "involuntary" in the same sense as childlessness because of biological sterility is involuntary. The factor which constitutes the parallel between the two is that in both cases it is not willfulness or selfishness that produces the abstention, but rather an elemental necessity: in one case a necessity of compulsion (as in sterility) and in the other a necessity of "ought" (as in responsibility conditioned by the situation).

We have been obliged to pursue this argument in order to secure a clear theological basis for the further question of how this responsible abstention from having a child (or another child) can be realized.

The following possibilities present themselves:

1. Abstention from cohabitation. Since coitus is not isolatable but is rather surrounded with an erotic atmosphere which extends into subtle expressions of fellowship (looks, voice, gestures), abstention from it means not only from the ultimate physical expression of the sexual relationship, but also an invasion of its wholeness. Worthy of note is the statement, which van der Velde cites and agrees with, made by a director of social missions to the effect that among all the

marriages in which permanent continence was required he had not seen a single one in which this requirement had been fulfilled or the marriage had not broken down under it.[15] Naturally, this does not mean abstinence for a limited time, which may be required for natural reasons (sickness, menstruation, etc.) or for spiritual reasons (I Cor. 7:5) and be in accord with the rhythm of life. Abstention on principle is a fundamentally different thing. It actually infringes upon sexual fellowship intended by the order of creation; and if—as we said—the focal point of marriage lies in the personal relationship, it means an assault upon the center of the marriage fellowship (not because cohabitation is this center, but rather because the fundamental absence of it affects the whole of the sexual relationship). The psychological effects of this absence—in the form of repressions—are symptoms of this disturbance.

2. Interrupted intercourse (*coitus interruptus*). Medical opinion is unanimous in rejecting this means because "it abruptly breaks off the rising curve of pleasure immediately before its climax" and in persons who are not altogether insensitive it leads in time to psychosomatic disturbances.[16]

3. Contraceptive measures. These involve a more or less active intervention in the processes of nature. Catholic moral theology rejects any physical devices or chemical means of preventing contraception and tolerates only the observance of the so-called infertile periods (*observatio temporum*), which it judges to be a *"res non in se mala"* on one condition, namely, that it serve as a temporary optional sterility and is not an expression of a permanent unwillingness to have children. This concession is made in view of the intrinsic value and the preservation of the personal fellowship of marriage.

In point of fact it is only a concession. The pastoral decision of S. Poenitentiaria of June 16, 1880,[17] answers the question *"An licitus sit usus matrimonii illis tantum diebus, quibus difficilior est conceptus?"* ["Is

[15] Van der Velde, *Die Fruchtbarkeit i. d. Ehe* (1929), p. 9; Bovet, *Die Ehe,* p. 162; Emil Brunner: "Asceticism within marriage *may* be a way; but it means terrible repression, which is dangerous both for body and soul." *The Divine Imperative,* p. 369.

[16] Bovet, *op. cit.,* p. 167.

[17] Stelzenberger, *op. cit.,* p. 232.

it permissible in marriage to make use of those days in which conception is more difficult?"] as follows: Under certain conditions which are described in detail such spouses are not to be disturbed (*inquietandos non esse*). The formulation makes it understood that this means it is only a "pastoral emergency solution." In like manner the Encyclical *Casti Connubii* maintains that "the observance of the infertile days is not against the order of nature, provided that the nature of the act and its subordination to the main purpose is not impugned." ("Those spouses are not to be said to act against the order of nature who use their right in a correct and natural way, although for natural reasons of time, or of certain defects new life cannot spring from this." Denzinger 2241.)

Nevertheless it is to be noted that even here a certain intervention in the processes of nature are held to be permissible and that a certain planning of the act of procreation may be possible. This would make sense only if the procreation of offspring were *not* made the chief purpose of marriage; and furthermore it could make sense only if here there were no complete identification of the order of nature with the order of creation. For surely even a "pastoral emergency measure" cannot be purely inconsequential; rather it can be legitimate only as a concession in view of a value the infringement of which would be a worse negation than the questionable concession itself. We have already seen that the Roman Catholic doctrine of marriage itself makes it only partially possible to discover in it lines which point to the same interpretation of the order of marriage which it would seem that one could indirectly infer from its position with regard to optional sterility.

The inconsistencies discernible here seem also to appear in the further question of how anyone can seriously justify making a qualitative theological distinction between different ways of influencing the processes of nature; in other words, by what right is the *observatio temporum* given ecclesiastical approval as a contraceptive measure while the application of technical contraceptives is condemned by the church. In the strict sense both are "unnatural," since they do not allow nature to operate blindly. The calculation of days by means of a calendar, mental arithmetic, and possibly a slide rule does not seem to be any less complicated and perhaps not even more sympathetic than the use of contraceptives. Here at any rate are some highly graduated distinctions whose theological relevance it is difficult to see, especially since, as we have seen, the theological distinctions fall at quite *different* points.

This exceedingly disparate value judgment upon the individual methods of prevention of conception may perhaps be more easily understood if we are allowed a pragmatic imputation: if even the slightest voluntary exertion of influence upon the natural processes of conception, even in the form of *observatio temporum*, is to be understood only as a concession granted with hesitation—and the frequent dogmatic statements insisting that the procreation of children is the chief purpose of marriage would certainly suggest this—then the slightest transgression of the conceded minimum would necessarily be illicit and evoke the fear that the observance of this minimum would become a very elastic thing in theory and in practice.

This concern must be taken seriously and respected even though we do not share its dogmatic presuppositions, its interpretation of the order of creation in marriage. In the next section we shall have occasion to show, in discussing the "manipulability of procreation," that our hesitation with regard to allowing unlimited freedom to use preventive methods in many respects agree with the hesitation of Catholic moral theology—though for different reasons.

## 3. The Population Explosion

A third factor which makes the question of birth control urgent is the rapid and progressive increase of the population of the earth, especially in the developing countries and particularly the countries of Asia. The geometrically progressive increase predicted as far back as 1798 by the English economist Malthus[18] did not come to pass—

[18] Malthus' theory (cf. Umbricht, *op. cit.*, p. 312) asserted that people who follow their natural urge increase very much more rapidly than do the means of subsistence. He maintained the thesis that population would increase in geometrical progression whereas the production of means of subsistence would increase arithmetically. (If this calculation were correct and the population of the earth were doubled about every twenty-five years, it would now total sixty billion people instead of two and a half billion.) Malthus therefore predicted mass misery—including moral misery—and expressed the fear that in the natural course of events overpopulation could be adjusted to the avail-

and it is to be hoped that many of the almost apocalyptic prognoses of modern statisticians will suffer a similar fate![19]—and yet the progress of medicine, especially of hygiene, presents another side of the picture in which the reduction of infant and child mortality as well as adult mortality itself may produce an increase of such proportions that it is being called a "population explosion."

This expected increase, which again—as in the case of Malthus!—is expected to result in a self-decimation of humanity through hunger and wars, has led to statements which declare that what is necessary is planned, state-controlled limitation of births, especially in economically underdeveloped but overpopulated areas like India, for example. By means of education, propaganda, and the availability of free-of-cost contraceptives the already dangerous threat must be met.[20]

It is a difficult and hazardous thing to set up decisive norms in the face of a catastrophic situation of which we can neither be sure that it actually exists nor foresee its possible proportions. If Catholic moral theology nevertheless feels obliged because of dogmatic reasons to set us such norms, it certainly must not have been easy for its representatives to do so. If according to the concept of a just war[21] it can be lawful to kill in a defensive war, then we must at least be allowed the question whether in a defensive war against a catastrophic biological flood it can be lawful to prevent or limit the birth of new life.

We intentionally choose this analogy between a defensive war and defense against a biological explosion in order to indicate that in the latter case it is difficult to express a "dogmatic" no, if one does not do so in the first instance. The difficulty of saying such a no in advance is further heightened by the fact that after all in the case of war it is a question of killing human beings, whereas a strategic program of birth control is only a matter of seeing to it that no life will be born

---

able means of subsistence only by hunger, epidemics, wars, etc. In this connection he recommended the limitation of births, though only through moral abstinence, whereas the advocates of Neo-Malthusianism who followed him (around 1850) recommended the far more radical measures of birth control (including artificial abortion and sterilization).

[19] On these statistics cf. what is said in the section on the "masses."

[20] Cf. *Universitas* (1960), 6, pp. 685 f.

[21] Cf. *ThE* II, 2, §3273 ff.

which would very probably be killed by a catastrophic lack of subsistence. The borderline situation always compels us to intervene more radically, whether it be in nature, in our constitutions, or in our codes of laws.

The theologicoethical problem here is that the preservation of a normative value can become questionable the moment another normative value is threatened by it, in other words, where a conflict (a conflict of values) arises.[22] Thus in this case it is possible that insistence upon the oneness of wedlock and parenthood as a normative value could be a threat to maintenance of a minimum assurance of life to the next generation.

The positions taken with regard to the problem reflect differences in the basic decisions concerning the question of birth control which we discussed above. The Roman Catholic bishops in the United States have taken an unequivocally negative position on the question whether American foreign aid may be used for the dissemination of birth control information in overpopulated countries. Even though, for the reasons given, we consider the dogmatic side of this position to be questionable and regret that the indicated conflict problem has obviously not been seen and evaluated for its theological relevance, nevertheless the pragmatic part of the statement is worthy of note and confronts us with problems which we too would recognize as criteria for the decision which is to be made.

The statement says, "It appears never to have occurred to them [the advocates of controlled population development] that the logical way out of the chronic situation in which there are more hungry people than food is not by way of reducing the population, but rather of increasing the production of the means of subsistence."[23] This reminds us of the inquiries made by the physician and temporary president of the United Nations Commission on Food and Agriculture, Josuede Castro, in his book *Geopolitique de la faim,* 1952, in which he comes to the conclusion that it is not overpopulation that leads to hunger but rather hunger that leads to overpopulation. That is to say, chronically insufficient nourishment leads to an intensification of the urge to propagate (hence the high birth rate among the Chinese, Indians, and Filipinos, etc.); and on the other hand the accumulation of property—which poses the problem of inheritance—and a higher living standard leads to a smaller increase of population. (*"Le monde ne trouvera donc pas le chemin de sa survivance en*

[22] Cf. *ThE* II, 1, §721 ff.
[23] *Universitas* (1960), 6, p. 685.

*essayant, comme le veulent les néomalthusiens, d'éliminer les exces de population, ou de contrôler les naissances, mais en s'efforgant de rendre productifs tous les hommes qui vivent sur la surface de la terre. La faim et la misère n'existent pas dans le monde, parce qu'il y a trop de gens, mais parce qu'il y a trop peu de gens pour produire et beaucoup de gens pour manger.*") This reversal of the causal relationship between hunger and overpopulation, based upon professional analysis, is thought-provoking. An ethical indifferentism which has no fundamental inhibitions, religious or otherwise, with regard to unlimited birth control and therefore all too quickly recommends it as a patent solution will hardly be in a position to evaluate or even to see the possibility of reversing this causal relationship.

Among Protestants, James A. Pike (Protestant Episcopal Bishop of San Francisco) and John C. Bennett (Union Theological Seminary, New York) have made statements on this problem and likewise a study group of Protestant, Anglican, and Orthodox theologians of the Ecumenical Council (Mansfield Report). Common to these statements is the position that a limited application of birth control in line with responsible parenthood is to be approved. According to Pike, this limitation is important also because the people in the underdeveloped countries, for whom the problem is especially urgent, are in a limited period of economic transition. In addition to this the Mansfield Report lays emphasis upon the point —with which, of course, the Orthodox members of the study group did not agree—that there is no ethical difference in value between the use of artificial methods of contraception and the *observatio temporum*.

Though it is true that our understanding of marriage and also our recognition of the problem of theological conflict do not permit us either to make an unequivocal decision with regard to warding off the population explosion or to reject outright the use of contraceptive means, we must nevertheless express some theological reservations of a quite *different* kind. The nature and value of these reservations might perhaps be best described as "reservation from the spiritual and pastoral point of view." There are three main reservations.

First, large-scale, state-controlled measures to prevent conception and their promotion would seriously blur the fundamental structure of the order of creation. After all, we have been able to say that birth control is ethically acceptable only insofar as it is carried out under the claim and also under the judgment of the order of creation, and hence insofar as one bows, in responsibility to the order of creation, to the "moral necessity" which we discussed above. But to leave contraception ethically wide open or, what is more, to elevate it to the status of a legal requirement would make the exception the rule, pervert the order of creation, and take away from the individual his obligation to make a responsible decision. This would be to enthrone not the unlimited monarchy of the libido but only its consequences.

*This would mean, then, that nature would no longer be transcended—as is permitted to, and required of, responsible parenthood —but rather all the human factors of the sex relationship that transcend nature would be naturalized.* Nobody who is going to make a responsible decision for this strategic, large-scale extension of birth control can be allowed to ignore this objection. It is hard to conceive how this objection can be overcome and what would be the nature of a state-controlled measure which would even approximately do justice to it. This objection could have just as limiting an effect as the *fundamental* rejection set forth by Catholic moral theology, even though its theological basis is completely different.

Second, an equally grave objection arises from the basic tendency which can be observed wherever technology impinges upon the human-biological realm and generates the idea that "anything can be made" ["*der Machbarkeit aller Dinge*"].[24] It is certainly true that technology has its part to play in the Creator's command to man to subdue the earth, but it is equally true that this purpose of technology is threatened when man no longer pursues this subduing of the earth to himself as a deputy and servant of God, but rather undertakes to do it in his own name. Then he is delivered over to the *hubris* of one who regards all things as subject to his manipulation and no longer respects any limitations put upon him by the Creator. Then for him the creation is no longer the receptacle of any normative structure whatsoever, but is merely material for his own self-realization, that is, material for acts in which he forms himself according to his own image.[25] So too the prevention of conception, which is a sign that man is given the task of responsibly transcending nature, can become a sign of an irresponsible *elimination* of nature. The technical pos-

---

[24] Cf. W. Schoellgen, *Aktuelle Moralprobleme* (1955), pp. 457 ff.
[25] Cf. Sartre, *ThE* I, §1972 ff.

sibilities which have been given into his hand (and these include certain methods of birth control) not only enhance his ability to transcend nature but also the danger of eliminating it. They can suggest to him the illusion that creation can be manipulated without limit and make him think that procreation is like a process of manufacture which permits one to expand or restrict the volume of production at will. Prevention of conception expanded to the proportion of a large-scale strategy opens up this apocalyptic prospect and gives cause for our theological concern lest man begin to think of himself as a biological Prometheus.

Third, the use of contraception, in the individual case and, in increased measure, in the form of strategic, large-scale planning, is always faced with two questions which call for ethical and spiritual decision.

1. The *spiritual* question runs as follows: By making what we think is a judicious intervention in the course of nature are we not allowing a calculating need for security to take precedence over confidence and faith in God? The bringing forth of children is *always* an incalculable venture; the bearing of a child is not without danger nor is its rearing without an element of risk. And there will *always* be difficulties that come from the external situation. From these "possibilities" there can come anxiety, which either becomes the material of faith (Ps. 73:23-28) or tempts us to meet it with the calculating prudence of security. The danger of this second reaction is that it may contain a demonic component. That is, it may turn out to be not only faithlessness (in the sense of a deficiency of faith) but may actually represent itself as being an act of responsible faith and thus put on the mask of an "angel of light" (II Cor. 11:14). Then what is represented to be a responsible act of omission (or procreation, for example) is in actuality only an untrusting anxiety which results in an excess of blind need for security.

It is very often difficult to draw the line between security grounded upon the responsibility of faith (naturally, this *too* exists, since faith does not exclude but rather includes reflection upon the consequences) and the need for security that grows out of unbelief. Birth control confronts us especially urgently with the question of *self-*

control, because the dangers and uncertainties (the symptoms of "being-in-the-world"[26]) are cause for constant anxiety and therefore furnish an inexhaustible stock of reasons which appear to give us the right not to allow new life to come into being. The ability we have to act upon these reasons at any time and without incurring any risk by the use of technical means increases our readiness to claim them.

Therefore faith will prove itself again and again, as Karl Barth so finely says, in "the conscious and resolute refusal . . . of the possibility of refusing, i.e., the joyful willingness to have children and therefore to become parents."[27] There can be no general regulation of birth control which does not leave open the chance for *this* form of abstention. This raises the question whether there can be any such general, strategic regulation at all, whether in any conceivable generalized form it would not choke off spiritual life at its root and therefore become more dangerous to faith than does atheistic propaganda. In posing this question we confess that we are not able to wring from it anything but this "rhetorical" meaning.

2. The *ethical* (using the term in its narrower sense) part of the question is whether the temptation which is inherent in the ease with which a strategic large-scale plan of birth control could be realized would not also have another effect, namely, that the fear, not to say the panic, which is unleashed by the expected population explosion tends to produce an attitude of mind in which one begins to apply a dubious—that is, panicky!—therapy before one has completed the diagnosis. That is to say, the fear robs us of the ability to be objective and calm, and all the more so since, after all, the ostensible cure is available in the form of organized birth control. To seize upon this therapeutic too quickly means to operate according to the law of least resistance and therefore the law of inertia.

This is why the question of the causal nexus of hunger and population increase is not calmly examined thoroughly or why it never even occurs to some to ask it, or why it is simply dismissed by doctrinaire ideological prejudice.

---

[26] Martin Heidegger, *Being and Time,* trans. by John Macquarrie and Edward Robinson (New York: Harper & Row, 1962), pp. 91 ff.
[27] *Church Dogmatics,* III, 4, p. 272.

This is a manifestation of the heuristic productivity of an attitude like that of Roman Catholic moral theology (and no blind Protestant zeal should prevent us from seeing this clearly). Since for dogmatic reasons (which we cannot accept) it has on principle barred the way to the path of least resistance and therefore *cannot* be subject to the temptation to solve the population explosion by means of planned birth control, the only possibility left to it is to keep on examining the explosion diagnostically in order to discover clues for a therapeutic attack upon it. Hence there are more solid sociological and economic insights emerging from this quarter than from the overhasty population manipulators.

It would be unfair to pass over in silence the fact that at this point the Roman Catholic reserve with respect to all contraceptive techniques proves to be fruitful and that we must not underestimate the importance of this warning voice in the clash of opinions. Our dogmatic starting point may be different from that of Catholicism and it may give us larger scope for the use of responsible freedom, but no one can ignore with impunity the historical vistas which are opened up by Catholic moral theology. And if we arrive at different decisions, we must first have passed through the barrage of its arguments. It will have the effect of a delaying action in the good sense and in any case it will be a reminder of that boundary line which must be observed at one point or another, but nevertheless observed, when we are dealing with the problem of birth control. To observe no boundaries—let us repeat once more—is not to transcend nature but to eliminate it. And wrong as it is to identify the order of creation with the order of nature, it is also wrong to separate them from each other and think that to ignore nature would not impugn the order of creation.

This conversation with Catholic moral theology has brought out a phenomenon which we have had occasion to observe elsewhere,[28] and that is that differences in theological principle do not necessarily involve differences in the realm of concrete action, but that on the contrary a common Christian program of action over against the "world" is very much a possibility. It is true that on the subject we

[28] *ThE* II, 2, §3950 ff.

have been discussing, different decisions are made on both sides with respect to *individual* life, but even here the criterion of the order of creation (even though it is differently applied) brings out the fact that we are both conscious of that borderline for which we are responsible and therefore constitutes some common ground. On the other hand, in the problem of life *beyond the individual* as represented by the question of population policy and organized birth control, both positions approach each other very considerably, despite the fact that they are based upon different reasoning. (Naturally we are speaking of the Protestant position *here* presented. Therefore this statement that the two positions are very near to each other cannot be applied to every position which is set forth in the context and in the name of Protestant theology.)

In the light of the principles set forth, the question of *sterilization* hardly requires any explicit treatment. Since it implies the decision in favor of permanent prevention of conception the decision to be made with regard to it is correspondingly more momentous, but not fundamentally different. Here the question of motive acquires added urgency. This applies especially to the question to be decided by the legislator who must determine to what extent the decision for sterilization shall be left free or even made a matter of legal disposition. Even though we cannot deny the right of society to protect itself against the birth of severely defective life or life generated by the asocial, it nevertheless appears impossible to us that the state should derive from this the right to interfere in the sexual nature of man against his will.[29] The consequence of such legislation would almost inevitably be the development of the ideological thesis that some life is unfit to be allowed to live ["*lebensunwerten Leben*"]. Here the philosophical eugenics of National Socialism should provide us with sufficient warning. In this matter the only legitimate reaction of the state must take the form of providing security measures or asylum. In view of the fact that abnormal and asocial individuals tend to propagate themselves more profusely than healthy people,[30] for the sake of the self-protection of society this right cannot be denied to the state.

In view of the fact that it would not by any means be only the normal people, finding themselves in a peculiarly tragic situation, but also the

[29] Cf. the Encyclical *Casti Connubii* (Denzinger 2245): Here one would be "arrogating [a] power to the civil magistrates which they never had and can never have legitimately."

[30] Stelzenberger, *op. cit.*, p. 337.

spiritually and morally subnormal people who would request sterilization, the state cannot start with the proposition that the decision with regard to sterilization is to be left only to the choice of the individual. On the contrary, it must undoubtedly assume that not everybody can see the full consequences of such a decision (especially since, unlike optional sterility, it is irreversible, certainly in the case of the man and probably in the case of the woman[31]). Therefore the appointment of an expert committee which would have the power of veto would be desirable.

The sole exception in which a constitutional, state-regulated compulsory sterilization (or castration) might possibly come under consideration would be the situation of a feeble-minded person who had been placed under guardianship, whose sexual impulses constituted a danger to those around him or there was the danger of his begetting abnormal children with another feeble-minded partner. The coincidence of two circumstances—namely, first, that the state (the community of law) cannot take over the responsibility for the begetting of severely diseased life, though it *must* do so where the person responsible cannot be called to account, and second, that the lifelong institutionalization of an otherwise "harmless" feeble-minded person might be an avoidable harshness—the coincidence of these two circumstances could make it debatable whether the representative (guardian, etc.) of the feeble-minded person might present such a request to the state. A measure thus safeguarded as far as possible from abuse would, however, come under the concept of a "constitutional, state-regulated compulsory sterilization (or castration)" only in a very limited sense, since the state does not possess the omnipotent power to dispose of such things and possibly does not even have the right to initiate such measures. The only situation in which this could arise would be in the possible case of a nonresponsible feeble-minded person who was unable to function in making the relevant decision and a representative had to make it for him, but that the state itself—which might be a "party" state, a potential ideological state—cannot be that representative, but is rather dependent upon the request of the guardian and the recommendation of an independent commission. We would see an ultimate theologicoethical argument for this proposal in the light of the order of creation in the fact that such measures could help to refute the argument of those who advocate the eugenic indication in connection with abortion. Since as a rule artificial abortion (see the next section) constitutes the most serious assault upon the order of creation, everything that diminishes the trend toward, and the temptation to, this assault has a certain ethical justification (though, of course, not blanket legitimation).

[31] Cf. Bovet, *op. cit.*, pp. 167 ff.

Catholic moral theology rejects any intervention for the purpose of sterilization or castration for the same reasons that are put forward in its rejection of contraceptive measures.[32]

[32] The literature includes: Jos. Mayer, *Gesetzliche Unfruchtbarmachung Geisteskranker* (1927); A. Niedermeyer, *Pastoralmedizin*, IV, pp. 145 ff.; Pius XII, address on Oct. 29, 1951, *Herder-Korrespondenz*, IV, 115, Nr. 27; Protestant statements: Bovet, *op. cit.*, pp. 167 f.; Søe, *Christliche Ethik* (2 ed., 1957), pp. 500 f.

# B. Interruption of Pregnancy (The Problem of Artificial Abortion)

Interference in germinating life confronts us, not with the question whether human life dare be prevented at its beginning—as in the case of contraception—but rather with the question whether human life dare be destroyed. This differentiation of the question is fundamental. A certain substantiation for the permissibility of preventing human life at its beginning in special cases might even employ the argument that in critical cases this conditional permission lessens the later temptation to do away with the unwanted life through artificial abortion. But in the very use of this line of argument the conditional permissibility of the one act underscores the unconditional forbiddenness of the other. This in itself should indicate that the conditional approval we give to contraception does not represent a tendency toward laxity, but would rather see the severity of the divine command concentrated upon the decisive point.

This decisive point is the sanctity of life itself, including germinating life.

By what right can anyone make this ethical distinction between the prevention of life that is coming into being and the killing of life that has come into being?

We have seen that under the conditions of "this aeon" a conflict can arise within the order of creation itself, in the sense that *one* side of its meaning and purpose—namely, the calling of men into a personal, responsible relationship with the Creator, which is granted only to man—can come into conflict with another side of its meaning and

226

purpose—namely, the created relationship between wedlock and parenthood. There can be no argument here about the fact of this conflict—at any rate in the simple form here described. For once impregnation has taken place it is no longer a question of whether the persons concerned have responsibility for a *possible* parenthood; they have *become* parents.

It is important, to be sure, that we should always see this problem from the point of view of the destruction of human life, but certainly we should not think only of the life of the nascent child, but also of the status of the already existent parenthood. This status means that the "office" of fatherhood and motherhood has been entrusted to the parents and that they are now enclosed in that circle of duties which obligates them to preserve that which has been committed to them, but also endowed with a blessing which is to be received in gratitude and trust—even though it be a gratitude expressed with trembling and a trust that is won through struggle. This makes it clear that here it is not a question—as it is in the case of contraception—whether a proffered gift can be responsibly accepted, but rather whether an already bestowed gift can be spurned, whether one dares to brush aside the arm of God after this arm has already been outstretched. Therefore here the order of creation is infringed upon in a way that is completely different from that of the case of contraception.

For this reason the Catholic theory of the animation of the fetus is not necessary here, though there is no question of the seriousness of the question, despite some of the rather odd flowers it has sometimes brought forth. What this theory *intends* to say is clear. Its purpose is to bear witness that the germinating human life is equal in status with the developing life of the child and the adult. The ontological structure of the thinking,[1] by the aid of which this explanation of the process from embryo to man is accomplished, entails the fact that it generates a series of further questions which lead to a sometimes fantastic speculation and which can obscure or even discredit the theological intention of the idea.

In the first place the question of the animation of the fetus raises the further question of the way in which it takes place. Does it occur "creationistically" through individual divine acts of creation (so Clement of Alexandria and Lactantius) or "generationalistically" through parental

[1] Cf., e.g., *ThE* I, §1148 ff.

propagation and transmission of the soul, which makes the child's soul an "offshoot" (*tradux*) of parental souls (so Tertullian and Appollinaris)? Likewise there must be an answer to the question *when* the animation of the fetus occurs and thus when an intervention in the germinating life becomes a "murder of the innocent."[2] The solution to this question was partially influenced, especially in scholasticism, by ideas that stem from Aristotle, namely, that the male fetus acquires a soul after forty days but the female fetus after eighty days. Thus the doctrine that there is such a thing as a *foetus animatus* and a *foetus inanimatus* had to be specifically rejected.[3] But even in the modern Catholic statements, in which such theories no longer play a part, the theory of animation asserts itself insofar as they seek to determine the precise period of time within which the impregnation occurs (forty-eight hours) and which represents the time interval within which in special cases (rape) a pregnancy may be manipulated by means of irrigations and injections.[4]

We on the Protestant side will do well not to allow these often rather strange questions and the dogmatic theories which evoke them to prevent us from taking seriously the *intention* of the doctrine, namely, that of distinguishing between potential life and actual life and thereby clarify the distinction of guilt between a permitted prevention and an interruption of pregnancy. One may regard the animation theory as a kind of mythological cipher for the thesis that germinating life is fully valid human life and therefore subject to the same protection as all human life. Everybody who holds this thesis is bound to give some kind of argument for it (even though in our opinion it recedes behind the thesis of full parenthood, which we mentioned above and which consists in the bestowal of the office of fatherhood and motherhood). This substantiating argument does not require any theory of animation. All that is needed is reference to some very plain biological facts. The fetus has its own autonomous life, which, despite all its reciprocal relationship to the maternal organism, is more than a mere part of this organism and possesses a certain independence. The embryo can die while the mother continues to live, and for a limited period of time in which the child can be kept alive the opposite is also possible. Just as both organisms have their own possibilities of living or dying so each of them can also have their own illnesses in which the other does not participate. The fetus has its own circulatory system and its own brain. These elementary biological facts should be sufficient to establish its status as a human being.

[2] Encyclical *Casti Connubii*, Denzinger 2243: "what reason can ever be strong enough to excuse in any way the direct murder of the innocent?"
[3] Innocent XI, "Various Errors," 1679, Denzinger 1184 f.
[4] *Lex. d. Kathol. Lebens*, col. 592.

The recognition of this distinction between the two cases has also had its effect upon secular legislation in that it makes abortion (fedicide or prolicide) punishable by imprisonment.[5] Naturally, the judgment pronounced by the Christian message goes beyond the conception of guilt implied by the penal sentence in several respects:

First, in the sense that it radicalizes the law. The murder does not begin with the active killing (Matt. 5:21 ff.)—nor in the killing of the embryo. It begins rather with the renunciation, the wishing away of the embryo (*orgizomenos to embruo!*); for here is a person who refuses to say Yes to a gift bestowed by God and a responsibility imposed by him. This is not only disobedience to the divine command but also ingratitude for the privilege offered to me in the talent and most certainly in the child entrusted to me.

Second, the legal concept of guilt is also transcended by the spiritual concept in that the divine judgment is not only more radical but more merciful than the judgment of men. For it does not only condemn the immediate perpetrator who produces an abortion of her unborn child (including her professional or quack helper), but rather sees this guilt of the individual incorporated in a totality of guilt; it is too compassionate to allow the chief fault to rest only upon *one* head (as human judgments must confine themselves mainly to the one person who can be determined to be the perpetrator of the offense). The eternal Judge is at once both more severe and more compassionate: more severe in that he sees the whole of human powers at work in any particular sin an individual commits; and more compassionate in that he thus does not make this individual the sole guilty one, but always turns to the others, asking which of them dares to cast the first stone (John 8:7).

This total guilt, in which the act of abortion on the part of a mother-to-be is incorporated, may equally include "the irresponsible and uninhibited sexual act of the man, moral carelessness, or depressing economic worries."[6] The temptation to commit abortion may thus arise from economic and social conditions which are partly the responsibility of the whole community and which lay upon Chris-

[5] Cf. Section 218 of the German Penal Code.
[6] Piper, *op. cit.*, p. 240.

tendom the obligation not merely to react to such cases from the point of view of "individual ethics," but rather by changing the conditions and eliminating the structural causes of such offenses by means of giving helpful assistance.

Among the most important "indications" which are adduced to justify artificial abortion, the so-called "social indication" is thus already shown to be illegitimate. There is no discernible reason that can justify us in allowing an external ("social") emergency situation to be made grounds for an abortion. This applies not only to the individual case of an intolerable economic, vocational, or housing situation (in which case what is demanded is the help of the "neighbor" in direct personal form or indirect institutional form) but also to the situation in which the law permits abortion in order to prevent overpopulation and establish a balance between production and consumers (in which case pragmatic considerations would be empowered to decide matters of life and death).

This latter course was subjected to a large-scale experiment in the Soviet Union in the years 1917 to 1936 when abortion was permitted. Here we refer to the decree of the Commissariat of Public Health, 1920, which along with the sanctioning of abortion contained the strict provision that the abortion must be performed only by approved physicians and also provided for free hospitalization. A further decree of the year 1924, necessitated by the overcrowding of hospitals with abortion cases, defined the degrees of priority. These definitions clearly indicate the pragmatic point of view: women who are engaged in production are given first consideration.[7] The results were devastating: in 1921 there were twenty-one abortions for every hundred births and in 1926 they had already reached ninety in every hundred births! The laws were therefore changed and all abortion was subjected to rigorous punishment.[8]

These catastrophic statistics cannot be cited in a theological ethics merely for the purpose of proving empirically the impossibility of a state-licensed abortion policy, that is, by showing what its social and population effects are. This would only be refuting a pragmatic policy by means of other pragmatic considerations! What we are saying here is that the prag-

[7] The decrees are reprinted in Soph. Benfey-Kunert, "Das Recht des ungeborenen Lebens," in *Hamb. Akadem. Rundschau*, 1947/48, pp. 44 ff.

[8] Cf. Jores, *op. cit.*, p. 49; August Mayer, "Erfahrungen mit der Freigabe der Schwangerschaftsunterbrechung in der Sowjetrepublik" in *Beiheft z. Zeitschr. f. Geburtshilfe u. Gynäkol.* (Stuttgart, 1933).

matic category has no competence whatsoever here and that it simply
cannot be applied to the question of the value of human life.

On the contrary we should have to uphold the inviolability of germinating life even if there were methods which would enable us to arrive at a
perfect medical, psychological, and political solution. But with this limitation we can point to these statistical facts and say that they also have
a theological force: they point to the fact that when the order of creation
is violated the punishment comes in an actual judgment in history[9] and
the fact that "sin is a people's ruin" (Prov. 14:34, Luther's translation).

The genesis of human life is a sacrosanct domain which dare not be
invaded by human hands or "rationalized," that is, subjected to
utilitarian considerations. And this inviolability over against any
pragmatic intervention follows not only from the order of creation,
the miracle of which has actualized itself and the violation of which
must be atoned for, but also from the order of redemption, just as
surely as Christ has bought man "with a price" and bestows upon him
an "alien dignity" (dignitas aliena).[10] This "alien dignity" expresses
the fact that it is not man's own worth—his value for producing "good
works," his functional proficiency, his pragmatic utility—that gives
him his dignity, but rather what God has "spent upon him," the sac-
rificial love which God has invested in him (Deut. 7:7 f.). Therefore
this "alien dignity" actualizes itself at the very point where man's own
value has become questionable, the point where his functional value
is no longer listed on society's stock market and he is perhaps declared to be "unfit to live."[11] And this actualization of man's "alien
dignity," which we have emphasized, may well exist at that point
where man is still a fetus and has no important pragmatic value or
may even be regarded as a burdensome, disturbing "enemy."[12]

The great majority of responsible physicians advocate the inviolability
of germinating life, the strict enforcement of Section 218 of the German
Penal Code, and hence the rejection of the "social indication." And they
do so even where they are not motivated by any directly Christian con-

[9] Cf. *ThE* II, 1, §2205 ff.
[10] Cf. *ThE* I, §705, 836 f., 1147, 1258.
[11] Cf. the section on euthanasia in the chapter on law.
[12] This plays a part, for example, in the "theory of self-defense," which
regards the fetus as an "unjust aggressor." It is explicitly rejected in *Casti
Connubii* (Denzinger 2243).

cepts, such as man's "alien dignity," but merely a *post*-Christian—but therefore, note, a post-*Christian*—concept of humanity. However, even here the idea is repeatedly expressed that the social indication may occasionally enter into the medical indication "to a certain degree, since we must judge a person in his entirety" and thus may run into an insoluble mixture of situational misery and psychosomatic effects.[13]

Since the eugenic indication plays a subordinate role, theological ethics must concentrate its inquiry upon the *medical indication*. In this case where the decision must be made between the life of the mother and that of the unborn child or even the decision between the life of the mother and the death of *both*, we have a borderline situation in which a strict prohibition of a medical intervention (aimed at artificial abortion) would be not only intolerably harsh, but would actually fail, for reasons which we shall discuss, to meet the demand of the order of creation.

In considering this borderline situation we are aware that the most careful self-control will be required not to neutralize our resolute rejection of abortion by opening a back door.

We shall dispense with any detailed description of the human side of such a case in which the mother of a family—perhaps the mother of small children—is threatened with death and could be saved by means of a "forbidden intervention" (a perhaps not legally, but theologically forbidden intervention). Since the possible harshness of an ethical demand does not affect its validity and the preservation of certain values may even demand the sacrifice of *life*, there is good reason for us to be on guard against emotions, however respectable they may be, and adhere rigorously to the facts when we are dealing with questions of principle.

But if we do this, then the question presents itself in this way: Can there be a situation in which I am allowed to destroy innocent life? Can I ever intervene as a judge when "nature"—to put it for the moment in this neutral way—allows two lives to be set in competition with each other? It is not only in the matter of abortion that this question becomes acute. It also arose in the concentration camps of National Socialism and the killing of the mentally ill, when the question

---

[13] Jores, *op. cit.*, p. 53.

was whether to sacrifice a few in order possibly to save a thousand others.[14] The fact that the possibility of a conflict of values exists is undisputed; and that it demands an interpretation which must employ the concept of a world which is no longer "whole"—this is recognized not only by Christian theologians on the basis of the story of the Fall, but also by the tragic poets.[15] The only question is, however, whether man is permitted to intervene in this conflict and solve it according to his judgment—no matter whether it is nature or history that confronts him with this conflict.

We respect the dreadful monolithic grandeur of the conception of Catholic moral theology, which sternly rejects such an intervention with the already mentioned argument that there can never be sufficient grounds to justify the "direct murder of the innocent."[16] Only indirect artificial abortion is recognized as permissible. By this is meant a medical measure which is undertaken for a purpose other than that of killing the fetus (therapeutic measures for the sake of the mother, for example), in which, however, abortion may result and possibly may even be foreseen.[17] Even in the tragic case of conflict which presents the alternative between the life of the mother or that of the child, the mother is under the sacred obligation to bear the child to maturity. What strikes us as "grand" in these affirmations is not only the willingness to accept even the most extreme consequences, but also their strict antithesis to any pragmatic considerations whatsoever.

This pragmatic weighing of values seems the obvious and natural thing to do right here where the conflict occurs, and the question presents itself which life is the more "valuable," that of the mother—upon whom the care of the family and the rearing and education of the children so largely depend—or that of the fetus—which has still to face the test of life and which at first appears to be only a burden and

---

[14] We have analyzed this case in detail as a particularly significant model of the borderline situation and here refer the reader especially to the section on "The Conflict between Life and Life," in *ThE* II, 1, §739 ff., especially the footnotes to §744, and also the bibliographical references given there.

[15] Cf. *ThE* I, §1330 ff.

[16] Cf. besides *Casti Connubii* the addresses of Pius XII on Oct. 29 and Nov. 28, 1951, *Herder-Korr.* VI, pp. 113 and 171.

[17] H. Noldin and G. Heinzel, *Summa theologiae moralis* (1952), II, pp. 328 ff.

not to have any productive value whatsoever. If we understand Catholic moral theology correctly, it would not simply dismiss the question of the relative rank of the two lives, but would only draw different conclusions from the answer to this question. That is to say, it would see the higher "value" of the mother, which presumably it would not dispute, precisely in the fact that the mother is capable, as an ethical personality, of making her own decision and thus of making the sacrifice of her life, whereas the unconscious fetus may be merely the object of hostile manipulations directed against it. Does not the relative rank of man consist precisely in his ability to sacrifice, in his quality of being able to make decisions?

We have not found this argument stated in just this way in Catholic literature (which does not mean that it may not be there) and perhaps we have overinterpreted the position of our partners in this discussion; if so, however, then certainly in their favor, in order to make it as difficult as possible to meet them. For the seriousness of the decision demands that one seek to meet the other's position at its optimum and not content oneself with the rather easy emotional objection that here Catholic moral theology is allowing a cold doctrinaire attitude to triumph over every impulse of the human heart. It may well be—in any case we are assuming this—that some completely different and highly "humane" thoughts are in the background here, namely, the appeal to the one who ranks higher—*noblesse oblige!*—to sacrifice himself instead of allowing the innocent life to be destroyed in his stead. Here the higher rank would be honored not by acknowledging a *privilege* (the one who is more important to society being spared) but must rather prove itself in the acceptance of higher *duties*. This is what we meant by saying that the Catholic position expresses the extreme antithesis of all pragmatic criteria of value.

Before we proceed, let us say that we see no possibility of contradicting this idea of sacrifice—except, of course, on the *one* condition that it be not put forward as a law whether of the state or of the church. It is only at this point that the gist of our opposition could lie; and here it must be expressed, since the Roman Church, by its strict prohibition of artificial abortion in *every* case, demands the sacrifice of the mother. Here the sacrifice to be made by the one of higher rank is simply drained of its meaning, because through this legalistic regulation the mother is made the object of a medical act of omission—on the part, say, of strict Catholic physicians or nurses. Casuistical regimentation of the case cancels out the freedom which alone could provide the basis for the higher duty of the one who has the higher rank.[18] If this freedom is granted, then the freely made decision of the mother to offer the risk of her life and not allow the fruit of her body to be touched can only be respected by Christian ethics.

Naturally, there is also a subtle form of noninstitutionalized legalism that could threaten such a sacrifice. This is the case when a mother acts in the name of, and under the pressure of, a supposed dogma of the order of creation which possibly is not to be held in this form at all. This confronts us with the real question that concerns us here in this *special* connection, exactly as it did in connection with the problem of contraception, namely, the question of how far and in what way the demand of the order of creation is to be obeyed. Here again we must be prepared to meet the question whether, under the conditions of this fallen, no longer perfect world, the direct application of the order of creation might not be "fanatical" ["*schwarmerisch*"] and therefore destructive; whether, therefore, there is not theological significance in the fact that Jesus did not simply make the protological law of the original state and the eschatological law of the Kingdom of God the law of this aeon, but rather allowed both to be the *corrective* which calls in question this aeon.[19] There is no need to emphasize particularly the fact that when we face the question of killing, which is at issue here, the "brokenness" of the claim of the

[18] Cf. on the problem of casuistry *ThE* II, 1, pp. 3 ff., II, 2, §4354 ff. [Cf. "The Freedom of Decision: The Impossibility of Casuistry in Ethical Christianity," in Thielicke, *The Freedom of the Christian Man* (New York: Harper & Row, 1963), pp. 148 ff. Trans.]

[19] The fact that this does not relegate the eschatological and protological demands to the status of Platonic marginal phenomena of the ethos, but rather possess an enormous historical immediacy, we have set forth in detail in the "ethics of politics"; cf. *ThE* II, 2, Index, "Bergpredigt," especially § 562 ff., 665-668.

order of creation[20] needs to be dealt with far more carefully than when we are facing the question whether possible life may be prevented from coming into being.

On the question of the *claim* of the order of creation there is a profound difference between the Catholic and the Reformation teaching concerning the relationship of creation and sin.[21] The reduction of the Fall to a mere injury inflicted upon nature (which remains otherwise intact), as Catholic theology teaches, makes possible a certain analogy and continuity between the norms of the original state and those of the (partially) fallen world. The doctrine of natural law formulates and systematizes these enduring normative axioms.[22] Its presupposition is that the Fall represents only an accidental break in the structure of the order of creation, that in establishing the ethical norms one can—to express it somewhat sharply—almost "pass over it." Over against this, Reformation doctrine is impressed by the elemental changes which sin has wrought within the very structure of the world.

Therefore Reformation doctrine arrives at a different doctrine of orders. It says that the orders—with the exception of the prototype [*Urbild*] of marriage and family—must be understood, not as orders of creation, but rather as orders of necessity in the fallen world, as measures which God provides to preserve the fallen world.[23]

With respect to the medical indication of abortion, this break between the original state and the conditions of this aeon becomes acute in that the conflict between life and life does not occur in the original order of creation and therefore the order of creation cannot provide a direct solution of the conflict. This is also evident in the example of the just war, which is justified only insofar as its purpose is to protect life which is committed to the care of the state, but which can do so only by destroying other life. This analogy of war is applicable only in a very limited sense, not only according to Catholic but also our opin-

---

[20] Cf. the discussion of this under the theme of how this transposition of the original "natural law" is to be made in the circumstances of this aeon in *ThE* I, §2054 ff.

[21] Cf. *ThE* I, §1001, especially 1014.

[22] Cf. *ThE* I, §2010 ff.

[23] Cf. *ThE* I, §2144 ff.

ion, since in a just war it is presupposed that the life which is to be destroyed is that of an aggressor and thus of one who is "guilty," whereas the unborn child is certainly not to be thought of as an aggressor in this sense at all, but rather as innocent life.[24] Here the point of comparison between war and abortion does not consist at all in the guilty-aggressive or innocent competition between two lives, but rather in the fact that both are opposed to the order of creation, that originally (*ap' arches*) life was not pitted against life, that it was incorporated in an order cosmos which had been wrested from the chaos (where everything was pitted against everything else). Because all life was "under God" and related to him, all life was at peace with all other life. Because the vertical dimension was in order, the horizontal dimension too was in order. We have repeatedly emphasized and shown the biblical basis of this relation between peace with the Creator *and* the peace of the creatures one with another, between breaking away from the peace of the Creator *and* the loss of peace within the creation itself.[25]

The consequence of this interrelationship is that what we see in the world as disorder can never be related directly to God's creator-hood and his government of the world. Where there is war in the world, it may be that God is giving us a mandate in it; but this does not mean that God "wills" war, that war is a part of the design of his creation. Where there is suffering and sickness, they cannot be interpreted as being the result of God's proper will (*voluntas Dei propria*), but are actually the reverse of this real will of God—though God still carries out his will in the midst of that which opposes it and is able to make even the forms of this opposition to "work for good" (Rom. 8:28). The eschatological emphases in the Bible make it clear that it is not God's *real* will that is at work in the perversity of the world: Jesus' healings of the sick are signs that point to the fact that in the Kingdom of God there will be no more suffering, no crying, no tears; his resurrection points to the destruction of the "last enemy" (I Cor. 15:26). It is not permissible (and, of course, we are not insinuating that our Catholic brethren do this!) to trace back directly

[24] Cf. *Casti Connubii*, Denzinger 2243.
[25] Cf., e.g., *ThE* II, 1, §2222 ff., 2234 ff.

and indiscriminately to the creative will of God both the birth of children and the crippling of children, both the blossom and the "frost that blights the springtime bloom"—and thereby transform him from the Lord of the order of creation into what is basically only the First Cause and a phantom of a philosophoumenon.[26]

This raises the question: When illness would make the bearing of the child a mortal threat to the mother, dare we say that what happens here is simply to be attributed to the will of God in creation? Dare we interpret the conflict between life and life that occurs here simply as a statute of his will to which we must submit? Is not all this rather the token of a creation that should accuse itself in the face of the *real* will of God? Or to turn the question around, would we not have to brand all medical action as rebellion against God, if we were to affirm that suffering, sickness, the hostility of the elements of the organism, and the hostility of the organisms to each other, are dispensations of God? Would this not mean that medical and nursing care flies in the face of God's will, prevents God's will from being done?

To ask these questions is to answer them in the negative. The order of creation is not an outline plan for what occurs in this case of illness, this conflict of two lives. I cannot incorporate it "directly" into this plan.

But, you ask, can I not do this at least partially, in *certain* relations? For example, by learning from the order of creation that God desires to preserve what he has created and gave it its *kairos*? True—but what does this mean when two forms of life created by him enter into mortal competition with each other? Our only point in asking these questions is to make it clear that the appeal to the order of creation becomes problematical insofar as one seeks to obtain direct answers concerning its demand in this case of conflict. Outside of the conflict the demand may be clear and unambiguous and there can be no question whatsoever about the prohibition of abortion, and yet it appears to become ambiguous as soon as the conditions of this aeon and the order of creation are seen to be incommensurable.

Here we are faced with the alternatives. The first is whether we

[26] Cf. Thielicke, *Tod und Leben* (3 ed.), p. 213.

should obey the demand of the order of creation by simply accepting the condition of this fallen world as a judgment and then interpreting a mother's dying because of her child as a kind of vicarious sharing in this sentence of judgment. But if we do this, are we really refraining from intervening in the order of *creation?* When all this happens, is it really the order of creation that is involved at all? Are we not rather refraining from intervening in the order of *judgment* when we simply allow the decree of judgment to take its course? And when we do this, are we not at most merely paying respect to the order of creation by regarding it only as a judgmental law which applies the standard of the original state and condemns our fallen world?

Or—and this would be the other alternative—do we not rather observe the claim of the order of creation if we grant to medical assistance the mission to set forth in a signlike (though admittedly imperfect) way God's *real* will for the world and allow it to be a reminder of the original perfect creation and a promise of the world to come? Is not the healing which is committed to the physician actually a part of the signlike struggle against the brokenness and disturbance of the creation? And is not his struggle actually a battle that is waged with means (medicines and techniques) which he can draw from the surviving store of created things? In this reaction of the medical man is there not a manifestation of that mystery of the world in which in this aeon the conflict is carried right into the order of creation itself and the fact that we always find it there whenever we ourselves begin to act; in other words, that the conflict of values manifests itself in the conflict of the elements of creation with each other, that the physician fights against the alien elements in creation in the *name* of creation and with its *means*, that, indeed, nature is marshaled and mobilized against nature?

Here we catch ourselves arguing by means of questions. This may be owing to the fact that here we are confronted with that utmost limit, where the exceptional case lands us, where even theological thought reaches its limit: where we get no further by making subsumptions under given dogmatic axioms and even the concept of the order of creation loses its applicability. True, we may be able to say why it is that we face this limit of theological thought and to that extent we shall be arguing theologically. We can show how in the borderline situation there appears that distortion of perspective which demonstrates all too clearly the derangement of the order of creation and the conflict of values which has intruded into it. All this we can state at the level of theological argument. But we cannot proceed with the same style of argumentation and "solve" that conflict. For in order for us to be able to proceed in this way the order of creation would have to be an immediately applicable standard. But this it is not.

The order of creation would be this kind of standard only if we did not view the incursion of sin as radically as did the Reformers, in other words, if we did not interpret it as a break in the continuity between the original state and the fallen world. If, however, one accepts this almost unbroken continuity and introduces the doctrine of original sin accordingly,[27] then both members of the continuity remain commensurable and the order of creation can be taken as a critical rule and standard and applied directly to the realities of our world. This experiment took form in the Catholic doctrine of natural law![28] If, however, we are compelled to hold a doctrine of sin which almost completely breaks the commensurability of the original state and this aeon in certain borderline cases, then it is impossible to lay one's finger directly upon the claim of the order of creation. To adhere to this commensurability under all circumstances leads, it is true, to a more "practicable" moral theology. For then one "knows where one is" with all the certainty of juridical deductions; one has fixed standards. And even though their application—as in the case of the absolute prohibition of abortion—can lead to extreme practical harshness and the reproach of doctrinaire disregard for life, it is nevertheless a triumph of practicability to achieve a situation in which the framework of standards remains unmoved and every case can be localized within it.

---

[27] Cf. *ThE* I, §991 ff., 1366 ff.

[28] However, even here certain changes are not entirely lacking when the norms of the order of creation are applied to this world. Here too a distinction is made between absolute and relative natural law. Nevertheless the break between the original state and the fallen world is viewed in a way completely different from that of Reformation theology. Cf. *ThE* I, §2016 ff.

In saying this it should be understood that we are by no means saying that this whole Catholic conception was contrived for reasons of practicability, that it is therefore pragmatic in a very remote sense. On the contrary, we are simply clarifying for our own benefit why it is that we often admire the impressive clarity of this conception and its rigid consistency, why it is that we too "would like to have something like it"—since, after all, if we had explicit directive norms at our disposal, this would reduce the hazardousness of making decisions—*and* why it is that we must nevertheless renounce all of this.

The desire for practicability, for some handy moral-theological application of the order of creation, must rather be subjected to the discipline of the question of truth. And the question of truth is this: Can we, dare we, interpret sin in such a way that this continuing analogy between the created world and the fallen world can be accepted and that therefore a commensurability exists between the two, and that thus the order of creation becomes a directly applicable standard? We cannot.[29] But then this means that we can no longer decide with precise theological exactitude—remembering clearly that this applies only within this very limited radius of the borderline situation where life is in competition with life—what the basic alternative shall be: whether the mother should sacrifice herself or not; whether the fatality of this split world should be passively endured or resisted in the name of a signlike medical intervention; whether we should accept the order of creation as a condemning law or whether the life that creation desires should be saved at least partially and possibly at the cost of another life.

Here it becomes very clear that nobody can relieve us of this decision and that the only help we can get from a theological ethics is that it may help us to see what the alternatives are and thus prepare the material for our decision.

Is it necessary to point out that in a concrete situation where this dilemma occurs this clarification is certainly not to be presented in this abstract form which we have had to traverse in the theological workshop?

---

[29] The more precise reasons for this are set forth in our doctrine of sin, which we have developed in constant discussion with Catholic theology. Cf. *ThE* I, index.

What we have here thought through reduces itself in the acute situation to some very simple questions: Whether a young mother sees that for her obedience to God means sacrificing herself for the nascent child, or whether she is prepared to give up her child in order to go on living in love for her family and to conceive life again for renewed service to God. Whether because of her desire to go on living, her elemental instinct for self-preservation, she wants to see the fruit of her body dealt with like a cancer which one simply excises, or whether in the knowledge that it is her child she makes the maternal sacrifice for the sake of the others for whom she must be preserved in order to go on being a mother to them. This, or something like this, is what the questions would be in the context of pastoral care. But the pastor must have previously thought through these questions theologically in order to be able to put them in this way and not simply to regard softness of heart (or weakness of nerve) as the expression of a compassion which would permit one to take the path of least resistance.

In the borderline situation the overwhelming force of these questions which cannot be decided with strict theoretical clarity brings out very clearly what is always the case, namely, that we can decide only subject to forgiveness. For we know that there are no "slick" solutions, either theoretical or practical. We know that whatever we do we incur guilt. We understand the physicians who, faced with a borderline situation where the medical indication is present, have performed an artificial abortion and are shocked by a sense of guilt, which for lack of a better word they describe as metaphysical guilt, as an offense against life—and yet not knowing how they could have done otherwise. But would a physician who chose the opposite course and allowed a young mother to die without intervention be free of this guilt, this "metaphysical guilt feeling"?

All this goes to show that the sin is not confined to one particular decision and that the choice of another alternative would mean the avoidance of sin. Rather here it becomes clear that we are moving in a world that is saturated with sin and that no one can pass through it without incurring guilt.

This is nothing more than what the theologians have been trying to say from time immemorial in the doctrine of original sin. In that doctrine they have been saying that sin attaches not only to our actions but also to the very status of our being which is antecedent to all our acts—indeed, that it attaches equally to the very status of this aeon which again is antecedent to our individual existence. The intention of the doctrine of original sin has always been to affirm this super-personal background of sin.

Therefore it is also a part of the task of theology to show that the structures of this superpersonal background—meaning the "orders" —exist in a twilight zone between creation and Fall, partaking of both, and to interpret them not only as realizations of the will of God but as being at the same time self-realizations of the world which is no longer the intact world that God created.[30]

Only as we start from this point of view can we judge what it means to live by the justification of the sinner and be comforted by the knowledge that, as Luther said, "even in the best of lives" what we do is in vain. In the borderline case we do not even "know" what we are doing or what we should do. Even our knowing and not-knowing is subject to forgiveness. But the fact that we live by forgiveness does not mean that we are without discipline (Rom. 6:15 ff.); rather we act on the basis of a new relationship (*douleia*).

To these fundamental theological considerations we may add another thought which comes from empirical observation and may perhaps be helpful in the concrete situation of decision insofar as it may under certain circumstances mitigate the harsh alternative of "either the life of the mother *or* the life of the child." However, it cannot help us to escape fundamentally the pressure of the borderline situation.

Obviously there is a difference between the relationship which we have with a living person and that which we have with a human life which is beginning to germinate. This difference manifests itself, for example, in the fact that many, for whom the rejection of euthanasia and perhaps even of capital punishment presents no problem, decide, when confronted with the conflict between the life of the mother and that of an unborn child, in favor of sacrificing the fetus. Even the theological affirmations that the fetus is already a "human being" and that (according to the thesis of Catholic moral theology) the *animatio foetus* takes place at the moment of impregnation show, by the very fact that they are affirmed as a warning and admonition and as a kind of protest against instinct and mere appearance, that people are not altogether under the impression that

[30] This is what we have attempted to do in our doctrine of orders: *ThE* I, §2144.

germinating life possesses that *humanitas* which they would unquestionably attribute to another person or even to an infant. If we are not greatly mistaken, there is at least a widespread "feeling" that the embryo, despite its relatively autonomous life, is nevertheless only a part of the maternal organism, and that in the case of conflict the whole takes precedence over the part. Therefore the mother must be saved.

The only question is, however, whether this feeling is right and whether this relationship of whole and part is correct. Certainly it is not correct! It certainly requires no special theory of animation to reject this idea of the relationship of the part to the whole. We point to the plain biological fact that the embryo has its own autonomy, on the basis of which the germinating life must be interpreted as the developing of a *humanitas* which is already there.

Nevertheless, the question arises whether this does not require some further distinctions. And here we come to our empirical observations. In a normal, healthy mother it is usually the case—and similar tendencies are also to be observed in the animal kingdom—that she is prepared to protect with her life even the smallest child and that in the case of conflict the idea hardly occurs to her to consider her life as "more valuable" and to draw from this the conclusion that she should be spared. So here the case of conflict is generally decided very unequivocally and quite independent of any pragmatic motives.

It is significant that this unequivocal willingness of the mother to sacrifice herself for the sake of the fetus is not so absolute and unconditional that the question cannot at least be discussed, whereas, characteristically, nobody even thinks of discussing the other case of destroying a child already born. (Where would one find this theme mentioned even in casuistical moral theologies?) This difference in which one is made a theme of discussion and the other is treated as if it were simply to be accepted as a matter of course certainly cannot be explained by saying that the situation of conflict between the life of a child *already born* and that of the mother is much more rare. (When does a mother ever get into the situation of having to jump in and save her drowning child? And when it does happen, is not this merely a spontaneous instinctive act which occurs quite outside the zone of ethical reflection and decision?) Very certainly the time during and after the Second World War, the air raids, and the exigencies of refugees raised this conflict in countless cases, and in not a few cases the conflict was such that the sacrifice of the mother was not a matter of spontaneous reaction but of conscious decision (over against death by starving, freezing, being buried by rubble, etc.). But quite apart from the frequency or infrequency of such cases of conflict, it is quite sufficient to visualize them in imagination.

Must not this difference in attitude toward these two situations—the general tendency to take it for granted that a mother will sacrifice herself for a child already born and the question that is raised about her willingness to sacrifice herself for an unborn child—must not this difference give us pause? Therefore, even though we hold that this realm of nascent life is sacrosanct and that only the medical indication is admissible, should we not make a *justified* distinction between the child already born and the unborn child—a distinction, be it noted, only in the face of that dreadful conflict in which it is clearly a question of a fundamental choice between two lives? Should we not be permitted to make this distinction even if the justification of it cannot be demonstrated in strict theological terms? Would it really be a case of falling under the verdict of "natural theology" if we felt obliged to interpret the differing way in which the maternal instinct obviously reacts here as not being an absolute unfaithfulness to the clear intention of the order of creation?

Again at this extreme limit situation we fall into the style of *interrogative* argumentation—a style which is obviously determined by the very subject with which we are dealing. We find ourselves in the realm of the nondeducible, the realm where the order of creation is at its extreme of incommensurability, and therefore in the realm where we are in utmost need of forgiveness—even for our *thinking!*

We continue our questions: Should it not give us further pause—on this same empirical level—that in medicine and in criminal law a distinction is usually made between the ovum which has just been impregnated and the developed embryo, some time after the first signs of life and movement, so that an abortion in the latter case is more serious than in the first? Is not this an expression of the assumption that the prenatal process is one of *becoming* a human being and not simply that a human being has already come into being through the impregnation? And should not the fact that this is a being in the process of becoming a human give us a certain right not to regard the diminutive embryo as human in the "same" sense as the nine-month embryo or the mother herself? The fact that the diminutive embryo is actually human life and therefore is just as sacrosanct as any human life remains beyond question. But the case of conflict in the borderline situation—and *only* it!—is characterized by the fact that it confronts us with an alternative which must be traversed even if it is not accepted but rather—as in Catholic moral theology—rejected. But this situation of having to choose compels us to assert not only the qualitative point of view (the fact that human life in every form is sacrosanct) but also the quantitative difference (which form of life has the higher sacrosanctity). This, of course, is precisely the friction that is engendered by the borderline case, a difficulty to which thought, and by no means only ethical decision, is exposed; for here there is a shift from one category to another (*metabasis eis allo genos*) and the category of the qualitative is mixed with the quantitative. It is important also to see this epistemological problem which is evoked by the borderline situation!

Even though we are aware that when we are in this realm of decision only a paper-thin wall separates us from sacrilege (from "metaphysical guilt") and that all such decisions can be made only under the shadow of saving grace, it would seem that these quantitative distinctions do not destroy ethical responsibility but are rather a part of it. That it involves the danger of slipping is obvious and that every application of balancing quantitative criteria has a tendency to lead us to the pragmatic point of view is likewise obvious.

Such dangers, however, always go with freedom and therefore cannot signify the contradiction of freedom. Those who want to avoid them can do so only by setting up a rigid dogma, such as the Catholic theory of animation. The thesis that the fetus acquires a soul at the moment of impregnation makes it fundamentally impossible to apply the quantitative criterion. To this extent it removes the burden of deciding what is to be done in a concrete case and what constitutes obedience; this question it decides beforehand. The burden is reduced to the question whether I am now willing to carry out this previous decision no matter how hard it may be. And no matter how hard it may be—and, after all, willingness to sacrifice the mother is a dreadfully hard thing!—this still provides a certain relief, because the stress of decision and the tendency to become soft which accompanies it is excluded, because the legalistic-dogmatic solution gives support to the weakness of human nature.

In saying this—and with all respect saying it *polemically*—we are saying that we are not trying in libertine fashion to soften the borderline situation and make it easier in a cheap way when we find it impossible to accept the theory of animation and are therefore compelled to turn to these quantitative differentiations within our basic affirmation of the sacrosanctity of human life. Greater freedom increases the burden; it does not lighten it. And in any case, we are not *seeking* greater freedom; it is rather imposed upon us all. And when Sartre says that we are "condemned" to freedom[31] we can accept the statement even though we have not traveled *his* road to arrive at this knowledge. By nature we all seek for the easier law which will relieve us of the burden of responsible decision even though it lays upon us the burden of stricter demands.

There are two ways in which we can seek a way out of the domination of the law: *either* the way of libertine freedom which permits us to act

[31] Cf. *ThE* I, §1975.

according to the law of least resistance and breaks down all sense of obligation; *or* the way of those who are free and yet bound, which means to *seek* the way in obedience, not the way that I choose but the way of him who has chosen me, not the way of prescribed legality, but the way of him who justifies me, however laden with guilt I may be.

Our concern is to leave no doubt whatsoever that this is how we wish this freedom with respect to the medical indication in pregnancy to be understood: as costly and not as cheap freedom. Only from this point of view can the quantitative criterion of which we spoke enter into consideration. And even there it enters into consideration only when the elemental conflict between the life of the mother and that of the unborn child permits—and not only permits, but then also demands—that a decision be made.

# C. Artificial Insemination

Artificial insemination is one of those borderline cases which pose far more fundamental questions than are contained in the purely casuistical side of the problem. Because it confronts the sex relationship, and particularly marriage, with an "extreme" question, we need to know what is the nature of it. Because it brings into discussion a peripheral possibility of parenthood, it compels us to draw the line from the center to this periphery.

First we need to consider the facts. Artificial insemination means the introduction of male semen into the vagina or uterus by means of instruments. The purpose of such a measure is to satisfy the wish to have a child in cases where it cannot be satisfied, because of physical or psychic reasons, through the normal sex act or where this act is not desired. In the first case the reason may lie in the impotence or in an organic impairment of the man. It is also possible that the normal marital procreation is not desirable because of an unfortunate incompatibility in the Rhesus Factor. Because of this incompatibility of blood structure the life of the child may be endangered before, during, and after birth, so that there may be the wish to employ other and physiologically unobjectionable semen for the impregnation. In the second case the reason for not desiring cohabitation may lie in the frigidity of the wife or in the ethical, social, and other inhibitions of an unmarried woman.

The semen employed in the artificial insemination may be that of the husband, so that the artificial insemination consists in medical aid given to married persons in procreation. This we speak of as homologous insemination. Or the semen may come from an outside donor.

248

In this case we speak of heterologous insemination.[1]

The positions hitherto taken with respect to the question of artificial insemination—no matter whether they come from doctors and lawyers, from Catholic or Protestant theologians—exhibit a confusing diversity. This confusion of opinions can be reduced to some kind of statistical order only to the extent that we can say that on the medical side there are advocates of both homologous and heterologous insemination, whereas homologous insemination finds fairly unanimous acceptance on the part of jurists and divided recognition on the part of theologians, and heterologous insemination is very generally rejected by the jurists and radically rejected by the theologians.

This extraordinary diversity in opinion can be illustrated by two statements chosen at random. An American account closes with these words: "Artificial insemination is providing an increasing number of involuntarily childless wives with a means of satisfying the yearning for motherhood, and bringing joy to thousands of families."[2]

On the other hand, a Danish report which describes a particular case of artificial insemination says this: "The father of the artificially procreated child is an unknown semen donor. The transmission was undertaken at the request of the married couple since the sterility of the husband would not permit the begetting of children. And yet even during the pregnancy there developed in the husband a hate-complex toward the unborn child, which, as the very well-known gynecologist who was acting in the case expressed it, had become for him 'a symbol of his own weakness.' This led to tension in the marriage which ended in divorce. The child has now come into the world utterly unwanted and fatherless. The physician, who had recommended the artificial insemination to the couple, says that after this experience he will never again advise this method."[3]

The arguments *against* artificial insemination are, as might be expected, significantly more multistratous than those presented in its defense. Thus on the *medical* side attention is called to the danger of incest: since in heterologous insemination the semen donor remains

---

[1] Perhaps the more common designations in English are A.I.H. (artificial insemination from the husband) and A.I.D. (artificial insemination from an anonymous third-party donor). (Trans.)

[2] Ratcliff, *loc. cit.*, p. 80.

[3] *FAZ*, 1935, Nr. 237, p. 5.

unknown (in order to eliminate any psychic ties of the wife with the biological father) it is possible that half brothers may later marry half sisters. This has led to the grotesque-sounding procedure of English doctors to limit the semen donations of a man "so that not more than 100 children can have the same biological father."[4] An *ethical* objection, which is also put forward by the theologians, affirms that here the psychophysical unity of the sex relationship is dissolved, that the element of personhood in it is expunged in favor of purely biological processes, indeed, that here the bios is mechanized again and that in doing this one is rising not only against creation but against nature itself. But *imagination* too can revolt against a world which is populated by artificially propagated human beings—the kind of world that Aldous Huxley conjured up in his novel *Brave New World*. The imagination is likewise exposed to extreme disquietude by the American report that during the Second World War ampoules containing the semen of 20,000 soldiers were sent back from the front to make possible the impregnation of their wives at home. And finally, too great a strain is put upon what I would call *metaphysical taste* by the technical terminology that has grown up around this subject: the talk about "test-tube babies"[5]; the references to the method of preserving semen through freezing and storing it for use as the maintenance of "semen banks," from which one could select the type of father according to color of hair and skin, mental and physical characteristics, and determine almost synthetically the kind of baby wanted; the designation of the mixing of the sperm of several men (in order to insure the anonymity of the donor) as a "semen cocktail"; the labeling of the donor as a "spermator" and the use of his virility as the "human stud farm" or "spawn trade."[6]

And yet, when one recalls how the first railroads were said to be injurious to health, eyesight, and nerves, one may be rather skeptical of all such objections and even more of the irrational inhibitions, and this means that we shall have to be quite objective and go to the bottom of the question. In doing this we shall orientate ourselves upon a

---

[4] Ratcliff, *loc. cit.*, p. 79.
[5] Dölle, *loc. cit.*, *Die Gegenwart*, p. 367.
[6] Dölle, "Die künstliche Samenübertragung . . .," p. 241.

theological understanding of man and the sexual relationship, leaving out of account the legal problems. We shall also leave out of our discussion the question of how the artificial insemination of unmarried women is to be judged, since the ecclesiastical statements on this question are unanimous and since what we shall have to say with regard to heterological insemination is related to this question.

The problem that confronts us can be stated as follows: Why is it that the artificial insemination of animals can receive general and—apart from details—undisputed acceptance, while it is vehemently contested in the case of human beings?

If we see aright, the objections which are raised in the name of humanity (*humanum*) focus on two essential points. First, as has already been indicated, artificial insemination threatens to remove the biological process of procreation from the psychophysical totality of the marital fellowship. This would appear to infringe upon the personal character of this fellowship, since it is deprived of one of its essential purposes, namely, the physical fellowship, which allows the inward fellowship to become outward and symbolic and thus "total" and which completes this expression in the will to have a child together. One cannot say (and we have given the reasons *why* one cannot say it) that the will to have a child does not exhaust the purpose of marriage. This would reduce it to a mere means. Every human fellowship bears its purpose within itself. The divine commission given to marriage in creation is to the effect that both are created for each other (as a polar unity, Gen. 1:27) as "one flesh" (Gen. 2:23-24) and that *in* this oneness they are to satisfy the command, "Be fruitful and multiply." The personal unity of man, wife, and child would therefore be ruptured by any isolation of the biological act of procreation. This objection must be taken the more seriously since we have fallen upon times when depersonalization has become a disease and this tendency is also invading our marriages and encouraging the cleavage between our biological life and our "human" existence in the narrower sense.

Related to this objection is a second, that, according to a statement by Otto Dibelius,[7] every artificial insemination is an act contrary to

[7] Dölle, "Retortenkinder," *loc. cit.*, p. 368.

nature insofar as it reduces the deepest mystery of human life to a technical process and degrades the woman at the ultimate depth of her spiritual life. These words will be properly interpreted only if one finds expressed in them not merely the general contradiction between nature and technology, bios and mechanization, but rather interprets the term "nature" to mean the nature of *man* and hence regards Dibelius' declaration as a statement concerning the nature of the *humanum*. Then this statement would say that procreation which is accomplished by applied biology, by science and technology, is an infringement upon the mystery of the source of life. One can in fact speak here of a mystery without exposing oneself to the charge of tending toward irrational fuzziness; for what is meant by mystery here can be very precisely defined. It is the mysterious, rationally unexplainable bond between the personal act of human communication—which, according to its purpose, is love—*and* the biological creation of a new life, which constitutes the pledge of this bond.

A proper estimate of these two objections can be formed only if we go beyond generalities and differentiate very carefully between the individual forms of artificial insemination. We shall therefore discuss first homologous and then heterologous insemination.

## 1. HOMOLOGOUS INSEMINATION

This is defined as the artificial transmission of semen from a husband to a wife. It is employed as an expedient when for the reasons stated above a normal emplacement of the semen is impossible. In this case it is a matter of medical aid to fertilization, to which serious objections can hardly be raised if all medical efforts to make the normal act of procreation possible have been without result. For in a marriage thus handicapped it is entirely possible that there can be a personal and sexual fellowship which is in accord with the meaning and purpose of marriage. The sole handicap—and I choose the word deliberately—consists only in the fact that a particular physical particle or a psychic condition is missing and that this blocks the way to the fulfillment of the marriage in having a child. Though this may seem obvious, there are nevertheless a number of objections, of which we shall discuss two serious ones and two unimportant ones.

### a. *Serious Objections*

In the first place it is conceivable that the childlessness in a marriage may not be caused by the handicap we have mentioned—whether it be physical or psychic in nature—but rather comes from a deeper disorder in the marriage. We may think, for example, of the case in which the couple stand in an obviously unerotic relationship to each other and this makes them incapable of performing the sex act.[8] But if "human" prerequisites for the progenitive act are lacking, then, naturally, an *aid* to procreation becomes problematical. Then, instead of being an aid, it becomes a substitute for intercourse. In this borderline case it is not easy to take a decision that escapes the charge of being doctrinaire. For though it is true that the problem actually comes to a focus here, it is nevertheless a question whether these intimate, personal areas can and should be regimented. Obviously there is no doubt that we can say that medical assistance to procreation dare be given only when the intimate prerequisites of marriage are incontestably present and it is only a matter of eliminating a handicap. Though it should be the duty of the physician to investigate the physical and psychic condition of the married couple he is treating and to express any doubts he may have, nevertheless one can neither bind the physician to legal rules nor make the wish of the couple for artificial insemination dependent upon a personal decision of the physician himself—in any case not if this decision goes beyond exclusively medical criteria and if it were to be based upon an attitude that he has taken toward the intimate sphere of the spouses and toward the thesis, however justified it may be theologically, that marriage is a psychophysical unity. The intimate sphere, like the realm of religious duty in marriage, is not "juridifiable"; it cannot be subject to laws and regulations. No third person can make any decisions in these two realms,[9] not even by health authorities or state-appointed commissions, which are recommended by many as courts of deci-

---

[8] An extreme example of this is the "companionate" marriage often entered into by homosexuals. In this case the psychophysical unity which is essential to the nature of marriage is lacking.

[9] This is also the problem inherent in so-called "pastoral medicine."

sion.[10] Right here any kind of institutionalizing is especially irrelevant and incompetent (*sachwidrig*), or better, inimical to personhood (*personwidrig*). In this realm the only thing that can be done is to give responsible help toward the making of a decision, which the married couple *themselves* must make. Even in a marriage which is erotically unsatisfactory or for other reasons infirm, the couple may entertain the hope of gaining new ties to each other by having a child and thus change the usual sequence of cause and effect. Even though as a rule this hope is an illusion and its fulfillment is a rare exception, who dares to thrust himself into this realm of personal venture with the criteria of a theory of probabilities? Who dares to do more at this point than at most give a warning and refuse to accept personal responsibility? The very personhood which many an opponent of artificial insemination wishes to safeguard is undoubtedly severely threatened—assuming that it is permitted by law—when the power of decision and thus the responsibility for it is delegated to a party or court outside the marriage. Even in the *medical* consideration of the case, the acting gynecologist should be bound to undertake the insemination only on condition that if there were no marital handicap a child could be engendered in the natural way.

It therefore appears to be important that the claims of personhood (understood in the Christian sense) and the sexual life which is determined by this personhood should not only be asserted *against* artificial insemination but also examined on the *basis* of artificial insemination.

Serious objections to homologous insemination, which cannot be brushed aside, would appear to be justified in the case where natural procreation is not basically impossible, but perhaps only temporarily prevented. Among these cases is, for instance, the example we cited above of "long-distance" impregnation through American soldiers at the front. Even if one takes into account the hazardous situation of the soldier at the front and his desire to leave behind offspring in case of his death, one must constantly bear in mind that artificial insemination can be an exception which can be conceded only in case the

---

[10] In Sweden, for example: Dölle, "Die künstliche Samenübertragung . . . ," pp. 236 ff.

"impossibility" of the act of procreation has been proved; it cannot be a security measure against threatening "possibilities." This particular instance has exemplary significance for the postulation or non-postulation of the "possibility." If the mere "possibility" is not radically rejected as a legitimation of artificial fertilization, the result would be the prospect of an almost unspeakable perversion: one could then foresee the rise of companies to insure the production of progeny, which would deposit ampoules of sperm in their banks before long journeys or extended separations which would make possible posthumous fertilizations in case of accident or even after an estrangement. One need think only of the increasingly excessive need for security in the face of the mass of anxiety in life to envision the semen ampoules becoming a reserve for all eventualities in life—including its most subtle and intimate areas. If we cast about for an analogous example in which the fateful role of mere "possibility" is eliminated, we might think of the political prisoner condemned to death, who desires that his as yet childless marriage be given a child and who as a condemned man is in a situation that rules out natural conception.

### b. *Unimportant Objections*

1. An objection coming from church circles in England, made in opposition to a statement of a commission appointed by the Archbishop of Canterbury which expressed itself as being unconditionally in favor of homologous insemination, argued that the masturbation which the operation necessitates is contrary to Christian moral law.[11] This objection might apply in the case of heterologous insemination, where, as we shall see, the semen donor plays an exceedingly dubious role. In homologous insemination, however, this objection is hardly valid, since it is based upon a theologically untenable doctrine of works. For Reformation thinking, at any rate, the worth or unworth of a "work" depends not upon its isolated form as such, but rather upon the state in which the person is with respect to God, and also the intention or purpose he is pursuing in this work or act.

[11] *Church Times,* Mar. 25, 1949, p. 182.

Thus Paul can say that the eating of meat offered to idols (I Cor. 8:8 ff.) can have a completely different meaning for two Christians: the one may possibly be spiritually immature and may still believe in the existence and the power of idols. If he eats of this meat, he is denying his Lord and resorting to a demonic altar. The other may perhaps be a mature Christian who knows that idols are nonexistent. Obviously, he can eat this meat without scruples of conscience. By eating it he can actually show his contempt for the idols and magnify his Lord. Hence what for the one is a work of denial is for the other an adiaphoron, an ethically neutral, but in no way evil, act. Therefore one cannot say that the eating of meat offered to idols is "in itself" a good work or an evil work. It depends on who is eating and why he is eating. When two persons do the same thing it is not necessarily the same thing.

This is precisely what has to be established with regard to the question of masturbation. Masturbation is as a rule regarded as offensive for the following reasons. First and above all because in masturbation sex is separated from the I-Thou relationship and thus loses its meaning as being the expression and consummation of this fellowship. Second, because the sexual phantasy is no longer bound to a real partnership and therefore roves about vagrantly. Third, because as a rule the absence of this bond leads to physical and psychic extravagance. The ethically decisive thing is therefore not the offensiveness of the physical function as such—in this area the criteria of taste, hygiene, etc. are involved rather than theological criteria—but rather the personal situation that underlies the masturbation, the very invertedness which in the spiritual realm Luther called man's being turned in upon himself [*incurvitas in se*]. All acts which are centered not upon God and my neighbor but upon my own self are actualizations of sin. This is what sets in motion the three stages of descent we mentioned above.

Now it must be admitted that the personal situation which underlies a masturbation for the purpose of homologous insemination is fundamentally and radically different. It is performed in the climate of a real sexual fellowship and its purpose is the *fulfillment* of this sexual fellowship. If one were to dispute this, one would be obliged, for example, to condemn *coitus interruptus,* not only because of its undoubted hygienic dubiousness, but its ethical wrongness, because it has analogies with the situation of masturbation. Therefore Catholic moral theology quite consistently says no in *both* cases. But it can do this only because it has a different concept of sin and works (because, that is to say, it operates with a concept of works being as such good or evil in the ontological sense and does not see them from the point of view of their personal background). At any rate for Reformation thinking it is impossible to isolate the act of masturbation as such and extract it from the context of situation and intention. Therefore the offensiveness of the masturbation required by insemination cannot be weighted with a theological argument.

2. Nor can the distinction between "natural" and "unnatural" be brought to bear against homologous insemination, at any rate not when this is understood in the sense of "natural" and "artificial." For, since man as the image of God transcends nature and is empowered and bidden by the command of creation to use nature and subdue it to himself,[12] his life is one constant intervention in nature, no matter whether he is cultivating the wilderness and turning it into a garden or allowing a doctor to intervene in the natural course of a disease and swallows some medicine. Intervention in nature and thus the employment of artificial means is not in itself questionable, but paradoxically is a part of "nature," that is to say, the nature of man himself. The problem arises only when two questions must be asked: first, whether this right to intervene and thus to subdue or eliminate extrahuman nature is *unlimited*, and second, what *kind* of nature is being subjected to this intervention.

As far as the first question is concerned, one must seriously ask whether our unrestrained elimination of day and night and cold and heat by means of modern technology, whether our passive acceptance of a canned, secondhand intellectual life (radio, television, picture magazines) and our avoidance of firsthand individual encounter with the countryside are not a more momentous and perilous intervention in nature and, what is more, an indirect intervention in the nature of man himself.

As for the second question (concerning the *kind* of nature in-

---

[12] Cf. the section on "The Permissibility of Intervention in Nature," pp. 209 ff. above.

volved), the difference between an intervention in a "natural" cancerous tumor and "natural" germinating life immediately suggests itself. In the first case it is a matter of the nature which from man's point of view should *not* be and in the second case of the nature which *should* be. In the first case we are dealing with a morbid growth which goes contrary to the design of creation, in the second case with the *fruit* of creation.

This cannot help having an effect upon the ethical quality of the specific "intervention." But does what should be according to creation demand that man must simply *let* things happen; does this mean that there should be no regulative intervention whatsoever? Even the Catholic Church does not, as we have seen, draw this conclusion; for even though it prohibits the use of contraceptive means, it nevertheless allows that cohabitation may take place in the so-called "safe period." Even though this is not a matter of artificial intervention but rather of playing off nature against itself, we must be under no illusion about the fact that this game of playing off natural forces against each other is actually directed by man and that consequently it constitutes an intervention.

The real crux of the controversy is therefore the question of the range and the limit of such interventions. Does artificial insemination transgress this limit when it is used as an aid to procreation in the case of two married people? We have sought to show that homologous insemination does not appear to do this—in any case not in principle—when certain reservations are kept in mind. But however one may decide at this point, the distinction between natural and artificial cannot be applied wholesale as a theological argument. The discussion must center rather upon some other very different questions, such as, for example, the question of what are the *limits* and in what *kind* of nature are interventions permissible.

## 2. HETEROLOGOUS INSEMINATION

Here we shall not deal with the legal problems that cluster about this subject.[13] The psychological problems, indicated by the Danish re-

[13] Cf. Dölle, "Die künstliche Samenübertragung . . . ," pp. 242 ff.

port cited above, do concern us very much as soon as we refrain from regarding them as isolated phenomena and rather see them only as symptoms of a deeper disorder (*inordinatio*), which prevails in the foundations of human existence and which a theological anthropology is indeed especially competent to deal with.

The problem is presented by the fact that here a third person enters into the exclusive psychophysical relationship of the marriage, even though it is only his sperm that "represents" him. Whether this formulation "represents him" is correct or not, we must now subject it to examination.

At first sight this assertion appears to be inapt. For naturally one cannot simply call this kind of interference adultery. Adultery requires a personal act of infidelity, a betrayal of a fellowship based upon fidelity by entering into another relationship. Therefore marital infidelity requires the interruption of the psychophysical fellowship by means of another psychophysical experience. When the Sermon on the Mount says "Every one who looks at a woman lustfully has already committed adultery with her in his heart" (Matt. 5:28), it is calling attention to this personal side of adultery and saying that it is the really decisive element. For what it is saying is that in adultery it is not primarily the body or the genitals that are involved, but rather the heart. In the language of the Bible, however, the heart always means the personal center. This is why the infidelity can begin way back there where the physical consummation of an adultery does not occur at all.[14]

But this element of infidelity appears not to be present in heterologous insemination. There are two main arguments in favor of this assertion.

First, the motive of the physician which is operative here is that of helping and of helping in such a way that he aims to eliminate the intervention of a third party precisely by reducing the process of procreation to a "purely" biological act. Second, heterologous insemination of a married woman is undertaken only when both husband

---

[14] Paul, too, agrees with this in I Cor. 6:12 ff. (cf. *ThE* I, §336 ff.) when he speaks of becoming "one body" (*en soma*) with a prostitute. The *porneia* breaks into the personal center. For *soma*, in contrast to *sarx*, is a synonym for the psychophysical ego itself.

and wife desire it. Their consent therefore excludes the infidelity of the one toward the other. Indeed, what is more, the wish to satisfy the will to have children not by adoption but rather in such a way that the artificially engendered child may be at least 50 per cent physically a part of the marriage can undoubtedly spring subjectively from the desire to fulfill one's own marriage and to find a special psychophysical relationship to the child thus begotten. One would cherish the hope that precisely to the degree that the marriage is founded upon love the husband will gain, by way of his love for his wife, a "stronger" tie with "her" child than is possible with an adopted child —especially since this tie need not be disturbed by any thoughts about a rival.

Hence it is possible that this reduction of the process of procreation to a purely biological act may not necessarily—as it seemed at first sight—be based upon a tendency toward depersonalization, an abandonment of the psychophysical relationship, and thus upon biological materialism. On the contrary, a completely opposite motive may be at work here, namely, that of biologizing the process for the precise purpose of safeguarding the personal character of the marriage and therefore of radically excluding any personal tie to a third person whatsoever. Accordingly, it would not be fair summarily to cast moral discredit upon heterologous insemination. Our arguments against it will be sound only if they are relevant, not only to the abuses of it which undoubtedly exist, but also to the *optimal* argument for it. We are striving therefore—against whatever emotional reactions to which we may incline—not to repudiate the biologizing of the process forthwith, but rather to take into account the possibility that —at least so far as its subjective purpose is concerned—it may be grounded precisely upon an earnest acceptance of the personal character of marriage.

With this in view, then, we must first examine the biological procedure.

There are two main factors which bring out clearly this reduction to the biological and show the concern—at any rate in the first of the two points—to exclude the personal intervention of a third party and, it must be admitted, in a way far beyond that which the intervention itself would demand.

1. The first point is that every effort is made to insure the complete anonymity of the donor. This is the reason back of the increasing tendency to refuse to allow a relative, say a brother of the husband, to function as the donor. The desire for this tie of kinship is understandable, since the family blood of the husband is thereby passed on to the child and in this way there is a continuation of a motive which is also present in the Old Testament levirate (marriage to a deceased husband's brother) and endogamous marriage (marriage within the tribe). The reason that leads to rejection of this form of insemination lies in the fear that the third party may intervene. It is feared that the mother may feel a tie to the biological father, even if he is the brother of the husband. Thus the personal element of fidelity is respected. This is also the only reason that motivates the advocating of the practice of mixing the semen of several donors—possibly containing the semen of the husband ("semen cocktail"). The intent here is to create the possibility, which is supportive of the marriage, that the child may after all turn out to be the husband's (in the form of a homologous insemination) and also to deindividualize and depersonalize the biological father, to render him completely unsubstantial as a person and thus to prevent the person of the married father from being supplanted.

What is amazing, however, is the great extent to which this, in our opinion optimistic, view of heterologous insemination which respects personhood is missing in the literature on the subject. What we have here interpreted as having positive value apparently does not accord with the self-understanding of most of the medical men who advocate this kind of fertilization.

As the specifically stated reasons are concerned, it must be said, unfortunately, that what they do is simply to explain the reduction to the biological itself by resorting again to biological terms. This should give us pause. And this brings us to the second point.

2. In order to demonstrate that it is an ethically natural matter, the biological-technical side of the artificial fertilization process is often placed on the same level as a blood transfusion or the transplantation of a cornea. Subjectively, this identification would indicate that here the impersonality of the process is not understood as a means to personal ends (as we assumed above), but rather as an

end in itself. Objectively, this identification undoubtedly rests upon a fallacy—even on the biological level itself. For both blood and cornea become impersonal things in the genuine sense when they are separated from their original biological "owner." This is already manifest in the fact that they are amalgamated with the new body and the alien blood eventually becomes one's own blood. The fusion of sperm cell and ovum, however, is not simply a matter of its amalgamation in the female organism. On the contrary, in the genesis of the child an independent "third person" comes into being. This is not without its consequences for the mother, but it can—as the Danish example shows—have an extreme effect upon the father. Even though it *need* not be so, the possibility is nevertheless there that the father may react in an emotionally hostile way to a child which to him appears to be a constant reminder of his own weakness. This understandable psychological reaction would then be the symptom of a far deeper, "existential" fact, namely, that the psychophysical totality of a marital fellowship is indivisible.

Even if we can imagine the exceptional case in which the husband for love of his wife desires that she attain fulfillment through motherhood and thus by consenting to a heterologous insemination performs an act of sacrifice which is an expression and not a sabotage of this fellowship, he thereby calls into play other psychic and physical realities which override this initial motive and acquire their own autonomy, realities which no longer follow the lead of a responsible marriage but begin to take the lead themselves. Since the totality of the personal relationship obviously will not tolerate the splitting off of the biological, one will not be able to justify or recommend heterologous insemination even if it does *not* result in such catastrophic symptoms. We are against it, therefore, not primarily because we fear the symptoms, but rather because the possible symptoms betray the violation of the far deeper *mysterium* of marital fellowship.

This violation also manifests itself when the fulfillment of motherhood which is not accompanied by the fulfillment of fatherhood breaks down the personal solidarity of the married couple. How else can this solidarity express itself except through the sharing of a common lot ("If one member suffers, all suffer together," I Cor. 12:26)?

And how else in this case could this sharing of a common fate be realized unless the wife shares the biological fate of her husband and both satisfy their desire to have a child by adoption? This is the only way in which their relationship to the child in the personal realm can become one that is more nearly shared and thus again more concentrated upon a love of neighbor that binds them more closely together and thus removed from the twilight of half-parenthood as well as the dividedness of a broken psychophysical relationship.

We have purposely spoken only of the psychological "symptoms" of a rupture of the marital fellowship brought about by heterologous insemination. Our intention here is to indicate that the psychological reactions are merely secondary, that they must not be overrated, and that they also may not occur. The American doctors whose reports are so extraordinarily favorable and who are apparently quite unaware of these negative symptoms, certainly are not simply lying, though they surely are not without one-sidedness and bias. But if we are properly to evaluate this diagnosis that the process is harmless, we shall not be able to ignore the following question: Is it not conceivable that married couples for whom the idea of a marital fellowship determined by personhood has become unattainable and who therefore have sunk to the level of a superficial, biologically orientated sex community or an economic community of labor and business, would not feel that heterologous insemination is anything more than such a sexual or economic matter, and therefore would also be immune to these problems which arise from the realm of the *humanum?* Would we not expect that there should be a large number of such couples in a technicized civilization, in a time when men are reduced to masses and depersonalized? Has not the sex act been repeatedly explained by the so-called glass-of-water theory and equated with the simple act of stilling one's thirst? But if coitus has thus become a purely biological process, why then should we not be allowed to substitute for it *another* biological process, namely, heterologous insemination? And if countless people in this new world no longer live close to nature but rather in a climate of the artificial— artificial light, heat, and locomotion—why should this further detachment from the natural by means of artificial fertilization constitute any problem worth mentioning?

It is quite possible, therefore, to explain the absence of the negative symptoms in this way. The only point is that then we differ from these American doctors in that this absence does not prompt us to optimism. On the contrary, we can conclude here that these negative symptoms point only to a disorder in existence, but that the *absence* of these symptoms point to an even deeper disorder. If the doctor feels that he is competent to deal only with painful psychic and physical changes, then he can dissociate himself at this point and with an innocent face write out a certificate of success and health. But if he is aware of the deeper disorders of life, he will be shocked by the fundamental lesions of the marital organism which lie deep beneath its smooth and healthy-looking skin and he will recoil from the shallowness of his superficial diagnosis.

In making this statement we find that on this subject of artificial fertilization we have been speaking less of the institution than of the persons who are involved in it. And this, of course, is no accident, if we take the personal, psychophysical relationship as the criterion of all our judgments, and if—in accord with the whole orientation of a Reformation ethics—we understand the order, not on the basis of their institutional structure, but on the basis of their function, namely, that of being a binding medium between I and Thou, between persons. When Luther repeatedly declares that our actions even within the orders—in marriage, in law, in the state—must be determined by the motive of love of one's neighbor, it follows that the specific of the orders lies not in their objective structure but rather in their function with respect to persons, in the function of presenting an ordering and ordered possibility for the meeting of persons. Therefore it makes theological sense that we should first have thought through the question of artificial insemination from the point of view of the persons involved and their condition, in order on that basis then to face the question whether homologous and heterologous insemination can be a possible institution, an "order."

Having discussed the persons in the marriage and their possible motives and situations, but above all their existential situations, we must now take a look at the "third man," the semen donor. From this personal point of view he is quite as important as the others. And in his case, too, the same problem arises: whether and to what extent the biological act of semen donation can be separated from the person and whether the attempt at such a separation does not destroy the psychophysical totality in him too.

Indirectly, we already made our decision on this question when we discussed the masturbation which is necessary for the semen donation. That which makes masturbation legitimate in homologous donation, namely, its incorporation in the marital I-Thou relationship, does not exist in the case of the extramarital donor. Even if, as American doctors recommend, young physicians and medical students are employed for this donation, this objection is still valid. And this vision of a student working his way through college is not without an element of the macabre and gruesome.

Who else should be considered as a "spermator"? Naturally, what is wanted is men with healthy genes and irreproachable character traits. But does not this desire in itself lead to a contradiction, since the main or part-time job of the semen donor presupposes an existential disease, namely, a pathological divorce between the physiological and the personal dimension of the sex realm? What degree of human degeneration or what degree of primitive underdevelopment in instincts and ideas is required to play the role of an anonymous spermator? Here again every analogy with blood donation deserts us. The parallel with prostitution does, however, suggest itself (though, of course, only with respect to this one aspect of the semen donor). For here, too, the sex process becomes anonymous and impersonal. The prostitute exchanges her partners at will because she has no personal ties and because the choice of this partner is made not from the point of view of communication but rather of the fee that is paid. Even those who advocate prostitution as a stop valve for sexual pressure and for sociological reasons would not idealize it, but would rather regard it as a measure of necessity,[15] whereas in some quarters heterologous insemination comes very near, if not exactly to being idealized, then to being treated as a quite harmless matter, and with its increasing spread and general sanction on the part of society

[15] Adolf Schlatter, *Christliche Ethik* (1929), pp. 365 f.

it would certainly be drawn into this perilous descent. But it would never occur to anyone—and here even the analogy with prostitution deserts us—to beget a child by means of a prostitute, who was *only* a prostitute for the person involved, in order to realize the desire for fatherhood. It is true that the fact that this case would hardly occur is certainly due also to the fact that the desire for nonmarital or extra-marital fatherhood can as a rule be satisfied in other ways, whereas motherhood is impossible if the husband is sterile. Nevertheless, the determinative reason may well be that generally one does not look to the prostitute for those qualities which one wishes to pass on to one's child and that moreover the very idea of wanting a child engendered in prostitution for exclusively physiological reasons and therefore anonymously and impersonally must necessarily strike at the very root of fatherhood.

We come, then, to our conclusion. As we said at the beginning, we certainly cannot say that the purpose of marriage is the propagation of children. This would be to depreciate the independent worth of the human fellowship of the married couple. Moreover, this defini-tion of purpose would make childless marriages, and marriages at advanced age, nonmarriages. Nevertheless, the child has its place in the relationship of the sexes according to the order of creation. There-fore where childlessness is not consciously desired or wherever it must be temporarily accepted because of compelling circumstances, and thus is not a fault, it is a deprivation that must be accepted. True, we are bound to combat the suffering. In this creative function within the disordered creation the medical vocation has its meaning and pur-pose, for God does not will that there be suffering in the design of creation. But the means through which the suffering is combated dare not contradict the meaning of suffering in life. Thus euthanasia, for example, which ends the suffering by prematurely induced death, is contrary to the meaning of the life of the sufferer. For man, unlike the animal, is a being who can suffer ethically. Therefore there can be a *"coup de grace"* for a dog, but not for man. In the same way heterol-ogous insemination, as we have now shown, combats the suffering of childlessness with means that contradict the meaning of the sufferer's life. These means wound his existence.

There may be special situations in which this may not be so. In the realms of ethical decision we can never live without the category of the exceptional, just as we can never live in the realms of legal decisions without the category of the rule. The exception must be assigned to the realm of personal venture and responsibility. Ethics can illuminate the problem as such and clarify the decisions with which the person is faced only at the moment when he is confronted with his exceptional situation.

In the course of our thinking we have repeatedly run into problems which go far beyond the "case" of artificial fertilization and point to the horizon of anthropology. In closing we mention one of the last of these problems. There is a suggestion in the technology of our mechanized world that is leading our generation more and more to believe in a dogma which we described earlier as the doctrine that "everything can be made" [Machbarkeit aller Dinge], that ultimately there is nothing that man cannot do. Man's potentialities are expanding to enormous proportions. Are there really any fateful, unpredictable facts left to daunt men, unalterable facts that have to be accepted— perhaps even accepted as "visitations" of God? True, there are such things still. And death will remain one of them. But they are being pushed farther and farther back. Even climate can be changed; even "human relations" can be influenced by synthetic means. This dogma of man's ability to do anything and everything constitutes the Promethean variant of our time. It is a new excess of misunderstood human autonomy. It is not that man can do so much which is godless. Man can also do these things under God, if he does so as administering the talents entrusted to him. But to believe in man who thinks he can do these things by his own power—this leads to excess and hubris. There is one thing that this man who can do everything cannot do: He is no longer capable of accepting suffering. He can no longer accept, because he no longer knows the One who gives and sends all things.

In this whole complex there are many tendencies which have associated themselves with artificial insemination and which move beyond the concept of homologous aid to conception. He who no longer knows God eventually loses the sense of personhood too. And he who has lost the sense of personhood no longer sees or understands the crisis that inheres in the breakdown of the psychophysical sex relationship. Therefore the symptoms of the crises which we spoke of (referring again to the Danish example) are no longer alarming. For these symptoms themselves subside when the disease of lost personhood has passed a certain point. Then the organism is, as it were, no longer capable of producing a fever.

Therefore the discussion necessarily thrusts away from the mere "case" of artificial fertilization and demands a discussion of the theological background. It is the fatality and the blessing of our time that its human questions always face man with the ultimate. It is always a question of rebellion or obedience. What it involves is the decision between the dogma that man can devise and manipulate and do all things and the willingness to "accept." The sense of responsibility that lies behind these decisions will recoil from heterologous fertilization. That sense of responsibility will turn the yearning for a child into a search for one's neighbor, for the child of other parents who is seeking a home.

# D. The Problem of Homosexuality

## 1. The Literature of Protestant Theology

One cannot expect to find in the theological ethics of German-speaking Protestantism a clear, consistent attitude toward homosexuality simply because hitherto the writers on ethics have taken little or no notice of the mere fact itself and therefore a body of opinion—to say nothing of a unanimity of judgment—is almost nonexistent. The indexes of many well-known works on ethics do not contain the word at all. Examples of this failure even to mention the fact are the more recent ethics of A. Schlatter, A. de Quervain, E. Brunner, A. D. Müller, W. Trillhaas, and (if we may mention a Danish ethics, but widely read in German translation) N. H. Søe. When homosexuality is dealt with—almost always incidentally—the statements teem with analytical data which are not in accord with the findings of medical and psychological research. A theology of orders [*Ordnungstheologie*] which is often handled in a doctrinaire way, obviously not having allowed itself to be called in question by any pastoral encounter with these persons and frequently betraying no sympathy with them whatsoever, tends simply to reject the whole thing in the name of its dogmatic axioms or in the fundamentalist form of biblical quotations. At the same time, however, there is little or no indication of what kind of constructive counsel the author as a pastor would give to a homosexual.

This inability to deal with a phenomenon which is felt to be religiously taboo is also evidenced in the fact that homosexuality is constantly being referred to the competence of the physician.[1] We

[1] Otto Piper, *Die Geschlechter. Ihr Sinn und ihr Geheimnis in biblischer Sieht* (1954), p. 274.

find statements which from the point of view of objective accuracy are more than questionable, such as that "innate homosexuality in the real sense . . . is extremely rare" (otherwise "the hereditary homosexuals would soon die out . . . because they do not reproduce themselves"). We also find it asserted that acquired homosexuality can be dealt with through medical care, so that in the great majority of cases adequate help can be given to those who are thus afflicted. It is also said that "medical experiments with sex hormones have met with good therapeutic success."[2] Such evidences of misinformation and half-information occur again and again.

Doctrinaire prejudices, which at the same time distort the *theological* problem presented by homosexuality, manifest themselves also in the fact that the value-judgment "homosexuality is sinful" is not isolated from an objective assessment of the phenomenon but is rather projected into it, and the result is that one arrives at an a priori defamation of those who are afflicted with this anomaly. Thus it is stated that especially in the last two world wars "weak-charactered, unstable homosexuals were preferentially employed for all kinds of treacheries."[3] Similarly, even such an otherwise pastorally open-minded author as Van Oyen says that innate homosexuality is "rooted in glandular and hormonal structures" and labels it as a pathological phenomenon which is generally associated with "psychopathic characters, schizophrenics, debilitated and underdeveloped infantile types."[4] Similar statements are made by Otto Piper, who likewise speaks of the pathological infantility of homosexuals,[5] relegates them as a rule to the puberty phase of development,[6] or explains them by saying that it is a substitute action because of the lack of a heterosexual partner.[7] He also says that is a perversion in that it practices merely physical excitation and is incapable of achieving a "sexual encounter."[8] Refreshingly different from these attitudes is the unbiased objectivity of The Wolfenden Report (see below) in its

[2] W. Becker, *Informationsblatt* (1954), 17, pp. 268 ff.
[3] *Ibid.*, p. 269.
[4] H. van Oyen, *Libe und Ehe* (1957), p. 132.
[5] O. Piper, *op. cit.*, p. 274.
[6] *Ibid.*, p. 90.
[7] *Ibid*, p. 182.
[8] *Ibid.*, p. 83.

reference to the findings of physicians: "Many of them [i.e. homosexuals] are valuable and capable members of society; thus they by no means correspond with the common prejudice that a homosexual must necessarily or with considerable probability be vicious, criminal, debilitated, or morally corrupt" (German ed., p. 9).

All of these statements indicate how an ethical value judgment can distort even the phenomenality of the thing which is to be evaluated. Moreover, these authors have obviously never experienced the tragedy that they might have felt in an encounter with an ethically upright, mature homosexual who is struggling with his condition. The theologian who speaks of the dubious character of homosexuality— and he would be blind or forgetful of his mission if he ignored it— must in any case look at another side of the matter and dare not defame the *humanum* of the person so conditioned in order to make his negation easier.

This inability to deal with the phenomenon which is conditioned by theological or psychic aversion to it can lead even such a prominent thinker as Karl Barth[9] into such an astonishing confusion of terminology that he is capable of putting such heterogeneous value judgments as "sickness," "perversion, decadence, and decay" on the same logical level. Thus alongside of the ethically neutral designation of homosexuality as "sickness," as pathological constitution, we find it abruptly denounced ethically and religiously as a "refusal to recognize God and a failure to appreciate man, and thus humanity without the fellow-man."[10] Apart from the *logical* dubiousness of such a juxtaposition of terms, at least the *question* must be raised whether the Platonic *eros* perhaps did *not* refer to fellow men and whether it is really only a matter, as Barth says, of "corrupt emotional and finally physical desire" and therefore only a matter of what Piper understands by mere "physical excitation." It is true that the homosexual relationship is not a *Christian* form of encounter with our fellow man; it is nevertheless very certainly a search for the totality of the other *human being*. He who says otherwise has not yet observed the possible human depth of a homoerotic-colored friendship. More-

---

[9] Karl Barth, *Church Dogmatics*, III, 4, p. 166.
[10] Cf. also *ibid.*, III, 2, pp. 229 ff.

over, the perversion inherent in the reduction of sexuality to mere "physical excitation" is also to be found in heterosexual relationships. To make this charge refer especially to homosexuals shows ignorance or prejudice. Barth, as a theologian, is right only insofar as he rejects the idealization and sacralization of homosexuality and takes away from it its "redolence of sanctity." As a matter of fact this idealization of homosexuality would lead to the same blindness of the phenomenon as does the negative counterpart of idealization, namely, defamation. Because Barth does not escape this latter danger, his ethical *directions* also miss the point. He who misinterprets the *factum* will also, logically, be unable to see the *faciendum*. One such direction which Barth gives is this statement: "The decisive word of Christian ethics must consist in a warning against entering upon the whole way of life which can only end in the tragedy of concrete homosexuality."[11] Here we should have to direct to Barth the question what this warning can mean for the constitutionally predisposed homosexual. For this person is already in this "way of life"; his somehow abnormal constitution is already there before any decisions are made. What is the person who is so constituted by "fate" to think of himself from the theological point of view? This is after all the real question. And then how shall he act on the basis of this self-understanding? Shall he live out his "natural" impulses, shall he suppress them, shall he sublimate them? *How* should he master his conflict situation? And here too we may be permitted to ask whether Barth has ever accompanied a homosexual pastorally on the "way" he has to travel. We suspect that if this had been so the fundamental theological orientation of this position would have been different.

As far as we know, the only two voices which have allowed a *different* tone to be heard in German Protestantism are those of two non-Germans. The first is the Swiss psychiatrist Theodor Bovet, who in numerous, wide-read publications has cultivated the borderline area between pastoral care and psychotherapy, medicine and Christian ethics. His book *Sinnerfülltes Anders-sein* (*Living Meaningfully as a Homosexual*) contains not only a careful medical phenomenology, but also a welcome demolition—based upon an evident knowl-

[11] *Ibid.,* III, 4, p. 166.

edge of the pertinent theological literature—of the value judgments which have been projected upon the phenomenon. He says that homophilia "as such has nothing to do with morals or with sin." One can "live morally or immorally as a homophile just as a 'normal' person can"; both "participate in exactly the same degree in sin, but also in forgiveness." And in the same way homophilia is "not to be characterized without reservation as sickness or a crime."[12] The anonymous author of the book, of which Bovet desires to call himself only the editor, regards as questionable the purely sexual extensions of homophilia. Accordingly the pastoral and psychiatric treatment would concentrate above all upon the sublimation of the impulse. Regardless of whether this solution is the only one to be considered or not, the important and refreshing thing about this book is its pastoral aspect of positive helpfulness, which avoids a purely sterile, "legalistic," negative attitude toward the endogenous and therefore incurable cases and gives to the homophile the creative task of filling his "differentness" with meaning. This explains why Bovet challenges the competence of criminal judges to deal with these cases and why he calls the Swiss Penal Code "exemplary," since it "punishes with imprisonment homosexual acts with minors or dependents, but not the voluntary relations of adults."[13]

The other voice is that of the English theologian, Derrich S. Bailey,[14] who, in connection with a careful analysis of the medical facts and a thoughtful evaluation of the biblical and traditional statements in addition to the well-known English Report, arrives at the thesis that in those cases in which the personality structure cannot be altered by medical treatment the most effective help is that "which enables the person to accept his handicap as a task that must be endured in a positive spirit." This is one of the pre-eminent tasks of pastoral care.[15] His unwillingness to classify homosexuality as a criminal offense, provided that there is no offense against public and order and no violation of minors and dependents, is similar to that of Bovet. It

[12] Theodor Bovet, *Sinnerfülltes Anders-sein. Seelsorgerliche Gespräche mit Homophilen* (Tübingen, 1959), p. 9.
[13] *Ibid.*, p. 10.
[14] Cf. his article "Homosexualität," in *RGG*, 3 ed., III, col. 441 ff.
[15] *Ibid.*, col. 441.

is significant that the only two theological or lay-theological authors who have explicitly pursued the problem of homosexuality and orientated themselves in the medical literature without desiring to compromise the normative criteria of theology—thinking of these criteria not as *given* doctrinaire propositions, but rather *seeking* for them—both recognize the exclusive competence of the physician and the pastor and reject that of the criminal judge. This should give us pause.

In this context is also the statement made by the Swedish bishops, published in a pastoral letter in 1951. It deals in concentrated form with questions of sexual ethics such as extramarital sexual intercourse, abortion, sterilization, artifical insemination, and homosexuality. The statement on homosexuality,[16] though it declares homosexual acts to be offenses against God's command (without giving any explicit theological reasons), approves the elimination of the penal clauses with respect to homosexuality in the new Swedish Penal Code. We are, of course, not to conclude from this elimination that homosexual acts are *ethically* justified. The right view, on the contrary, is "that means other than imprisonment are required in order to save a man with homosexual tendencies." The homosexual who is honestly struggling would "receive all the understanding and all the encouragement that Christian love can give." The pastoral letter does not indicate what the objective purpose of this pastoral love should be in dealing with homosexuals (since the phenomenon as such is not interpreted theoretically, it is, of course, impossible to make out from the statement what direction the pastoral "therapy" is to take), but rather limits itself to an appeal for medical help and prophylactic social measures to guard against possible infections. Therefore, care must be taken that homosexuals be not allowed to deal with young people. Moreover, society must fight against every form of homosexual prostitution. In our particular connection the most important point is the statement's insistence that a criminal prosecution of homosexual relations between adults is out of the question, since this is a matter of ethics and not of criminal law.

---

[16] Reprinted in *Monatschrift für Kriminologie und Strafrechtsreform* (1955), p. 193.

The recommendations of the English reports move in the same direction. This applies not only to the "Interim Report" of the Church of England[17] but also to "The Wolfenden Report," a statement which is a very thorough piece of team work by a committee appointed by the British Home Secretary (departmental committee under the chairmanship of Sir John Wolfenden).[18] The most important relevant statement is found in Section 355, Recommendation I: "That homosexual behavior between consenting adults in private be no longer a criminal offense." In Recommendation II it is stated "that questions relating to 'consent' and 'in private' be decided by the same criteria as apply in the case of heterosexual acts between adults."

We cannot discuss in detail the position taken by *Catholic* moral theology, which is based partly upon natural theology and partly upon biblical injunctions. However, it is noteworthy—to indicate at least one similarity to the statements just mentioned—that the very carefully prepared English Catholic statement, published in 1956 by the Roman Catholic Advisory Committee under Cardinal Bernard Griffin ("The Griffin Report"), though it rejects on the basis of moral theology all homosexual activity, nevertheless affirms that such offenses should be dealt with in the confessional rather than in the courts.[19] The definitive principles are stated in Paragraphs VII and XIII:

Paragraph VII: "It is not the business of the State to intervene in the purely private sphere but to act solely as the defender of the common good. Morally evil things so far as they do not affect the common good are not the concern of the human legislator."

Paragraph XIII: "It is accordingly recommended that the Criminal Law should be amended in order to restrict penal sanctions for homosexual offenses as follows, namely, to prevent: (a) the corruption of

[17] Cf. D. S. Bailey, *Sexual Offenders and Social Punishment* (London, 1956 [Church of England Moral Welfare Council]), p. 40.

[18] *Report of the Committee on Homosexual Offences and Prostitution,* Her Majesty's Stationery Office (Comnd. 247), 1957. (The Wolfenden Report.) German edition and commentary by A. D. Dieckhoff (Hamburg, 1957).

[19] "Report of the Roman Catholic Advisory Committee on Prostitution and Homosexual Offences and the Existing Law"; text in *The Dublin Review,* No. 471 (Summer, 1956), London, pp. 60-65. German edition, Hamburg, n.d., J. R. v. Deckers Verlag.

youth; (b) offenses against public decency; (c) the exploitation of vice for the purpose of gain."

In summing up the positions taken up to this time, the following may be said:

First, the result of the development of the medical disciplines (especially psychiatry and neurology) which have investigated homosexuality, wherever Christian theology has taken cognizance of it, has not been to divest it of its dubiousness or even of its character as sinful disobedience. It has, however, contributed to the fact that homophilous tendency and thus homosexual *potentiality* are not subjected to the same verdict by some Christian ethicists, but are rather regarded as subject to ethical treatment. But even in the cases where the homosexual syndrome becomes an overt act there is a clear tendency to refer them to the physician and pastor, but not to the courts (except in the borderline cases of abuse of juveniles and dependents). The degree to which even Christian theology, insofar as it has seriously concerned itself with the problem at all, is prepared to revise its taboo attitudes may be apparent in the difference between present-day *openness* to a pastoral attitude of service (which is more observable in practice than in theory) and the positions taken in seventeenth-century Lutheran orthodoxy. The kind of taboo-inspired judgment, which distorts the medical as well as the theological view, pronounced by Benedict Carpzov, the Lutheran professor of church and criminal law, would be impossible for even the most conservative theologian today. In his *Practica Rerum Criminalium* he lists the sequelae of homosexual vice: "Earthquakes, famine, pestilence, Saracens, floods, and very fat, voracious field mice."

Second, one detects in certain areas of the relevant Protestant (but also the Catholic) literature not only an unexamined rejective attitude on principle, but also a natural—and to that extent understandable—rejective *instinct* with respect to the phenomenon. This rejective instinct must be (if not eliminated, then certainly) brought under control and regarded in the epistemological sense as a discriminatory prejudice, not only in the name of the demands of scientific objectivity but also in the name of pastoral ministry. The person who has to deal with such cases as a pastor or even as a physician will find that a real personal encounter with this threatened and often unhappy neighbor will help him to get beyond this instinctual inhibition that blocks his judgment. It must be said, however, that the person who is more or less discernibly inhibited by this instinct is hardly likely to be consulted as a pastor or a physician by the person thus afflicted, so that it is extremely difficult to eliminate this prejudice and hence the diminished objectivity that goes with it. Similar problems may exist for the jurists and thus may complicate the discussion of the facts from the point of view of criminal law.

All the more worthy of note, then, are the English reports and the pastoral letter of the Swedish bishops, which up to now are without parallel in German Protestantism. In the framing of these documents it was doubtless the team work of experts, which is especially fruitful in this area, that largely contributed to the overcoming of this inhibition.

## 2. The Theologicoethical Aspect of Homosexuality

According to the Protestant principle of Scripture, the theological interpretation of homosexuality cannot ignore the relevant statements of the *Bible*. However, we would not be satisfying this principle of Scripture if we merely cited the Holy Scriptures instead of interpreting the quotations in accord with the kerygmatic purpose. A merely legalistic citation of Scripture which did not inquire into its significance would lead—by no means only in the subject under discussion—to the most fantastic combination of heterogeneous elements. This is demonstrated by the jungle of doctrines produced by the sectarians, all of whom appeal quite positively and unreflectively to the Bible.

As far as the *Old Testament* is concerned, it is uncertain whether the passages concerning "sodomy," which have been traditionally authoritative, actually refer to homosexual acts at all. In any case, Isaiah 1:10, 3:3, Ezekiel 16:49, and Jeremiah 23:14 characterize the sins that were responsible for the downfall of Sodom quite differently.[20] Apart from this there can be no doubt that the Old Testa-

[20] Cf. Gerhard von Rad, *Genesis A. Commentary,* trans. by John H. Marks (Philadelphia: Westminster Press, 1961), pp. 212 f.

ment regarded homosexuality and pederasty as crimes punishable by death (Lev. 18:22, 20:13). Whether direct injunctions are to be derived from this for Christians must remain a matter of discussion, at least insofar as behind this prohibition there lies the concept of cultic defilement and thus the question is raised whether and to what extent the Old Testament cultic law can be binding upon those who are under the Gospel and to what extent it places them on a wholly new level and frees them from the Law. Here the problems of theological principle which are referred to in technical terminology under the subject of "Law and Gospel" become acute. Even the nontheologian can see the scope of this problem when it is realized that in the Old Testament the prohibition of divination, the drinking of blood, sexual intercourse with a menstruating woman, and many other things are put on the same level with the capital offense of homosexuality. It would never occur to anyone to wrench these laws of cultic purification from their concrete situation and give them the kind of normative authority that the Decalogue, for example, has.

In the *New Testament* homosexuality is again listed in catalogue fashion with other forms of disobedience, such as idolatry, fornication, adultery, greed, drunkenness, thievery (I Cor. 6:9-10; cf. I Tim. 1:9-10). Accordingly, there can be no doubt that Paul regards homosexuality as a sin and a perversion of the order of human existence willed by God, even though within this catalogue of vices it is not accented as being *especially* horrible, as many moral theologies would make it appear.[21] The listing of homosexuality with heterosexual offenses like adultery and fornication would rather suggest the problem of whether, along with the total rejection of homosexuality, we must not also consider the question to what extent this refers to the libido-conditioned disregard for one's neighbor, in other words, a particular *way* of homosexual behavior (possibly analogous with adultery, polygamy, etc.). In any case, it is worthy of note that, according to the Synoptics (in which the subject of homosexuality does *not* appear), Jesus dealt with the sensual sinners incomparably

---

[21] W. Schoellgen, for example, when he says that "in the picture of the natural man, as painted in the Bible, homosexuality represents almost the darkest shadow, the extreme of ethical darkness" (*Konkrete Ethik* [1961], p. 410).

more leniently than he did with the sinners who committed the sins of the spirit and cupidity.

For the theological evaluation of the Pauline statements concerning homosexuality it is especially important to note the way it is dealt with in the most familiar passage about it: Romans 1:26 f. And here we cannot dispense with a number of hermeneutical comments.

This section deals with the question of why it is that the natural man, the "heathen," does not know God, even though the Creator is manifest in his creation. The answer given to this question is that man refuses to accept his creatureliness, that he does not acknowledge God and therefore does not know him. The natural man is not *in* in the truth and therefore he does not recognize or know the truth.[22] The wrath of God over this hubris expresses itself in God's giving man over, abandoning him (*paredoken*) to the consequences of this his fundamental attitude, leaving him, as it were, to the autonomy of the existence which he himself has entered upon. In consequence of this autonomy of judgment, then, *religious* confusion also leads to *ethical* chaos. It consists in confusion of the eternal with the temporal. That is to say, finite entities are vested with the sovereignty of God and men worship idols (Rom. 1:23). Because the lower and the higher, the creature and the Creator, are exchanged ("perverted"), the result is a perverse supremacy of the inferior desires over the spirit. And in this context the *sexual* perversions are mentioned as further marks of this fundamental perversion (Rom. 1:26 f.).[23]

What is theologically noteworthy and kerygmatically "binding" in this exposition of Paul's is the statement that disorder in the vertical dimension (in the God-man relationship) is matched by a perversion on the horizontal level, not only within man himself (spirit-flesh re-

[22] On this interpretation cf. my book *Theologie der Anfechtung* (1949), pp. 21 ff.

[23] Hans Giese (in his article "Zur Psychopathologie der Homosexualitat," in *Praxis,* 1961, No. 48) proposes that we make a distinction between the terms "abnormal" and "perverse," the latter term to designate only "psychopathological forms of psychically abnormal sexual conduct." When we occasionally use the term "perverse" here in a different and more general sense we do so only because in our special connection we wish to make use of the etymology of the Latin word *pervertere* for the analogy between what happens in the vertical dimension (the perversion of the hierarchy of Creator and creature) and what happens in the horizontal dimension (the perversion of the order of the sexes).

lationship) but also in his interhuman contacts. One of the fundamental lines that runs through the Bible is that the analogy between the vertical and the horizontal relations is maintained and given theological foundation. An outstanding example of this two-dimensional view is the story of the Tower of Babel (Gen. 11:1 ff.) in which man's rebellion against the Creator (vertical movement) brings with it the "dispersion," that is, the destruction of human community and thus the perversion of the fellow-human relationship along with the confusion of tongues (horizontal movement).[24]

The point of the Pauline statement lies precisely in this correspondence between the two dimensions. The individual demonstrative references, including the reference to sexual perversion, are simply illustrations of this point. They come from the stock of the tradition with which Paul was surrounded, above all the Stoic catalogues of vices and their Jewish counterparts, such as the "wisdom of Solomon," Philo, Josephus, and the Sibylline Oracles.[25]

There can be no question that Paul is here rejecting homosexuality, otherwise he would not characterize it in this passage (even more sharply and more incriminatingly than in I Corinthians) as a symptom of original sin. Nevertheless, as far as the relative theological emphasis is concerned, it is significant that it is not made the subject of separate theological statement, but that it appears only in the context of *another,* theologically fundamental, statement and as an *illustration* of it. This cannot be without significance for the interpretation of it. For we must reckon with the fact that Paul's conception of homosexuality was one which was affected by the intellectual atmosphere surrounding the struggle with Greek paganism. For the thinkers and especially the moral philosophers of late antiquity (and by no means only for the Christians living at that time), pederasty, however, was regarded as a sign of depravity and a decadent culture.

The fact that this status of homosexuality as an "illustration" within the context of a completely *different* statement is not irrelevant may become evident in another instance in which Paul employs an

---

[24] Cf. the interpretation of this story in my book *How the World Began* (Philadelphia: Muhlenberg Press, 1961), pp. 273-87.

[25] H. Lietzmann, *Kommentar zum Römerbrief* (4 ed., 1933), pp. 33 ff.

illustration to set forth a fundamental statement. In I Corinthians 11:2 ff. his concern is to argue against the putting of the sexes on the same level, or stated positively, to provide a Christological basis for the man's position as the head of the woman. This he illustrates by the fact that the man as the "image of God" (v. 7) should keep his head uncovered at worship, whereas the woman should wear a head covering or else her hair should be cut off. Here again the essential *intention* must be distinguished from the illustration. His essential *intention* is to combat the idea that there is no difference between the sexes, argued erroneously on the basis of the solidarity of all men before God, regardless of sex; the *illustration* is taken from the contemporary regulations for dress. And these in turn were probably so firmly bound up in Paul's "conception" with his idea of the difference between the sexes that he himself was not capable of realizing the difference in quality between the *intention* of statement (which is related to these differences) and the *means* employed in his statement (the symbol of the difference in dress). But the moment when men who are no longer bound to that contemporary situation (as we are not today) ask what is the kerygmatic bindingness of such statements, this difference in quality becomes highly important. The point is that the differentiation between the sexes, which is the point that Paul is here stating, is just as important for *us* today as it was then. It would never occur to us, however, that when we accept these statements of difference between the sexes we must also take over the dress regulations which had symbolical force at *that* time. We have the freedom to choose *other* symbols of this difference which come from our own time and situation.

Obviously, the statements concerning dress and those concerning homosexuality are different in importance; this is immediately clear from the text. And yet the fact that homosexuality here appears in the context of the symbolical and illustrative statements and thus is a *means* of statement and not the object of the statement of *intention* itself, gives us a certain freedom to rethink the subject. This freedom should be used to reflect upon the question of how homosexuality must be interpreted theologically if it is to be the independent subject of a statement (as it is *not* in Paul). In view of the difficulty of the problem and the fact that most of the traditional statements are not applicable, we have been obliged to go through these methodological considerations in order to gain a proper approach to our question.

In this area of legitimate inquiry thus opened up the first thing that must be said is that for biblical thinking and the Christian thinking which follows biblical thought, it is impossible to think of homosexuality as having no ethical significance, as being a mere "vagary" or "sport" of nature. The fundamental order of creation and the created determination of the two sexes make it appear justifiable to speak of homosexuality as a "perversion"—in any case, if we begin with the understanding that this term implies no moral depreciation whatsoever and that it is used purely theologically in the sense that homosexuality is in every case *not* in accord with the order of creation. (Therefore in ordinary usage Giese's term "abnormal" would in fact, be appropriate.) In this sense homosexuality falls on the same level with abnormal personality structure (= psychopathy), disease, suffering, and pain, which likewise are generally understood in the Bible as being contrary to God's will in creation. This points, then, to the hidden connections between the Fall as a disordering of creation and the pathological changes in existence in the world as a whole. In this sense the miracles of Jesus are understood to be a kind of reminder of what God originally intended the creation to be in a world in which his creation has been disordered. In the same sense, the eschatological statements concerning a coming world in which there will be no more suffering or crying or death are to be understood as allusions to the restoration and continuation of the original intentions of the Creator.

The disturbed original status of the world, however, must be strictly separated from its actualization, just as original sin (*peccatum originale*) is distinguished from the concrete sin (*peccatum actuale*). Applied to the case of homosexuality, this means that theologically one dare not put an endogenous homosexuality, which is a kind of symptomatic participation in the fate of the fallen world, on the same level with concrete acts of libidinous excess, no matter whether these acts are the result of the actualization of this inherited constitution or of infection by a diseased environment in the form of an induced or a

merely meretriciously misused homosexuality. The predisposition itself, the homosexual potentiality as such, dare not be any more
strongly depreciated than the status of existence which we *all* share as
men in the disordered creation that exists since the Fall (*post lapsum*).

Consequently, there is not the slightest excuse for maligning the
constitutional homosexual morally or theologically. We are all under
the same condemnation and each of us has received his "share" of it.
In any case, from this point of view the homosexual share of that condemnation has no greater gravity which would justify any Pharisaic
feelings of self-righteousness and integrity on the part of us "normal"
persons.

For the disorder of creation which manifests itself here we must
point out the promise that lies in making use of the possibilities of relative healing inherent in creation. In this sense medical treatment is,
from the theological point of view, symbolically significant of the preservative will of the Creator which still continues to be in force in the
created world (Gen. 8:21 f., 9:13-16); and at the same time the
healer may think of himself as one who carries out this will and as one
whose vocation it is to serve his neighbor.

Applied to our particular subject, this means that homosexuality
cannot simply be put on the same level with the normal created order
of the sexes, but that it is rather a habitual or actual distortion or depravation of it. It follows from this that the homosexual is called upon
not to affirm his status a priori or to idealize it (on this point Karl
Barth is quite correct)—any more than any other pathological disorder can be affirmed a priori—but rather regard and recognize his
condition as something that is questionable. (This does not rule out
the possibility that it can become the vehicle of a blessing and a creative challenge.) The homosexual must therefore be willing to be
treated or healed so far as this is possible; he must, as it were, be willing to be brought back into the "order." Since sexuality has an affinity
to the totality of man, this would mean not only the willingness to consult the physician but also to be receptive to pastoral care.

But now experience shows that constitutional homosexuality at any
rate is largely unsusceptible to medical or psychotherapeutic treatment, at least so far as achieving the desired goal of a fundamental

conversion to normality is concerned. Thus it becomes properly a theological and ethical problem. Since, contrary to certain popular opinions which are frequently accepted by theologians, the great majority of homosexuals belong in this classification and their number is considerable, the church is here confronted with a grave problem in the area both of fundamental reflection and practical pastoral care.

The first thing that must be said about it is that here our attitude toward an ailment that is recognized as incurable *changes*. That is to say, we must "accept" it—which is different from the attitude which we described above, in which illness is declared to be contrary to creation and is attacked with the will to heal and be healed. What, then, does "acceptance" mean here? It can mean to accept the burden of this predisposition to homosexuality only as a divine dispensation and see it as a task to be wrestled with, indeed—paradoxical as it may sound—to think of it as a talent that is to be invested (Luke 19:13 f.).

Does this acceptance mean, then, that a person thus constituted may act in accord with his constitution, that this fateful *habitus* may be actualized? This is the most ticklish question of all. It can be discussed at all only in the framework of that freedom which is given to us by the insight that even the New Testament does not provide us with an evident, normative dictum with regard to this question. Even the kind of question which we have arrived at, namely, the problem which is posed by the "endogenous *habitus*" of homosexuality, must for purely historical reasons be alien to the New Testament. In the light of the findings of medical research to which we owe our understanding of the inseparable interinvolvement of the total personality structure (urges, character, disposition, etc.), the question must necessarily be faced afresh—in exactly the same way as in the age of the democracies, for example, the problem of the "governing authorities" must be rethought and cannot be settled by recourse to a timeless dictum of the New Testament concerning the state (concerning the necessarily contemporary state and its contemporary structure).

Perhaps the best way to formulate the ethical problem of the constitutional homosexual, who because of his vitality is not able to practice abstinence, is to ask whether within the co-ordinating system of his constitution he is willing to structure the man-man relationship in an *ethically responsible* way. Thus the ethical question meets him on the basis, which he did not enter intentionally, but which is where he actually finds himself, into which, as Heidegger would say, he has been "thrown." A certain analogy with this situation may be seen in the Old Testament chapter concerning the Noachic covenant (Gen. 9:1 ff.). Here what has erupted in the world is attributed to the sinful disordering of creation which works itself out in the structure of society. But now God in the way in which he "deals with" the fallen world places himself on the *basis* of the disordered world: from henceforth force will be combated with force, or better, illegal force will be opposed with legal force. It is in this principle that penal law finds its theological foundation.[26]

In accordance with this conception we may assume that the homosexual has to realize his optimal ethical potentialities *on the basis* of his irreversible situation. Here one must seriously ask whether in this situation—naturally only in the case of adults!—the same norms must not apply as in the normal relationship of the sexes. This is the question with which the "sympathetic" pastor is confronted. It is the question of how the homosexual in his actual situation can achieve the optimal ethical potential of sexual self-realization. To deny this would in any case mean a degree of harshness and rigor which one would never think of demanding of a "normal" person. *Celibacy* cannot be used as a counterargument, because celibacy is based upon a special calling and, moreover, is an act of free will. That such a homoerotic self-realization can take place only among those who are similarly constituted and that, besides, it cannot be an open and public thing, because it falls outside the bounds of the order of creation, hardly needs to be pointed out.

Anybody who is willing as a Christian theologian to concede the idea that it is possible to achieve ethical realization on this questionable but noneliminable basis will be able to carry out this venture—for this is what it will always be, since there are never any "patent" solutions for the borderline cases[27]—only if at the same time he persistently addresses himself to the pastoral problem involved in this

---

[26] Cf. *ThE* II, 2, §1050 ff.
[27] Cf. the analysis of the "borderline situation" in *ThE* II, 1, §688 ff.

ethical realization. On this the following may be said. Even though it be true that the "normal" basis of the created order of sex relationship is fraught with hazards and temptations to go contrary to the order (cf. the Pauline catalogues of vices!), it is not difficult to see that the homosexual is exposed to even greater dangers, which in many cases where the help of the physician and pastor is lacking simply cause him to succumb to certain temptations. We mention only a few symptoms of this threatening descent.

1. The homosexual does not have the benefit of living within a supporting order that is informed by a traditional ethos such as that of the institution of marriage. Instead of having at his disposal a set of prefabricated decisions which are made for him by the tradition and make it easier for him to find his way about, he is to an unimaginably greater degree thrown back upon himself. Since he generally begins only gradually to recognize his disposition, he goes through phases of terrible loneliness and stages of groping and uncertain improvisations.

2. Otherwise than in the "normal" sphere, the noningrained normative attitude easily produces a propensity toward the excessive, toward rapidly changing partnerships (promiscuity) and thus a sabotage of even that relative "order" which the homosexual *could* achieve even on his basis.

3. The ostracism the homosexual suffers through the criminal law and the defensive instinct of society leads him to frequent very dubious circles. He cannot risk any public attempt to make advances. Whereas the "normal" person is permitted to regard a representative of the other sex as a potential partner and is exposed only to the possibility of being refused (without thereby being socially or morally compromised), the homosexual runs the danger of encountering a "normal" person, with all the consequences that this may involve. This search for a partner of his own kind in the shady areas of society means an extraordinarily heavy spiritual burden and, what is more, a dangerous temptation especially for the person who really wants to live an ethically responsible life.

4. The same burden and temptation result from the fact that the homosexual must wear a mask and act like a hypocrite before friends, acquaintances, and as a rule even in his own family, but nevertheless live in constant fear of discovery and its consequent compromise of

character.[28] Thus he is thrown into a situation of permanent conflict.

From all this it follows that the homosexual in a very special way needs intellectual and spiritual guidance or at least care, which will give him a constantly renewed stability on the slippery ground of his existence. The temptations of the homosexual which we have described are so great that we must appreciate why it is that Christian theologians often despair in the face of the minimal chances of being able to live ethically with homosexuality and achieve an acceptable partnership. And we ourselves do not venture to credit these chances with anything more than being a possible exception.[29]

Therefore Christian pastoral care will have to be concerned primarily with helping the person to *sublimate* his homosexual urge. But this cannot be done by exposing the homosexual to defamation of his urge. On the contrary, it is possible only if we are able to help him to see the tasks and the potentialities that are inherent in his abnormal existence. Not infrequently these consist in a pedagogical *eros,* in any case most often in a heightened sense of empathy. Therefore the goal of this sublimation will be found precisely *in* the actual danger zones, because here is where the "charism"—the possible "charism"!—of the homosexual is presented with appropriate tasks. Responsibility toward those who come in contact with persons who are thus constituted requires, of course, that these opportunities be recommended or opened only to those homosexuals who indicate that they are ready for such sublimation and evidence their stability. In most cases even these persons need the continuing ministry of their medical or pastoral counselors.

## 3. The Theologicolegal Aspect

From what has been said it is apparent that it is our conviction that homosexuality is primarily an *ethical* question, insofar as it is not a matter of the seduction of youth or the exploitation of relation of de-

[28] Abundant clinical material has been assembled in the book by Hans Giese, *Der homosexuelle Mensch in der Welt* (Stuttgart, 1958). Among the statistical materials there are also important documentations of relationships which manifest ethical fidelity; cf. especially pp. 133 ff.

[29] We say this despite certain rather astonishing statistics which Giese cites concerning stable, "monogamous" relationships among homosexuals. Cf. *ibid.,* pp. 133 ff.

pendency or a recognizable danger of infection. *Therefore it is not the concern of criminal law.* (Otherwise adultery and fornication would also have to be prosecuted as criminal offenses and action would have to be taken even though no charges were lodged [cf. Wolfenden Report, Section 14]). This is the more true since the "homosexual constitution," lived within the limits we have defined, is not even to be *ethically* disqualified *a limine,* but is capable of realizing relative ethical values within the questionable framework of this disposition and it is possible for it to be a relative ethical order, even though in principle it is contrary to the order of creation (understood in the theological sense!). But even for those who are *not* impelled by their pastoral experience to accept this theological interpretation of homosexuality and consequently regard even that homosexual existence which is lived within the narrowest limits as not worth discussing from an ethical point of view, homosexuality can have only an *ethical* and not a *legal* relevance. In any case, this is the consistent opinion of those who have dealt with the problem *in extenso* from the ethical as well as from the theological point of view. On this point there is a clear, unmistakable consensus in the English reports (including the Roman Catholic!), the Swedish pastoral letter, and the two authors whose work should be taken with special seriousness (Bovet and Bailey).

One may also deal with the noncompetence of criminal law, within the limits discussed, from the point of view of the nature of the punishment.[30] Of the recognized purposes of legal punishment, expiation, deterrence, and reform, the first is in this case more than questionable, while the last does not apply at all. On the other hand, if we illegitimately incorporate facts which should be evaluated ethically into criminal law, this leads to distortions which produce fresh ethical *and* penal complications. We need only to think of the practice of blackmail this gives rise to and the ethically and legally dubious expedients of self-defense by which homosexuals seek to escape this danger.

When the argument in Section 216 (amendment of the hitherto

[30] The chapter on law in the still unpublished Vol. III of *ThE* contains an extended discussion of this.

existing Section 175) in the draft of the new Penal Code [of the German Federal Republic] points out (on p. 348) that "homosexual" unchastity between women entails "less drastic consequences for life together in human society" and therefore "does not require that it be combated by means of criminal law," then the very considerations we have just discussed would prompt us to ask whether here cause and effect are not being confounded. Is female homosexuality really not punished because it is socially less harmful? Or is it possibly just the other way around, that it is less harmful in the legal, criminal sense precisely because it is *not* punished, because it is left as being ethically questionable or reprehensible and no attempt is made to juridify the ethical? May not the fact that female homosexuality is less harmful perhaps be due to the fact that it is not to the same degree driven into shady circumstances and is not compelled to resort to dubious means, exposing itself to blackmail and its accompanying reactions of compliance or self-defense? We simply cannot see any theological, philosophical, legal, or psychological reason why—apart from this explanation—the two forms of homosexuality should be differentiated in value. If the consequences were not so hazardous and dreadful, one might almost venture to propose that we make the experiment of subjecting female homosexuality to punishment in the name of the principle of the equality of the sexes.[31] The probability is that then we would very soon be speaking of the social danger of sexual misconduct between women.

As we have said, the only kind of homosexuality which is not the concern of criminal law is that which does not affect minors and dependents and, by being confined to those who are clearly of the same constitution, does not infect others, that is, does not lead to induced homosexuality in normal persons or even bisexual persons. It is true that the explanatory preamble of the new draft of the Penal Code adopts this justifiable prophylactic point of view and for this very reason intends to insist upon legal punishment of *all* kinds of homosexuality (in the sense of acts of sexual intercourse). Nevertheless it is difficult to see why this prophylaxis cannot be achieved in another

[31] In Austria both are subject to penalty, though in practice they are dealt with differently.

way: it is already present to a large extent in the fact that in society a very clear and universal aversion to homosexuality exists and is also ineradicably embedded in human nature. This by itself constitutes a considerable antitoxin to the threat of infection. From this "view of the great majority of the population" (Penal Code, p. 347) criminal law should draw the conclusion that what must be done is to form a concept of "public offense" under which drastically conspicuous or actually soliciting forms of homosexual conduct would be subsumed. This would be the most that criminal law can accomplish here. In this way criminal law could also prosecute those forms of conduct which the new draft fears would become uncontrollable if the sections bearing on this matter were omitted (p. 348, middle of col. 1).

In conclusion we may address ourselves to the possible objection that the position taken here represents a dubious liberalization, not to say an ethical "softening of the bones." We are not unaware that this danger is an actual threat. Whenever the principle of criminal law based upon motivation (*Täterstrafrecht*) supplants criminal law based purely upon the actual deed committed (*Erfolgsstrafrecht*), or even becomes codeterminative, the question of motives, of ethical quality, in short, the inner nature of the culprit arises. Two consequences follow from this:

First, it results in an increased reluctance to give in to the tendency to give legislative form that which is only ethically relevant. In the mixed form of both concepts of criminal law, which appears in the new draft (in our theological opinion quite legitimately!), the ethically relevant can be given additional legal force only if the act constitutes a threat to society and its basic order of law.[32]

The second consequence that follows from including the point of view of a motivational concept of criminal law is what we may call, in rather pointed polemical fashion, the domination of the expert. In the context of our subject psychologists, psychiatrists, and neurologists are necessarily involved to a large extent. And here the question

[32] The sole exception to this which I have been able to detect is in the new draft of Section 218 (sexual misconduct with animals), the argument of which is based only upon the concept of dishonoring the human dignity of the person who commits the act (p. 351, col. 2). We have tried to show that this verdict does *not* necessarily apply to certain forms of homosexuality.

arises whether the endeavor "to understand all" does not also entail the tendency "to forgive all" and whether this may not tend to weaken the whole concept of punishment, obliterate clear norms, and transform the infliction of punishment into a visit to a social sanatorium or protective hospital or nursing home. The concern for a clear and unambiguously applied system of norms explains why it is that occasionally there emerges something like a longing for the kind of criminal law which is based purely upon the act committed (*Erfolgsstrafrecht*),[33] such as that which prevails in England and also in the Soviet Union. Would it not be fundamentally more "salutary" for the culprit and would he not react with more willingness to amend his ways if he were confronted with clear norms based upon actual deeds, whereas in the other case everything is open to debate and then is discussed away?

It is precisely when we face such a complicated and basically insoluble problem as that of homosexuality that this question is likely to arise. On the other hand, we must not overlook the fact that the alleged clarity and unambiguousness of purely factual norms does not spring from a discernment of the nature of law and ethos, but is rather pragmatic in character. For these so-called "purely factual norms" [*Tat-Normen*] consist of postulates which are set up for the purpose of making the law easier to apply in a practicable way. One can leave open the question whether this practice is actually permissible or even to be recommended in areas which have to do with external social life (for example, the problems connected with traffic laws). But where the core of personhood is as directly affected as it is in the case of homosexuality, such pragmatic regulations must inevitably result in appalling outrages upon the humanity of those who are already suffering severely from their disposition; they would be an assault upon the dignity of the person because they do not inquire into the condition of the person, and they do not do this because in this way the practicable application of the law remains or becomes easier to "handle."

We can summarize our conclusion by accepting as essentially our own the recommendations of the documents we have cited (The Grif-

[33] Cf. Schoellgen, *op. cit.*, pp. 407 ff.

fin Report, 1956, The Wolfenden Report, 1957, and the pastoral letter of the Swedish bishops, 1951), namely, that homosexuality is to be subjected to legal prosecution only under the following cases:

1. Acts committed against minors and dependents;
2. Acts committed against public decency (scandal);
3. The mercenary exploitation of homosexuality.

Our arguments have been in many respects different from those employed in these documents, and we have addressed ourselves to a number of points of view which play no part in them. The result with respect to the legal punishment of homosexuality, however, is the same.

# V    CONCLUSION

# Historical Changes in Our Understanding of Eros

In the course of our discussion we have been repeatedly confronted with the fact that the norms of sexual behavior are exceedingly variable. This is true not only of the changes they have undergone in the course of history, but also of the great breadth of variation of standards to be found in ethnological groups. The variety of sexual norms is apparent not only in different times but also in different places. Related to this, as we have seen, is also the fact that even the relevant biblical statements must be separated from the contemporary setting which often conditions them and interpreted in the light of our changed situation today. Only so can we see that they are still binding upon us. The preceding chapter on homosexuality provides an impressive illustration of this.

Therefore, I should like to conclude with a discussion of this fundamentally important variability in our understanding of *eros*. Christians and secularists and Christians among themselves so often speak at cross purposes concerning questions of the ethics of sex, become intolerant, and cast unjustified reproaches upon one another because they do not adequately see and evaluate this problem of variability.

In the presentation of the biblical and Reformation understanding of marriage we must have been struck by the extent to which the individual *eros* recedes into the background as a positive value. In the Old Testament it plays only an incidental, almost anecdotal role, while elsewhere attention is wholly directed to marriage as an institutional ordinance and is more a concern of the tribe than of the individual. In the New Testament marriage appears in the Gospels as a gracious order created by God; and probable as it may be that it included *eros* between the sexes, there is no mention whatsoever of any special significance it may have had for the inception of a marriage or within the marriage itself. When it is mentioned, as in Paul, this is done with a definitely negative accent. Here it may possibly be understood as representing the libido, which needs to be domesticated in the emergency institution (*Not-Institut*) of marriage and is otherwise only a hindrance to unbroken devotion to the Lord. When in contrast to this New Testament view modern theology without exception speaks of an affirming of the body and sexuality[1] and, despite the investigation made, still declares that it is moving on a line marked out by the Scriptures, it undoubtedly cannot document this by a biblicistic use of quotations. This theology can appeal to the Bible (and also to the Reformers!) in support of this position only by finding in biblical theology areas in which they can find room for a changed attitude toward reality—just as the writers of the Bible filled these areas with *their* understanding of reality. So here we cannot simply quote, but must rather interpret, and hence we are again confronted with the task which we have repeatedly mentioned before, namely, the hermeneutical task of separating the kerygmatic kernel from its contemporary husk. For our present topic this task would mean raising the question whether and where in the biblical orders of creation and redemption there is a theological place where *eros* and the modern understanding of reality affected by it can be "settled," in exactly the same sense in which the ancient classical understanding of reality was able in many different ways to find room for itself here. This question involves the task of distinguishing between the abiding net of the orders of creation and redemption *and* those variable en-

---

[1] "The Christian discrimination against *eros* as such is undoubtedly a very old mistake." Karl Barth, *Church Dogmatics,* III, 4, p. 126.

tities which it catches up within it at any specific time. We have been familiarized with this task of discriminating in our day by the discussion of the problem of hermeneutics. The problem has even become popularly known through the distinction that has been made between the kerygma and the mythical and philosophical forms in which it expresses itself, and in connection with Bultmann's hermeneutics has evoked discussion on many different levels.

Therefore we need to discover the ethical variants of this originally dogmatic question. And it is plain to be seen that actually there is only one variant in question here: for since we have the right to understand the temporally limited world view or the mythical ciphers as mere media of expression for the kerygmatic kernel and thus set ourselves the task of transposing the kerygma into *our* media of expression (instead of anachronistically, and therefore untruthfully, retaining the outworn media and burdening the faith with them), we also have the right to understand men's feeling about life and attitude toward reality and the reflective forms which these take as the same kind of variable medium through which the kerygma expresses itself at any given time.

This would mean therefore that with Paul the medium that determined him was a certain Hellenistic feeling about life which was hostile to the body and that this therefore constituted the medium out of which and within which he perceived the kerygma. But then this would also mean that this clearly discernible insensitivity to *eros* is not a part of the Christian message *itself,* but is rather to be assigned —to speak in Kantian terms—to the "categories" and thus to quite special anthropological presuppositions.

Only when things are seen in this way does the second part of the question follow, namely, the question whether the kerygma admits of being taken into completely different categories; in other words, whether people with entirely different anthropological presuppositions can be touched by it and find themselves in it: Jews and Greeks (Acts 18:4, 20:21; Rom. 3:9; I Cor. 1:22 f.; Gal. 3:28; Col. 3:11), people with ancient, classical minds and people with modern minds. Thus, for example, we should have to examine the concept of *soma* (body) in Paul to see whether it does not have in it a far greater potentiality of ways of understanding the body and corporeality than Paul himself, with his limited individuality and the limitations of his time, was able to see.

These attempts to discover in biblical theology places where modern forms of consciousness can be lodged have long since become commonplaces which are taken for granted in other areas of theological thought. One need only think of the controversy between natural science and Christianity.[2] Here too the concept of astronomy in Joshua 10:12 f. cannot be identified with the message itself, but must be distinguished from it. The act of making this distinction then implies the further question of where the affinity of the message with the changed scientific knowledge lies, or better, where its affinity with the modern scientific "knower" *himself* lies.

This distinction between the kernel of the kerygma developed only gradually as the doctrine of verbal inspiration, which identifies the two, was broken down by the pressure of the awakening historical consciousness. In any case, this breakdown of the doctrine of verbal inspiration constitutes one of the essential presuppositions for making this distinction. At first it was felt to be a threat to the substance of the Christian message and in many cases it was employed for just this purpose. In many respects Christianity is still suffering from this traumatic shock. In point of fact, however, what at first appeared to be a threat turned out to be an opportunity to advance theological knowledge and also to realize it pastorally in a wholly new way. Likewise, the historical and critical investigation of the Bible seemed dangerous at first, and it too tended at first to appear in the mask of a temple destroyer. (The name of David Friedrich Strauss will suffice as an illustration.) Finally here too it turned out that it was only this newly discovered polyphony of witnesses that brought to light the full breadth of the biblical pleroma.

However, in broad sections of the history of the church before the beginning of the modern era the media in which the biblical kerygma was expressed were taken over with the kerygma itself. This is evidenced in the area of *eros* in the fact that Paul's lack of appreciation in this dimension was handed on in the tradition along with the kerygma and thus in a calamitous way became a mark of what Chris-

---

[2] Cf. the dialogue between theology and biology in the chapter on "Man in the Cosmos," *ThE* II, 1, §1181 ff.

tianity was thought to be. In part, of course, this may also be owing to the fact that in many periods *eros* itself was still too much in a state of latency to assert itself as an independent theological problem. Here it is not an easy thing to avoid confusing cause and effect. That is to say, it is not easy to determine whether the lack of the human presuppositions prevented the corresponding theological questions from arising or whether the influence of a Christianity so understood prevented the human presuppositions from arising.

In any case, the fact remains that very generally marriage was not understood as a fulfillment, an enrichment of human life, a source of happiness, and that *eros* was not implicitly regarded as a motive that causes one to seek a lifelong relationship with a "thou" of the other sex. We shall not undertake a tour of inspection through the history of the church because we would hardly know where to begin and where to stop. In any case, wherever this positive view of marriage as a fulfillment continued to exist despite the general attitude, it was not inferred from the theological interpretation of marriage (for in this instance we do not mean by "positive" the *"justitia aliena"* of marriage as a helpful ordinance of God), but was simply the *humanum* (the specifically human element), which still continued to exist, stirring, delighting, and enrapturing men where they really should have been shamefaced. The polemical observation that Christianity is hostile to the body and *eros*, that it regards marriage as an "asylum for the sick," and that the new feeling about love—as it appeared in the poetry of the troubadors—forced people "to look for another object than one's own spouse,"[3] this reproach can avail itself of very considerable documentation in the history of the church. The somewhat melancholy reflection that may attach to this observation is disquieted by the question whether church history is really the textbook and picture book for a legitimate exposition of the Holy Scriptures and whether one can really depend upon it if one wants to know what is "Christian." The answer to this question can be only a criticism of the tradition and a call to go back to the immediacy of the Scriptures. (The fact that the Scriptures themselves are in turn a part of the tradition does not get rid of the question.) The answer would therefore

[3] Løgstrup, *RGG,* (3 ed.), II, 328.

begin with the polemics and the new departure of the Reformation on the basis of their *sola scriptura,* even though this principle will often enough be turned around and used critically against the Reformers, for *example* in the area of the theology of marriage.

The question which the modern person who deals directly with the Bible will address to it cannot be the question whether there are in it any indications that biblical man had an appreciation of marriage as a fulfillment of life or of individual *eros.* We have already pointed out a few of these indications in the Old Testament. But they are theologically irrelevant, since their presence or absence is to be charged to the account not of the kerygma but of the (variable!) categories.

The question must rather be whether the created order of marriage as a gracious help in making human life possible allows room, not merely to "justify" modern man's affirmation of life and its fulfillment of the individual *eros* and the richness of human communication, but rather to include and interpret and fill it with its meaning. This task of taking something that had changed completely, something that had not yet appeared in the Bible at all, and nevertheless subjecting it to the norms and the interpretation of the Bible, setting it down under its light, is, after all, a task that confronts us all along the line. We have only to think of the task of finding theological meaning in technology or space travel or the "job" (which is an altogether different form of work from that of the old idea of a vocation) or democracy (a form of state which is strictly different from Old Testament theocracy as well as the authoritarian state of the epistle to the Romans).[4] There is no end to the instances once one begins to count them.

We now simply have to reckon with the fact that there is a changed feeling about life, a new relationship to work,[5] to the world around us, to *eros.* Here we have become aware of hitherto hidden values which can never again be made to disappear (and should not be). It would therefore be unreal—quite apart from the false interpretation of Scripture—to desire, for example, simply to reproduce Luther's understanding of marriage or even to preach a wedding sermon in his

[4] *ThE* II, 2, §20 ff.
[5] *ThE* II, 1, §1429 ff.

style. We can no longer go back behind these established facts. It is entirely clear to us that in the realm of exegesis we cannot go back to the time before the advent of historical and critical study of the Scriptures, in order to make our own the supposedly still sound exegesis of the Reformers (though naturally we gratefully use it as a corrective and a stimulus).

We must deny ourselves this recourse, not only for the sake of honesty, but also because otherwise we would be throwing away the wealth of new growth in our knowledge. In view of this new understanding of reality, do we have the same resolute determination not to pass by the new-found values and simply go back to the time before they existed? If one reads the liturgical forms for marriage in the service books, one might well doubt whether we have this determination. Here we cannot simply "quote" the Bible any more than we can elsewhere. We must interpret it—interpret it in the light of the changed consciousness of reality. Merely to quote Paul on the subject of marriage would actually be offensive to countless persons. They would not recognize their own "happy" marriages in these statements of his and they would probably disassociate themselves from these texts with the sad conviction that this was a blind man talking about color (and with all respect to the Apostle they perhaps would not be far wrong).

On this break between the modern attitude toward life and that of the time before Romanticism (to take a very rough periodization but by no means the only possible one), we mention only the very diverse examples of Luther's theology and that of Pietism.

For *Luther,* as Løgstrup has pointed out, "sexuality and Christian faith are undergirded by the same understanding of life; the psychological question whether they could both exist in the mind at the same time never even occurred to him."[6] Seen from the point of view of God the primary purposes of marriage, namely, the procreation of children and the satisfaction of the sexual libido, belong together, for he uses the desire of the sexes to achieve this purpose, even though the lovers need have no conscious realization of this.[7] One may perhaps compare this *cum grano salis* with Hegel's "strategy of the Idea": just as the "world-his-

---

[6] *Op. cit.,* 327.
[7] *WA* 34, 1, 59, 40.

torical individual" pursues his own ends and satisfies his urge for power without suspecting that he is thereby realizing the purposes of the World Spirit, so man satisfies his sexuality without realizing (or at any rate not having to realize) that he is thereby serving the purposes of the order of creation.

In *our* connection what concerns us theologically at this point is that in Luther the place of the psychic experience remains undefined. The experience is simply observed as being a fact. God knows why he allows us to have it. One can also formulate the purpose of God in theological terms, as Luther occasionally does. But to make this *eros* experience the subject of theological interpretation and to evaluate its peculiar quality— as a gift to add fulfillment to life or even as something that binds persons to each other—this lies beyond the range of his reflection. But this is just what strikes us as being "medieval"; here there is no echo of our own *eros* experience. There are only a few faint advances in another direction but these are hardly utilized theologically. Thus Luther is occasionally capable of describing sexual love even apart from the purposes of procreation as the indispensable bond of marriage[8] and even goes so far as to say that God laughs and rejoices when two married people get on well together.

*Pietism*, in contrast with Luther, raises the psychological question. It had to arise for Pietism if only because even in the realm of piety it always started out from *experience,* the experience of conversion, regeneration, repentance, joy in the Lord. In conformity with this interest in the psychic experience the *eros* experience also called for interpretation and theological evaluation. And yet this question was not posed in such a way that the *eros* experience as such, having its own value as an encounter with the created world, became the object of the question. Hence this kind of psychological interest, despite its new sensitiveness, was not capable of opening the way to a relationship with modern forms of experiencing *eros* and marriage. Rather in Pietism the psychological question was focused on the compatibility of the *eros* experience with the experience of union with Christ. But since the *eros* experience as such was not thought through theologically and thus remained a spiritually unsubdued element of strong psychic force, its relation to the religious experience could be regarded only as competitive. Here was a power that sought to fill up the whole of the psyche to the limits of its capacity.

The tendency to think of this threat of the elemental *eros* in this way may have been strengthened by tradition; for in tradition the libido had always been thought of as something that must be tamed and domesti-

[8] *WA* 34, 1, 61.

cated. And in line with this tradition, for Pietism it remained something to be ashamed of (a *pudendum*), something which at most was merely tolerated by God.

Nevertheless this psychological focus of the question led to a direction different from that of the past; for in Pietism the *eros* experience was not something to be dealt with by coercion and kept within bounds. Anybody who is aware of psychological realities, as were Zinzendorf and Spener, for example, and is equipped with the kind of sensitive organs of perception which they possessed, knows—what is obvious to any psychoanalyst today[9]—that forms of experience are not to be influenced merely by negative means. They therefore opposed the *eros* with the weapon of psychological sublimation.

Given the psychic structure of the Zinzendorf type of piety, the only means of sublimation could be the assimilation of the *eros* experience into the *religious* experience. The religious eroticism, as it is expressed in the framework of Zinzendorf's "Jesus-love," is well known in the documentary evidence.

This sublimation may, however, express itself in the opposite direction, that is, by "sanctifying" the sex act itself, whether this be by consummating our sexual life in the same attitude in which we go to the Lord's Supper (thus Zinzendorf), or by reducing the lust to a minimum by concentrating upon Christ and so practicing an *"exercitium apathias,"* or by having the first cohabitation of the newly married take place in the presence of representatives of the congregation acting as "marriage helpers" and garnishing the affair with a liturgy for sexual intercourse [*Beischlafliturgie*].[10]

It requires no illustrations to show to what inhibitions and distress such an *eros* experience would lead, striking with elemental force the receptivity of people who were sensitive to the experiential, almost trained, disciplined, and oriented to be receptive to experience, and yet an *eros* experience which was not accepted and affirmed and which could not be fitted into the theologically prescribed mental structure. Then this unsubdued *eros* became something that must be all the more checked, controlled, mistrusted, and extravagantly sublimated. This then leads to the disparagement of even the slightest signs of *eros* in relation with other persons, as it did, for example, in Spener.[11]

One understands then how violent the reaction would be to a "Christian" tradition which culminated in this disparagement of *eros* at the very threshold of the modern age. And again, as so often, the new atti-

[9] Cf. Pfister, *op. cit.*
[10] Cf. Tanner, *op. cit.*, pp. 76, 127, 135, 163, 168, 182, 235.
[11] *Ibid.*, pp. 186 f., 239.

tude toward reality made such great headway that it called forth secular protests against these narrow "Christian" inhibitions and anxieties and (again, as so often) this initial polemic continued for a long time afterward to cast suspicion on the new-found attitude toward *eros* in the eyes of the pious. Even the new cosmology initiated by the astronomy of Galileo and Copernicus was for a long time subject to the verdict of being anti-Christian. It was Romanticism that allowed the modern attitude toward *eros* to break through with elemental force.[12]

There should be no disputing the fact that *eros* has in the way we have described entered into our consciousness as a newly discovered, independent value. That *eros* is one of the determining motives in the choosing of a marital partner is so taken for granted that it hardly needs to be stated. Likewise, marriage is thought of only very peripherally, even among Christians, as being an institution whose purpose is to domesticate the sex urge. In the foreground marriage stands as a positive good, a complementation of the particularity of the individual and a fulfillment of life in the almost countless ways in which it is actualized in a total life relationship.

Now, what is thus an unquestionable phenomenological fact is still fraught with theological problems. It is, after all, theoretically conceivable that this vitalization of the individual *eros* may represent a wrong development, which would not permit us simply to accept it because it is a given fact and grant it "the normative force of the factual" simply on the basis of its factuality. We know from the history of theology to what disastrous heresies this theological sanctioning of the given facts has led, whether we think of the "serious" forms of such theological approval—such as the principle of legitimacy enunciated by J. Stahl and A. F. C. Vilmar[13]—or of the unserious forms in which a downright "natural theology" seeks to "sacralize" certain historical epochs or political and biological ordinances and bestow upon them the dignity of institutions of creation.[14] Theology un-

---

[12] Cf. Friedrich Schlegel's *Lucinde*. Also W. Dilthey, *Das Leben Schleiermachers* I (2 ed., 1922); also Schleiermacher's *Hausstandspredigten* in the year 1818, especially the first sermon.

[13] Cf. W. Hopf, *A. Vilmar* (1913); H. F. Hedderich, *Die Gedanken der Romantik über Kirche und Staat* (1941).

[14] Recall the "German Christians" under Hitler; cf. P. Althaus, *Politisches Christentum* (1935); Thielicke, critique of natural theology, in *Theologie der Anfechtung* (1949), p. 14.

doubtedly must have the courage to say that public opinion and the "things an era takes for granted" (Gogarten) are wrong, instead of merely accepting them in the sense of being willing to give them a theological interpretation.

The question of conscience addresses itself to the theologian in two ways:

First, it appears in the question whether he is so much and so naïvely a child of his time that he quite naturally regards the current value structure as a domicile [*Gehäuse*] in which and on the basis of which his theological positions can also be built. On this aspect of the question of conscience we may remark that it could not have arisen for Paul and the Reformers in just this way, since the idea of "our age," "the present time," as a period of time distinguished from other phases of history, did not exist for them at all; what we have here is rather a typically modern concept which could arise only as the result of a "historical consciousness."[15] The unreflective way in which Paul, for example, takes over contemporary ordinances as theologically valid[16] could be for a—*horribile dictu!*—"modern theologian" a grave fault. As the intellectual scale has grown richer new degrees of possible guilt also arise.

The second form in which the question of conscience is addressed to the theologian is determined by the self-critical consideration of whether he is not behaving in a way that is just the opposite of those who in naïve contemporaneity give theological validity to the normative force of the factual. This reversed procedure would consist in the fact that he completely overlooks the changes that have come with time and from an exalted, superhistorical place condemns every epoch as apostasy, as being "below the line of death."[17] In this case he would come to the conclusion, in the name of his doctrine of sin and the alleged "infinite qualitative difference between time and eternity," that all ages are on the same level, which would make it seem unlawful for him to see any "theological" problem at all in the awakening of the individual *eros*—except that it is a confirmation of his theological theory that history is *de facto* nothing more than a

[15] Cf. H. Heimpel, *Der Mensch in der Gegenwart* (1954), pp. 9 ff.
[16] This applies, e.g., to his regulations for the dress of women in church, I Cor. 11:5, 13, or to his position with respect to slavery, Philem. 11-19.
[17] Thus Barth in *The Epistle to the Romans.*

permanent variation of original sin.

In that we are fully aware of these critical questions which theology addresses to itself and take them seriously, we answer them by asking the further question whether and where the theological point is to be found from which the individual *eros* can be interpreted theologically. We have already answered this question thetically by saying that the order of creation in marriage does contain this theological basis and that it provides the possibility for understanding marriage, not merely as a hindrance to evil (*arcere malum*), but also as a positive fulfillment of life and *also* to think of it in terms of individual *eros*. Our interpretation of the creation of man, especially the woman (Gen. 2:18 ff.), has shown that here the order of creation for the man-wife relationship is only sketched in outline and that it allows broad latitude for filling it with content. There is no reason why the wife's being a helper (Gen. 2:18) cannot be understood as a diffraction of what Paul means by being helpers of each other's joy (II Cor. 1:24, AV), and why the leaving of father and mother and thus "cleaving to the wife" and "becoming one flesh" (Gen. 2:24) should not also leave room for interpreting this in the sense of individual *eros*.

The obvious breadth of this outline provides room for the most widely different attitudes and feelings. Thus it is altogether possible to think of the wife being a helper in the sense of being a nurse in Luther's "hospital for the sick" and thus serving to canalize the torrent of the libido. Probably this would cover only one aspect of the text but it would not exhaust its possibilities. However, it cannot be denied that this interpretation has a place in it.

But we have just as much right to interpret this being a helpmeet positively as a fulfillment of life.

Like the order of creation, the order of redemption also provides room for this interpretation. For it would be an unjustified simplification in line with natural theology if one were to interpret the contribution of the individual *eros* to the fulfillment of married life only one-sidedly as a fulfillment of the design of creation, a way to the full measure of creaturehood. Even if we were to take this course in the direction of the fulfillment of the design of creation—and here every statement must be made with extreme caution—we should still have to remember that there is no form of development of the created being in which the Fall is not involved. Any attempt to retract or ignore it or to allow it only partial validity would be misusing the doctrine of creation for an act of self-redemption (Rom. 1:18 ff.). This becomes exemplary clear precisely in the area of *eros*, and it does so in two respects:

First, it must not be forgotten that in mythology *Eros* had the position of a God or a daemon and that therefore there is reason to expect that wherever it is in the picture its claim to occupy the throne will always be potentially present. In this connection we do not even need to think in terms of excess of passion, of ecstasy and the total possession it takes (though this too may have something to do with this claim to divinity). We need only to think of the well-known and widespread way in which *eros* becomes the dominant criterion of the relationship of the sexes. Here it is capable of crowding out the deeper levels of communication, in which fidelity, self-sacrifice, and reverence for the other person hold sway, for the sake of a momentary effervescence of temperament. Thus it can deliver the relationship of the sexes to extreme instability. The fact that the divorce rate has risen in direct proportion to the increasing prevalence of the individual *eros* is undoubtedly connected with this. The attempt to explain this increase merely with the argument that in times past divorce was regarded as a disgrace whereas now it has become increasingly sanctioned by society is undoubtedly wrong. Rather it could be just the other way around. The increasing willingness to give this social sanction to divorce would not have been possible had there not been a corresponding increase in the valuation given to the individual *eros* in the occurrence, the continuance, and the possible ending of a marriage. In this connection it is not the individual *eros* itself which is dubious, but rather the high rank that is given to it, a rank that comes close to the deity it once had, but without the piety the original pagan brought to it and degraded by the pragmatic framework in which it appears: it has become the patron saint of eudaemonism. It raises happiness to the rank of being the real mark of a full life and above all of self-fulfillment. To achieve self-realization, to realize one's optimal potentialities and to "use" the other person to that end: this threatens to be the destiny of a dethroned god who seems to be staging his comeback in a secularized world.[18]

This pragmatic character of the *eros*-god, who has been reinstalled under changed conditions, is also discernible in the fact that the loved one remains in communion with me only as he satisfies the erotic claims which I can make upon him with respect to my self-fulfillment. When he no longer satisfies these claims (because of age or the deadening power of habit and familiarity, or boredom, etc.) he is dismissed. I no longer deal with him as a person with the "infinite value of a human soul"; I value him only for what he is worth, or to put it very crudely, I treat him merely as an erotic functionary whose importance to me stands or falls as he performs or does not perform his function for me. There is no room here for *agape,* which lives not by making claims but by giving and which by loving makes the other person worth loving.[19]

Second, the individual *eros* reveals its dark side in the very thing that qualifies it as a "gift," a development of the order of creation. The individual *eros* can grow only to the degree that the individuality itself develops. Where this development does not occur, the partner

[18] W. Schubart (*Religion und Eros* [1944] has revived this attitude toward *eros* which had its basis in Romanticism and was also incorporated in theology by Schleiermacher. These elements in his book rob it very largely of the productive function it might have performed even for Christian ethics, namely, that of calling Christianity to account for its latent hostility to *eros* and failure to see that time has brought changes. "The beloved person embodies for the lover this oneness [add: in the sense of a divine wholeness] or offers himself as a medium and guide to this oneness. When two lovers find each other, then at one point in the cosmos the wound of loneliness is closed" (p. 84). "Genuine sexual love is a *testimonium Spiritus Sancti.*" "In the acts of love the lovers sense the connection between their bond and the divine breath of the All" (p. 85). In the "state of grace" which lovers attain when they have found their way out of tension into harmony, sexual love broadens out "into love of one's neighbor, into love of the All and of God." This is the "cycle of erotic love" (p. 231). Two things are clear in these quotations: the eudaemonistic urge to self-fulfillment (indeed, to cosmic fulfillment) and the assertion that *eros* has the status of deity. Here *eros* does not stand under the judgment and grace of the Father of Jesus Christ, nor is it in a state of tension with *agape,* but is itself the whole spring: even *agape* is only a rivulet that branches off from its stream.

[19] This *agape* is fashioned after the model of God's love: "*Amor Dei non invenit, sed creat suum diligibile; amor hominum* [= *eros*] *fit a suo diligibile*" (God's love does not find, but creates its lovable object; man's love is caused by its lovable object), *WA* 1, 354, 35. Cf. also A. Nygren, "*Eros and Agape,*" *ZsyTh* VI, pp. 690 ff., especially p. 720.

—so far as *eros* is concerned—is interchangeable. He lacks the mark of being unique, noninterchangeable. But development of individuality is identical with the formation of a higher differentiation. Thus we have "highly differentiated" individuals.

On the other hand this means a development of the "gift" of creation. For individual differentiation must not by any means be regarded only from the point of view of sin and judgment, as it is, for example, in the story of the tower of Babel (Gen. 11:8), where differentiation means isolation and dispersion. But the same individualization appeared in its unbroken quality in the order of creation when God brought forth the individual creatures "each according to its kind," that is, each with its own individuality (Gen. 1:11, 12, 21, 24, 25). What was abundance in the creation becomes in the Fall a deficiency. On one side, therefore, differentiation actually does have a positive intent in creation; in any case it can be thought of as a continuation of the initial intent of creation, and theologically, this can be covered by the term *conservatio*.

On the other side, however, differentiation also represents a "task,"[20] a responsibility imposed by the order of creation. For, having received this gift, we are faced by the demand that we pay due regard to the differentiated individuality of the other person, accepting him as he is. Not to accommodate oneself or even not to be *able* to accommodate oneself to the other person may wound and hurt him, and the discernment of this fact probably produced the typically modern idea of "mental cruelty."

The responsibility to which this demand calls us begins already with the choice of a partner. If this responsibility is lacking, that is, if both are not by constitution in the required relationship of complementarity to each other, this would imply that there are tensions which could easily become intolerable because it is difficult to expect that a developed individuality will be able to muster the permanent self-control to endure such a relationship or to submit to constant oppression. Here the possibilities of going wrong are far greater than they were in the preindividualistic era. To wound the status of

[20] The customary play on the words *Gabe* (gift, in the preceding paragraph) and *Aufgabe* (task). (Trans.)

another person through the status of one's own nature—and by no means merely through individual acts—is not a blameless thing. On a higher level Goethe has exemplified this conflict in the relationship of Faust to Gretchen.

It is also characteristic of this status of highly developed individuality that the *humanum* is more vulnerable than previously because it offers many more points of attack. These points of attack become more numerous as the individuality becomes more differentiated and more highly cultivated. Everyone knows that a person who is highly cultivated and sensitive in the realm of intellect and the arts is far more susceptible to undertones and overtones in a human relationship or even in a controversy than an uncomplicated extrovert who does not catch them at all. The one reacts perhaps to a blow with a club while the other dies of a pinprick. Even a complicated electronic brain is more susceptible to disturbance than a simple two-stroke engine. Symptomatic of this susceptibility of complicated cultured natures to disturbance even by subtle attacks are the usages of courtesy.[21] A clod registers attacks only if they are delivered point-blank; among diplomats, however, who may serve here as examples of developed cultural forms, even notes of protest and declarations of war are not wanting in a certain courtesy which an uncultured person is not able to impart even to his love letters. Here what the one thinks of the other, his disapproval or even his contempt, is written "between the lines"; but only the cultivated, sensitive ear can hear it. In the same way, even the most conventional civilities may harbor pointed allusions and poisoned darts which come near to being instruments of murder. In an encounter between a cultivated person and a more primitive nature this capacity for subtlety can become a deadly weapon of superiority, since the cultivated person secures the superior position by keeping "in form," while the uncultured person who is incapable of doing this is either reduced to impotent silence or reacts like a rowdy.[22]

It is important to clarify these complexities and subtleties in human

---

[21] Cf. the chapter on courtesy in *ThE* II, 1, §538 ff.

[22] A very illustrative example of this is the exchange of notes between the Vatican under Pius XII and the Hitler government.

intercourse, since they not only occur, but are even sharpened in the realm of the individual *eros* and therefore in marriage too. There are two ways in which this is true.

First, this possibility of subtle (or subliminal) attack upon the other person is no longer confined as it was in the past to court circles where courtesy was at home. What was formerly reserved to a small caste of highly cultivated people has now become, if not common property, at least very widespread. The refinement of manners and the fostering of individuality are a part of the stock of ideas of the democracies, expressed even in their basic laws.

Second, in marriage this subtle, subliminal element expresses itself in the lifelong intercourse of two individualities. Possible conflicts do not by any means arise only from verbally expressed differences of opinion. More sensitive natures, especially after long and intimate association, are able to interpret even the slightest gesture the other person makes. Disharmonies reveal themselves in symptoms which the outsider cannot perceive and which can hardly be conveyed to him in words. Anybody who has ever been a counselor in connection with marriages that are breaking down knows the helplessness which the persons involved often show in struggling for words to express what is separating and offending them, not by any means merely because the intimate realm is a *pudendum* (something of which one is ashamed to talk), but primarily because they are such small irrational things, which a poet would know how to put into words but are beyond the grasp of ordinary language. These include such subtleties as the tone and timber of a voice which has become unpleasant and uncongenial, an odor, a certain stereotyped gesture, to say nothing of the intimate realm itself. Thus in the *eros* relationship of two fairly strong individualities the law of attraction and repulsion leads to an inevitable tendency toward instability. When the idea of individual complementarity is held to be normative, the individuals are compelled to ask themselves constantly whether they "still" suit each other or whether they have not grown away from each other. The enlarged area of vulnerable surfaces, which each exposes to the other and which brings about a susceptibility to a whole gamut of subtle and intimate tensions, leads to tremendously increased possibilities of sinning and being unjust to each other—which, though of a different form, is as radical as that mentioned in this area by the Sermon on the Mount (Matt. 5:28). Thus there are subtle forms of breaking a marriage which are more grave than the physical act of adultery. But the opposite is also true: the physical act of adultery need not in every case seriously impugn a marriage which is still sound so far as subtle human contact is concerned. Here a couple's knowledge that they permanently belong together and are meant for each other (in an altogether earthly, erotic sense!) makes it possible for them to overlook intimate, but passing alliances, because they are sure that the other party will always come back home.[23]

What is of primary importance for us in this connection is not only to understand that the awakening of the individual *eros* is an increased development of the wealth of creation, but also to make it clear at the same time that this development entails an increase in the possibilities of incurring guilt. The more highly developed the individuality becomes, the greater and the more difficult to satisfy are the demands upon self-denial of individuality. This intensifies the need for *agape* as self-giving. Likewise, the danger increases that the individuality, one's own entelechy, will become the measure of all things and that self-fulfillment, *amor sui,* will become the criterion for all the decisions of life. The fact that the individuality can become an object of idolatry is unmistakable. The question "What do I get out of this?" supplants the question "Where and whom must I serve?" And this basic change in the question is not made any less perilous by the fact that the question "What do I get out of it?" does not necessarily need to be meant in a material, economic, sensualistic sense. It may lie deep in the realm of the sublime and be concerned with the "higher self" which must be realized. Faust did not sin against Gretchen in furtherance of his libido, but rather in furtherance of his metaphysically glorified Faustian "being," his entelechy. Thus the question can take on an ethical, indeed a religious, tone by being put

[23] However, almost without exception this is true only of the husband's "escapades," not those of a wife. Even in the first case this attitude is, of course, not the rule. But the fact that there are such cases at all in not too infrequent exceptions is important and must be pointed out.

in the form "What do I owe to myself?"

What we thus interpret theologically as an intermixture of creation and sin, a gift and a possibility of going wrong, is also important phenomenologically. That is to say, if, as they develop, the awakened individual *eros* and the awakened individuality also entail greater possibility of imposing injury, violation, and even cruelty upon the other person, there can be forms of marital breakdown which are irrelevant to the theological side of the problem of divorce. It seems to us unfortunate that this side of the problem has remained almost unnoticed by theology. When it does come up, it is usually dealt with only in negative terms. When a person wants to be free from a partner who threatens the development of his personality, he is usually told that he is taking too seriously his own individuality and what he owes to himself. We do not deny that often this reproach and admonition is not amiss, and that it is even a part of the protest that the Christian pastor is obliged to lodge against the idolatrous worship of individuality. The abuse of individuality, however, is not an argument against its legitimate use, as this has emerged for modern man (at least as a possibility), and as, in any case, with the awakening of the individual *eros,* it has become an indispensable responsibility which he cannot ignore.

It is precisely this legitimate use which the church apparently has not yet become aware of. At any rate, the public is not generally aware that the church does take note of it. This may be one of the reasons why those who are in marital difficulty very generally do not seek out the pastor but rather turn to the mental specialists or the agony columns in the newspapers. The church should not always justify the fact that it is being ignored with the argument that what people are looking for is greater permissiveness. This is only partly true. Rather people fear that the problem of individuality is not taken seriously in the church, that there is no theological place for it in the church. This is why we have endeavored to find a place for it and not to be content merely to establish sociologically that the times have changed.

Our purpose in all this is none other than to make known afresh the *vox ecclesiae perpetua* (the perpetual voice of the church) in the

Law and the Gospel, in judgment and promise: the *promise* in the sense that the awakening of individuality too is subsumed under it, that this awakening is a development, a proliferation, of the abundance of creation; the *Law* in the sense that the awakening of individuality at the same time brings with it increased possibilities of incurring guilt and a corresponding demand for *agape, diakonia,* and self-denial,[24] which we ourselves cannot meet, but which is promised to us.

Nor do we wish in the area of *eros* to tone down or give any different meaning to the old message in its severity and its kindness. We are sure, however, that the application of this message today cannot overlook the fact that this newly awakened individuality exists, and that it cannot be proclaimed either in a "reactionary" way or even in a timeless, supratemporal way. On the contrary, we are sure that theological reflection must come to grips with this fact, in order that pastoral care, theologically inspired and aimed, may reach the person as he actually is today and not be left to the individual pastor's theologically uncontrolled capacity for empathy, warmheartedness, and openness to the human situation. Faced with a concrete desire for divorce, it is all too easy for him simply to stick relentlessly to his mandate and therefore irresponsibly to overlook the fact of individuality, the *eros* which is related to it, and the complications it has brought with it. He can only preach a law that kills (II Cor. 3:6; Rom. 7:6, 4:15), and he is then talking beside the point and not addressing himself to the real situation. It is far more difficult, and also more convincing, when a pastor faces up to these complicating facts and still remains true to his commission, whether he has to summon troubled individualities to self-denial, to warn them against idolatry, or to lead them to the death of the old man and the rising of the new man; or whether he is to concede the intolerability of a bad marital situation and help them to see the necessity of forgiveness. In any case, one thing is certain, and that is that the deeper we penetrate into or experience creation, the more manifest becomes the rift in creation. Each intensification of humanity (and *eros* is a part of it) goes hand in hand with an intensification of the need for redemption.

---

[24] *haparnesastho heauton,* Matt. 16:24; cf. Matt. 10:38; I Pet. 10:21.

# Bibliography

I.  INTRODUCTION. THE DUALITY OF MAN: BIBLICAL ANTHROPOLOGY
OF THE SEXES

M. C. van Asch van Wijk, *Zweisam ist der Mensch,* 1952.
Karl Barth, *Church Dogmatics,* II, 4, 1951, pp. 127 ff.
Ch. v. Kirschbaum, *Die wirkliche Frau,* 1949.
Erwin Metzke, "Zur Anthropologie der Geschlechter," in *The-*
*ologische Rundschau,* 1954, p. 211.
H. v. Oyen, *Liebe und Ehe,* 1957.
Anna Paulsen, *Geschlecht und Person, Das biblische Wort über*
*die Frau,* 1960.


II. EROS AND AGAPE. THEOLOGICAL PHENOMENOLOGY OF THE HUMAN
SEX RELATIONSHIP

D. S. Bailey, *Sexual Relationship: A Guide to Published Litera-*
*ture,* London, 2 ed., 1957.
Th. Bovet, *Die Ganzheit der Person in der ärztlichen Praxis,* 1939.
Th. Bovet, *Die Ehe. Ihre Krise u. Neuwerdung,* 3 ed., 1948 (Eng-
lish trans., *Love, Skill and Mystery, A Handbook to Marriage,*
New York, 1958).
P. Christian, *Das Personverständnis im modernen mediz. Denken,*
1952.
Diotima (pseudonym), *Schule der Liebe,* 1930.
W. Fischer, *Neue Tagebücher von Jugendlichen. Die Vorpubertät*
*an Hand lit. Selbstzeugnisse,* 1955.

A. Gehlen, *Der Mensch. Seine Natur u. seine Stellung i. d. Welt,* 4 ed., 1950.

H. Giese, *Die Sexualität des Menschen,* 1955.

H. Gödan, *Die Unzuständigkeit der Seele. Eine Neufassung des Seele-Geist-Problems für Theologie, Medizin u. Pädagogik,* 1961.

J. Guitton, *Essai sur l'amour humain, Paris,* 1948.

H. Hunger, *Das Sexualwissen der Jugend,* 2 ed., 1960.

Ellen Key, *Love and Marriage,* 1911.

A. C. Kinsey, in P. H. Biederich and I. Dembinski, *Die Sexualität des Mannes, Darstellung u. Kritik des* "Kinsey Reports," 1951.

A. C. Kinsey, W. B. Pomeroy, C. E. Martin, *Sexual Behavior in the Human Male,* 1949.

K. Lorenz, "Uber die Bildung des Instinktbegriffs," in *Die Naturwissensch.,* XXV, 1937.

Margaret Mead, *Male and Female: A Study of the Sexes in a Changing World,* London and New York, 1949.

E. Michel, *Ehe. Eine Anthropologie der Geschlechtsgemeinschaft,* 1948.

A. Nygren, *Agape and Eros,* trans. by Philip Watson, 3 vols., London, 1932 ff.

M. Picard, *Die unerschütterliche Ehe,* 1942.

O. Piper, *The Biblical View of Sex and Marriage,* New York, 1960.

H. Prinzhorn, *Leib-Seele-Einheit,* Zurich, 1927.

L. Prohaska, *Geschlechtsgeheimnis u. Erziehung,* 1958.

A. de Quervain, "Ehe u. Haus," in *Eth. II,* 1953.

B. Russell, *Men and Women,* London, 1948.

Max Scheler, *Die Stellung des Menschen im Kosmos,* 1928.

H. Schelsky, "Die sozialen Formen der sexuellen Beziehungen," in H. Giese, *op. cit., pp.* 241 ff.

H. Schelsky, *Soziologie der Sexualität,* 1955.

M. Schmaus; *Kathol. Dogmatik,* II, 2, 1941.

A. Schuschkin, *Die Grundlagen der kommunistischen Moral,* Berlin, 1958.

O. Schwartz, *Sexualität u. Persönlichkeit,* Wien, 1934.

O. Schwartz, *Sexualpathologie,* Wien, 1935.

R. Siebeck, *Medizin in Bewegung,* 1949.

E. Spranger, *Psychologie des Jugendalters,* 24 ed., 1954.

Charlotte Strasser, "Seelische Gleichgewichtsstörungen im geschlechtl. Eheleben," in *Die lebendige Ehe,* 1948, pp. 203 ff.

W. G. Sumner, *The Science of Society,* I, 1927.

*The Lambeth Conference 1958,* London, 1958.

Kl. Thomas, "Sexualunterricht in schwed. Schulen," in *Wege zur Menschen,* 1956.

P. Tillich, *Love, Power and Justice,* New York, 1960.

P. Tournier, *Medicine de la personne,* 1940.

Th. van de Velde, *Die Abneigung i. d. Ehe,* Zürich, 1928.
O. Weininger, *Geschlecht u. Charakter,* 1922 (English trans., *Sex and Character,* London, 1906).
V. v. Weizsäcker, *Arzt u. Kranker,* 1941.

III. THE ORDER OF MARRIAGE

1. Marriage and Sex Relationship in the Bible and Primitive Christianity

Benzinger, "Familie und Ehe bei den Hebräern," *RE* (3 ed.), 5, 738.
Fr. Büchsel, "Die Ehe in Urchristentum," in *ThBl,* 1942, 5, 113 ff.
H. von Campenhausen, *Askese in Urchristentum,* 1949.
Adelh. Caspar, *Die Frau in der Bibel,* 1927.
G. Delling, *Paulus' Stellung zur Frau und Ehe,* 1931.
Elfr. Gottlieb, *Die Frau in d. frühchristl. Gemeinde,* 1927.
H. Greeven, on the New Testament statements concerning marriage, in *ZEE,* 1957, pp. 109 ff.
H. Greeven, "Die Weisungen d. Bibel über d. rechte Verhältnis von Mann und Frau," in *Kirche und Volk,* Nr. 12.
E. Kähler, on the "subordination" of woman in the New Testament, *ZEE,* 1959, 1.
Ludwig Köhler, *Hebrew Man,* trans. by P. R. Ackroyd, Nashville, Abingdon, 1957.
W. G. Kümmel, "Verlobung und Heirat bei Paulus," in *Bultmann-Festschrift,* 1954, p. 275.
K. Preisker, *Christentum und Ehe in den ersten 3 Jahrunderten,* 1927.
J. Wellhausen, "Die Ehe bei d. Arabern," *Nachr. d. köngl. Gesellsch. d. Wissenschaften z. Göttingen,* 1893, p. 43.

2. Marriage: the Sacramental and the "Worldly" Interpretation

P. Althaus, "Luthers Wort zur Ehe," in Th. Heckel, *Ehe und Familienrecht,* 1959, pp. 7 ff.
G. Baumert, "Ehe, sozial.," in *RGG* (3 ed.), II, 322.
H. Boehmer, "Luthers Ehe," in *Lutherjahrb.,* 1925, pp. 40 ff.
Ch. Buchow-Hohmeyer, *Die Zeitehe,* 1928.
Th. Bovet, *Die Ehe. Ihre Krise und Neuwerdung* (3 ed.), 1948 (English trans., *Love, Skill and Mystery, A Handbook to Marriage* [Garden City: Doubleday & Company, 1958]).
Th. Bovet, *Ehekunde. Die jüngste Wissensch. v. d. ältesten Lebensordnung,* 1961.
B. Dennewitz and D. Meissner, ed., *Die Verfassungen Mod.*

*Staaten. Eine Dokumentarsamml.*, 1947 (on Soviet family and marriage laws), I, p. 210.

Frz. Diekamp, *Kathol. Dogmatik*, III (10 ed.), 1942, p. 375.

H. Dombois, "Das Problem d. Institutionen u. d. Ehe," in *Familienrechtsreform*, ed. H. Dombois, 1955, pp. 132 ff.

H. Dombois, "Ehezerstörende Seelsorge" (on problems of mixed marriages), in *Materialdienst d. konf.-kundl. Insts.*, 1962, 1, 1.

W. Elert, *Morphologie des Luthertums*, II (2 ed.), 1953, pp. 80 ff.

Gottschick, article "Christl. Ehe," in *RE*, 5, pp. 182 ff.

B. Jordan, "Zur Entwickl. d. ev. Trauliturg.," in *Weltl. u. kirchl. Eheschliessg.*, ed. Dombois and Schumann, 1953, pp. 72 ff.

Count H. Keyserling, *The Book of Marriage*, 1926.

H. Leenhardt, *Le mariage chretien*, 1946.

B. Lindsey and W. Evans, *The Companionate Marriage* (Garden City: Garden City Publishing Co., 1929).

K. E. Løgstrup, article "Ehe, ethisch," in *RGG* (3 ed.), II, 325.

E. Michel, *Ehe* (2 ed.), 1950.

Kl. Mörsdorf, "Die kirchl. Eheschliessungsformen nach. d. Selbstverständnis d. christl. Bekenntnisse," in *Münchn. Theol. Zeitschr.*, 1958., p. 241.

H. R. Müller-Schwefe, *Die Welt ohne Väter*, 1957.

O. A. Piper, *The Biblical View of Sex and Marriage*, New York, Charles Scribner's Sons, 1960.

A. deQuervain, *Ehe und Haus* (*Ethik*, Bd. II), 1953.

Gertr. Reidick, "Die Mischehe," in *Una Sancta*, 1961, 16, pp. 212 ff.

Gertr. Reidick, *Die Hierarch. Strukt, d. Ehe*, 1953.

J. M. Schneeben, *Handb. d. kathol. Dogmatik*, IV, 1903, pp. 769 ff.

W. Schubart, *Religion und Eros*, 1944.

Siegmund-Schultze, *Um ein neues Sexualethos*, 1927.

R. Sohm, *Das Recht der Eheschliessung, aus dem dtsch. u. kanon. Recht geschichtl. entwickelt*, 1875 (excerpts reprinted in Dombois-Schumann, *Weltl. u. kirchl. Eheschliessg.*, 1953, pp. 11-26.

F. Tanner, *Die Ehe im Pietismus*, 1952.

W. Trillhaas, *Ethik*, 1959, pp. 257 ff.

Th. van de Velde, *Ideal Marriage, Its Physiology and Technique*, New York: Random House, 1930.

### 3. Divorce and Remarriage of Divorced Persons

G. Bornkamm, "Die Stellung des NT z. Ehescheidung. Ein Gutachten," in *EvTh*, 1948, 9/10, pp. 283 ff.

G. Gloege, "Das Ethos der Ehescheidung," in *Gedenkschr. f. W. Elert*, 1955, pp. 355 ff.

Mar. Hagemeyer, *Der Entw. d. Familiengesetzbuches d. DDR* (3 ed.), 1955.

P. H. Hanstein, *Kanon. Eherecht,* (3 ed.), 1953.

L. Richter, *Beiträge z. Gesch. d. Ehesch.-rechtes i. d. ev. Kirche,* 1858.

F. K. Schumann, article "Ehescheidung," in *RGG,* 336.

Anneliese Sprengler, "Um eine schriftgemässe Behandlg. d. Probl. s. d. Trauung Geschiedener. Zur Gesch. d. Wiedertrauungsfrage," in *Zeitschr. f. ev. KR (ZKR),* III, 1954, pp. 163 ff., 268 ff.

K. Staab, "Die Unauflöslichkeit d. Ehe u. d. sog. 'Ehebruchs-klauseln' bei Mt. 5:32 u. 19:9," in *Festschr. Ed. Eichmann,* 1940, pp. 435 ff.

Marianne Weber, *Die Idee der Ehe u. d. Ehescheidung,* 1929.

**4.** Special Problems of the Woman (Her Nature; Woman in Society; The Unmarried Woman; Vocation; The Problem of Equal Rights, etc.)

Simone de Beauvoir, *The Second Sex,* trans. and ed. by H. M. Parshley, New York: Alfred A. Knopf, 1953.

A. Böhm, "Die Frau i. d. modernen Gesellschaft," in *Wort u. Wahrheit,* 1954, 9/10.

Regina Bohne, *Das Geschick der zwei Millionen. Die alleinstehende Frau in unser Gesellschaft,* 1960.

F. J. Buytendijk, *Die Frau. Natur, Erscheinung, Dasein,* 1953.

H. Dölle, "Die Gleichberechtigung v. Mann u. Frau i. Familien-recht. Eine rechtspolit. Skizze auf rechtsvergl. Grundlage," in *Um Recht u. Gerechtigkeit, Festg. f. E. Kaufmann,* 1950, pp. 19 ff.

Herder-Korrespondenz, *Die Gleichberechtigung der Frau u. ihre Grenzen im Familienrecht,* 1950, 2, 89.

E. Kaufmann, *Die Gleichheit vor dem Gesetz. Veröffentl. d. Vereinigung dtsch. Strafrechtslehrer,* 1927, 3.

M. Köller, "Die Frau als gleichberecht. Gehilfin," in *Kirche i. d. Zeit,* 1954, 4. 75.

John Lawrence, *Women without Men,* 1954.

G. von LeFort, *Die ewige Frau,* 1940.

Elisabeth Pfeil, "Die Berufstätigkeit von Müttern," in *Veröffentl. d. Akademie f. Gemeinwirtschaft,* Hamburg.

H. Schelsky, "Die gelungene Emanzipation," in *Merkur* 86, 1955.

Alice Scherer, "Die Frau. Wesen u. Aufg.," in *Wörterb. d. Politik,* VI, 1951.

K. H. Schwab, "Ehe u. Familie i. Lichte d. Gleichberechtigungs-gesetzes," in Th. Heckel, *Ehe-u. Fam.-recht,* 1959, pp. 48 ff.

E. Stern, "Die Unverheirateten," in *Geschlechtsleben u. Gesell-schaft,* 7, 1957.

### 5. Anthropological Changes in Our Understanding of the Sexes and Their Relationship

H. J. Bothe, *Zuverlässige Beschreibung des nunmehro entdeckten Herrenhutischen Ehe-Geheimnisses. . .*, 2 vols., 1751 f.

Simone de Beauvoir, *The Second Sex,* trans. and ed. by H. M. Parshley, New York: Alfred A. Knopf, 1953.

Diotima (pseudonym), *Schule der Liebe,* 1930.

Dombois-Schumann, *Familienrechtsreform,* 1955 (cited as *FR*).

W. Jannasch, *Erdmuthe Dor. Gräfin v. Zinzendorf,* 1915.

A. Jeanroy, *La Poesie lyrique de troubadours,* 2 vols., 1934.

P. Kluckhohn, *Die Auffassung der Liebe in der Literatur des 18. Jahrhunderts und in der deutschen Romantik,* 1922.

O. Lätheenmäki, *Sexus und Ehe bei Luther,* 1955.

K. E. Løgstrup, article "Ehe, ethisch," in *RGG* (3 ed.), II, 325.

F. C. Oetinger, *Freimüthige Gedanken von der ehelichen Liebe,* in *Sämtliche Schriften,* ed. K. Ehmann, 1863, V.

O. Pfister, *Die Frömmigkeit des Grafen L. v. Zinzendorf. Eine psychoanalytische Studie,* 1925.

Bertrand Russell, *Marriage and Morals,* New York: Liveright, 1929.

L. L. Schucking, *Die Familie im Puritanismus,* 1929.

M. A. G. Spangenberg, *Apolog. Schluss-Schrifft, worinn über tausend Beschuldigungen gegen die Brüder-Gemeinen . . . beantwortet werden,* 1752.

Elis. Schwarzhaupt, "Kirchl. Stellungnahmen zur Familienrechtsreform in der Bundesrepublik und in der Sowjetzone," in *Evangelische Verantwortung,* 1956, 2.

F. Tanner, *Die Ehe im Pietismus,* 1952.

H. Weizsäcker, *Schleiermacher und das Eheproblem,* 1927.


### IV. BORDERLINE SITUATIONS

#### 1. Birth Control (The Problem of Optional Sterility)

Karl Barth, *Kirchliche Dogmatik,* III, 4, pp. 301 ff. (English trans., Vol. III, Part 4, pp. 268 ff.)

Maston Bates, *Die überfüllte Erde,* 1959.

Theodor Bovet, *Die Ehe,* 1948, pp. 158 ff.

Emil Brunner, *The Divine Imperative,* Philadelphia: Westminster Press, 1937, pp. 367 ff.

St. de Lestapis, *Geburtenregulung-Geburtenkontrolle,* 1962.

Jos Mayer, *Erlaubte Geburtenbeschränkung?,* 1932.

J. Messner, *Das Naturrecht,* 1950, pp. 571 ff.

E. Michel, *Ehe. Eine Anthropologie der Geschlechtsgemeinschaft,* 1948, pp. 127, 189, 196.

Alb. Niedermeyer, *Handbuch der spez. Pastoralmedizin,* 1950 ff., II, pp. 68 ff.

O. A. Piper, *Die Geschlechter,* 1954, pp. 235 ff.

Pius XI, Encyclical *Casti Connubii,* 1930 (Denzinger, 2241 and Herder-Ausgabe).

Pius XII, Address on Nov. 28, 1952, in Herder-Korrespondenz, VI, 172.

W. Schöllgen, "Zur pastoraltheologischen Beurteilung d. 'abusus matrimonii' (der Geburtenbeschränkung)," in *Aktuelle Moralprobleme,* 1955, pp. 300 ff.

Joh. Stelzenberger, *Moraltheologie,* 1953, p. 230.

Frz. v. Streng, *Das Geheimnis der Ehe,* (12 ed.), 1947.

W. Umbricht, "Geburtenüberschuss — Geburtenregelung," in *Civitas,* 1955, 7/8, p. 310.

"Umstrittene Geburtenkontrolle. Bericht über kirch. Stellungnahmen," in *Universitas,* 1960, 6, p. 685.

H. Wagner, *Geburtenregelung als theologisches Problem,* 1930.

H. Wirz, *Vom Eros zur Ehe* (rev. ed.), 1953.

## 2. Interruption of Pregnancy (The Problem of Artificial Abortion)

a. *On the Catholic theory of animation* (animatio foetus)

Innocent XI, *Various Errors on Moral Subjects,* Denzinger, 1151 ff., especially 1184 f.

Hans Meyer, *Thomas von Aquin,* 1938, p. 315.

Alb. Niedermeyer, *Pastoralmedizin,* III, pp. 101 ff.

J. H. Waszink, article "Beseelung," in *Reallex. fur Antike und Christentum,* 1950 ff., II, p. 176.


b. *On theological, medical and legal opinion*

Karl Barth, *Church Dogmatics,* III, 4, pp. 415 ff.

H. J. Gamm, "Schwangerschaftsunterbrechung als religiöses und erzieh. Problem," in *ZEE* 1961, 4, pp. 193 ff.

A. Jores, "Um den §218," in *Hamb. Akadem. Rundschau* 1947/48, 1/2, pp. 48 f.

Leo XIII, *Craniotomy and Abortion,* 1889, Denzinger 1889 f.

Otto Piper, *Die Geschlechter,* 1954, pp. 239 ff.

Pius XI, *Casti Connubii,* Denzinger 2242 ff.

Pius XII, "Address on Nov. 28, 1951" in *Herder-Korrespondenz* VI, 171.

Eberhard Welty, Herders *Soz.-Katechismus,* II, 1953, p. 95.

## 3. Artificial Insemination

F. Bloemhof, "Das Problem der künstlichen Insemination beim Menschen," in *ZEE*, 1958, pp. 15 ff.

H. Dölle, "Retortenkinder. Jurist. Aspekte der künstlichen Befruchtung," in *Die Gegenwart*, 1953, pp. 367 ff.

H. Dölle, "Die künstliche Samenübertragung. Eine rechtsvergleichende und rechtspolitische Skizze," in *Festschrift fur E. Rabel*, 1954, pp. 187-250.

J. D. Ratcliff, "Artificial Insemination—Has It Made Happy Homes?" in *Woman's Home Companion*, reprinted in *Reader's Digest*, June, 1955, pp. 77 ff. [Perhaps the book on which this article seems to be based will prove more helpful: Glanville Williams, *The Sanctity of Life and the Criminal Law* (New York: Alfred A. Knopf, 1957), pp. 112 ff. Trans.]

H. M. Schmidt, "Die künstliche Samenübertragung bei Menschen in der juristischen Diskussion in Deutschland," in *ZEE*, 1961, 4, pp. 193 ff. (Further references to the literature here.)

A. Schellen, *Artificial Insemination in the Human*, London and New York, 1957.

G. Trappe, "Einige moraltheologische Probleme der Insemination artificial," in *Civitas*, 1955, 7/8, p. 324.

P. Wirz, "Ärztliche Problematik der Insemination," in *Civitas*, 1955, 7/8, pp. 317 ff.

# INDEXES

# Index of Scripture Passages

## OLD TESTAMENT

## NEW TESTAMENT

# Index of Names

# Index of Subjects

*(For further information see Table of Contents)*